TIME TRAVEL IN NORTH VANCOUVER

A peek into the past

Revised & Updated 2018

SHARON J. PROCTOR

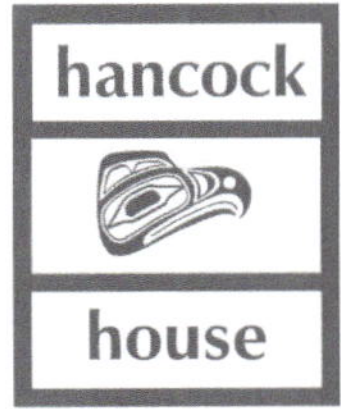

ISBN-13: 978-0-88839-200-8 *[2018 revised & updated edition]*
ISBN-13: 978-0-88839-629-7 *[2010 edition]*

Cataloging in Publication Data

Proctor, Sharon J., author
Time travel in North Vancouver : a peek into the past / Sharon J. Proctor. -- Second edition.

ISBN 978-0-88839-629-7 (2010 softcover)
ISBN 978-0-88839-200-8 (2018 softcover)

1. Historic sites--British Columbia--North Vancouver--Guidebooks. 2. Historic buildings--British Columbia--North Vancouver--Guidebooks. 3. Historic sites--British Columbia--North Vancouver (District)--Guidebooks. 4. Historic buildings--British Columbia--North Vancouver (District)--Guidebooks. 5. North Vancouver (B.C.)--History--Pictorial works. 6. North Vancouver (B.C. : District)--History--Pictorial works. 7. North Vancouver (B.C.)--Guidebooks. 8. North Vancouver (B.C. : District)--Guidebooks. 9. North Vancouver (B.C.)--Tours. 10. Guidebooks. I. Title.

FC3849.N67P76 2018 971.1'33 C2018-903479-3

Printed in the USA

Editor: Theresa Laviolette
Production: I. Luters & R. Groenhyde
Cover Design: M. Lamont
Cover Photo: Then: Lonsdale Below Esplanade, 1925 (NVMA 2006); Now: photo of the same location by Fernando Blendl, 2018

We acknowledge the financial support of the Government of Canada through the Book Publishing Industry Development Program (BPIDP) for our publishing activities.

Published simultaneously in Canada and the United States by

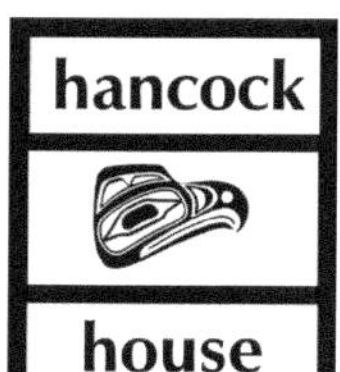

HANCOCK HOUSE PUBLISHERS LTD.
19313 Zero Avenue, Surrey, B.C. Canada V3Z 9R9
(604) 538-1114 Fax (604) 538-2262

HANCOCK HOUSE PUBLISHERS
#104 4550 Birch Bay-Lynden Rd, Blaine, WA U.S.A 98230-9436
(800) 938-1114 Fax (800) 983-2262

Website: **www.hancockhouse.com**
Email: **info@hancockhouse.com**

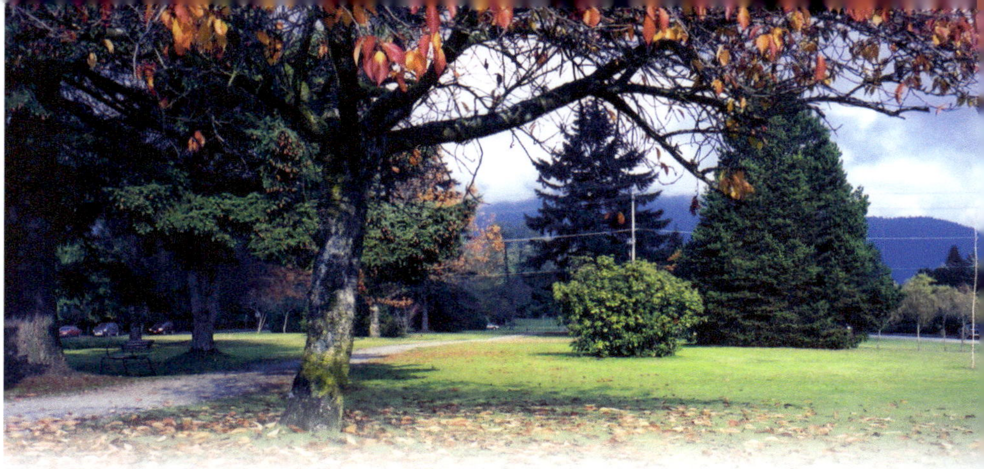

Contents

4. East to Deep Cove

5. Lynn Valley

6. Mountains

Picture Credits

Acknowledgements

This book grew out of my work as editor and writer of the *Express,* a local history periodical published by the Friends of the North Vancouver Museum & Archives Society. In my continuing search for fresh stories about North Vancouver's past, I interviewed people who had never been interviewed, visited old sites, read old newspapers, and examined diaries, memoirs, government records, and early and modern maps. At every turn I found myself comparing past and present. This book is the result. It's a Friends Society publication, a satisfying sidebar to my work on the *Express.* And everyone who helped me with *Express* stories, by default helped me with the book.

North Vancouver Museum & Archives staff, of course, gave me complete access to information, maps, photos, and memoirs located in the collections. I'd have gotten nowhere without Robin Inglis (former director of the Museum & Archives), Nancy Kirkpatrick (current director), Janet Turner, Shirley Sutherland, John Stuart, Francis Mansbridge, June Thompson, and Daien Ide.

Then there are the many wonderful seniors who shared with me their memories of growing-up in North Vancouver in the 1920s, 30s or 40s. Betty Poole, Carl Sparks, Marg Birtles, Leonora Dunse, Jim Lawrence, Frank Walden, Betty Brown, and Irene Ironside — all transported me back to earlier decades and showed me the past through their eyes.

I also am indebted to local historians and history buffs who had already researched various elements of North Vancouver's early days. They include Dick Lazenby, Roy Pallant, Eric Crossin, Henry Ewert, Suzanne Wilson, and Doreen Armitage, all of whom let me examine their research findings.

As for the book itself, Robin Inglis and Ray Van Driel (teacher at Ridgeway School) helped me search for good vintage photos. Nancy Kirkpatrick and June Thompson checked my final manuscript for accuracy, and Shannon Craver scanned the North Vancouver Archives' photos you see on these pages.

To all of you, I owe my deepest gratitude and sincere thanks.

Then there's my husband, David Rodger. He cheerfully put up with my neglecting him for two years; watched for oncoming traffic as I stepped onto busy streets to re-photograph old scenes; accompanied me when I visited original sites deep in local forests; and edited my texts. (There *was*, however, some grumbling about late dinners!) Thank you so much, David, for your help, patience and understanding.

— Sharon J. Proctor
March 2009

The Friends of the North Vancouver Museum and Archives Society thanks Sharon J. Proctor for preparing this new 2018 edition of Time Travel and re-photographing many of the featuured sites.

– Nancy Kirkpatrick, Director

North Vancouver Museum and Archives, June 2018

Introduction

We've come a long way...

Think of the two photographs on this page as a metaphor for North Vancouver's history. In one (A), you see the northeast corner of Moody and 7th, as it looked over a century ago. The other (B) shows the same location in 2007. They illustrate the dramatic changes that North Vancouver has experienced since the earliest settlers. And the changes keep coming.

Happily there are several excellent books that describe the main aspects of our history. This book is different!

It is more like a tour-book. It takes you to individual locations. At each place, you're transported back and forth in time so you can see for yourself how the site has changed. The original edition of *Time Travel* was published in 2010. Since then, the pace of change in North Vancouver has intensified. So this revised edition has many new photos and updates.

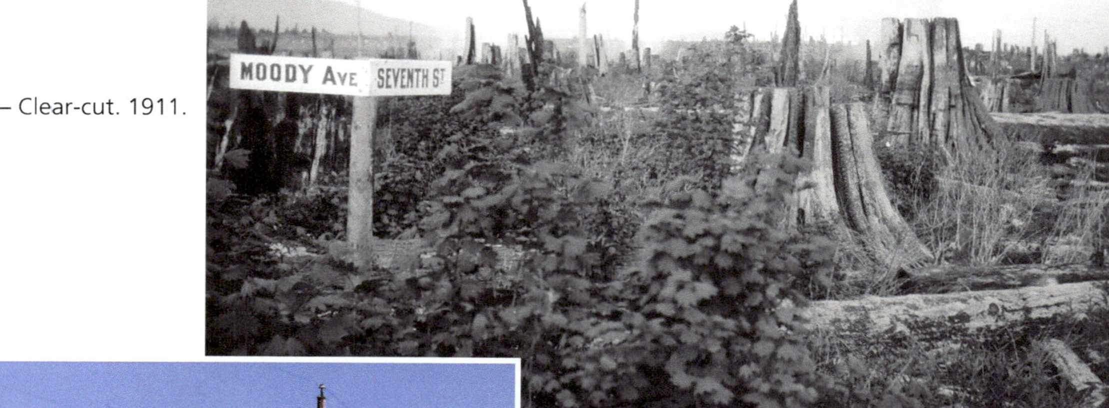

A – Clear-cut. 1911.

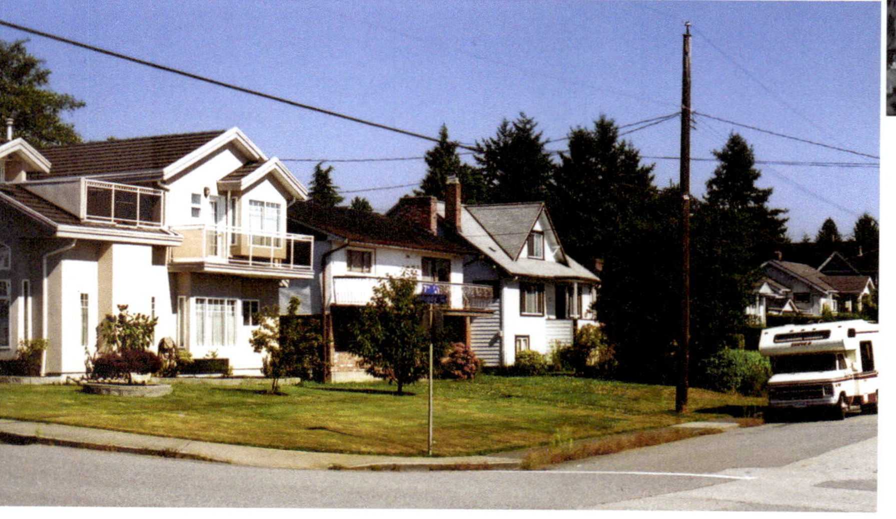

B – Residential area, 2007.

1 Lonsdale

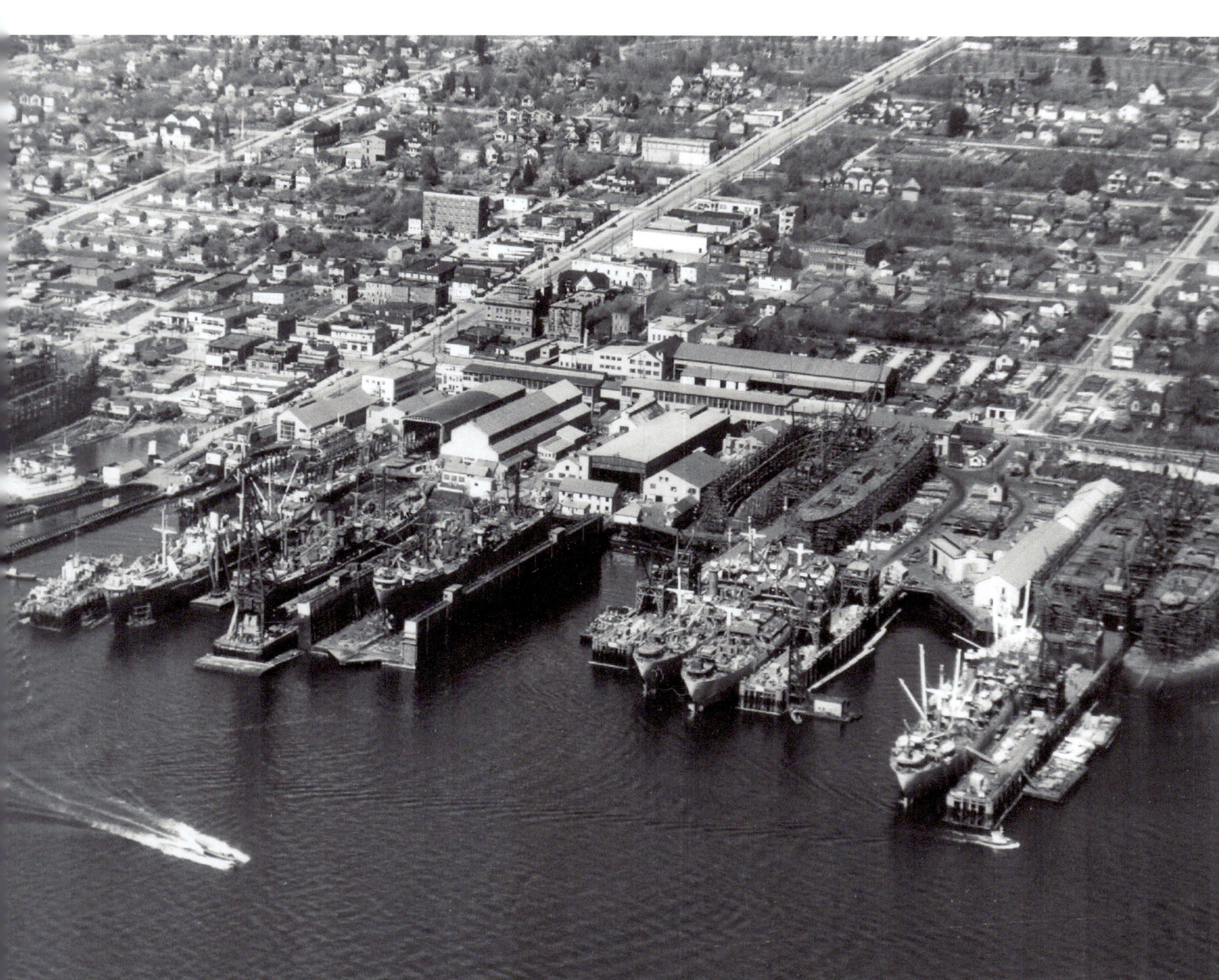

Esplanade

Originally this street was a true "esplanade" — a seaside promenade extending from Lonsdale to just past Chesterfield, seen in this 1907 view looking west (A). It was created in 1901 to accommodate the new Hotel North Vancouver. Summer crowds would arrive on the ferry and walk along here to spend a holiday at the hotel or participate in special outdoor celebrations. In the other 1907 photo, looking east from Chesterfield (B), we see Esplanade hosting a joint celebration of Dominion Day and the City of North Vancouver's incorporation. The same view in 2016 shows a modern street lined with commercial buildings (C).

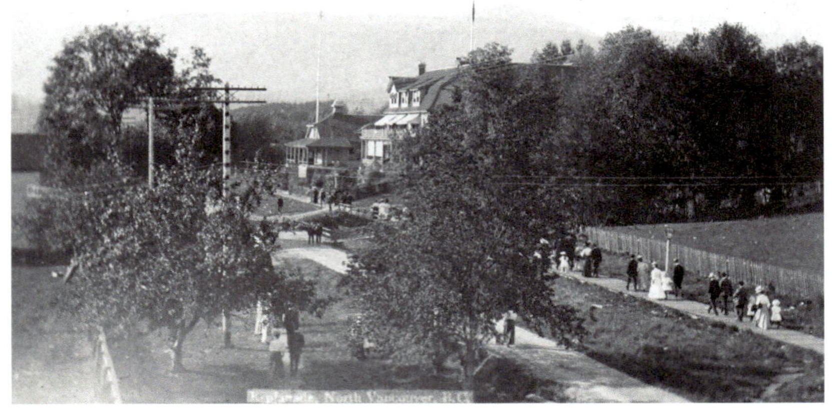

A – Esplanade, 1907.

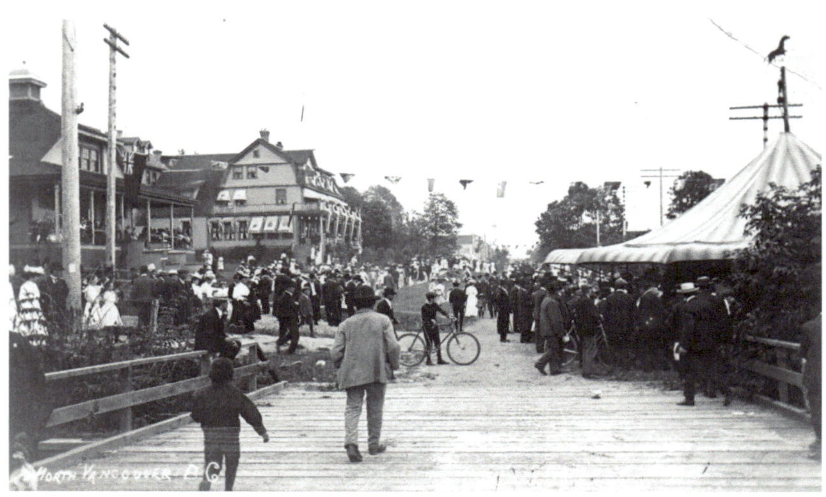

B – View from Chesterfield, 1907.

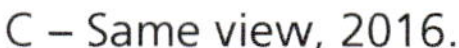

C – Same view, 2016.

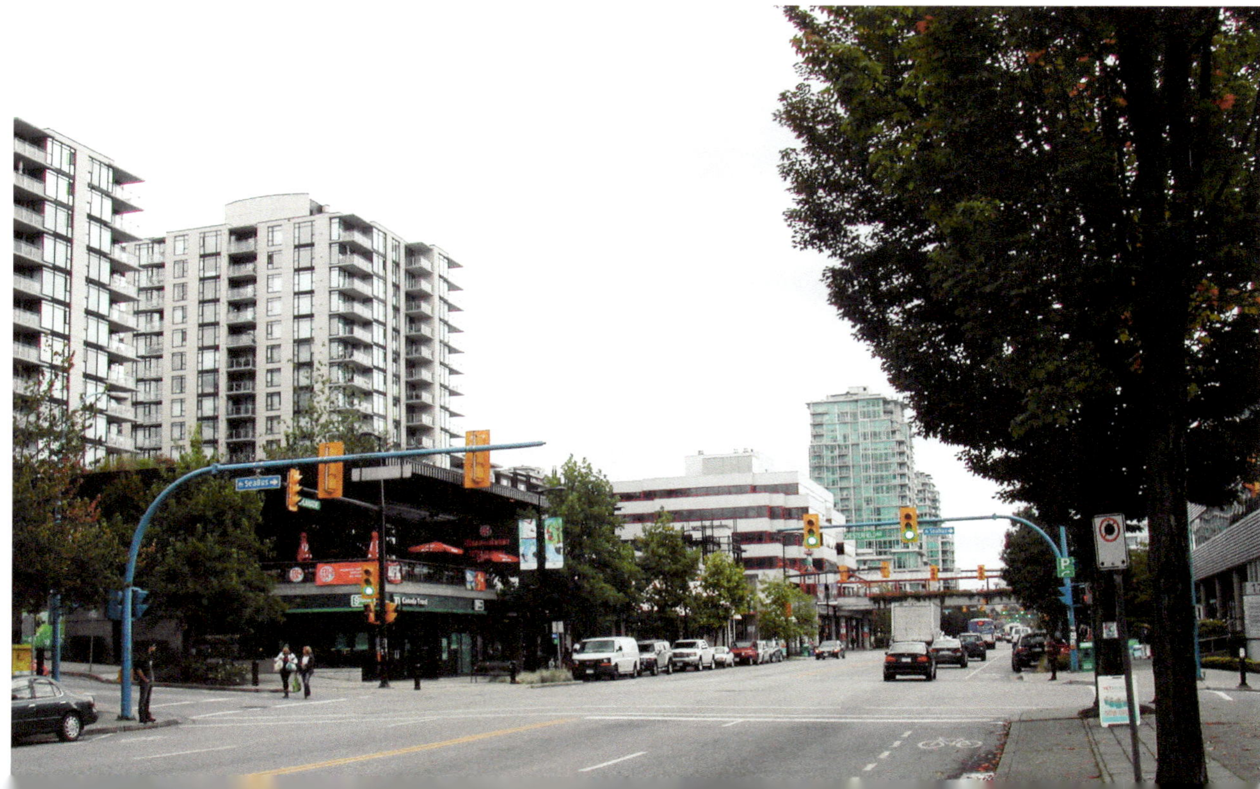

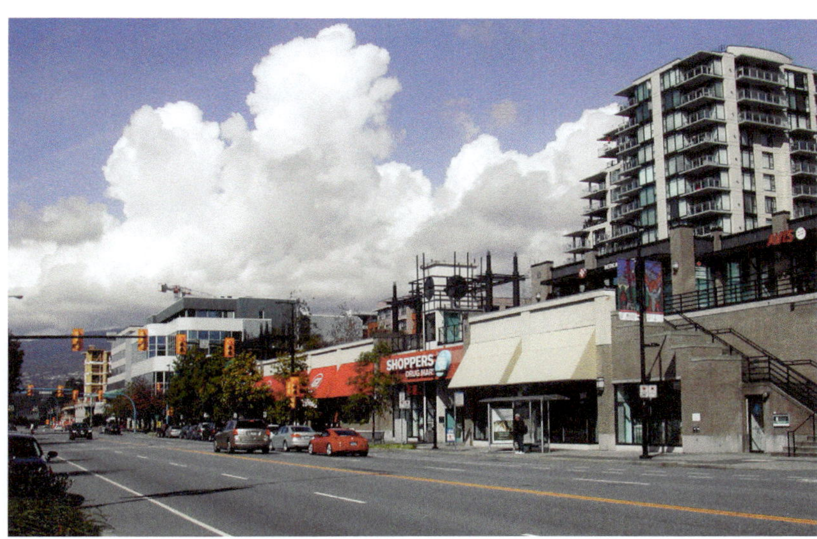

A – Modern buildings, 2016.

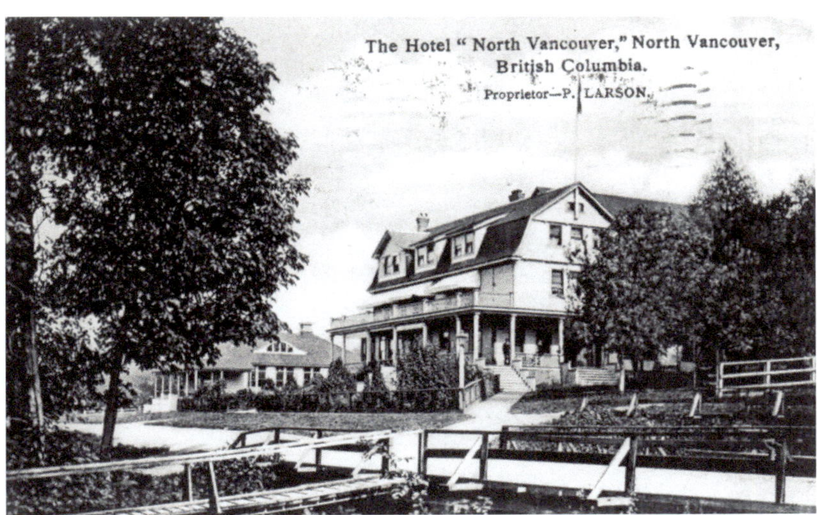

B – Hotel North Vancouver, c. 1912.

Hotel North Vancouver

Now walk east on Esplanade, from Chesterfield to Rogers Avenue, and look back (A). In 2016 we see a Shoppers Drug Mart on the right, then an IGA, then a Canada Trust and Boston Pizza on the corner of Chesterfield. Standing here in 1912 (B), however, you'd have seen the Hotel North Vancouver, its garden and its pavilion, respectively, on these three sites. The hotel was built in 1901, and its buildings and grounds covered both sides of Esplanade and extended down to a beach. Here's a 1908 view from the water (C). Overnight accommodations, fine dining, bar, lawns, shade trees, beach, picnic tables, bandstand, barbecue pit, changing rooms — no wonder people flocked here for vacations, meetings, family gatherings, concerts, dances, picnics, and barbecues!

C – View from the water, 1908.

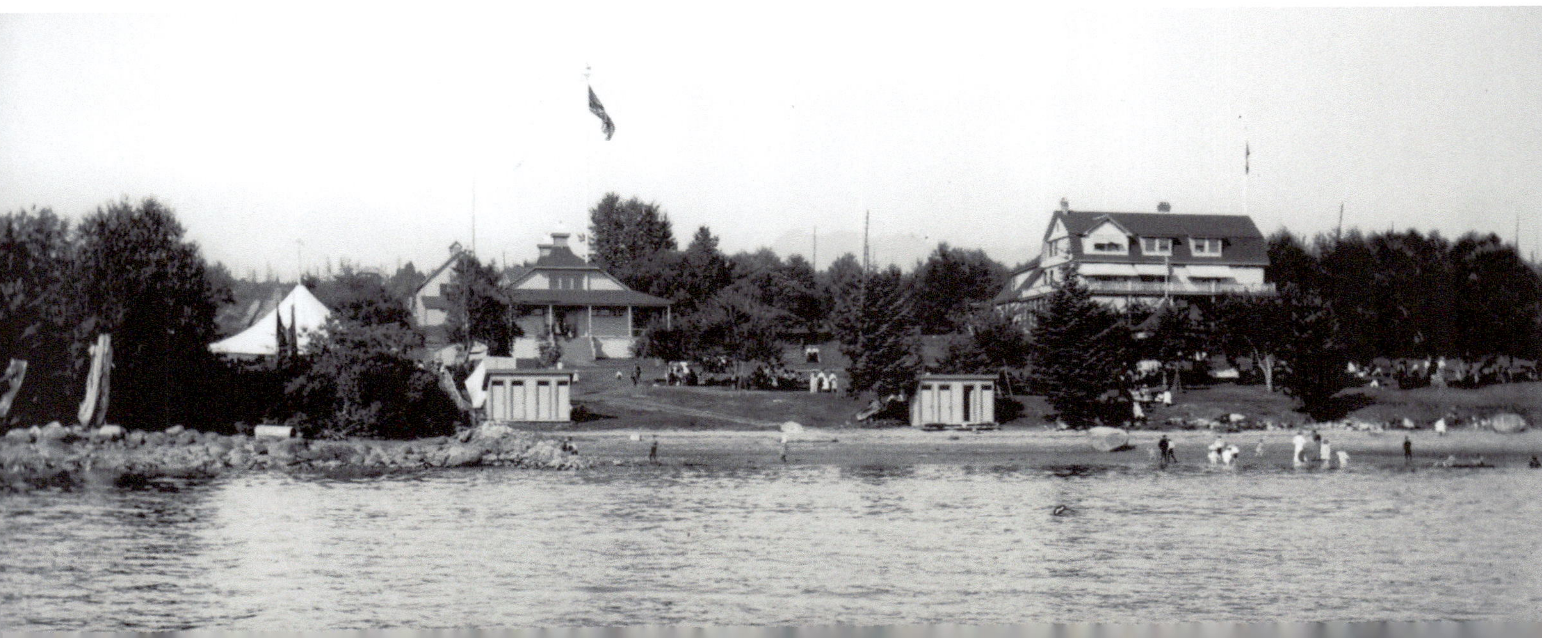

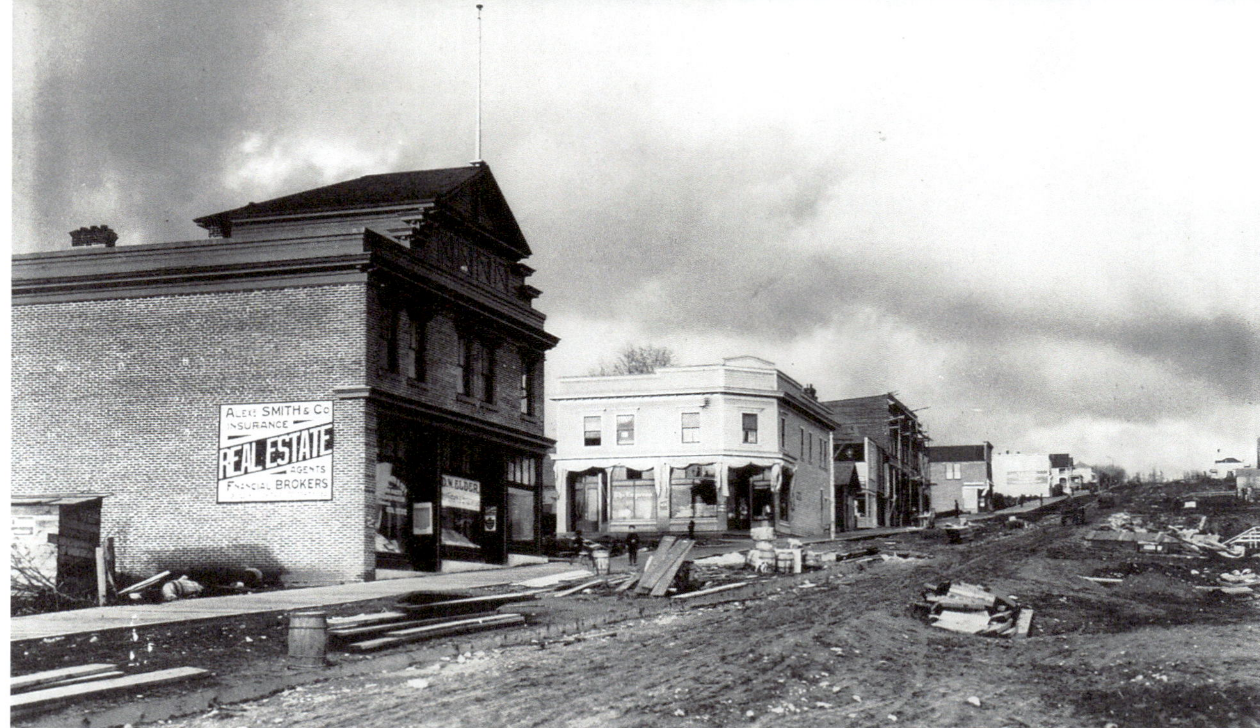

A – Lower Lonsdale, 1905.

Lower Lonsdale

Before 1902, the bottom few blocks of Lonsdale were virtually undeveloped, despite Lonsdale's connecting to a ferry wharf and ferry service to Vancouver. It was just a primitive road that led up the hill. Then, around 1902, businessman Alfred Hammersley purchased District Lot 274, which included this area. He improved the ferry service, upgraded the road, and convinced people to buy lots and set up businesses here. For a while the lower section of Lonsdale was a "work in progress," as you can see in this 1905 photo looking uphill from the wharf (A). Notice how the "street" proceeds *straight* up the hill. The same view today (B) reveals a modern street, modern buildings, and "terracing" (levelling-off) at each cross street.

B – Lower Lonsdale (southbound lane), 2016.

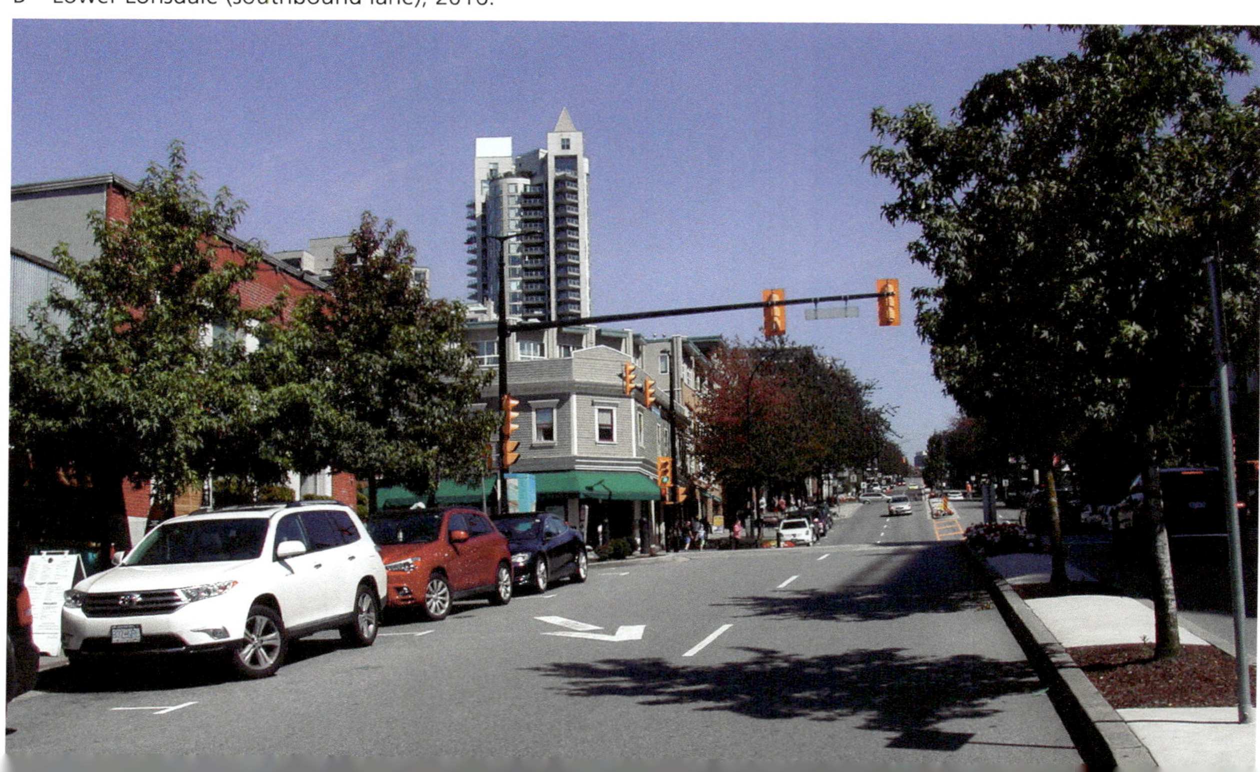

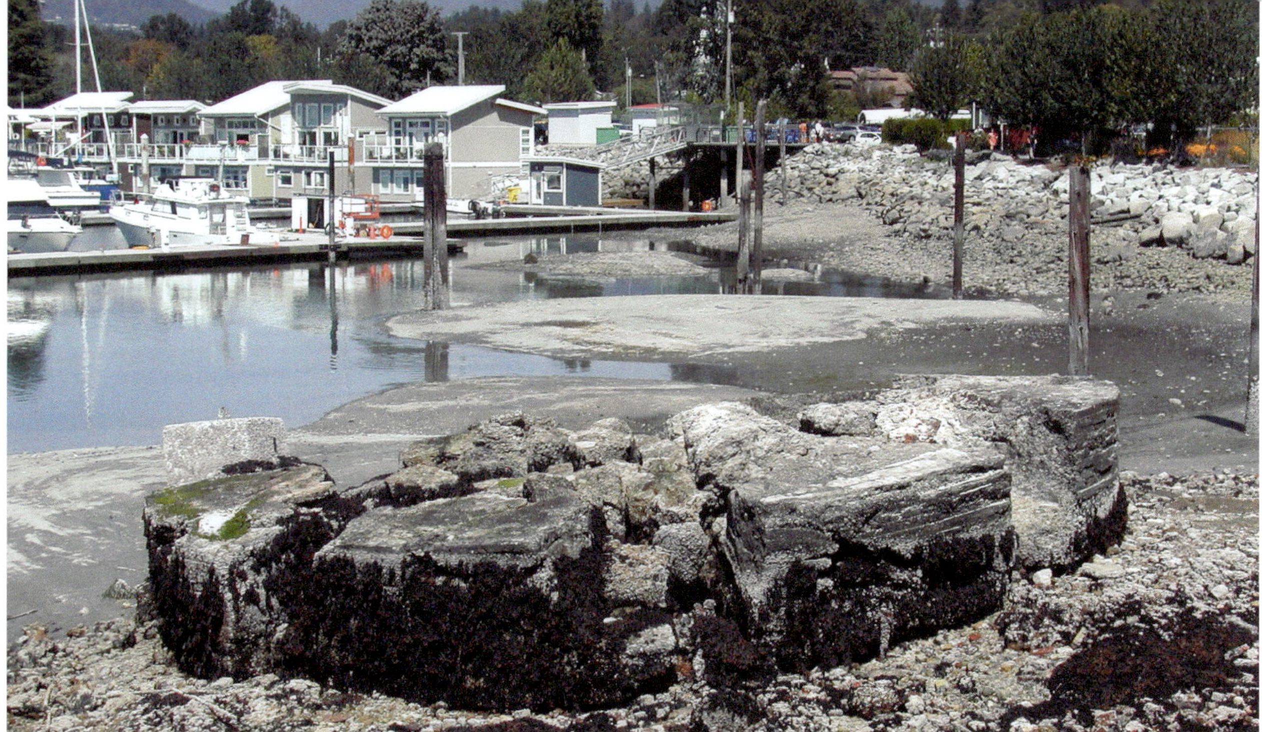

A – Concrete circle, 2016.

Horne Bros. Shingle Mill

Next time you visit Lonsdale Quay, take a short stroll westward along the seawall past the BC Institute of Technology's marine training school. After the path turns right, you'll see a circle of concrete chunks in the tidal area (A). The Horne Bros. Shingle Mill once operated here, and this circle is the remains of its waste-burner. You can see the mill in this 1927 aerial photo (B). That wide street at the top is Mahon Avenue. And the tower-like structure in the centre is the burner. For many years Horne Bros. burned wood waste and rejected shingles in this structure, but in later years used other means of waste disposal. The mill was shut down and demolished in the early 1980s.

B – Aerial view of mill, 1927.

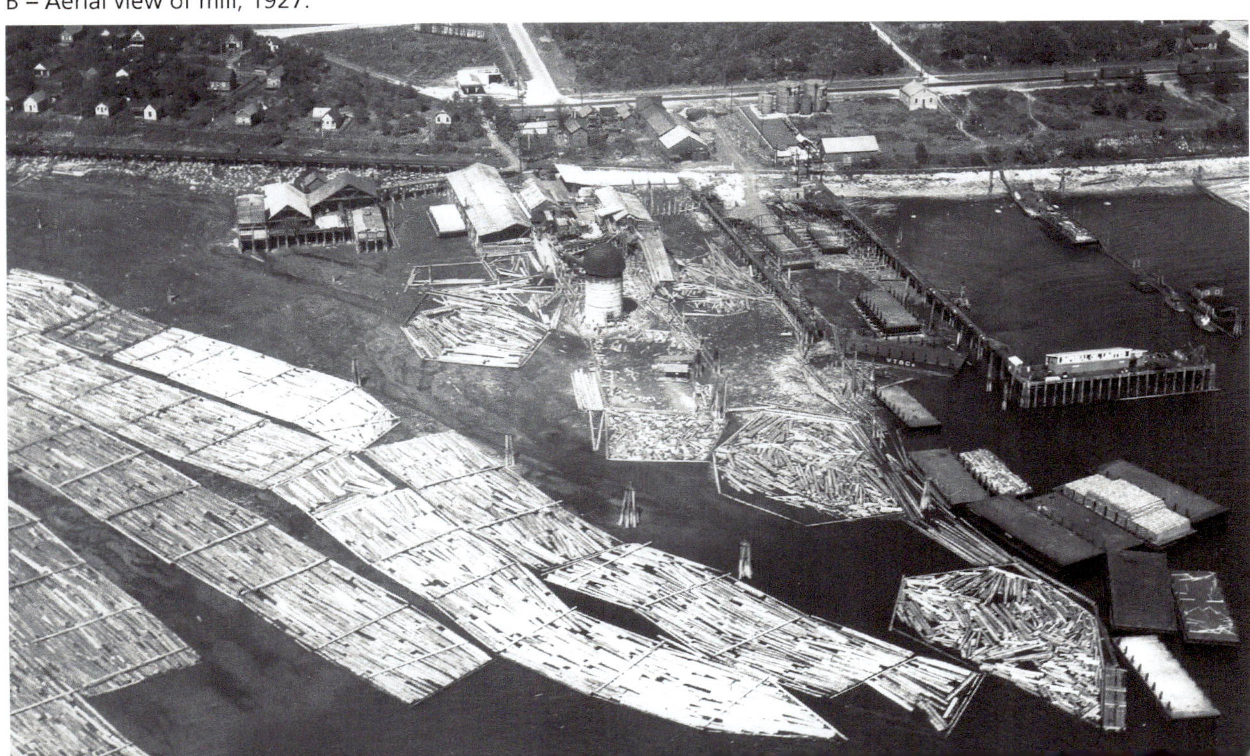

Ferry No. 5

North Vancouver Ferry #5 made its last scheduled trip to the Lonsdale wharf in August 1958 (A). A year later it returned to the foot of Lonsdale as a floating seafood restaurant called "Ship of the Seven Seas." It was later renamed "Seven Seas Seafoods," as you can see in this undated photo (B). The stunning neon sign on top, nautical décor inside, large seafood buffet (e.g. oysters on the half shell, curried Dungeness crab, blackened red snapper), and great view of the harbour made it a renowned North Vancouver icon. The Seven Seas closed in 2001 and was demolished in 2002. In recent years, its former berth at the bottom of Lonsdale has been mostly empty (C).

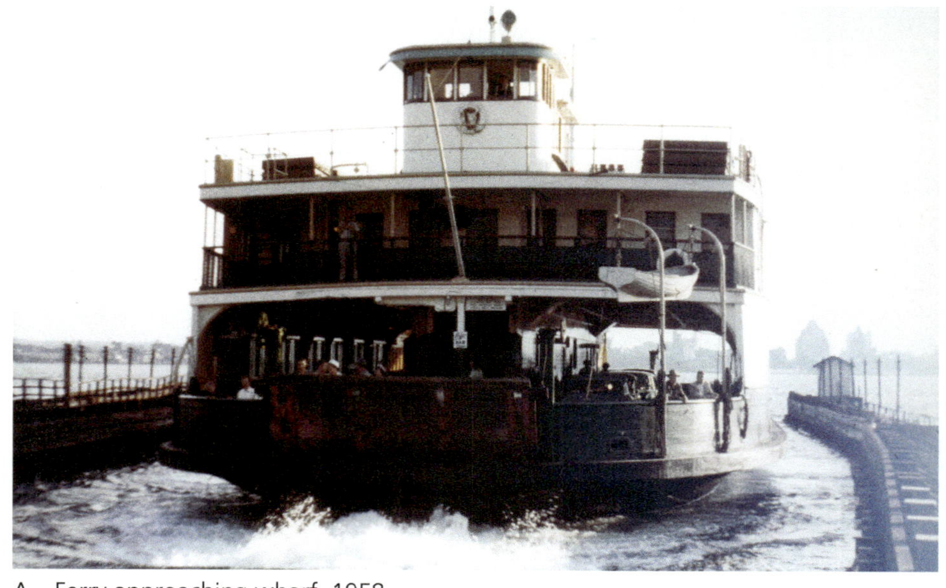

A – Ferry approaching wharf, 1958.

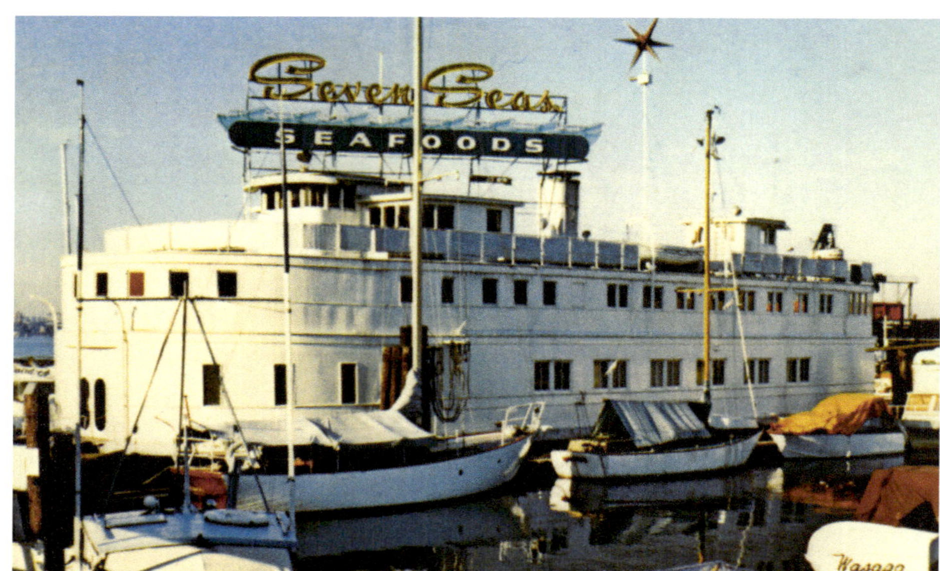

B – Floating restaurant, date unknown.

C – Former berth, 2016.

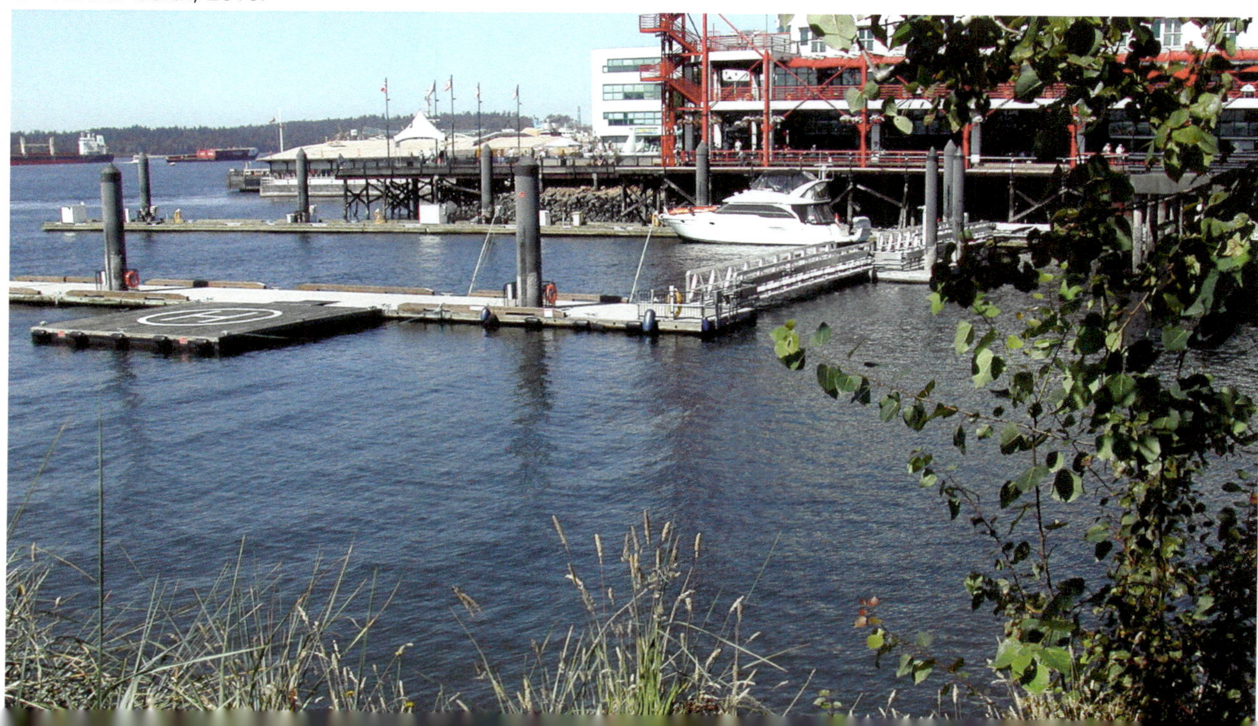

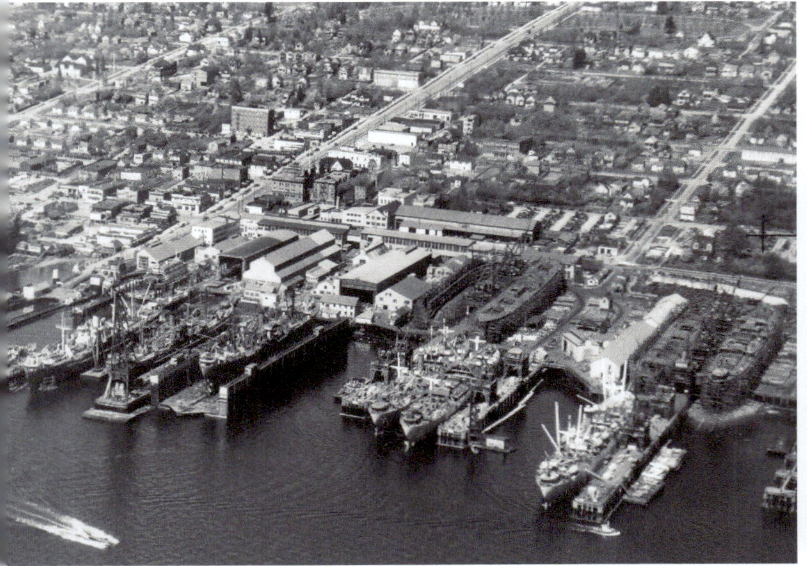

A – Burrard Dry Dock, 1944.

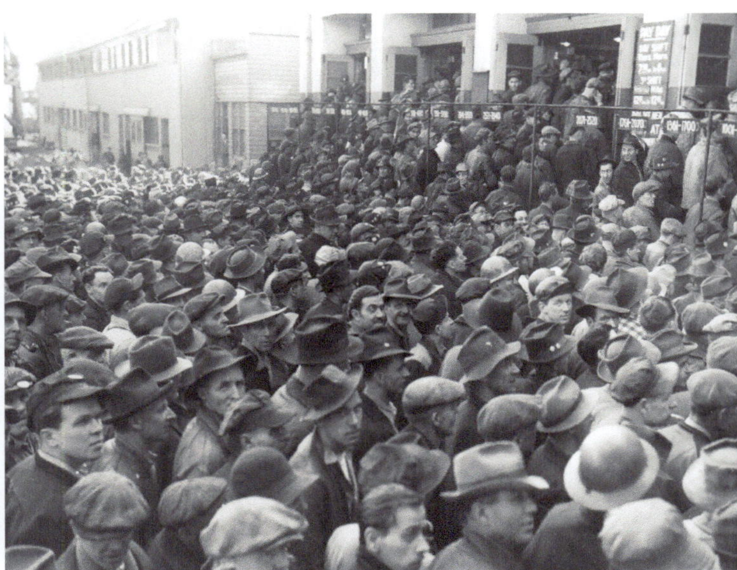

B – Quitting time, 1944.

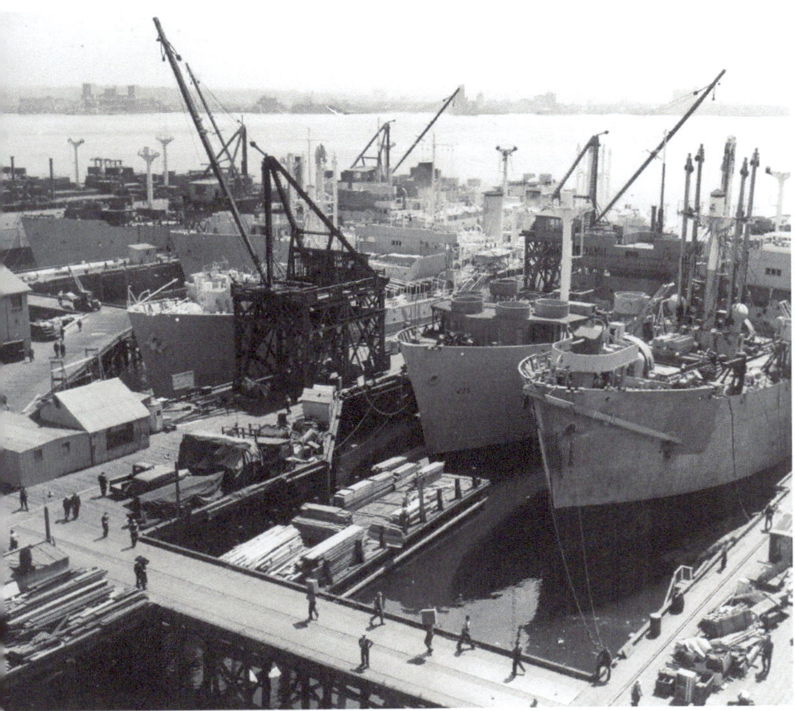

C – Ships under construction, 1945.

D – Two saved buildings and company crane, 2016.

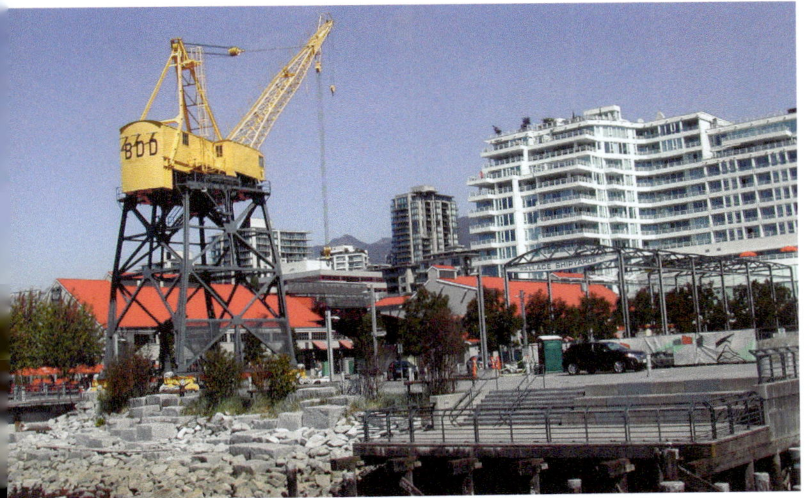

Burrard Dry Dock

During World War II, Burrard Dry Dock shipyard at the foot of Lonsdale was an impressive operation, seen here in 1944 (A). Thousands of workers toiled up to seven days a week, churning out 10,000-ton supply ships, escort ships, minesweepers, tugboats, landing craft, and other vessels. Indeed, quitting time produced a mass exodus onto Lonsdale, shown here in 1944 (B). Plus, the shipyard's waterfront was always full of ships under construction, pictured here in 1945 (C). The shipyard closed in 1992. For *years* afterward there was discussion on whether or not to preserve it. In the end, the Coppersmith Shop and Pipe Shop (D) plus Pier #3 were saved. Everything else was cleared away. Condominiums, shops, a hotel, and other facilities are gradually covering the rest of the site.

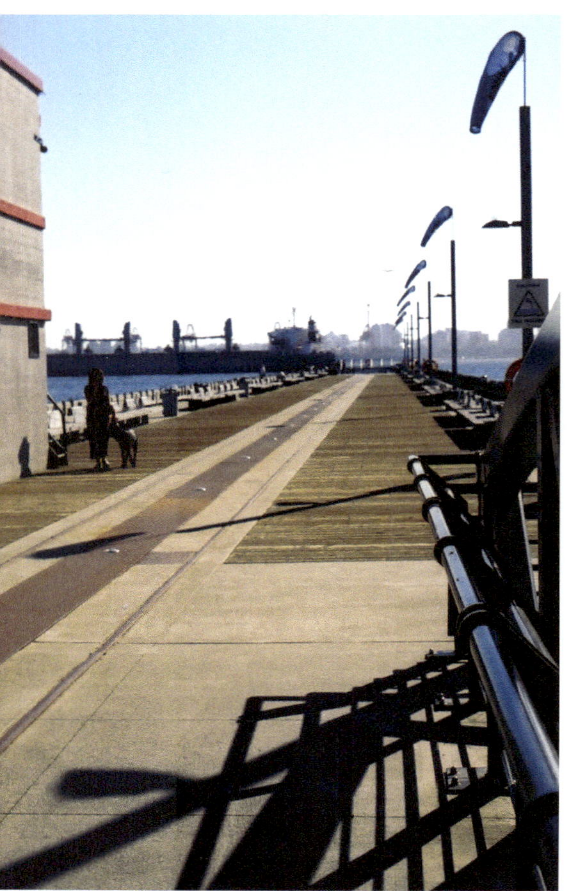
A – Restored pier, 2007.

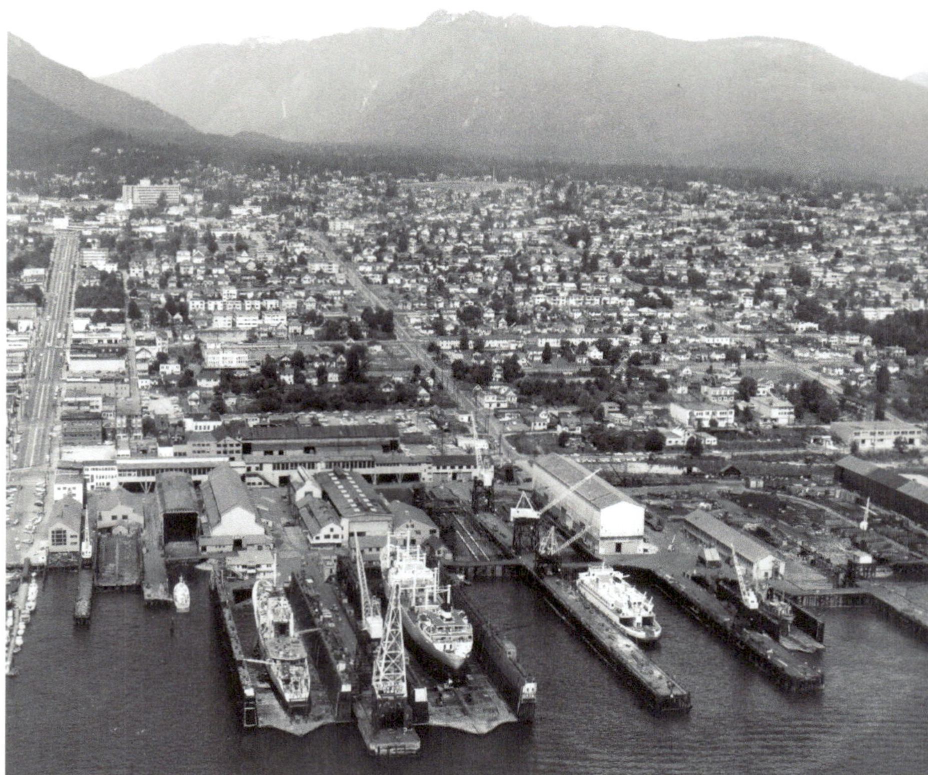
B – Aerial view, 1963.

Burrard Dry Dock Pier

Just east of the foot of Lonsdale is the restored Burrard Dry Dock Pier (A). This was Pier #3 of the Burrard Dry Dock shipyard (previous page). You can see it in the foreground (left of centre) of the 1963 photo (B). It was built in the 1920s and had a crane that moved on tracks, plus a stationary crane at the outer end, viewed here in 1953 (C). Besides building ships, ferries and other vessels throughout most of the twentieth century, Burrard Dry Dock did repairs. Pier #3 was used to repair 10,000–12,000-ton ships and ferries. If you walk on it now you'll see the old movable-crane tracks, as well as the four base pieces of the stationary crane — this one, for instance (D).

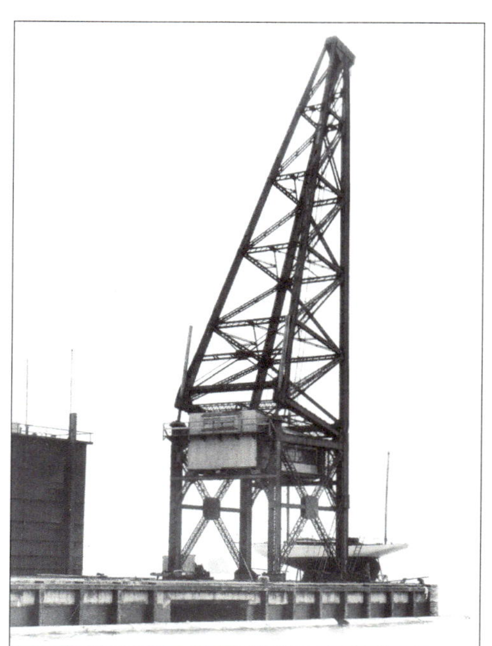
C – Stationary crane, 1953.

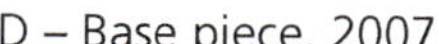

D – Base piece, 2007

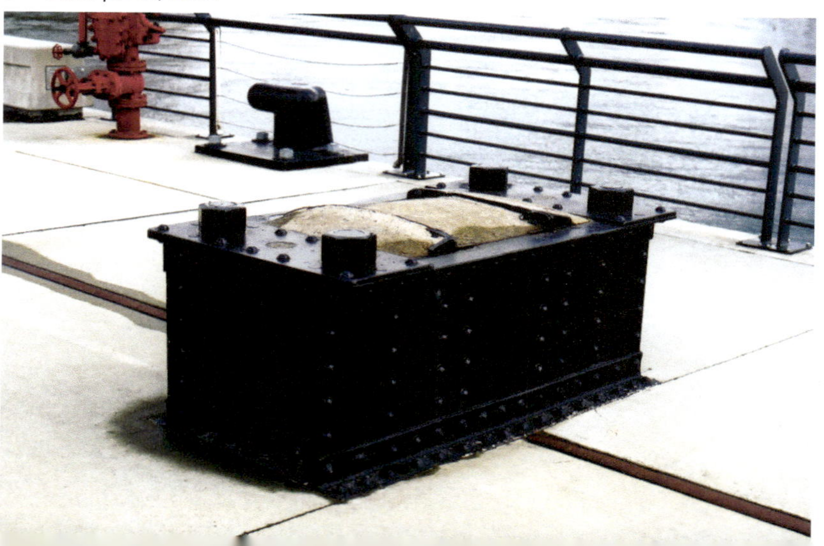

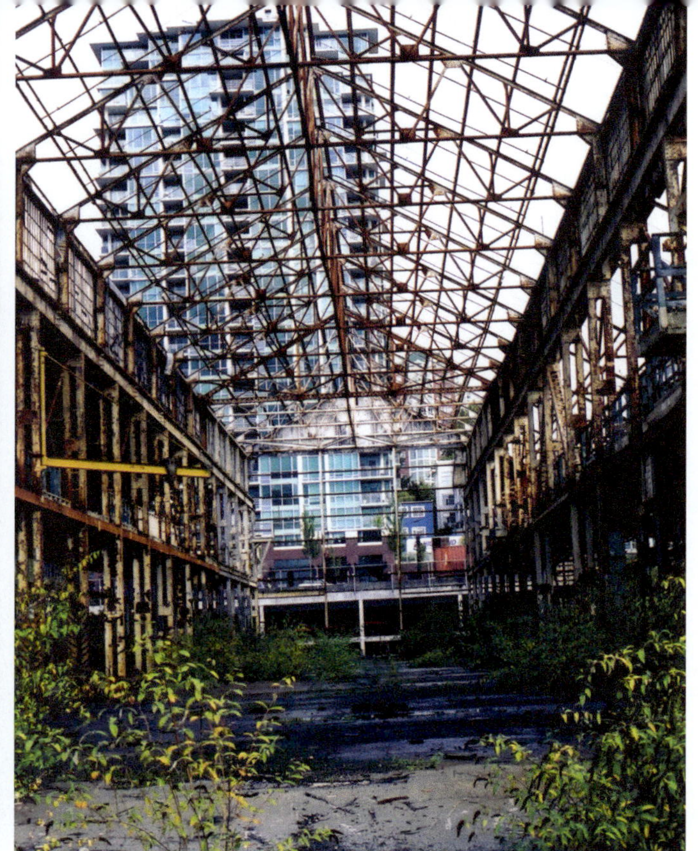
A – Machine Shop skeleton, 2007.

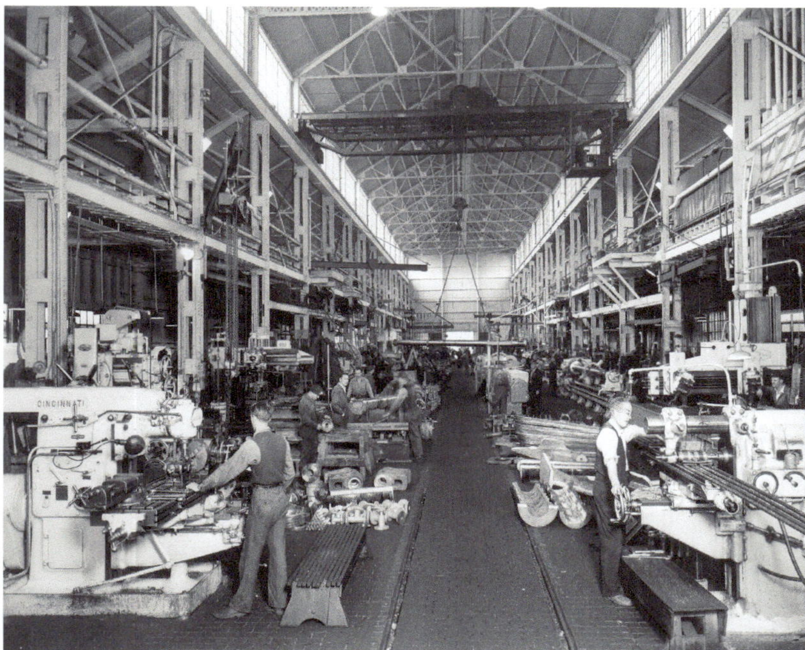

B – Interior, 1945.

The Machine Shop

In recent years, Lower Lonsdale visitors heading for the Burrard Dry Dock Pier on foot got to see the impressive building skeleton that fills this 2007 photo (A). This once was the shipyard's Machine Shop. Our modern photo looks straight north, up the centre of the interior. Check the same view in 1945, during World War II (B). The space is alive with workers operating lathes, milling machines, drill presses, grinding tools, and other equipment. Their job was to "fine-tune" new metal parts to precise specifications. As for the outside of the building, it looked like this in 1991 (C), when it was called "Fitters Shop." The building's remains are gone now, cleared away in 2008 (D).

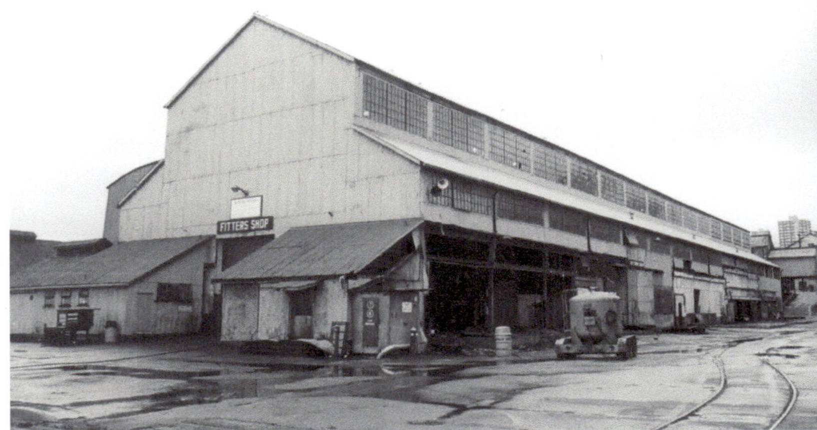

C – Exterior 1961.

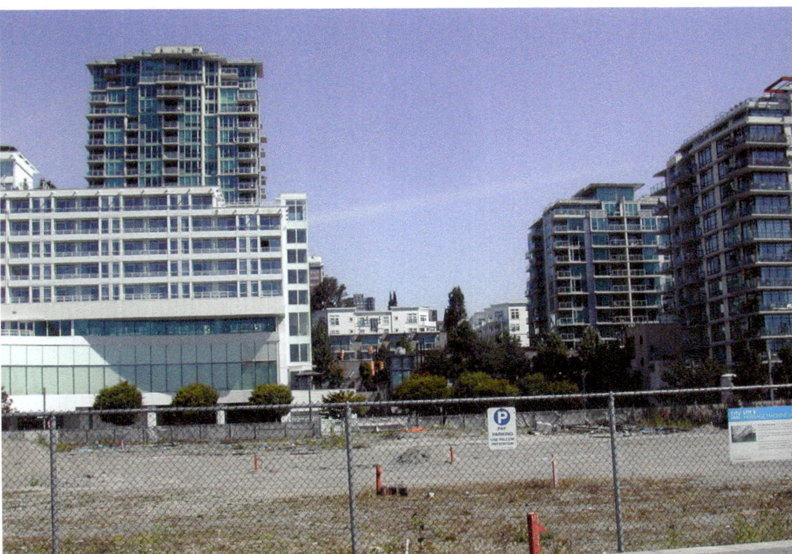
D – Machine Shop site, 2016.

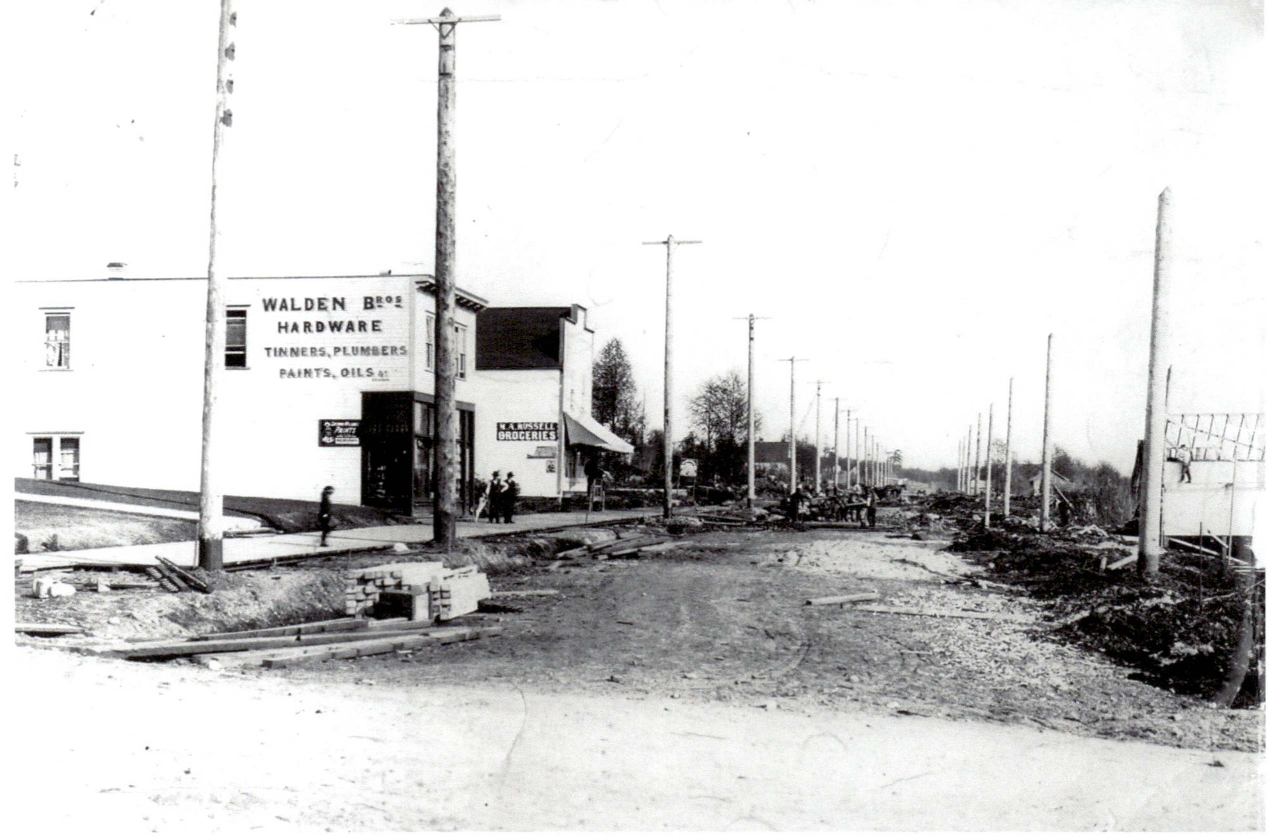

A – Looking east, c.1905.

East 1st Street

Around 1905, 1st Street was a mess, as you can see in this photo looking east from Lonsdale (A). There were few buildings (one was Walden Bros. Hardware on the left), and there was wood scattered all over from people clearing adjacent land. At least the electric power poles were installed (left). And so were the cable poles (right) for the streetcar line soon to be built. The same view in 2016 (B) shows East 1st to be an attractive modern street lined with a mixture of old and new buildings. The streetcar service came and went between photos (1906–1947).

B – Same view, 2016.

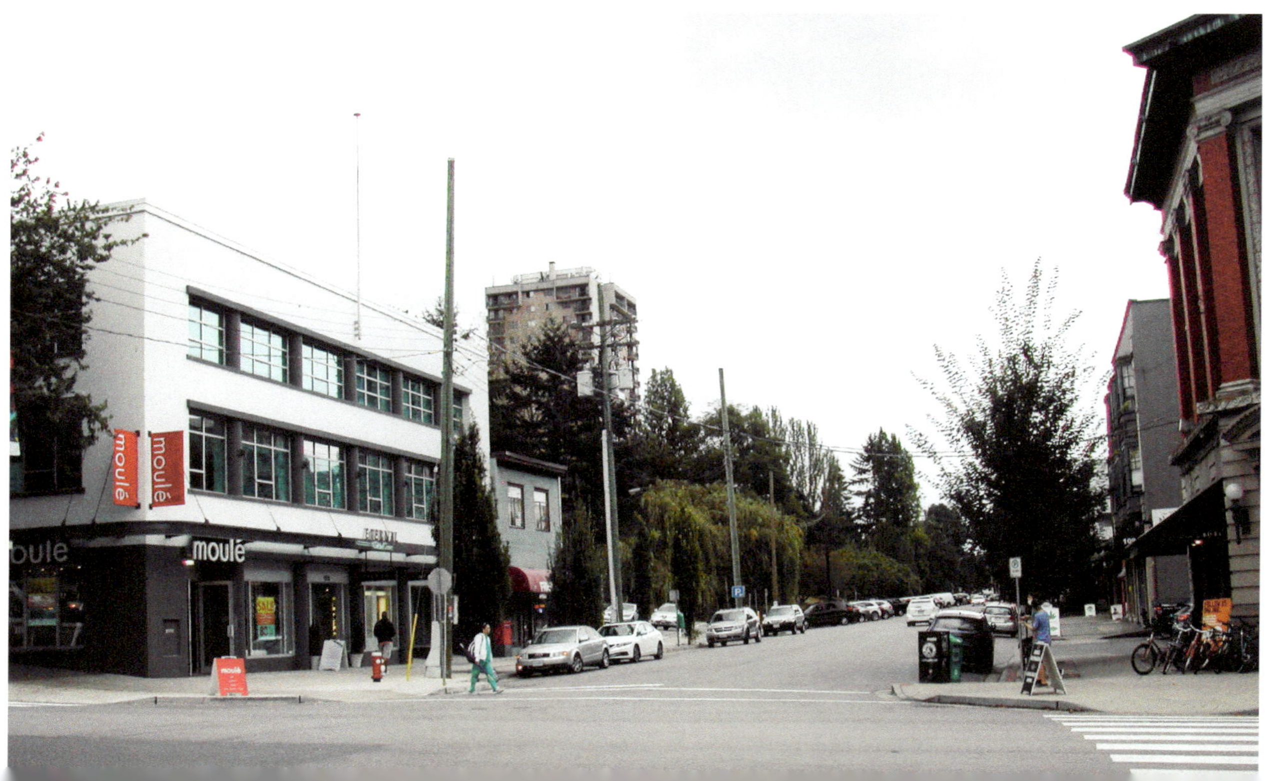

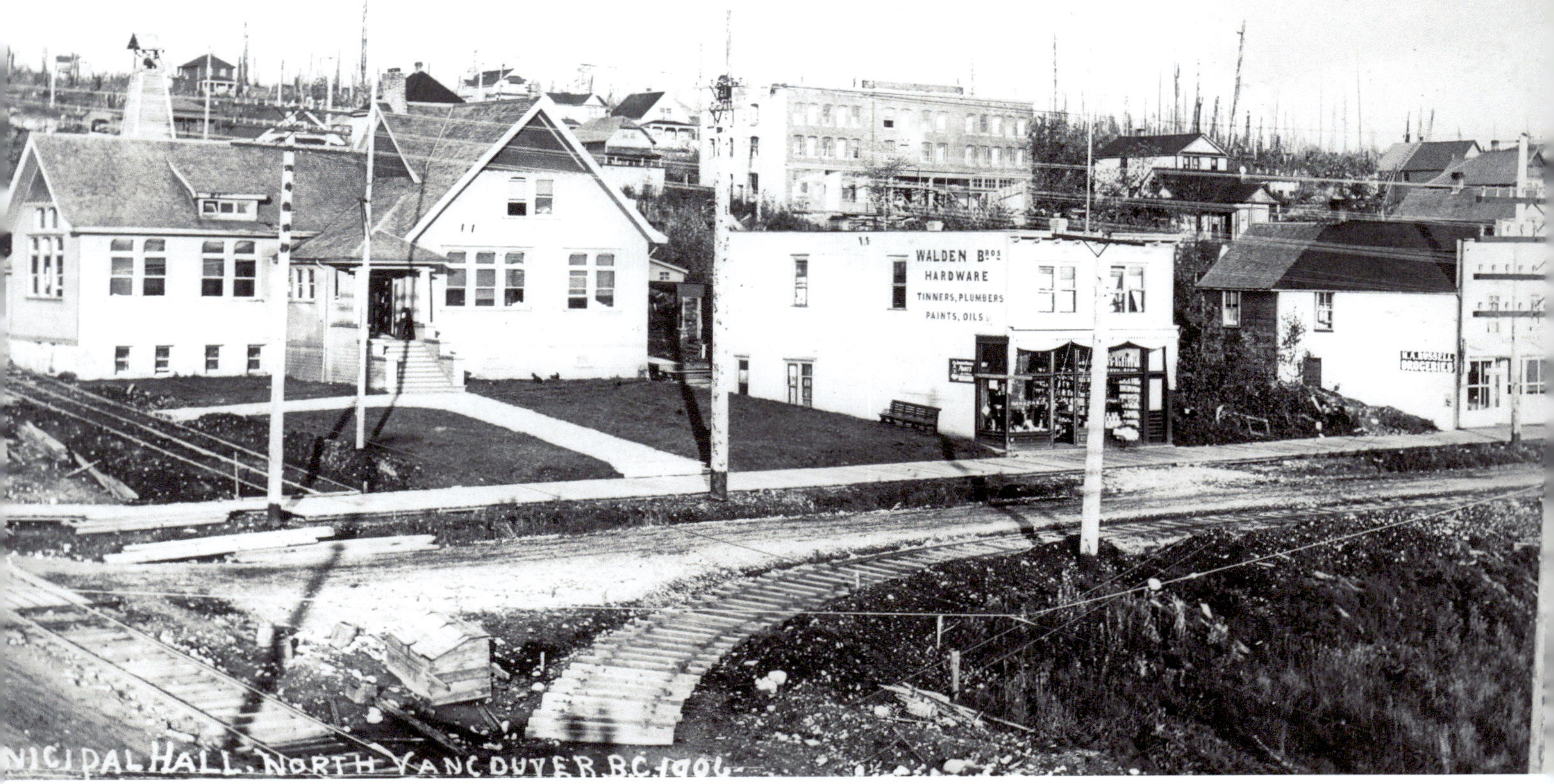

A – Northeast corner, 1906.

Lonsdale & 1st: northeast corner

The 1906 photo (A) shows North Vancouver's Municipal Hall (later the City Hall) on the northeast corner of Lonsdale and 1st. It was built when the City and District were one municipality. The building to the right of it is the Walden Bros. Hardware store, which supplied hardware, paints, oils, grates, tiles, and house furnishing to early residents. Now examine a 2016 photo of the same corner (B). A large white building covers the old Municipal Hall site. Built in the late 1940s, this was the post office for many years and presently contains private businesses. But notice the tiny building beside it, on the right. It's the old Walden Bros. building — now over 100 years old. Today it's the "Friendly Grocery," shown in this 2016 close-up (C).

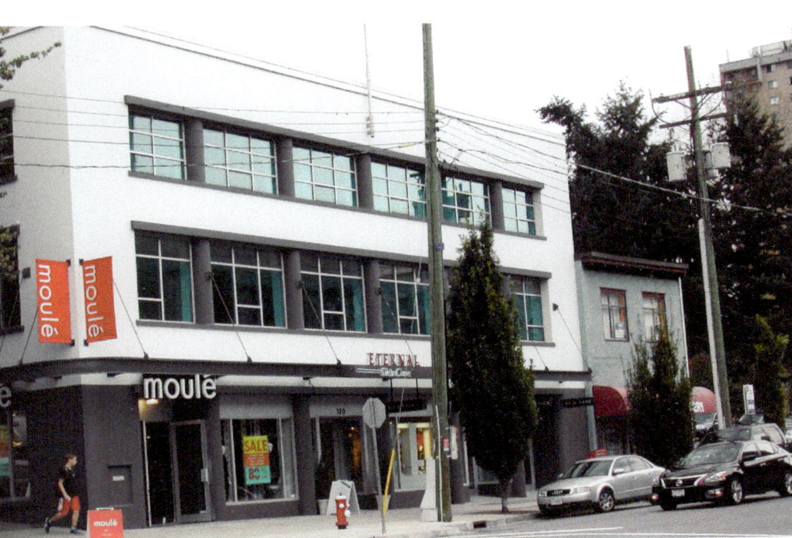

B – Modern view, 2016.

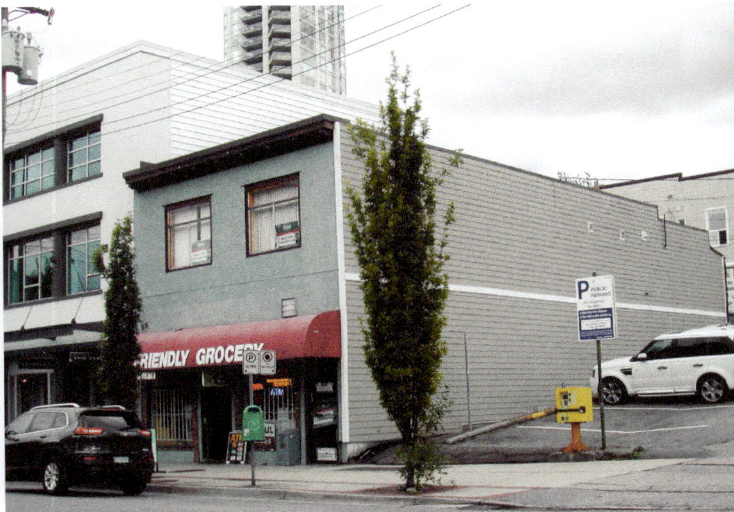

C – Friendly Grocery, 2016.

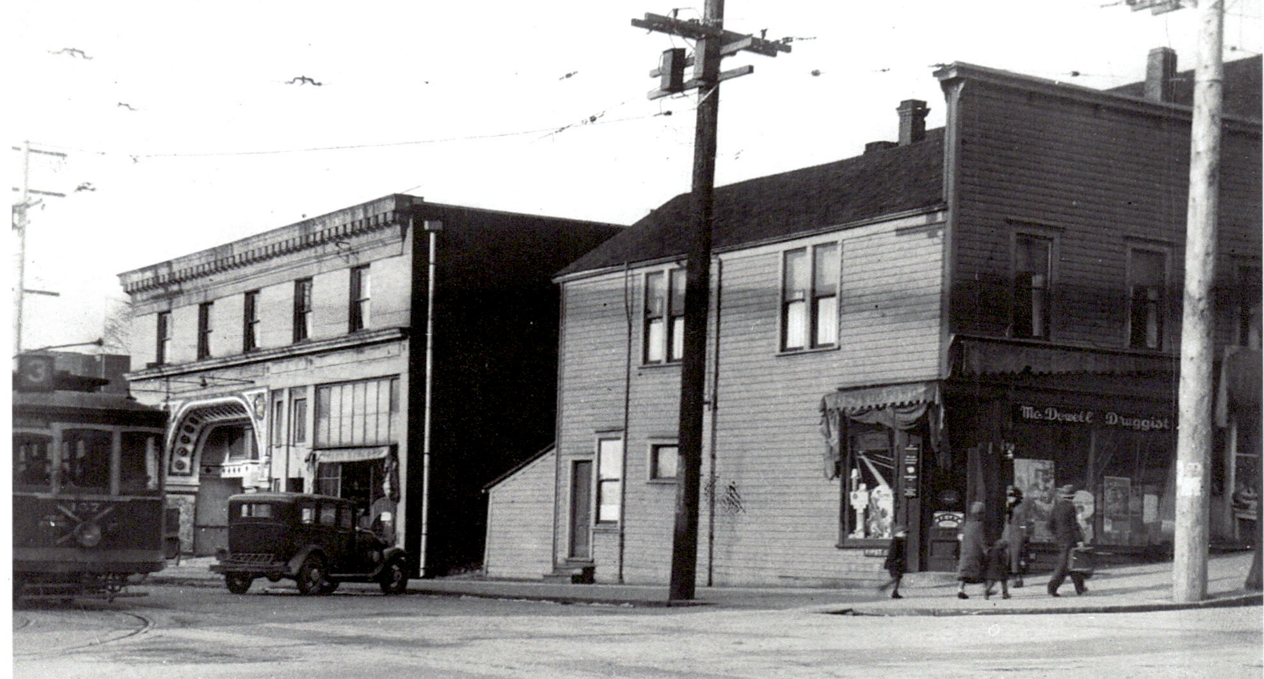

A – Northwest corner, 1936.

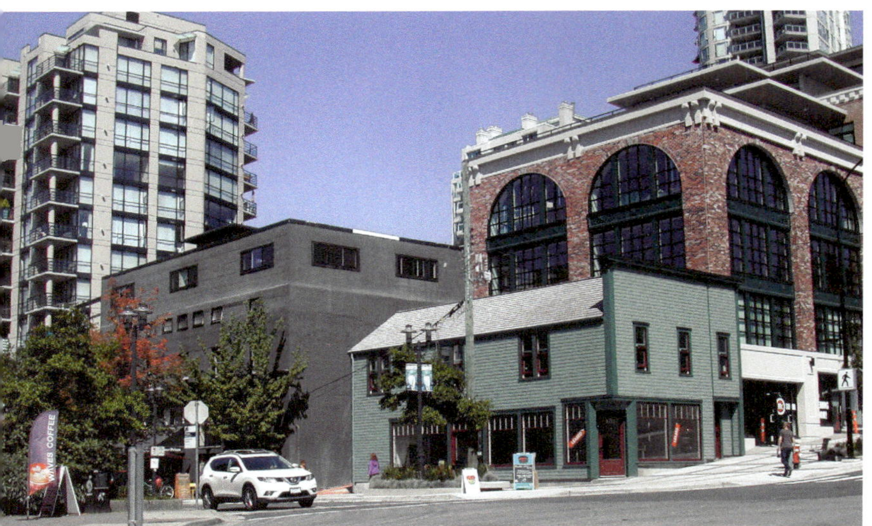

B – Same corner, 2016.

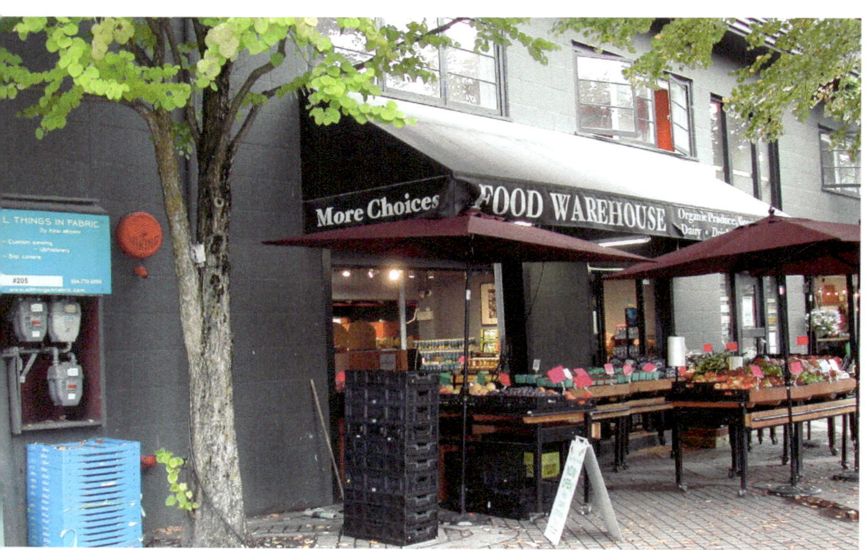

C – Food Warehouse entrance, 2016.

Lonsdale & 1st: northwest corner

In the 1936 photo (A) we see the Empire Theatre building on the left, at 110 West 1st (note the wide entrance). Built in 1912, the theatre presented silent movies and live vaudeville performances until it closed in 1934. On the right is the Beasley Block, which was built in 1904 at the corner of Lonsdale & 1st. In 1936 it still had its original main-floor tenant, McDowell's Drug Store. McDowell's stocked such medical ingredients as heroin, opium, mercury, strychnine, chloroform, and arsenic, which doctors continued to prescribe to patients in the 1930s. Both buildings are still there (B). The Beasley is now newly renovated, and the Empire is two storeys taller. A Food Warehouse occupies the theatre space, with its wide entrance and sloping inside floor (C).

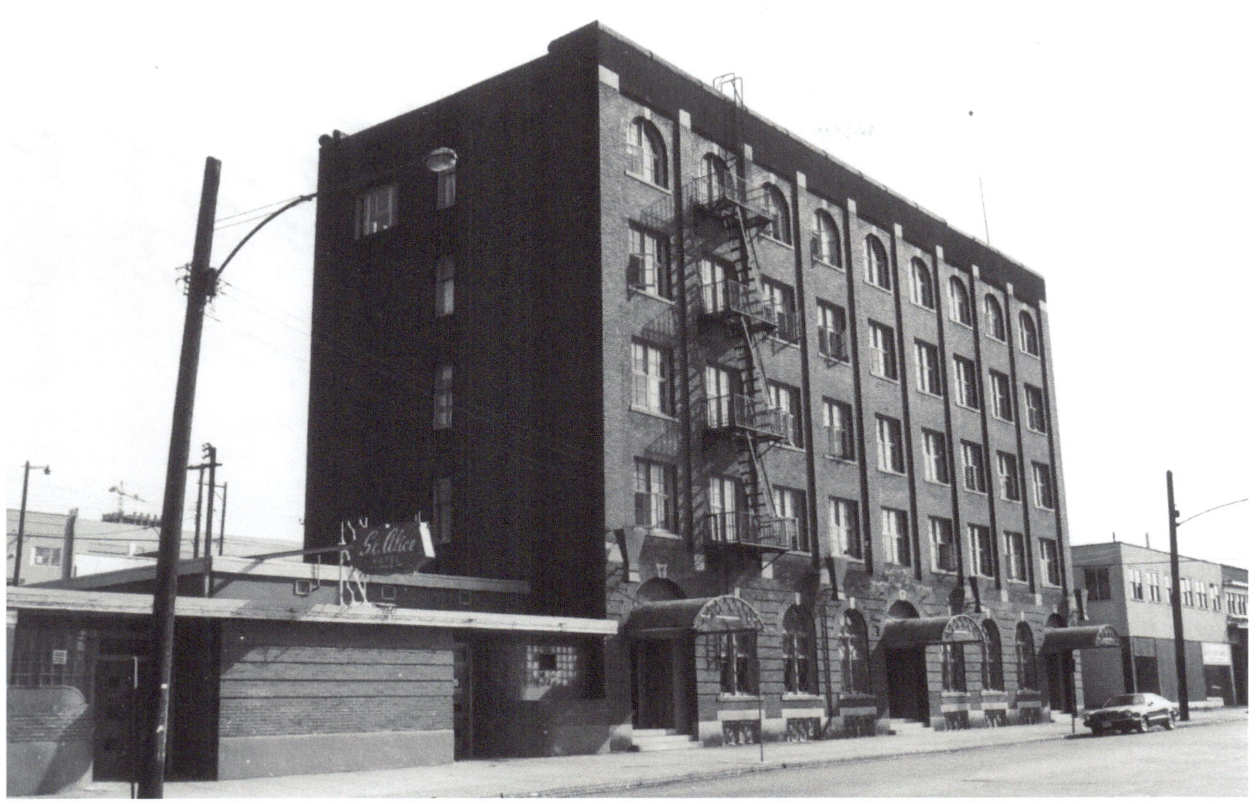

A – St. Alice Hotel, 1970.

St. Alice Hotel

The St. Alice, seen here in 1970 (A), was once called the "Grand Lady" of early North Vancouver hotels. It opened in 1912 to much fanfare, including a sumptuous banquet, speeches by the mayor and other dignitaries, and dancing to the music of a live orchestra. Five storeys high, it had 70 rooms, plus a dining hall, banquet room, lounge, beer parlour, and other facilities. Its glory, unfortunately, faded in later years. During World War II it was converted into a 35-unit apartment block for Navy families, and eventually it housed low-income men. The St, Alice was demolished in 1989, and a condominium tower called "The Observatory" was built on the site, 120 West 2nd (B).

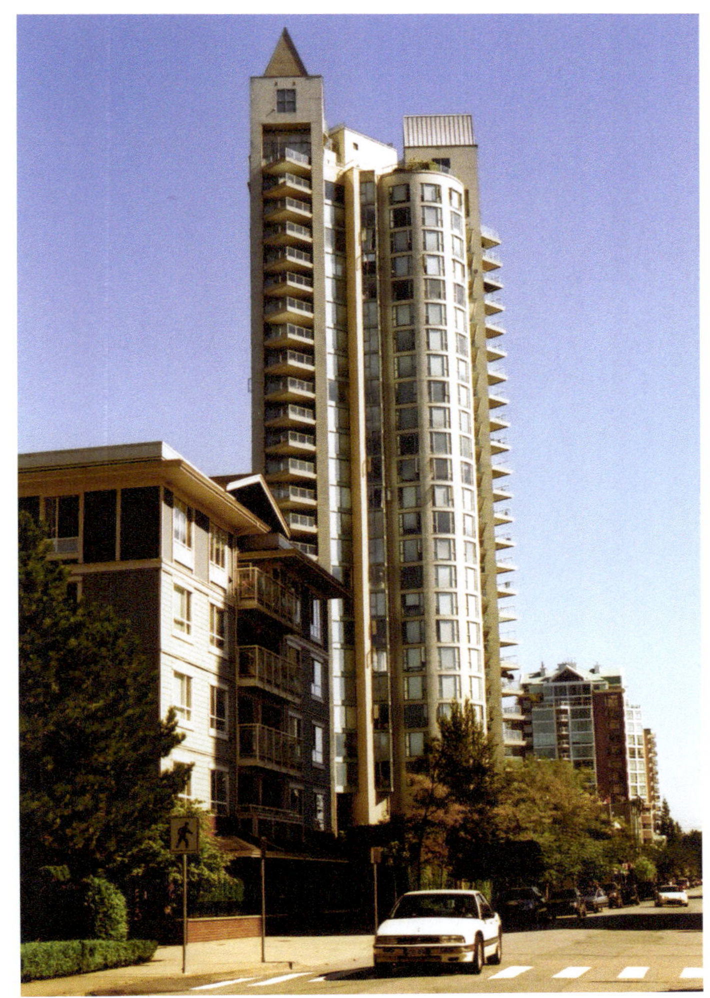

B – Condominium tower, 2007.

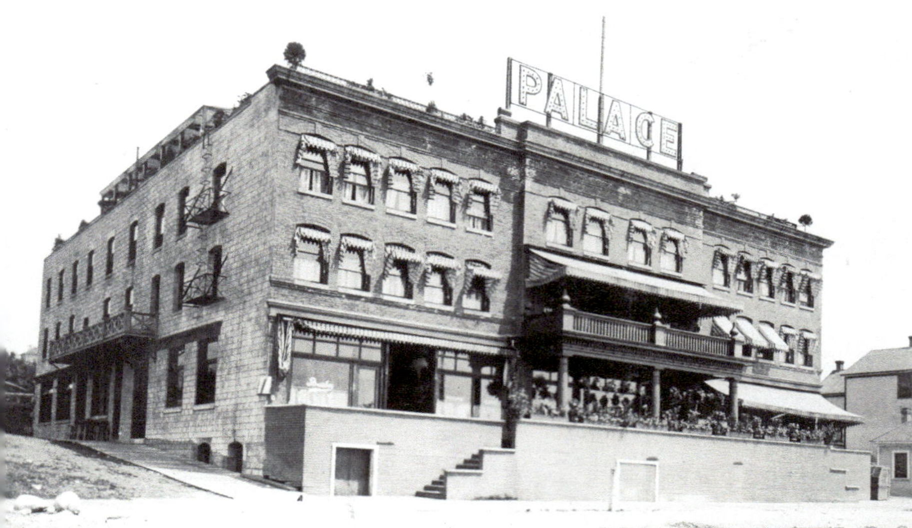

A – Palace Hotel, c.1909.

Palace Hotel

"The only hotel in British Columbia with a roof garden," proclaimed a 1909 advertisement. The subject was the elegant Palace Hotel on East 2nd, seen in this contemporary photo (A). Opened in 1906, it also boasted "100 rooms with hot and cold running water, electric lights, telephone, call bells, prompt and attentive service, $2/day and upwards." The Palace had a central courtyard (B), a ladies reception room (C), café & grill room, billiard room, bar, rooms "*en suite* with private bath," and many other conveniences. Later its name was changed to "Olympic Hotel." It declined over time and was demolished in 1989. It was replaced by a condominium high-rise called "The Olympic," 130 East 2nd (D).

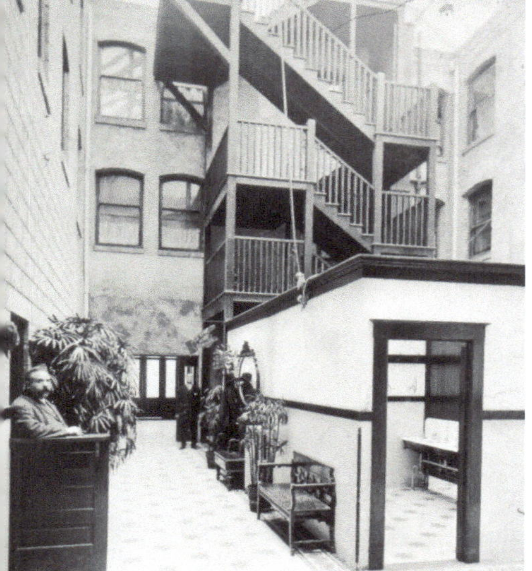

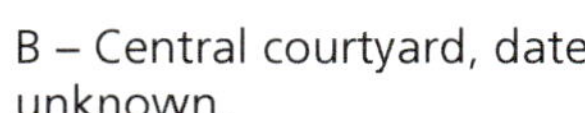

B – Central courtyard, date unknown.

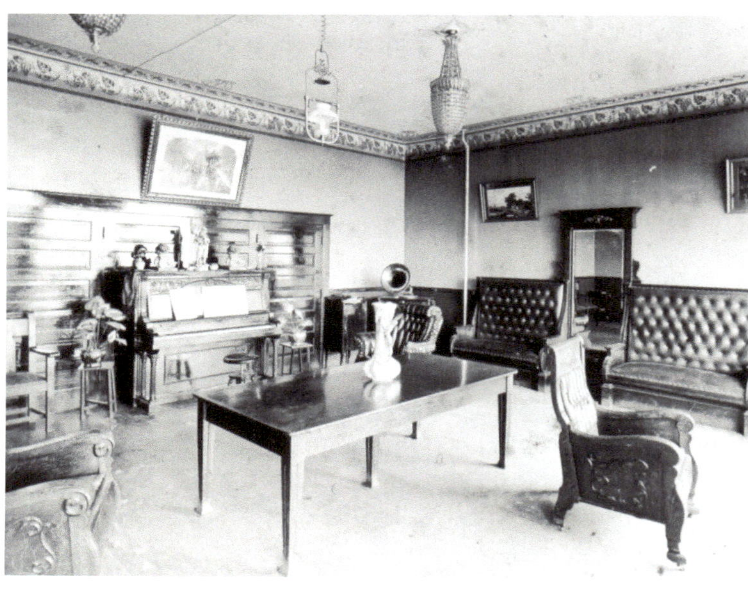

C – Ladies reception room, date unknown.

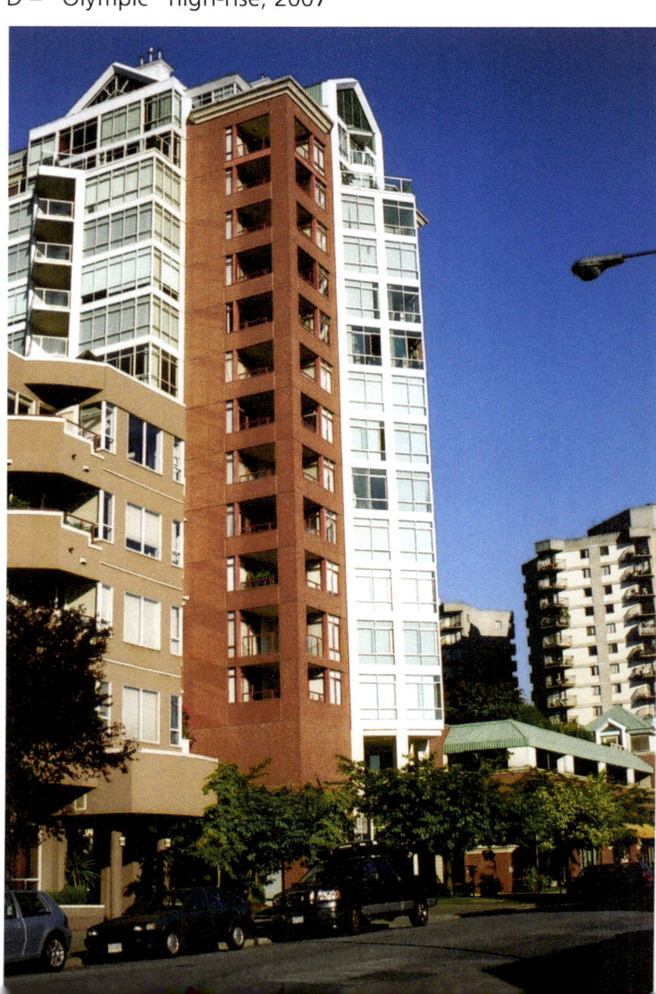

D – "Olympic" high-rise, 2007

Lonsdale & 3rd: northwest corner

Over the past century the northwest corner of Lonsdale & 3rd went from residential to business, then back to residential. In the photo taken around 1907 (A), we see the home of William Morden and his family, which stood here. Mr. Morden built the house in 1903. In the 1950s (B), the same corner was the site of Everett Motors Co. Ltd., a Dodge-DeSoto dealer that sold and serviced cars and trucks. In one ad, the company promoted "glamorous" Dodges and "dashing" DeSotos. A condominium complex now sits on this corner (C).

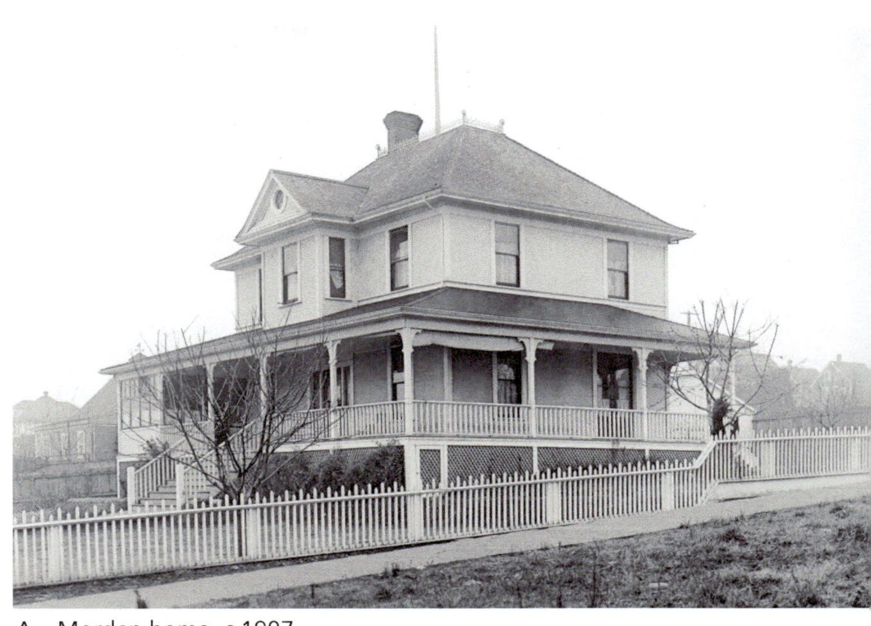

A – Morden home, c.1907.

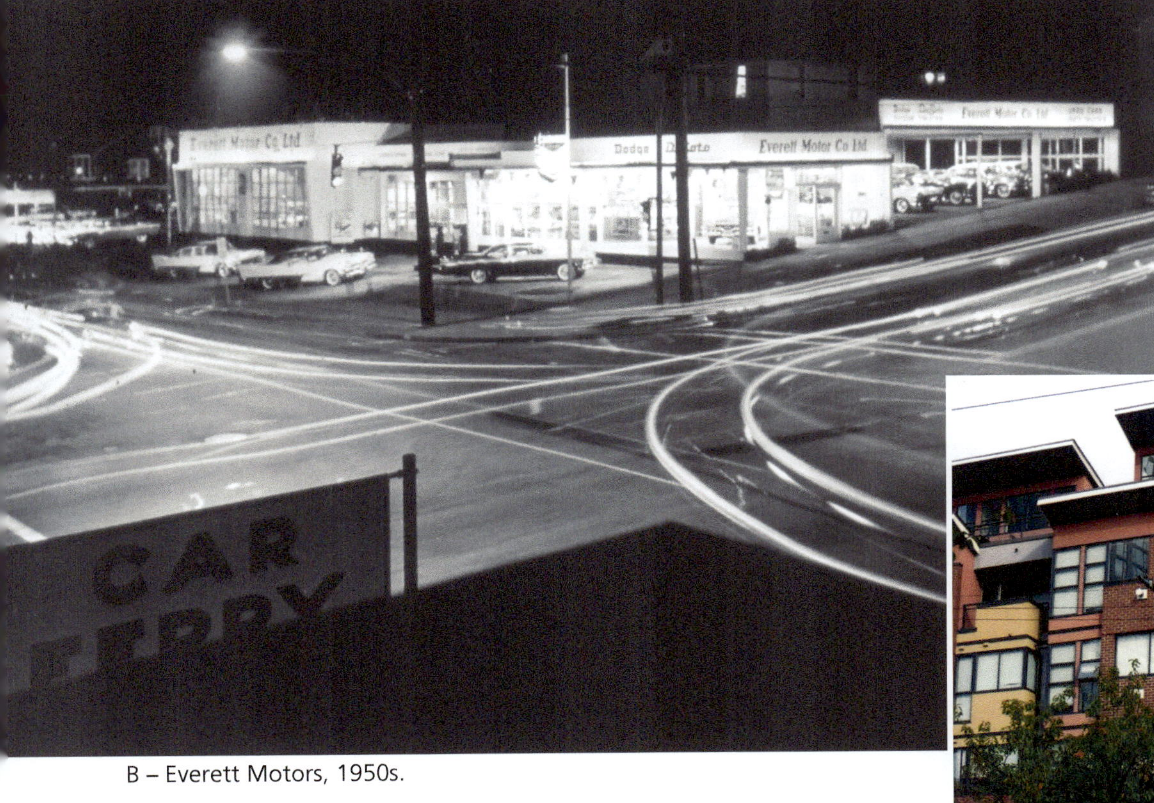

B – Everett Motors, 1950s.

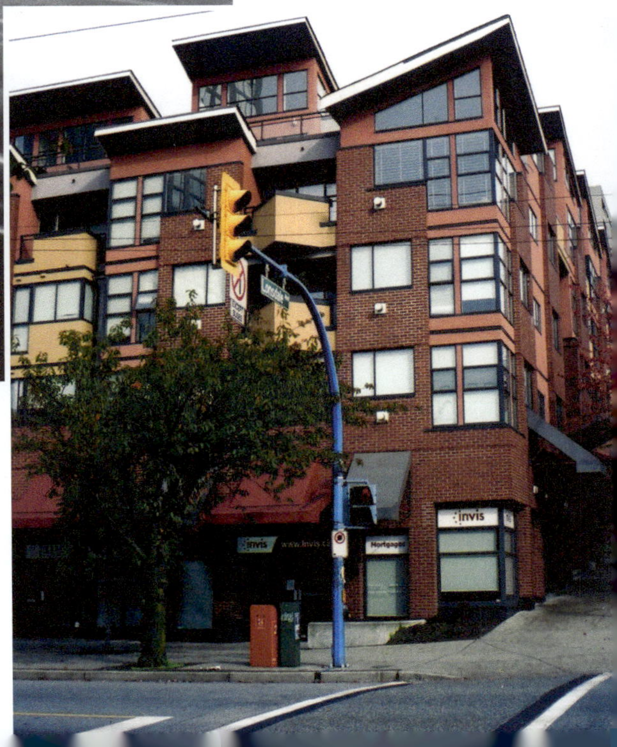

C – Condominium complex, 2007.

John Brind's Blacksmith Shop

When your car, van, or truck breaks down, you take it to a garage for repairs. Before cars, however, people drove horse-drawn buggies and wagons. And when these broke down, the owners took them to the nearest blacksmith shop, the equivalent of our modern garage. North Vancouver had several of these in the early years, including John Brind's establishment at 123 West 3rd, seen in the 1913 photo (A). A photograph taken in 1920 shows the inside (B). Brind and his staff heated irons in a hot forge and used them to build or repair wagon-wheel rims, horse harness fittings, and other metal parts. Now there's a one-storey "NIKI Design & Glass Studio"at 123 West 3rd (C).

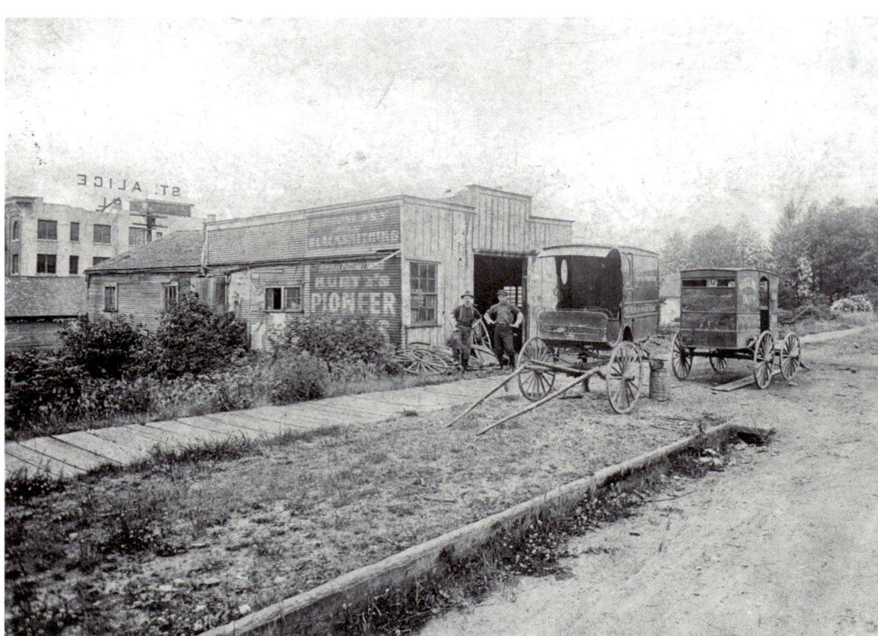

A – Blacksmith shop, 1913.

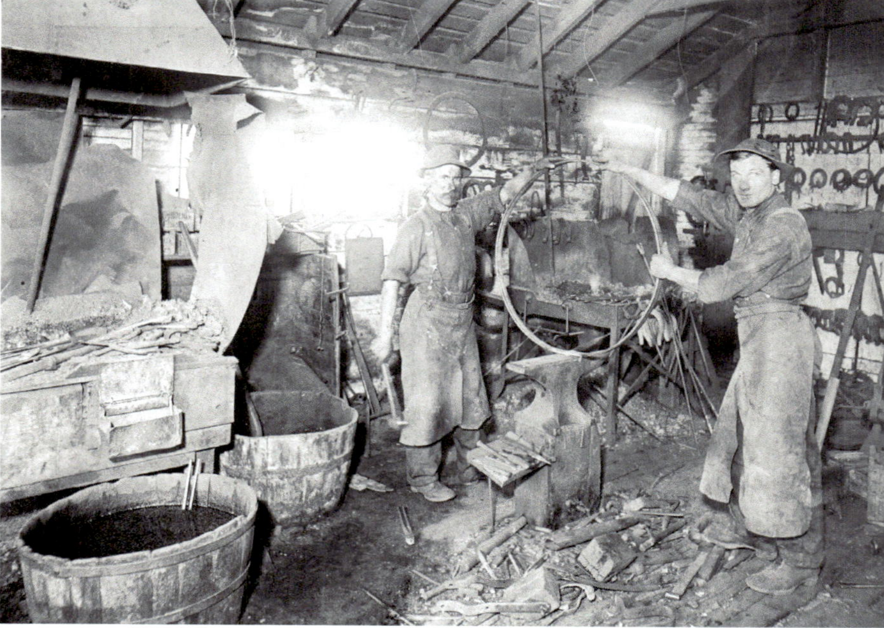

B – Interior, 1920.

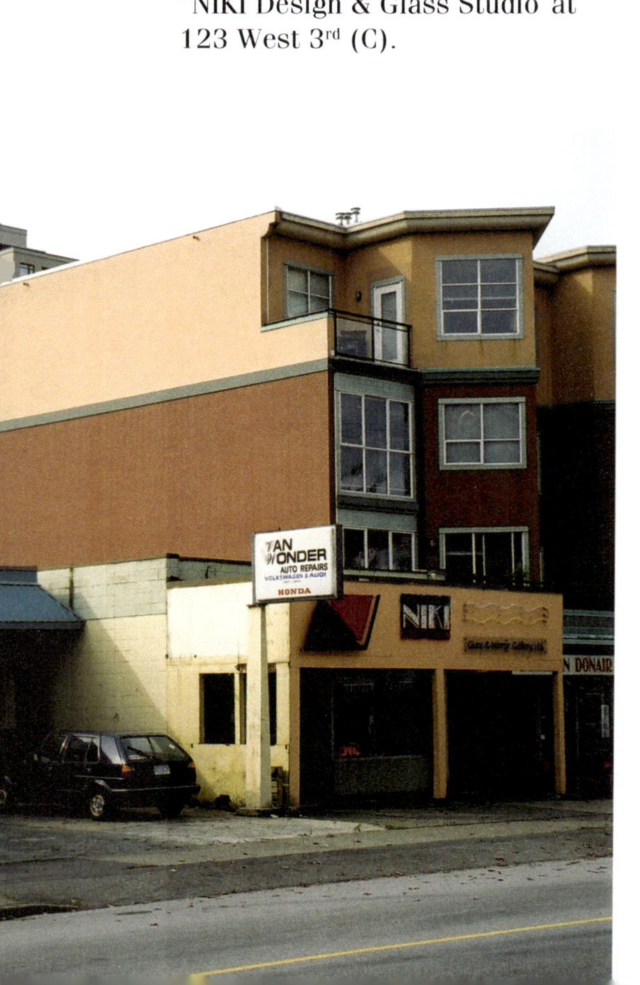

C – NIKI, 2007.

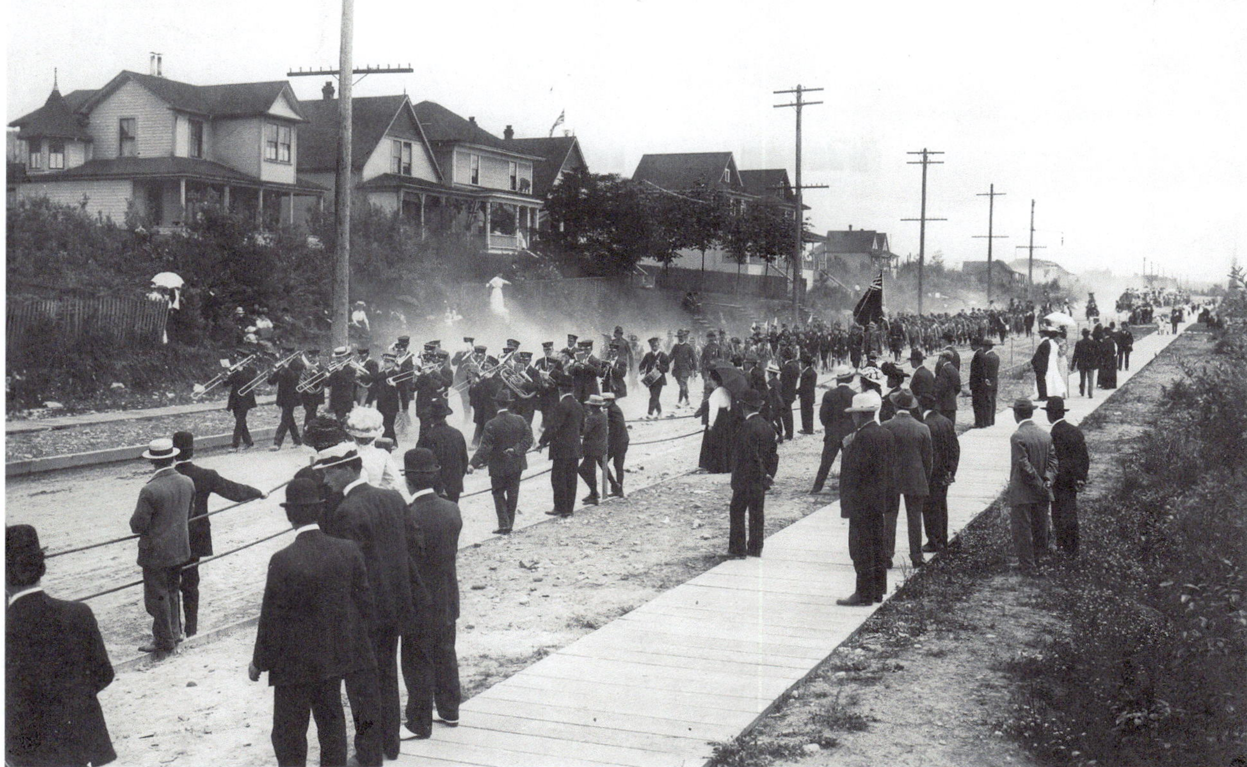

A – East 3rd, c. 1910.

100 Block of East 3rd

This 1910 photo (A) shows the 100 block of East 3rd Street on July 1st. In it we see the annual Dominion Day Parade marching westward toward Lonsdale. Notice the wooden sidewalk in the foreground and the four homes on the left in the picture. In the early part of the twentieth century, when our local hills were cloaked in old-growth forests, all North Vancouver sidewalks were made of wooden planks. The same view in 2008 (B) shows modern concrete sidewalks, apartments and condos — plus three of the homes in the 1910 photo. Actually all four are still there. The nearest has been moved forward on the lot, thus blocking our view of its immediate neighbour.

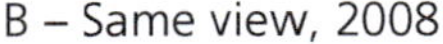

B – Same view, 2008

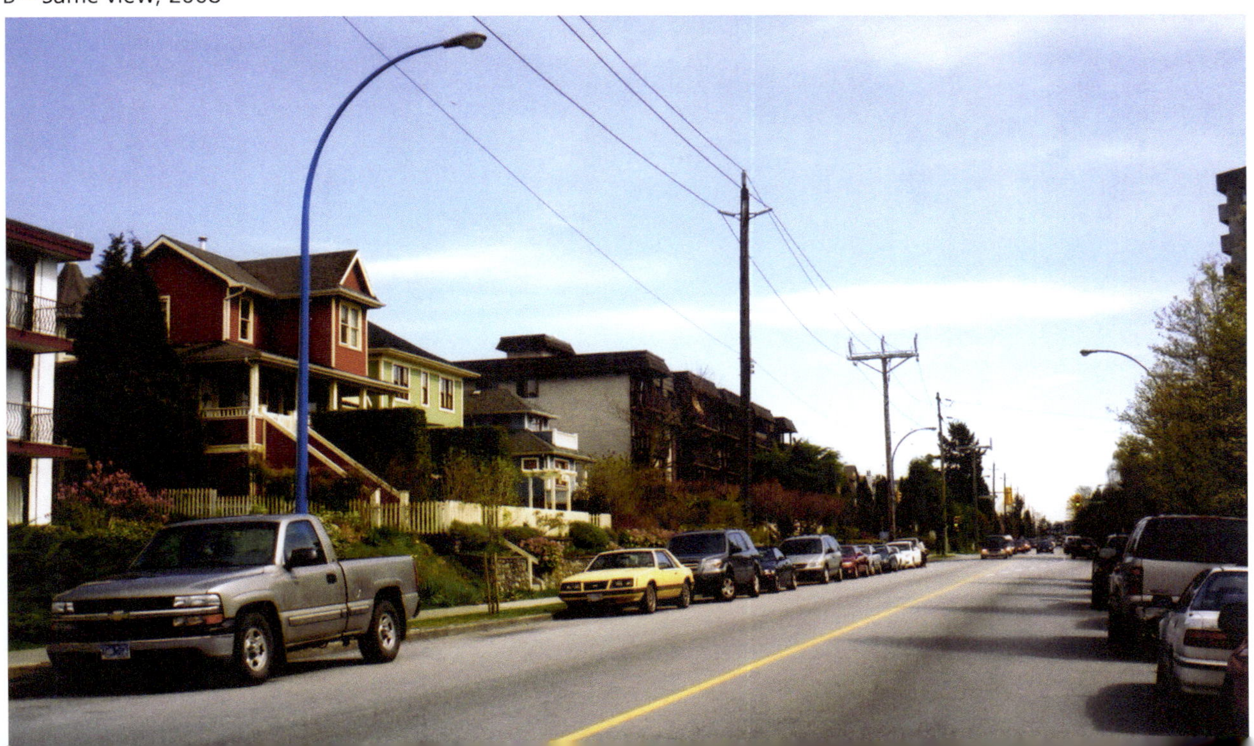

Funeral Chapel

For decades the Harron Bros. Funeral Chapel helped North Vancouver families make the final break with the physical remains of loved ones who once glowed with life. It was founded in 1913 by Andrew Harron, who built the chapel and his family's home back-to-back in the same building. The chapel faced south, at 122 West 6th. The family home faced north, at 123 West Keith. Notice what the front of the chapel looked like around 1950 (A). By the early 1960s, it was re-named North Vancouver Funeral Chapel and had a different appearance (B). The same 6th Street view in 2007 shows the rear of the Beaconhill Apartments high-rise and its parking area (125 West Keith), which cover the chapel's original footprint.

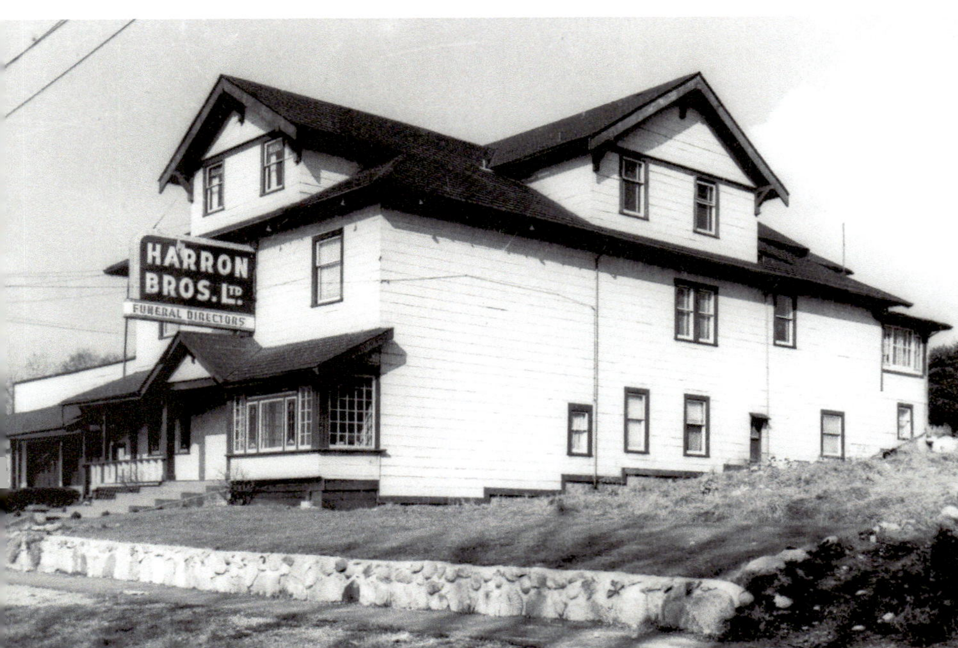

A – Funeral Chapel, c.1950.

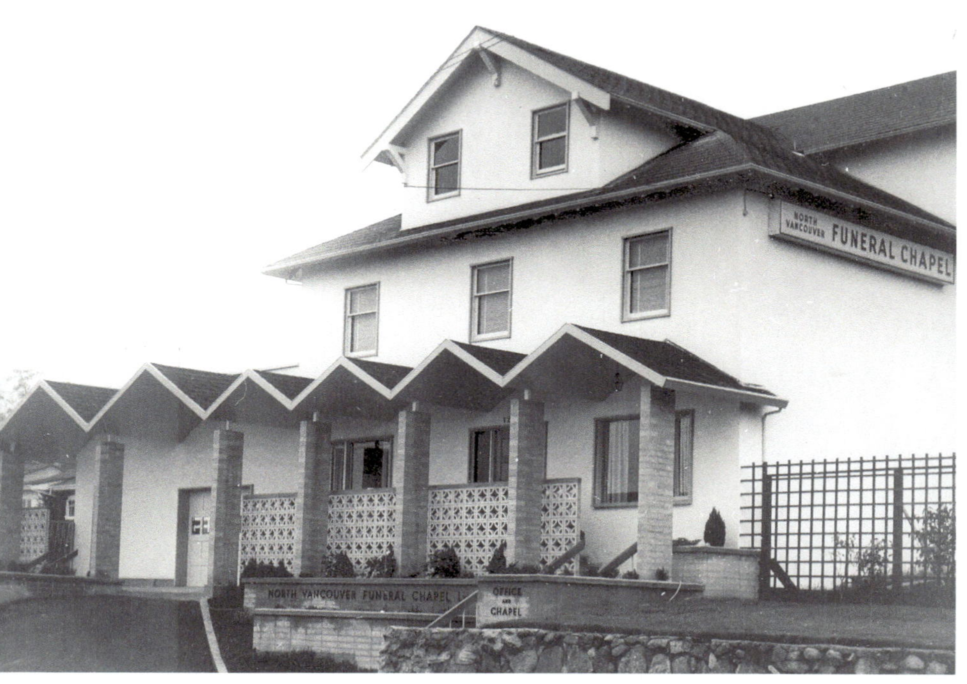

B – Chapel, early 1960s.

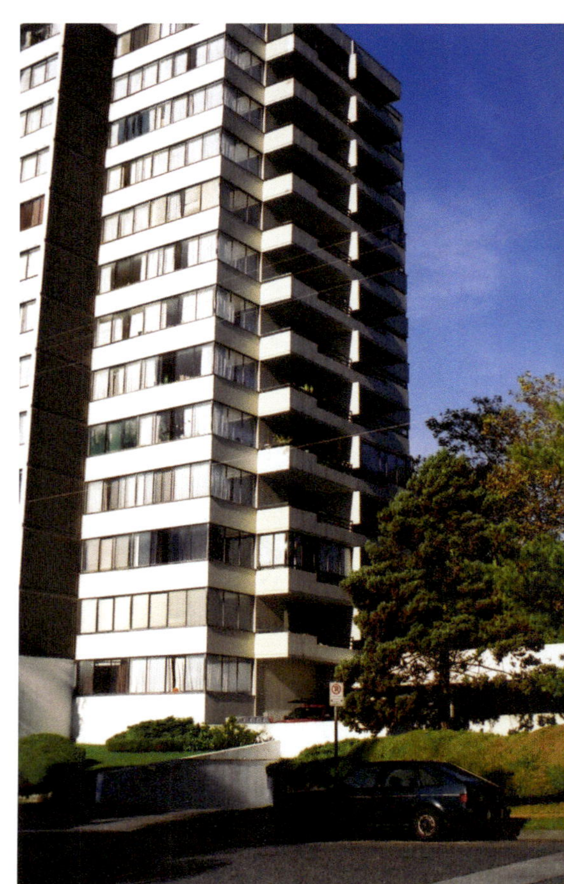

C – High-rise & parking, 2007.

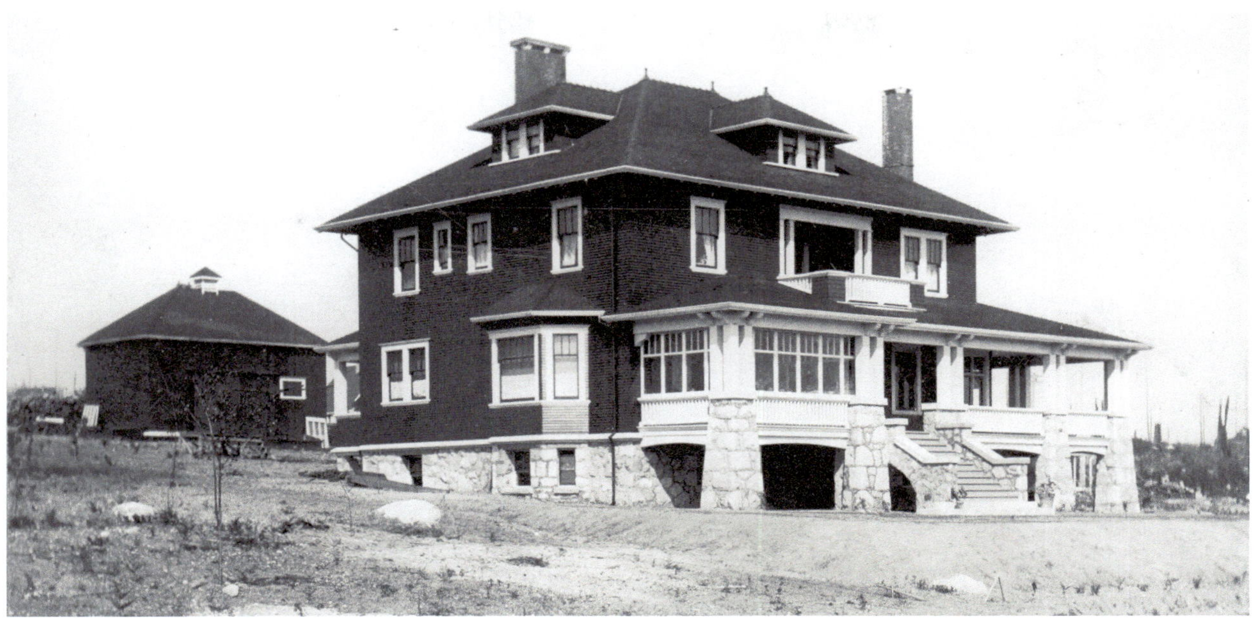

A – McNair family home, 1907.

The McNair Home

In the early 1900s, wealthy investor and shingle-mill owner James McNair owned the whole block (yes, all 16 lots) between St. Georges & St. Andrews and Keith Road & 6th Street. He built a spectacular home for his family on the 6th Street side. You can see it in this 1907 photo (A), taken just after it was built. The house is still there, at 256 East 6th (B). Of course, McNair's land is covered with condominiums now. The old house, in fact, is the centrepiece of a condo complex.

B – Part of a condo complex, 2007.

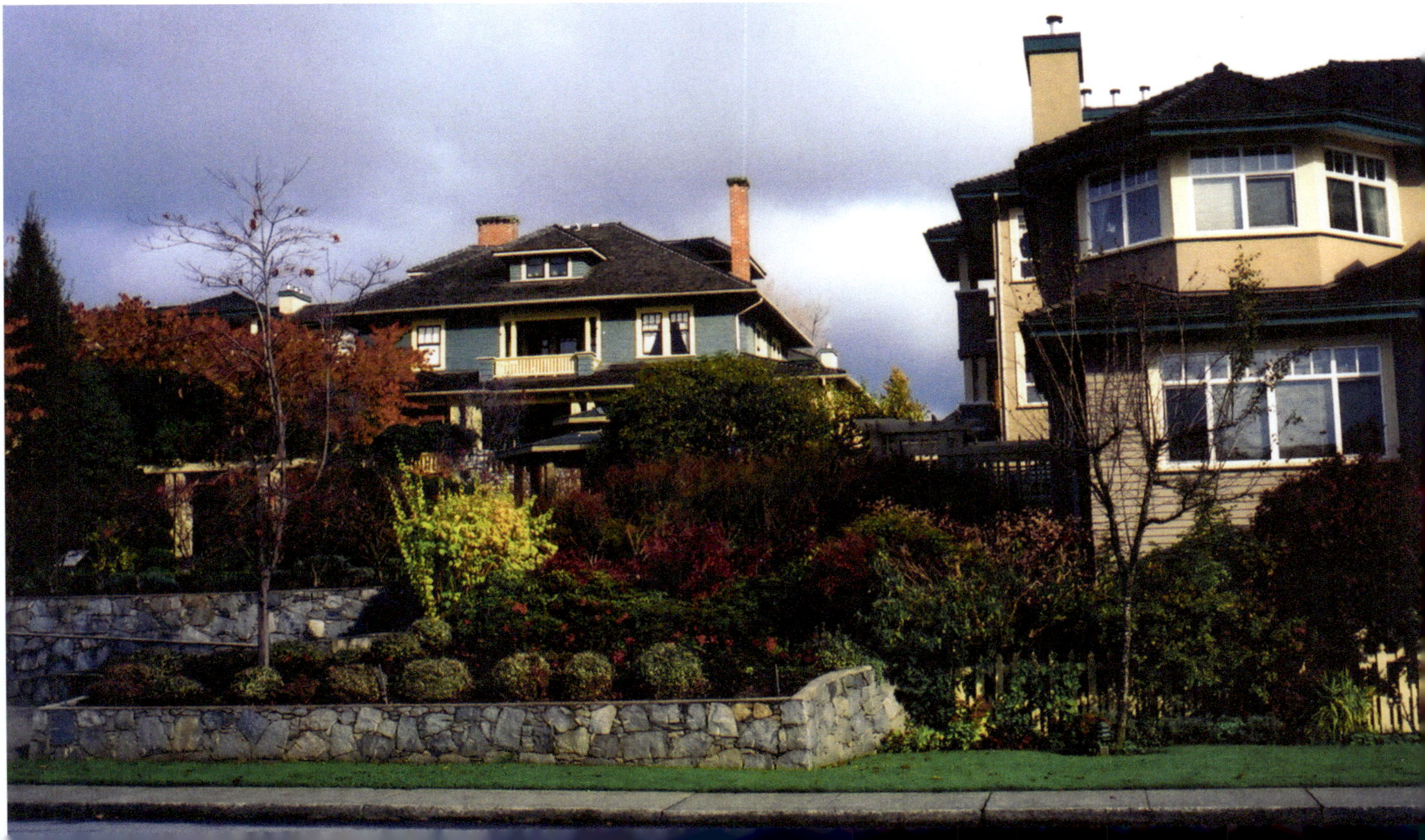

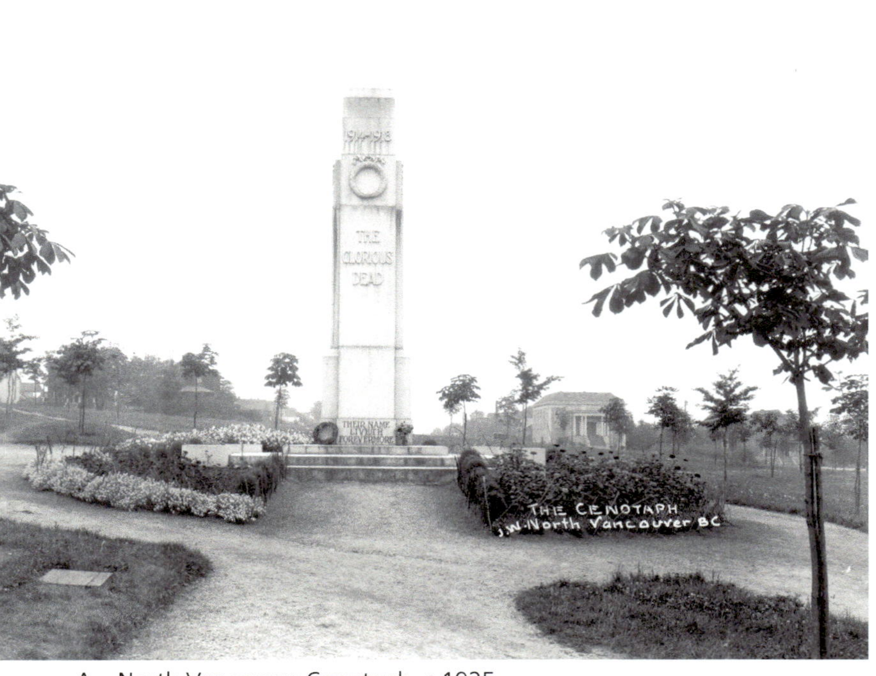

A – North Vancouver Cenotaph, c.1925.

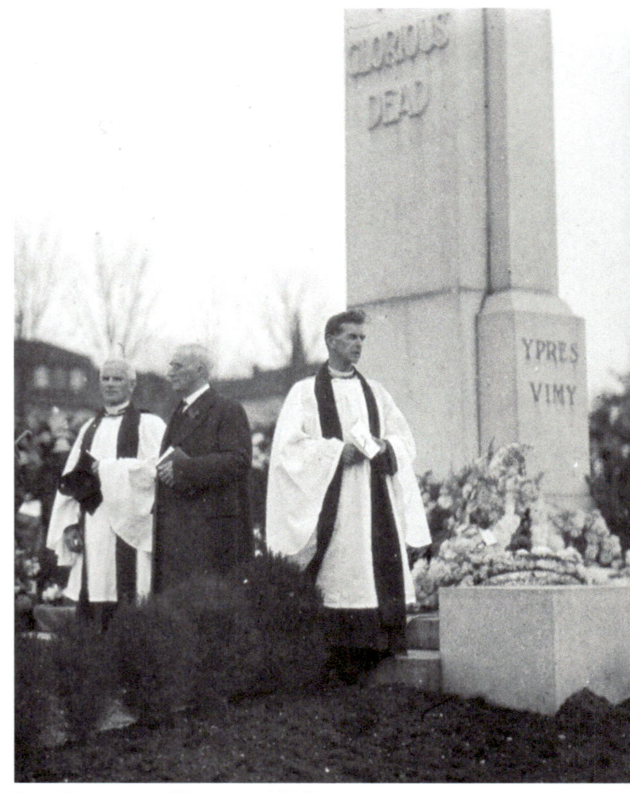

B – Close-up of base, c.1923.

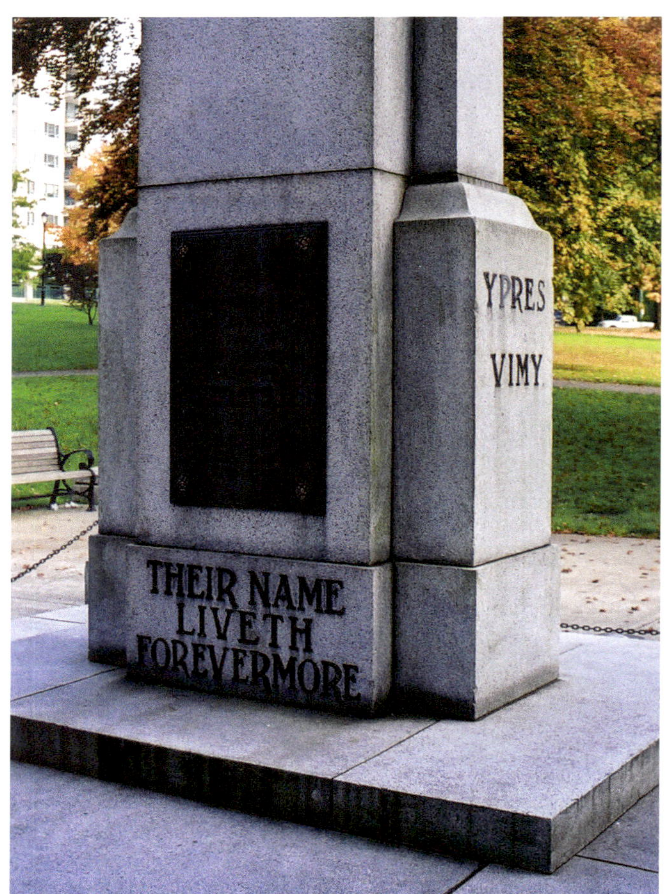

C – Added plaque: Boer War, World Wars I & II, 2007.

The Cenotaph

The young men from North Vancouver who fought in World War I faced trench warfare, explosions, poison gas, rotting corpses, mud, disease, and mutilation. Over 100 died between 1914 and 1918. Others returned home with shattered bodies and minds. In 1923, inspired by the Whitehall Cenotaph (London, England), North Vancouver erected a Cenotaph in Victoria Park to honour its World War I dead. Notice how it looked around 1925 (A), and in the close-up taken around 1923 (B). Since then, the Cenotaph has been altered to also honour North Vancouver's Boer War, World War II, Korean and Afghanistan casualties (C & D).

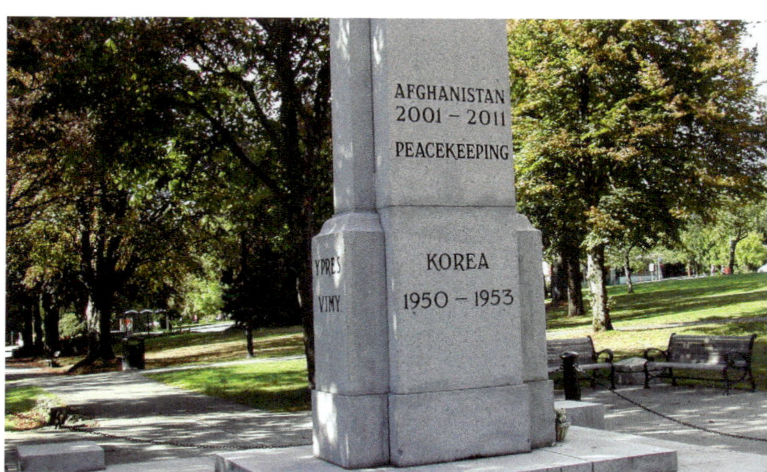

D – Korea and Afghanistan, 2016.

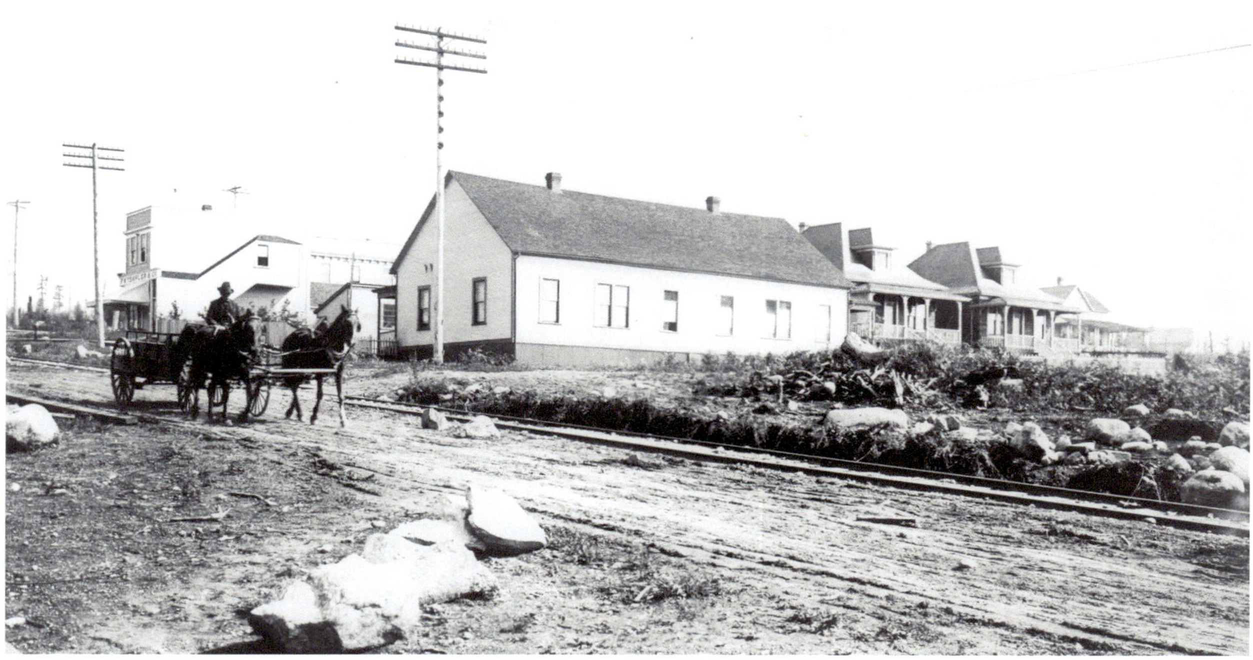

A – Morden Hall, c.1907.

Morden Hall

Morden Hall was one of North Vancouver's first gymnasiums. Built around 1902 on the northeast corner of Lonsdale and Upper Keith, it's the larger building in the photo taken around 1907 (A). Lonsdale was still unpaved — and that's the future Victoria Park on the right. While it hosted other activities, Morden Hall's main function was to serve as a gym for basketball players. Not just local players, but top players from City of Vancouver teams came here to practice and improve their skills. A few years after the photo was taken, however, the building was remodelled and turned into a residential duplex. It was demolished in 1965. An apartment building sits there today, across the street from Victoria Park (B).

B – Apartment building, 2008.

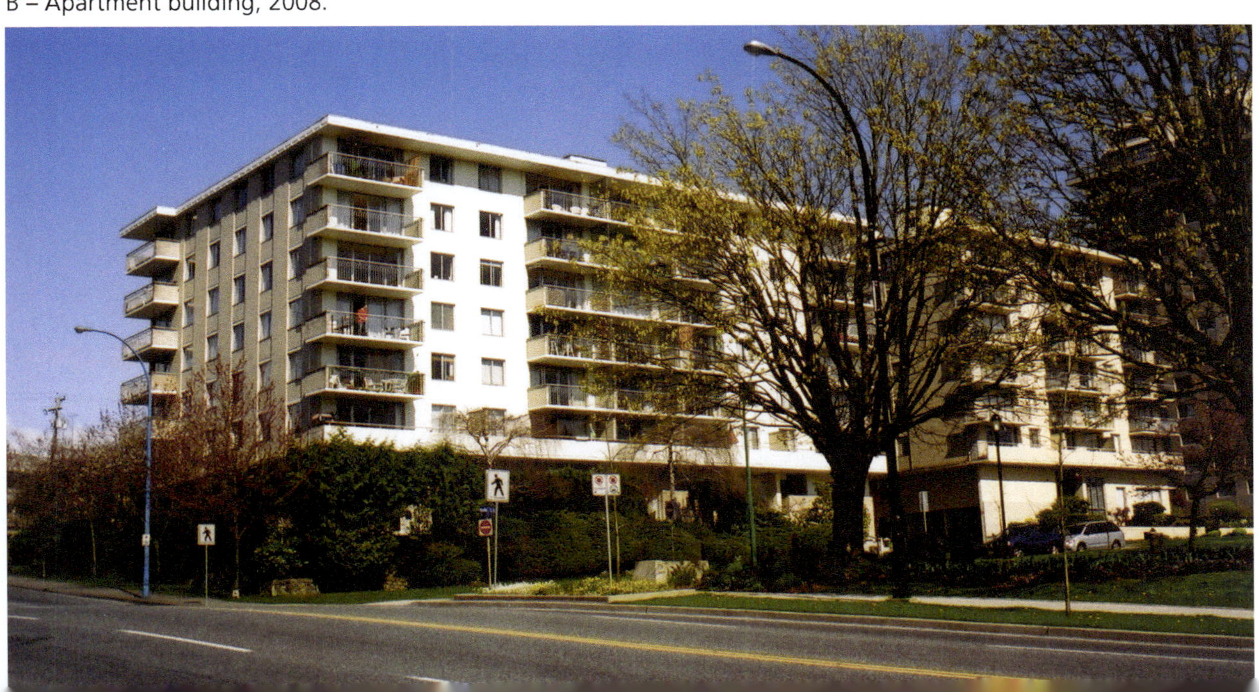

Corner of Lonsdale & 8th

On the northwest corner of Lonsdale & 8th (where Lonsdale bends) James Burnes and his family lived in a seven-room home, seen here in 1906 (A). The house faced 8th and its address was 112 West 8th. Notice the wooden-plank sidewalks, and the large burnt tree stump. The burnt stump was the result of a forest fire that swept through here in 1898. In the early 1950s the same corner was occupied by Webb's Drug Store (B), which had a Lonsdale address, tenants living upstairs, and two commercial buildings next door. The three business buildings are now gone, and the corner is occupied by a modern glass-walled office building with a Purolator branch on the main floor (C).

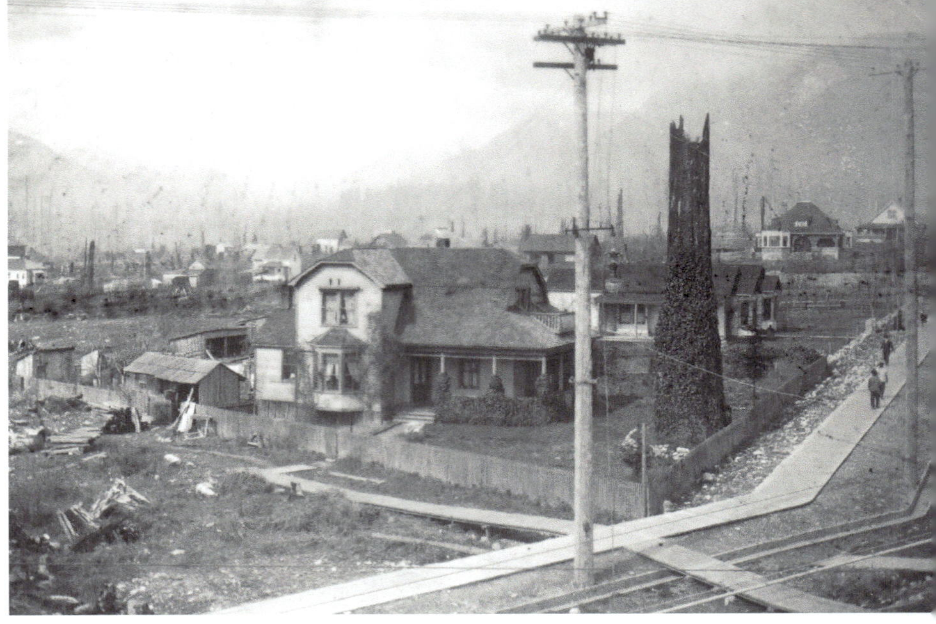

A – The Burnes home, 1906.

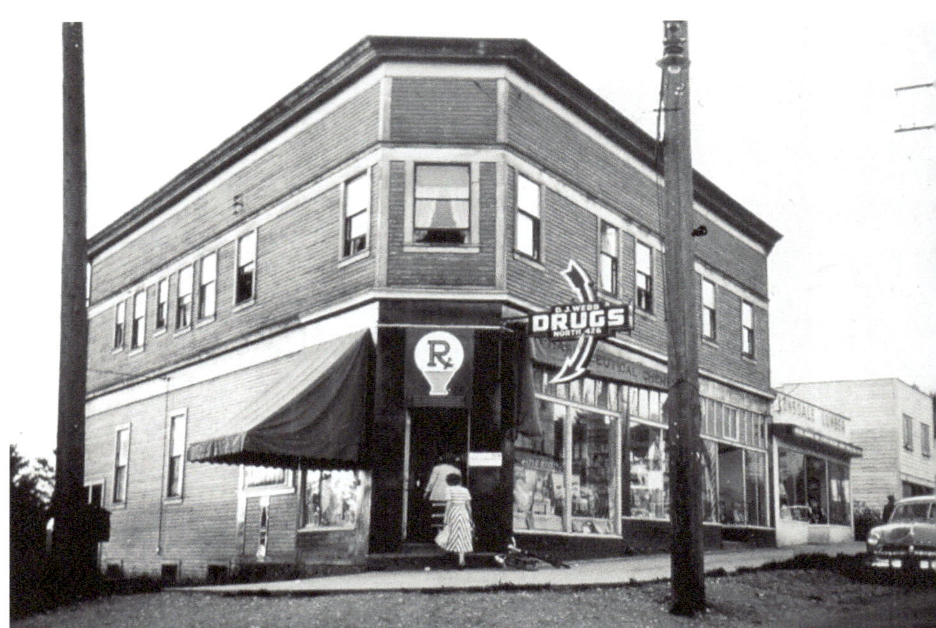

B – Drugstore, early 1950s.

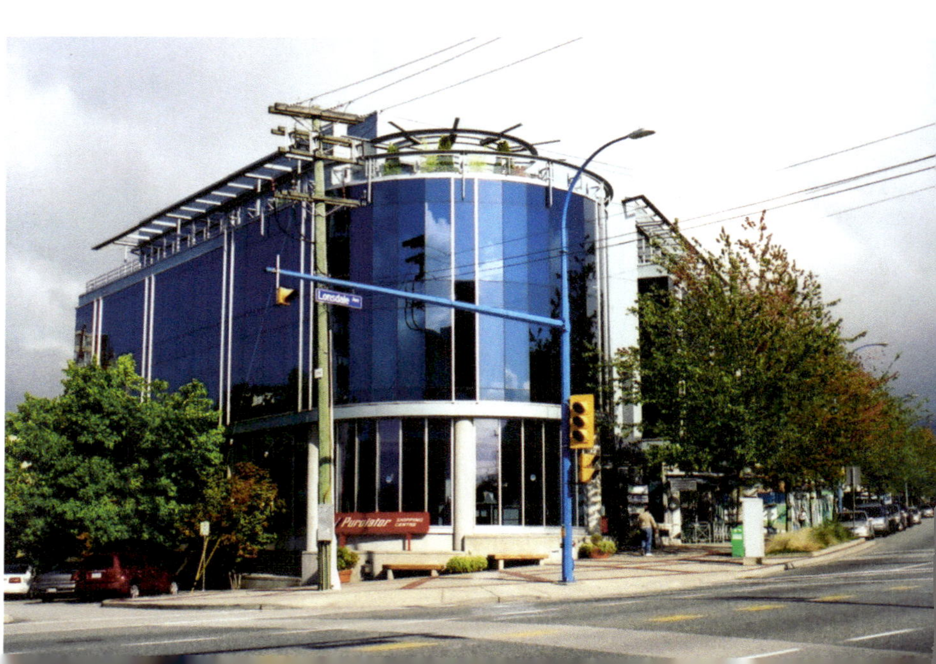

C – Office building, 2007.

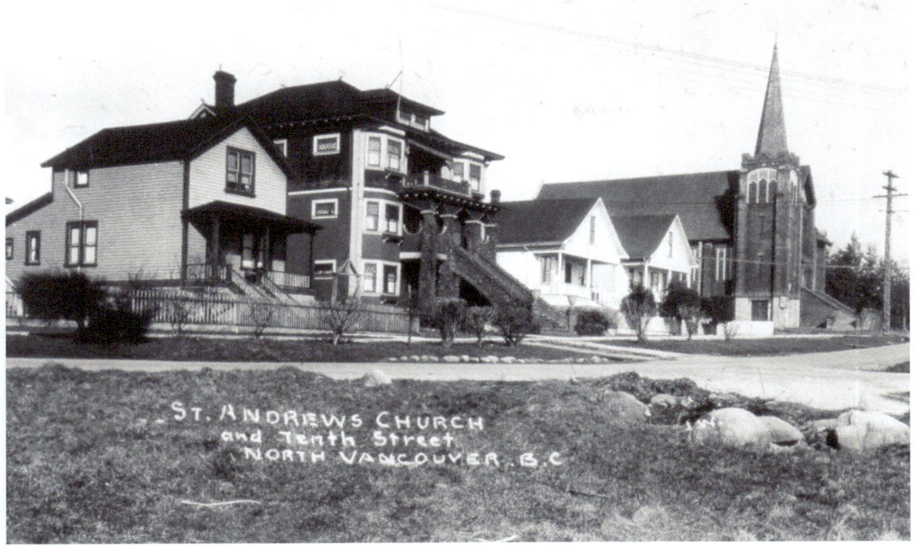

A – Five buildings, 1920s.

Vintage Buildings at 10th & St. Georges

The 1920s photo (A) shows five buildings that were built between 1910 and 1912. The same view in 2007 finds four still there (B). On the right is St. Andrews United Church at 1044 St. Georges. It was St. Andrews *Presbyterian* Church until 1925, when Presbyterian, Methodist, and Congregational groups merged to form the United Church. The large structure on the left is "The Colonial" at 160 East 10th, seen up close in a 2008 picture (C). It's an apartment block, built by a husband and wife from Germany. When it was finished, they moved into one of the suites, staying until their deaths in the late 1920s. The two houses in between are at 164 & 166 East 10th. Here's a better view of them in 2008 (D). All four buildings remain today (2016).

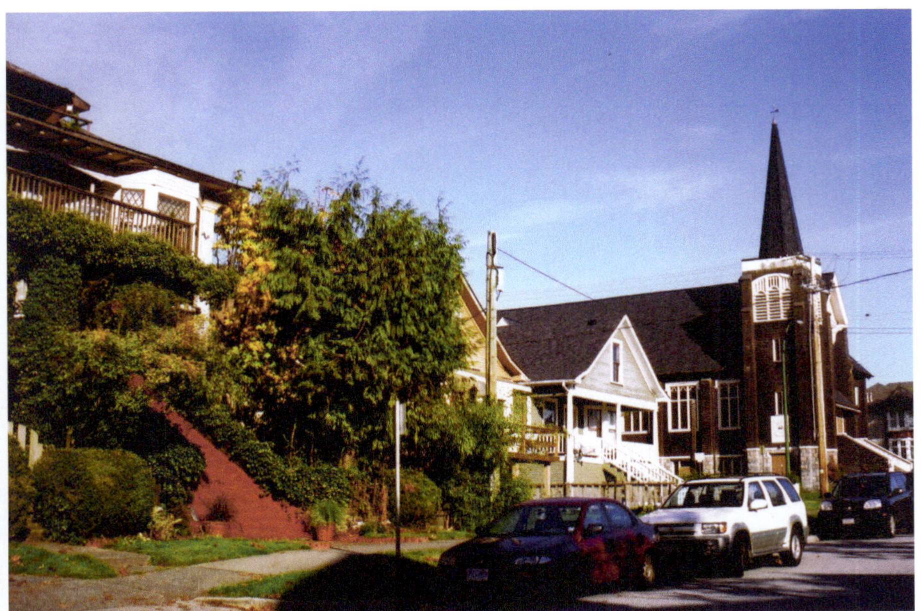
B – Four buildings, 2007.

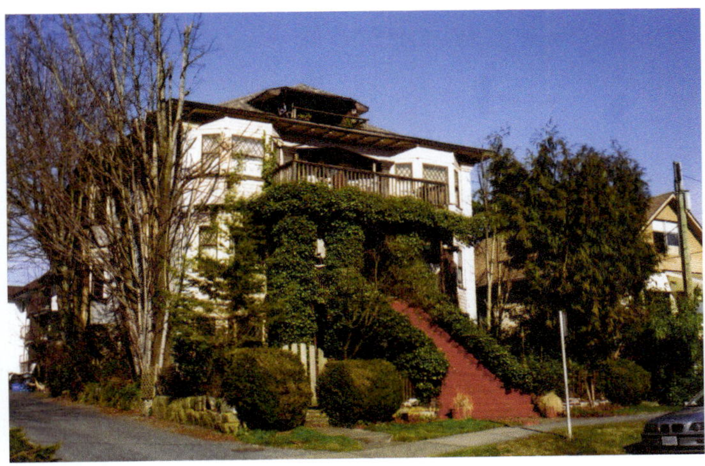
C – "The Colonial" apartments, 2008.

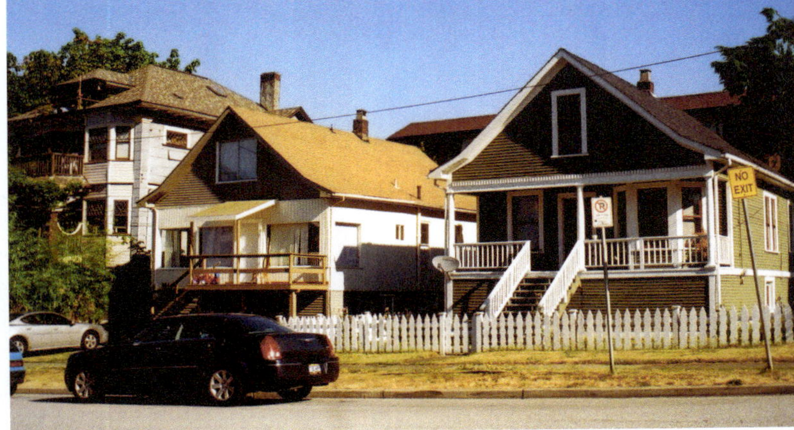

D – The houses, 2008.

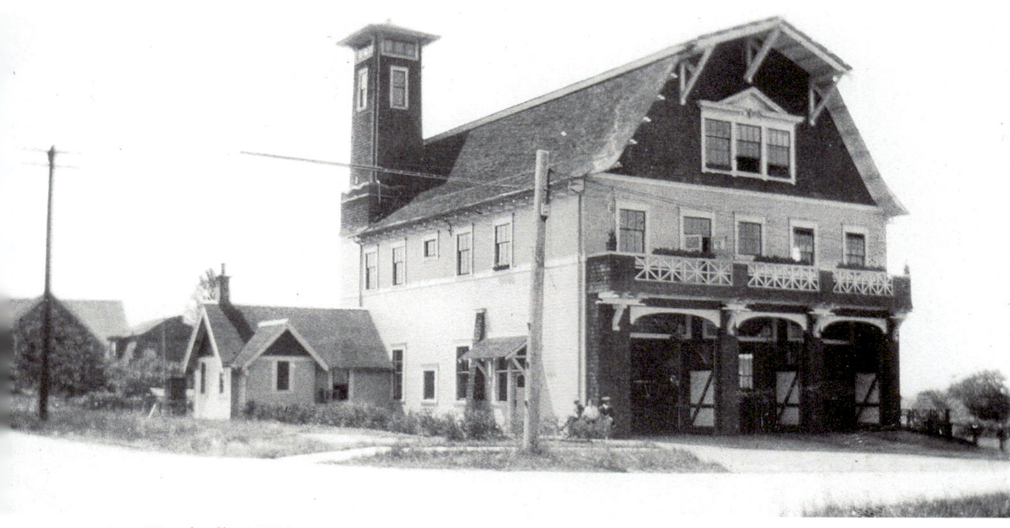

A – Fire hall, 1921.

Fire Hall

Since 1911 there has been a fire hall at the corner of 13th and St. Georges. You can see the first one in the 1921 photo (A). This facility contained not only fire-fighting vehicles and equipment, but also a gymnasium on the top floor where the firemen could work out or hold dances and other events. By the 1950s, however, the upper storey was gone (B). But notice the house next door. The fire chiefs used to live in this house, built in the mid 1920s. Today a modern fire hall sits where the house used to be (C). Once the new building was in place, the old fire hall was demolished and its site turned into a fire-hall parking lot.

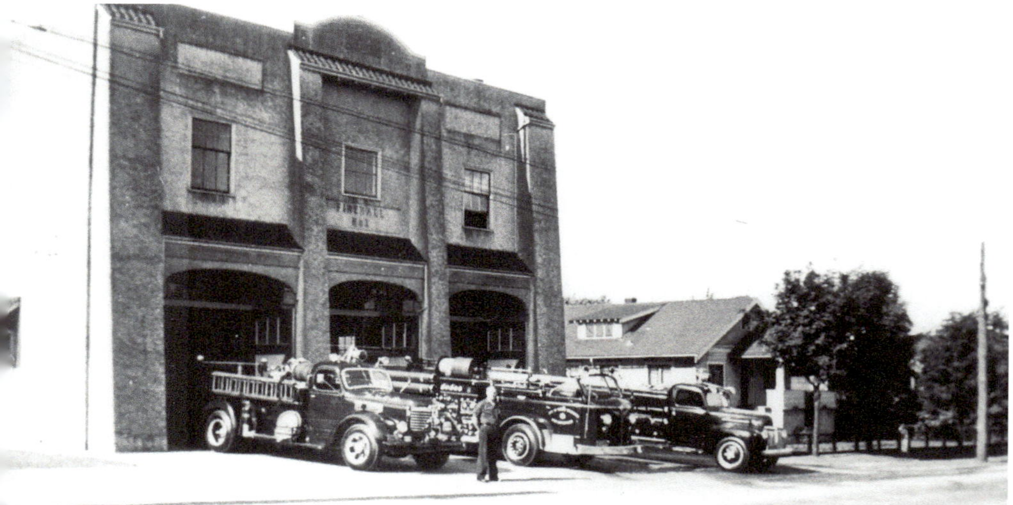

B – Fire hall, 1950s.

C – Modern fire hall, 2007.

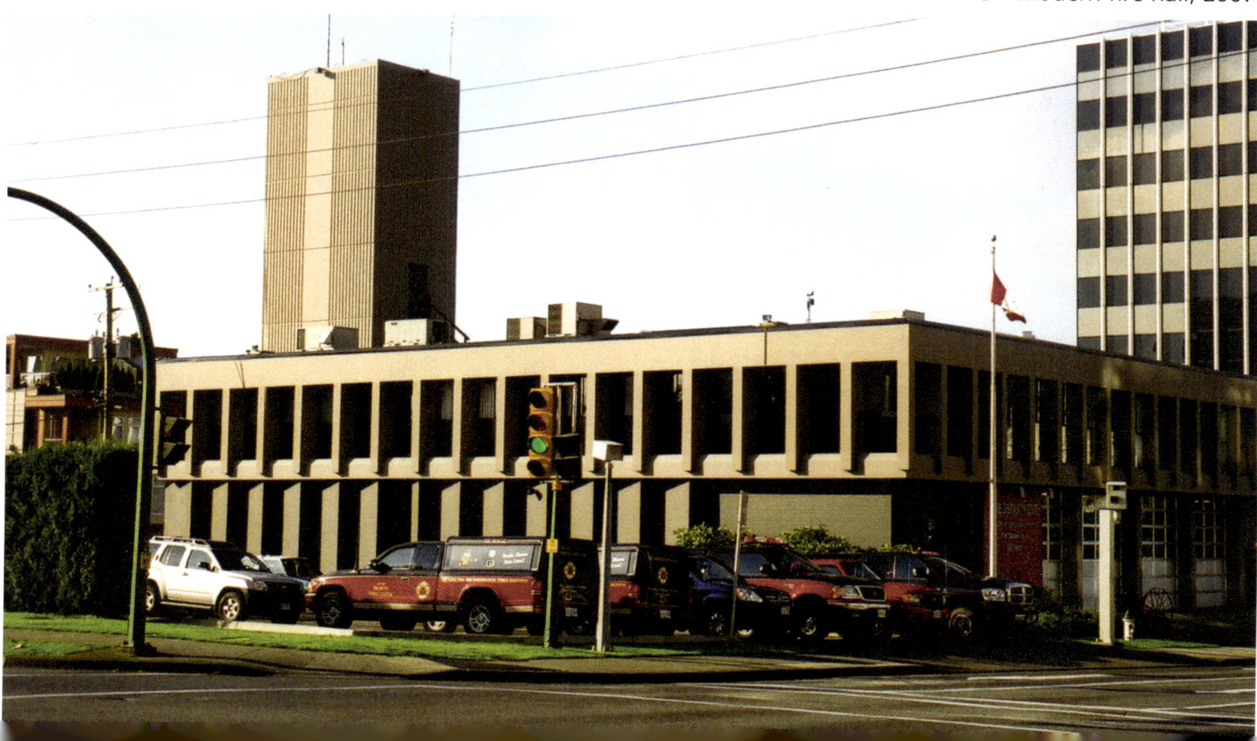

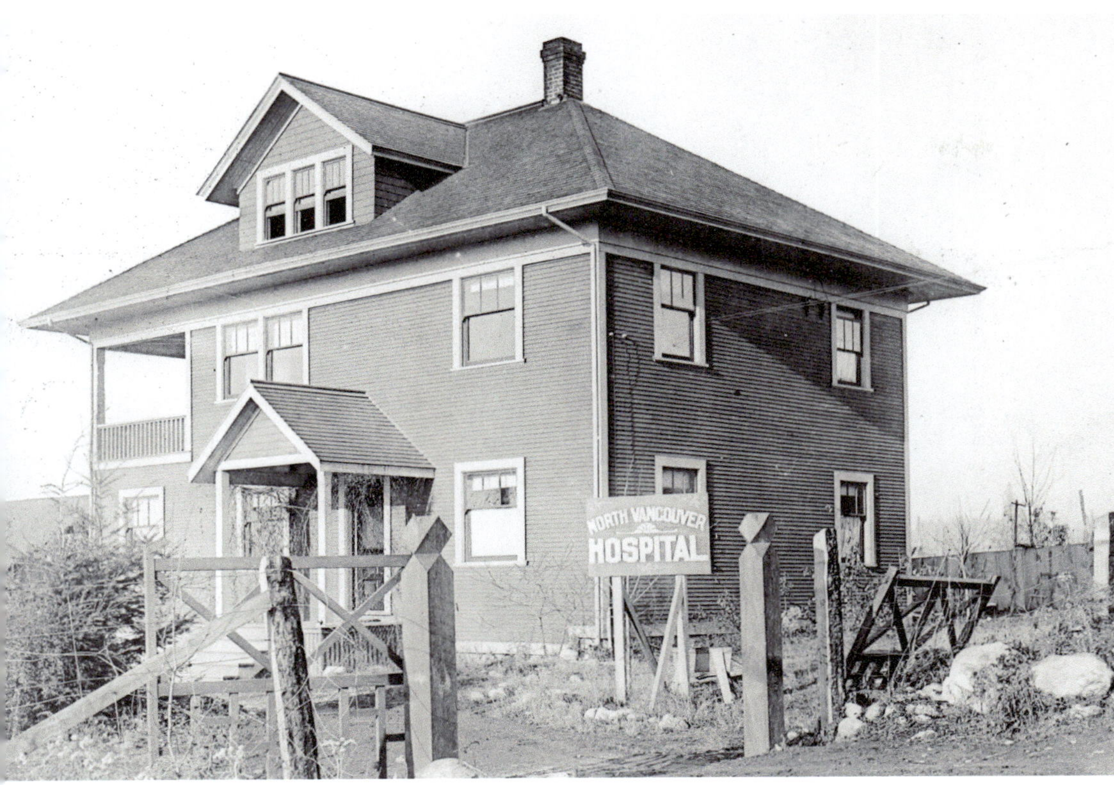

A – North Vancouver Hospital, c.1908-1910.

The First Hospital

At one time the nearest hospital was in Vancouver — *via ferry*. When local decision makers couldn't decide whether to build one on this side of the Inlet, three nurses took matters into their own hands. Mina and Jenny Dawson and their widowed sister (Mrs. Stephenson) rented a house on 15th Street near St. Andrews and turned it into our first public hospital. North Vancouver Hospital, shown in this vintage photo (A), opened in 1908. The sisters ran it themselves. They could comfortably accommodate six patients and handle any accident or illness that didn't require major surgery. By 1910, though, the facility was too small. So, the same sisters built a new one on East 12th, and closed the original. The Century Apartments, seen here in 2007 (B), now cover the first hospital site.

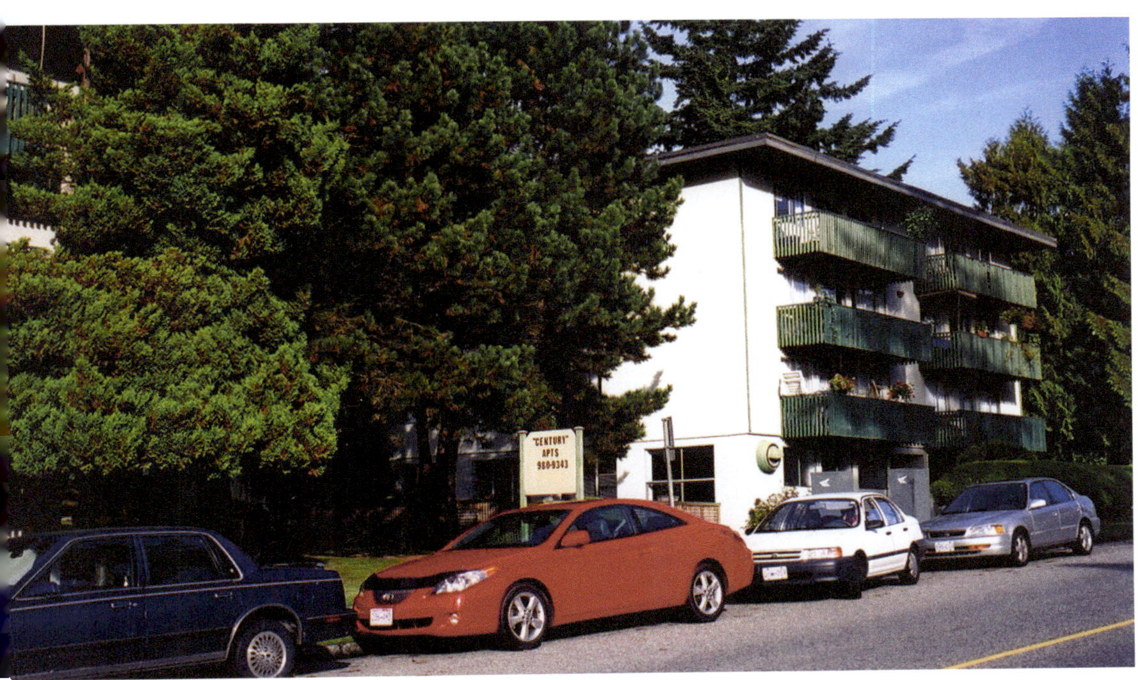
B – Apartment complex, 2007.

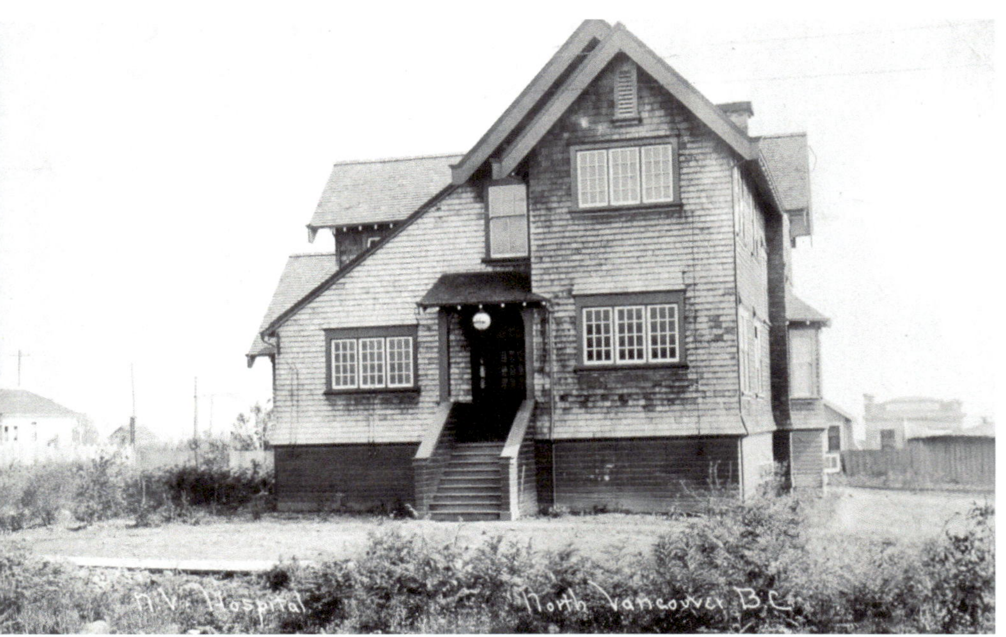

A – North Vancouver General Hospital, date unknown.

B – Lonsdale Private Hospital, 1983.

The Second Hospital

When the hospital on 15th became too small, in 1910 the aforementioned Dawson sisters built a new 15-bed facility in the 100 block of East 12th. This was the North Vancouver General Hospital, seen in an early photo (A). It eventually became inadequate due to an ever-increasing population, returning World War I soldiers, and a 1918–19 flu epidemic. So a new wing was added. In 1929 it was replaced by the second North Vancouver General Hospital on East 13th (which later became part of Lions Gate Hospital). The vacated building on 12th was converted to a nurses' residence. Around 1950 it became the Lonsdale Private Hospital, a privately owned long-term nursing and rest home, shown here in 1983 (B). A condominium complex at 145 East 12th sits on the site today (C).

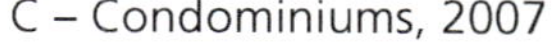

C – Condominiums, 2007

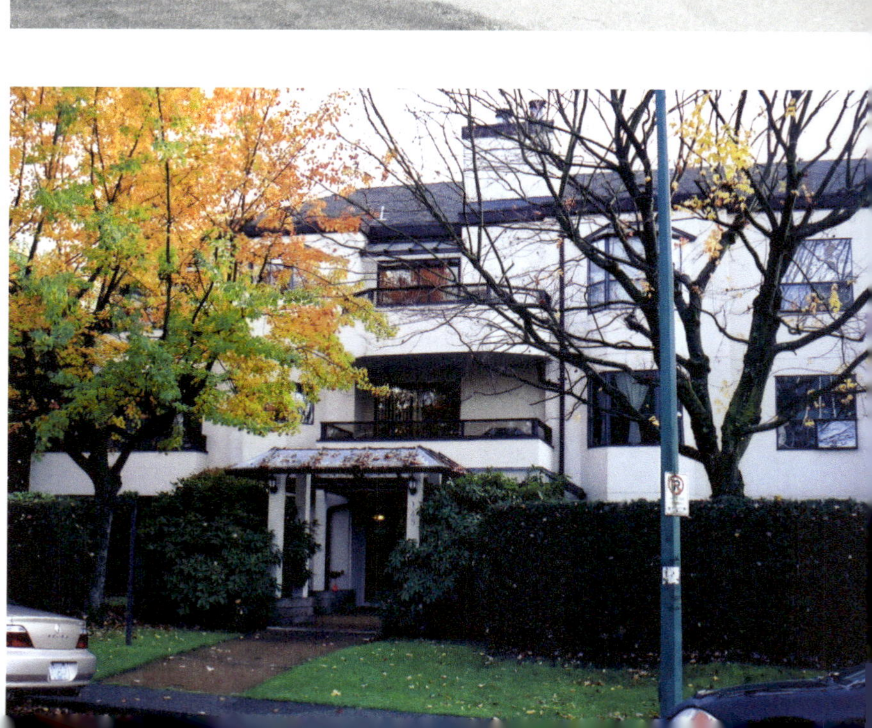

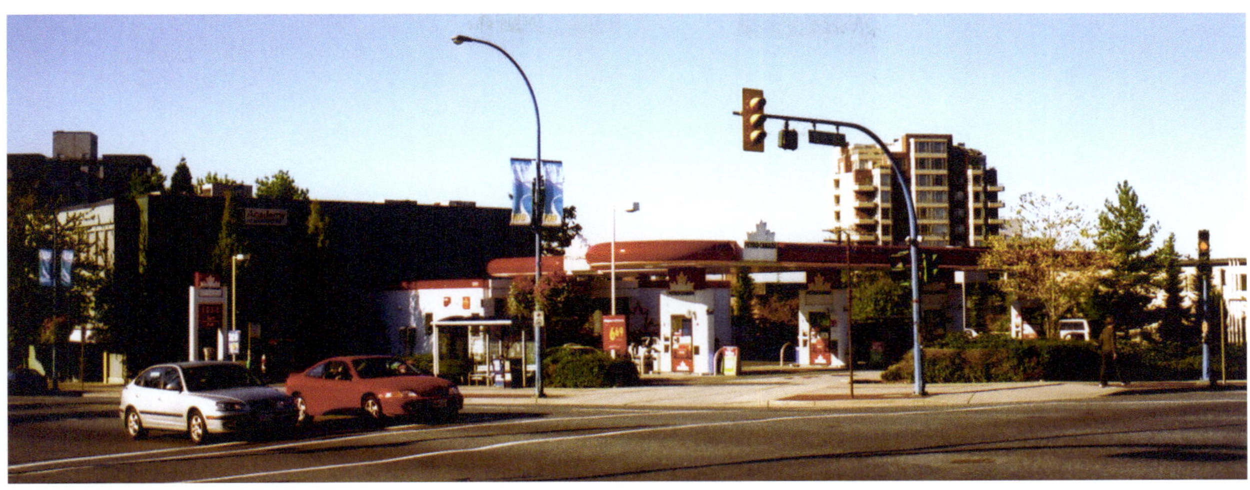

A – Petro Canada station, 2007.

The Curtis Home

A Petro Canada station and business buildings today line the west side of Lonsdale, between 12th & 13th (A). A century ago you would have seen a private home and beautiful gardens here. Well-known Vancouver architect George Curtis and his family lived on this property from 1906 to the 1930s. Their house was next to 13th, but faced 12th (B). From the front porch one had a beautiful view of tall trees, an arched bridge over a flowing stream (C), and flowerbeds extending the length of the property (D). The 1929 depression forced Curtis to retire and move his family to Vancouver Island. The house survived into the 1950s.

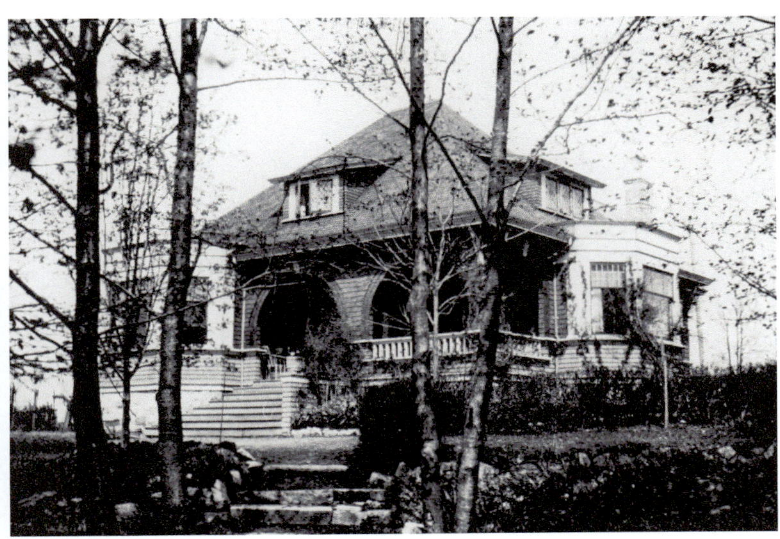

B – Curtis home, date unknown.

C – Bridge over stream, date unknown.

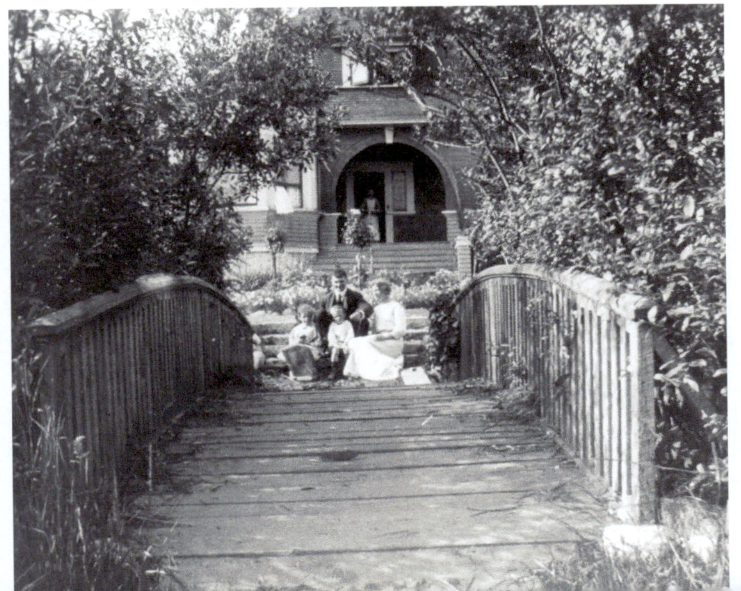

D – Flowerbeds, date unknown.

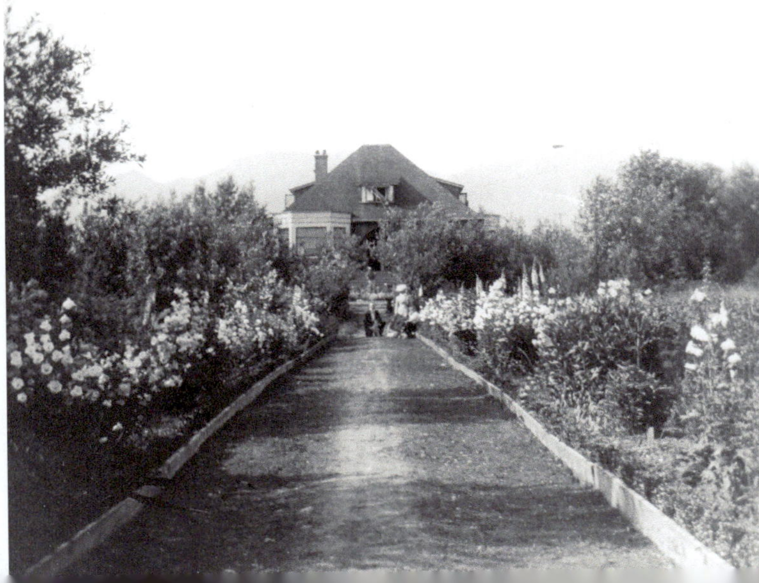

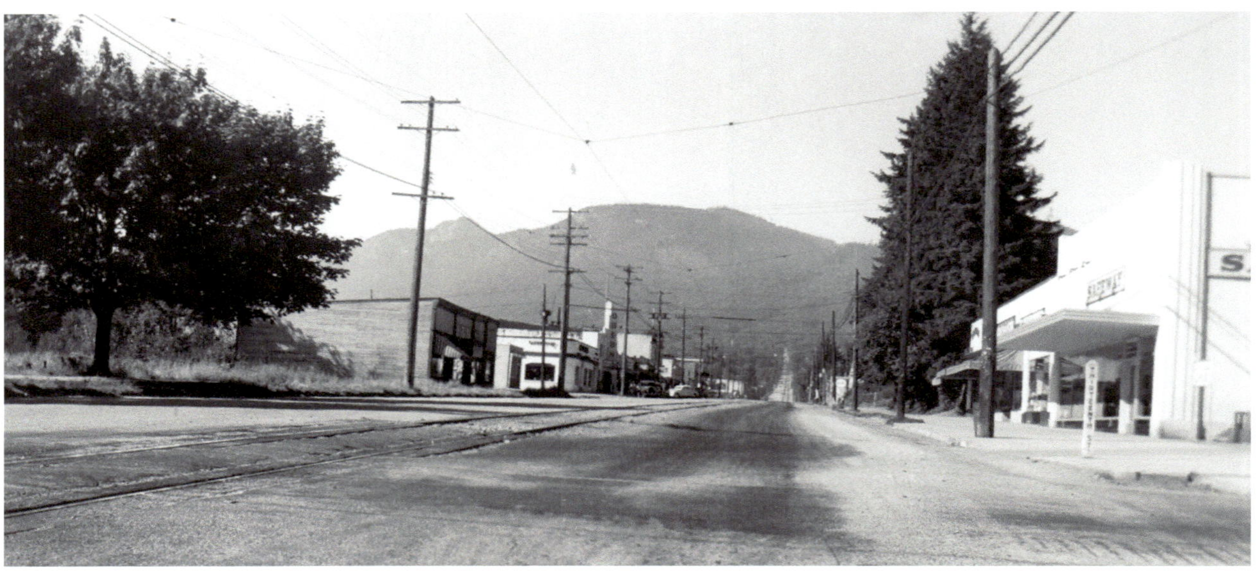

A – Central Lonsdale, mid 1940s.

Looking North on Lonsdale from 13th

Up to the mid 1940s Central Lonsdale was only lightly developed. As you can see in this 1946 photo looking north from 13th Street (A), there was still vacant land, and streetcar tracks ran up the centre of the street. Notice the Safeway grocery store on the right. In those days it was located immediately next to Lonsdale. Today, Central Lonsdale is lined with modern commercial buildings (B). The old Safeway was later demolished, and its site turned into a parking lot for the new Safeway set back from Lonsdale. Now both Safeway and its parking lot are gone, replaced with high-rises.

B – Central Lonsdale, 2018.

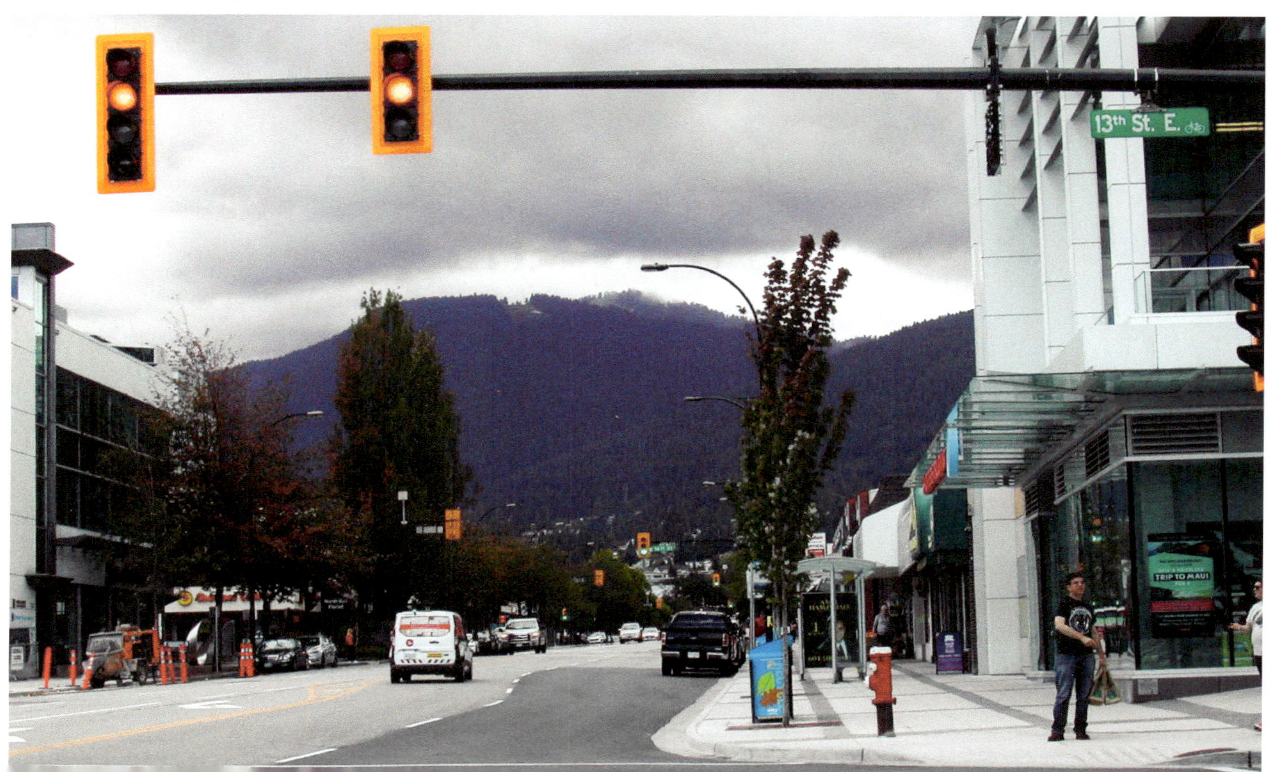

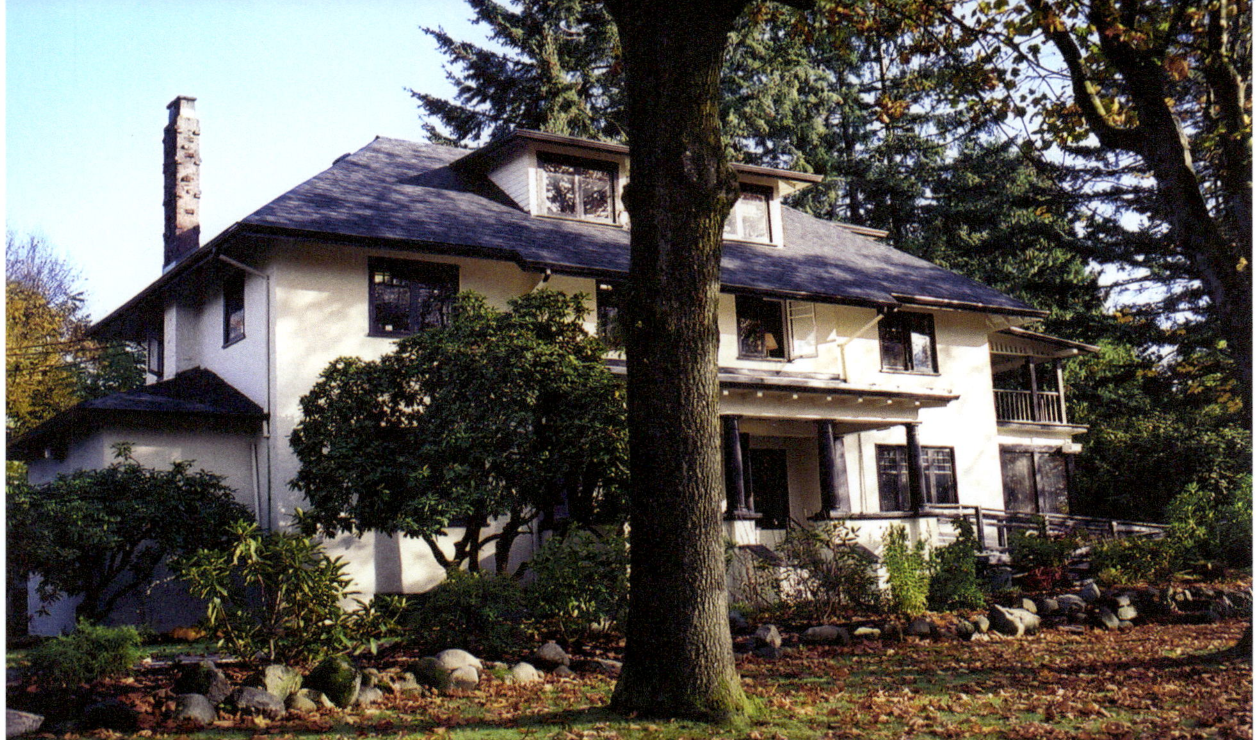

A – Psychiatric Services, 2007.

The Shakespeare Home

There's a building at 1350 St. Andrews surrounded by a generous yard (A). Owned by Vancouver Coastal Health Authority and close to Lions Gate Hospital, it houses an Occupational Therapy Program, which operates under Coastal Health's "Community Psychiatric Services." This was originally the family home (B) of a real estate and insurance broker named William Shakespeare (yes, that was his name!) and his wife, Winnifred. Built for them in 1912, it had a foyer, a living room, a front room with a fireplace, a kitchen, and several bedrooms. The old photo was taken shortly after they moved in. The Shakespeares moved out in the mid 1940s, and the house remained a private home until around 1970.

B – Shakespeare home, c.1912.

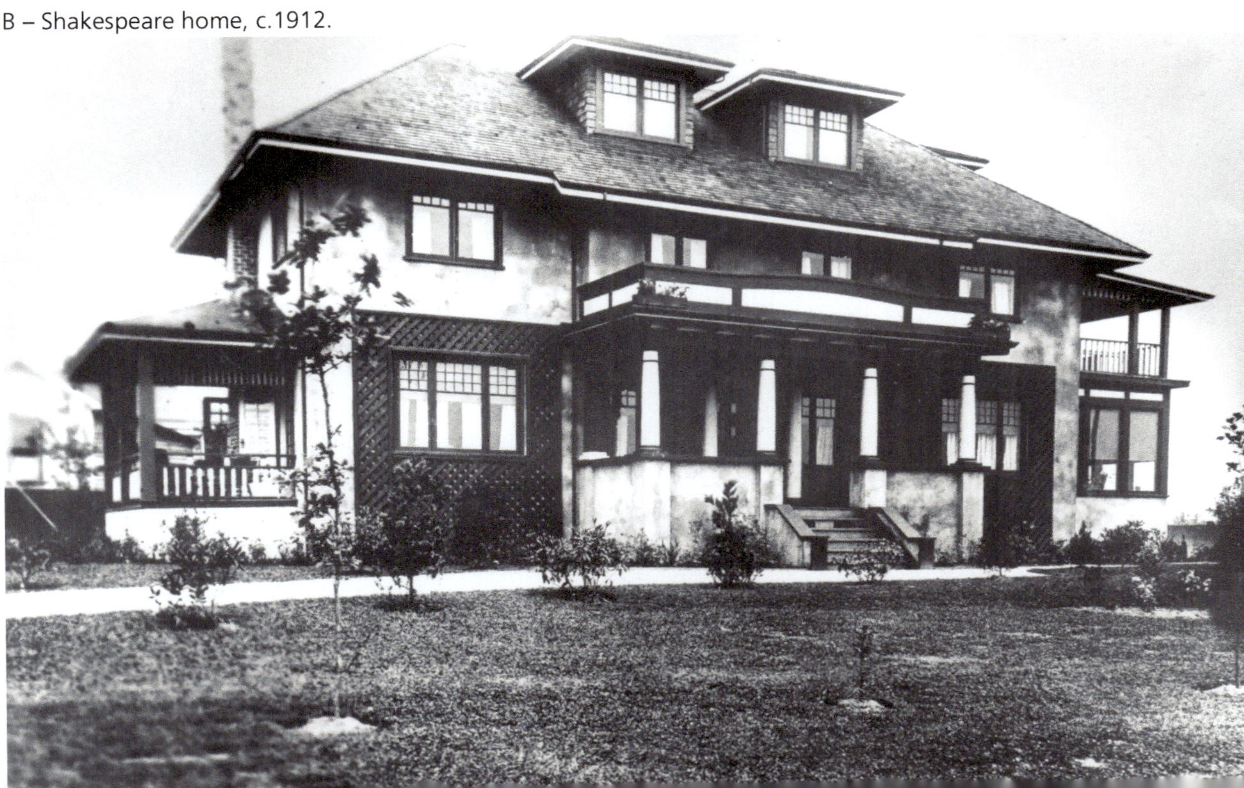

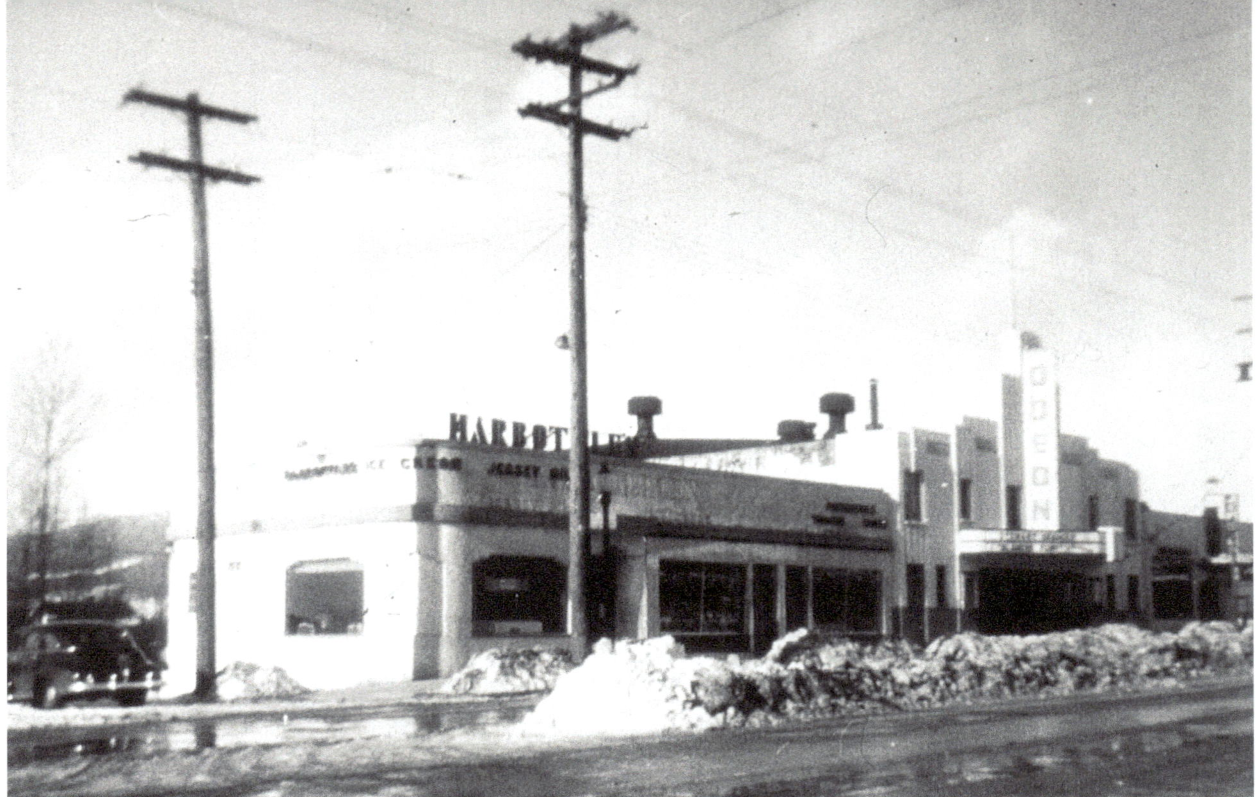

A – Harbottle's store, c.1950.

Harbottle's Jersey Products

In the 1930s Thomas P. Harbottle developed a successful dairy-products business. Not only did he deliver cream, butter, buttermilk, and fresh eggs to your home, but also he sold them in this retail store at 1401 Lonsdale, which opened in 1938. Here's what it looked like around 1950 (A). Throughout the 1940s, you could go in and choose from a full line of dairy products, or else sit at the counter and enjoy a milkshake, soda, or some other dairy treat. After Harbottle retired around 1950, the building was occupied by a succession of (mostly) coffee shops and cafes. It was demolished around 1980 and replaced by the commercial building shown in the 2008 view (B).

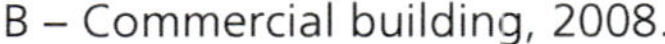

B – Commercial building, 2008.

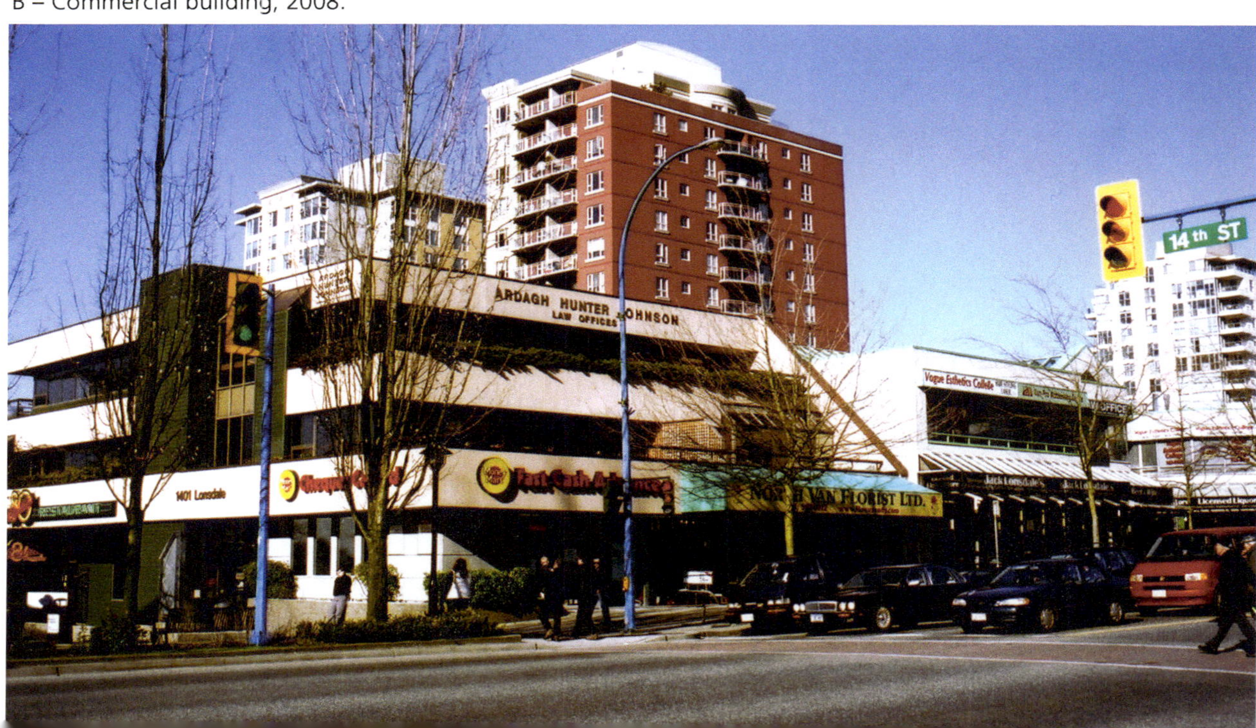

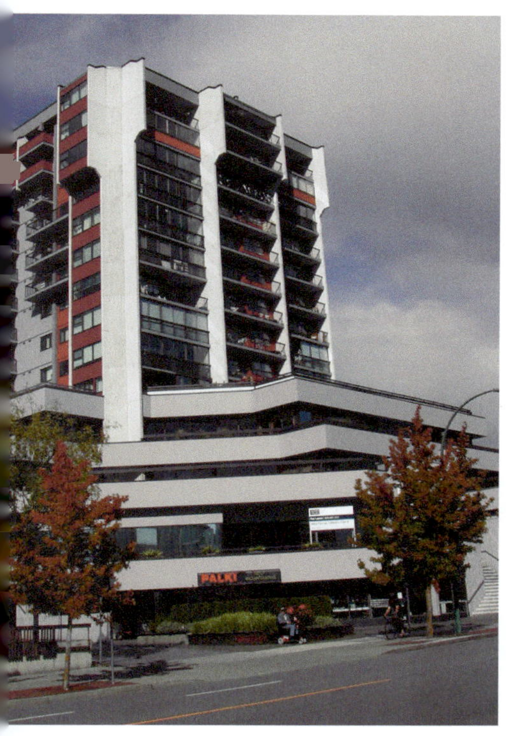

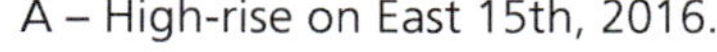
A – High-rise on East 15th, 2016.

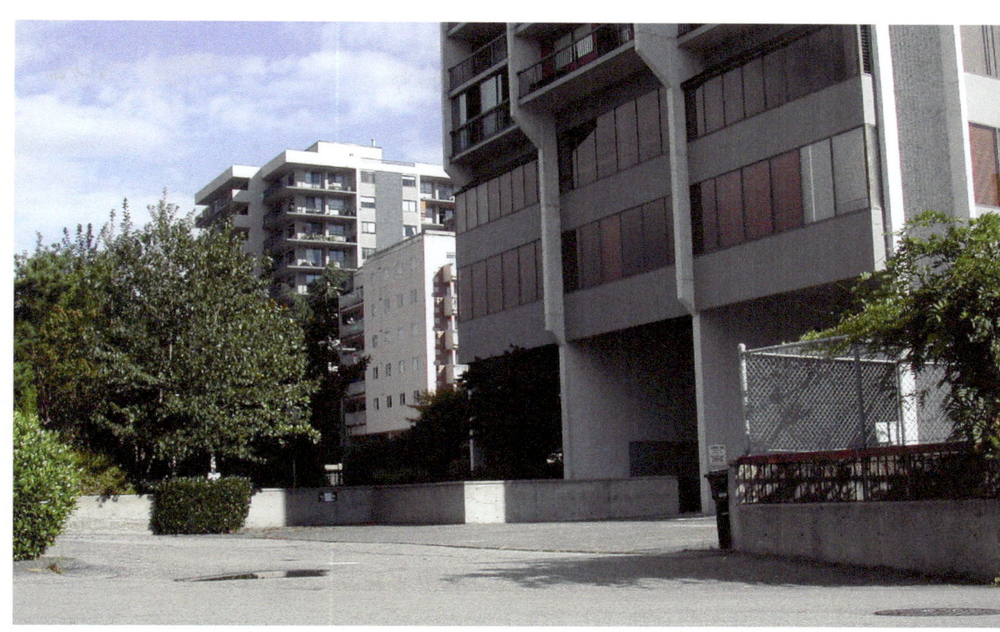
B – Parking in the rear, 2016.

The Irwin Home

There's presently a high-rise at 126 East 15th (A), with parking in the rear (B). The parking area is where the house in this 1910 photo (C) once stood. The house was built around 1909 for William J. Irwin and his wife Katherine who raised their family and spent the rest of their lives here. He founded Irwin & Billings, an insurance firm still operating in 2016. Originally the house sat on five acres that ran along 15th to 17th, and Lonsdale to Eastern. The Lonsdale half was sold in the 1920s. For many years the Irwin property was a scene rich in trees, gardens, and flowers, as you can see in this 1910 photo of the Irwin family (D). There was also a pasture for their cow!

C – Irwin house, 1910.

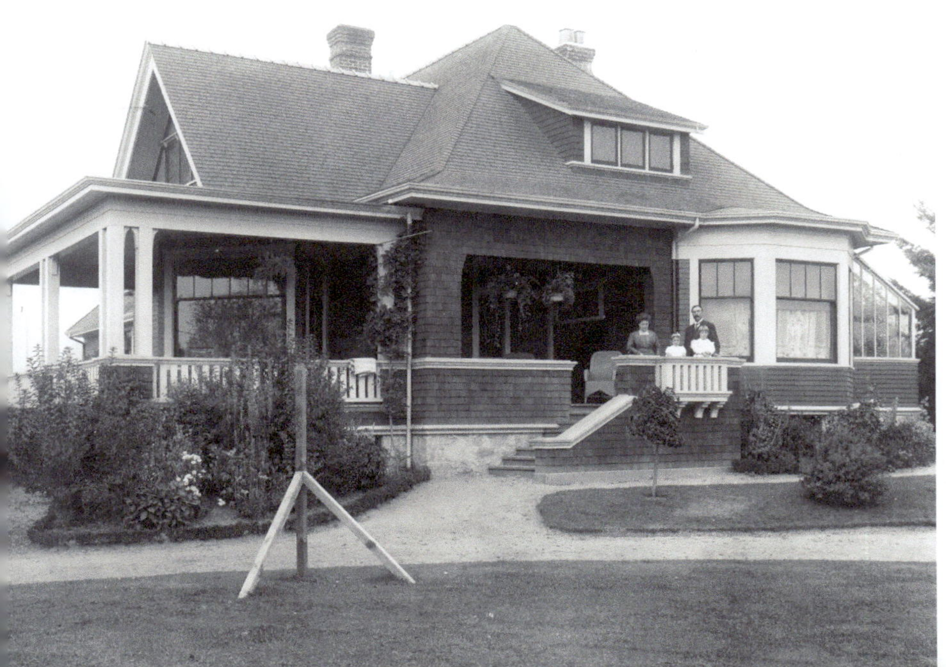

D – Irwin family on grounds, 1910.

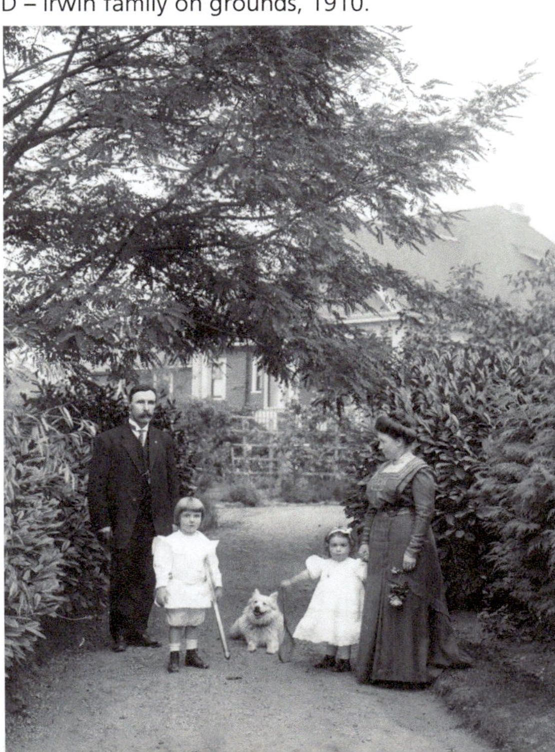

Lonsdale Theatre

The 1920s photo (A) shows the 800-seat Lonsdale Theatre that once stood at 1545 Lonsdale. It opened in 1911 to a packed house, seen in this photo shot from the stage on that occasion (B). Notice the different seating areas: the main floor, the horseshoe-shaped balcony, and box seats at the front overlooking the stage. From 1911 to the early 1950s, this theatre entertained North Vancouverites with top Hollywood movies, as well as operas, operettas, musical plays, and other live stage productions. When it shut down after 40 years, the Royal Bank moved into the building and stayed into the 1990s. The structure was demolished in 1997. A modern HSBC bank is there now (C).

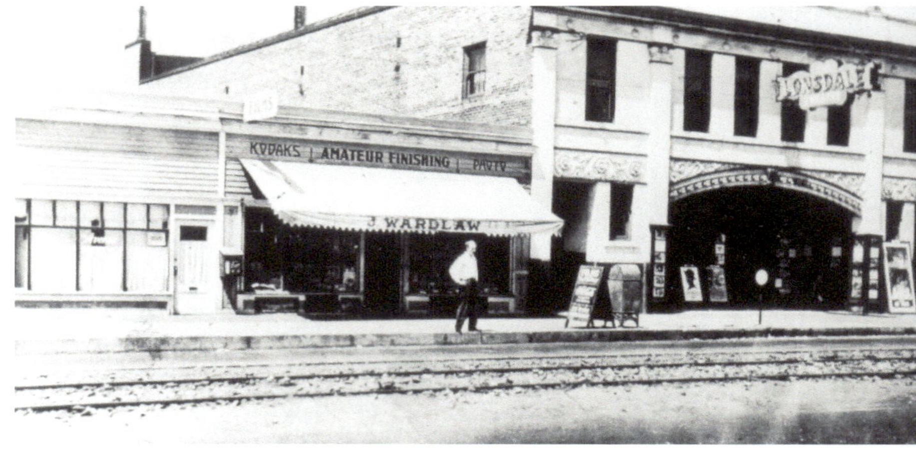

A – Lonsdale Theatre, 1920s.

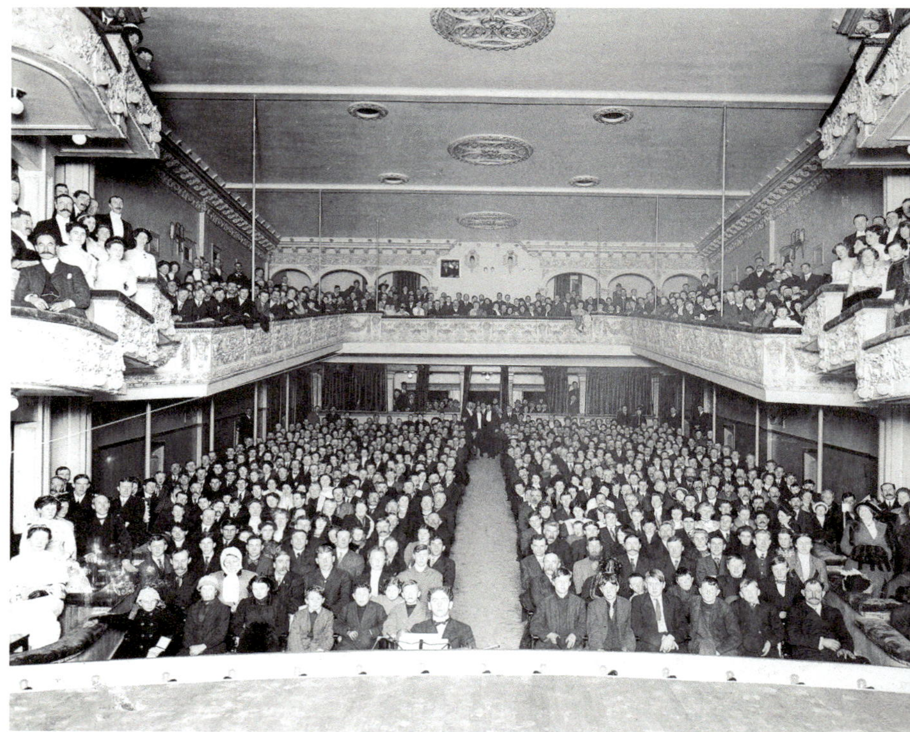

B – Opening audience, 1911.

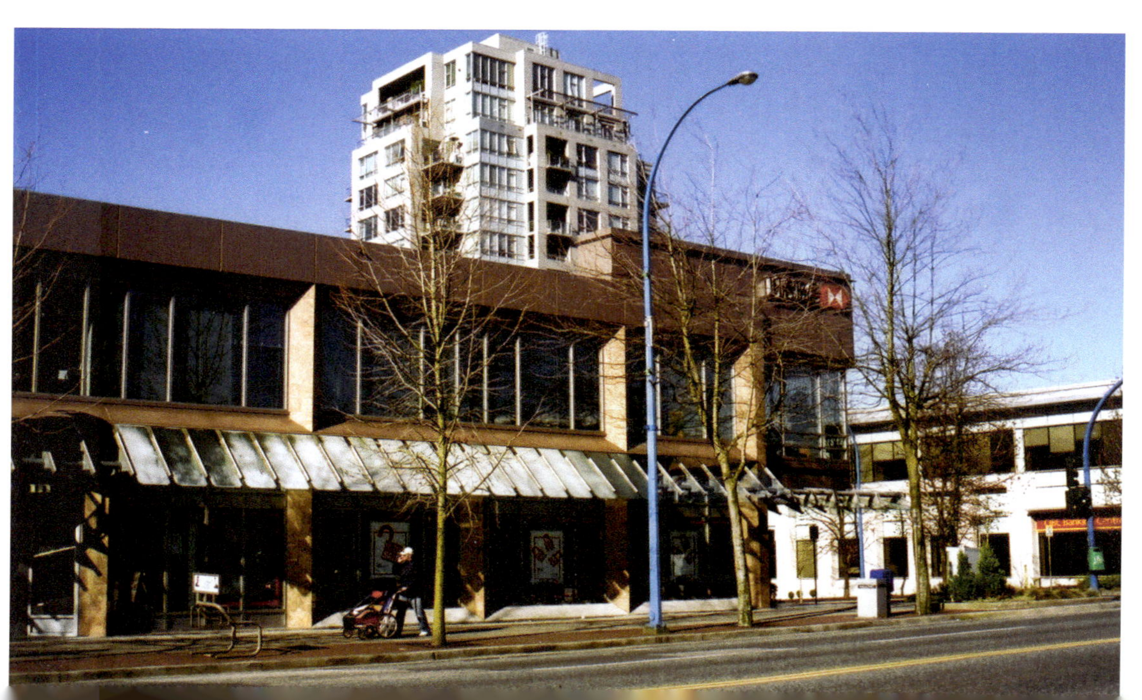

C – HSBC Bank, 2008

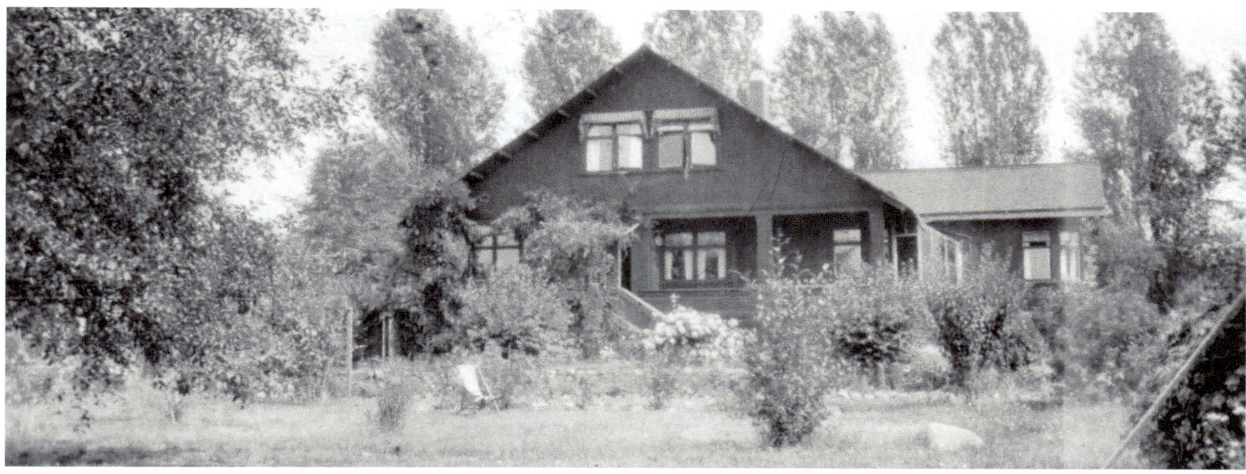
A – Jackson home, date unknown.

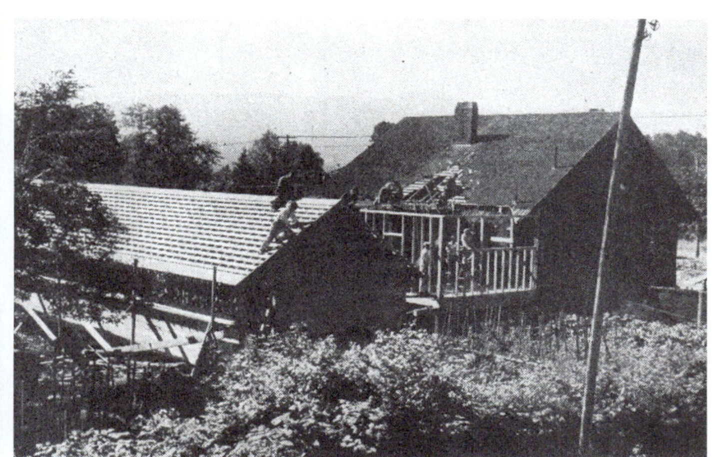
B – Shipyard staff at work, 1945.

The Jackson Home

In 1906, Vancouver merchant Colin Jackson built his family's home on 2½ acres of land at 225 East 15th (A). They stayed until the late 1920s, at which point Jackson lost the property to taxes. What's interesting here is that, in the early 1930s, the house and land became the well-known St. Christopher's Vocational School for mentally challenged boys. This school had amazing community support. The Fraternal Order of Eagles provided major funding annually. Wallace Shipyard staff volunteered their evenings and weekends in the 1940s to upgrade and expand the house (B), and local residents hired St. Christopher's boys to do odd jobs. Then, in 1960, the school moved to Lynn Valley, and the former Jackson property became Lions Gate Hospital's parking lot (C).

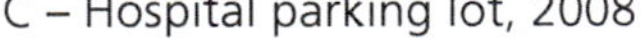
C – Hospital parking lot, 2008

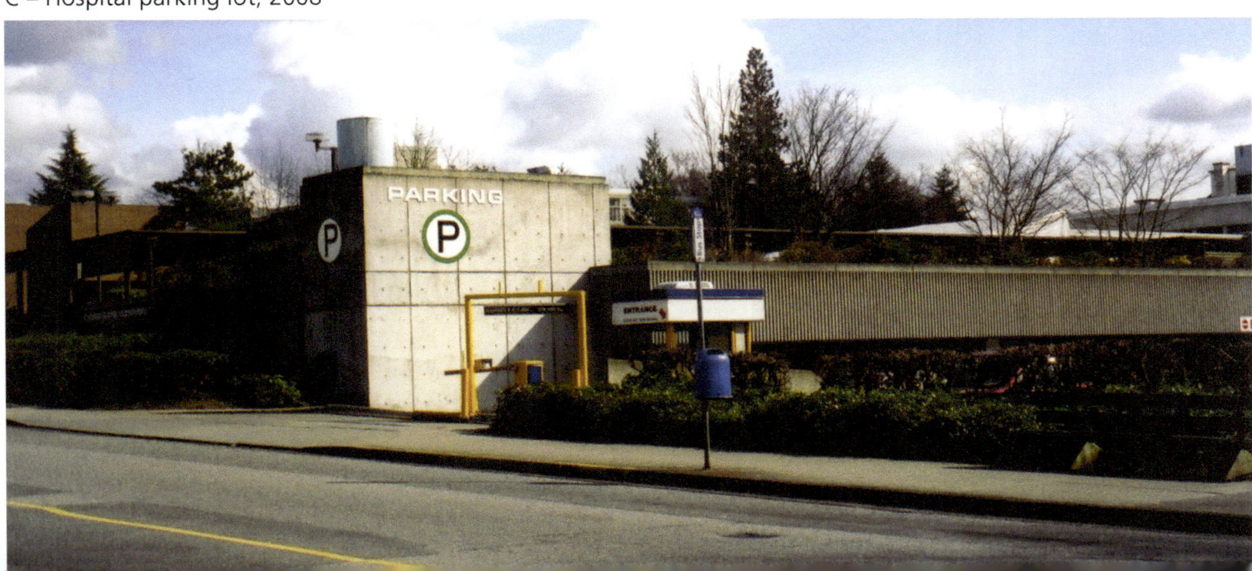

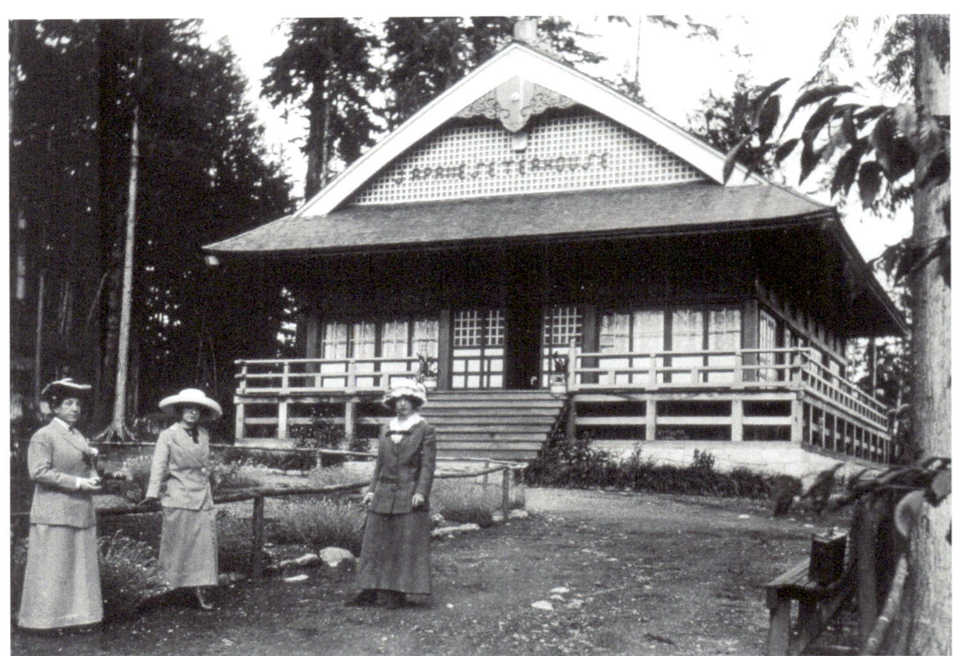

A – Teahouse, 1911.

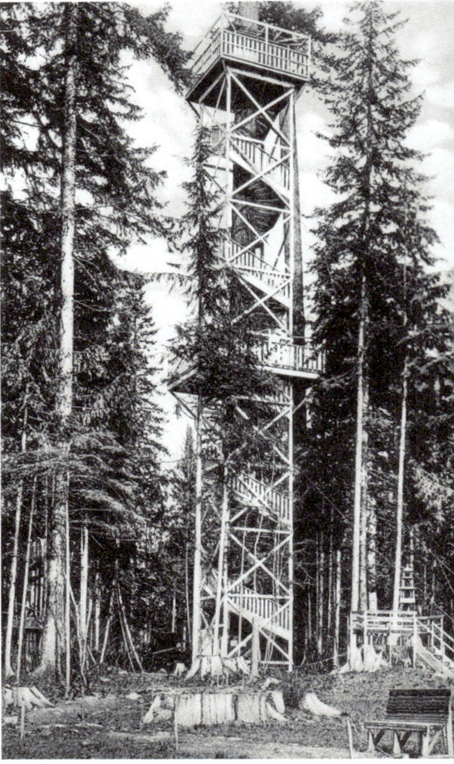

B – Tower, date unknown.

Japanese Tea Gardens

When BC Electric Railway Co. (now BC Hydro) was developing North Vancouver's streetcar service around 1906, it thought the "Lonsdale" line needed something extra at its 21st Street terminus to increase usage. So, the company had some land it owned at 21st and St Georges (Block 208) turned into a Japanese-theme attraction. The Japanese Tea Gardens, which opened in 1910, featured the teahouse in this 1911 photo (A), the tower in this undated view (B), and several other amenities. The tower had a staircase that spiralled around the trunk of a tall fir tree, to a platform 33 metres (108 feet) above the ground. The view was spectacular! A depression in 1913 forced the Tea Gardens to close, and the site became residential (C).

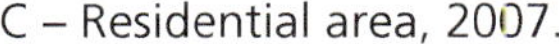

C – Residential area, 2007.

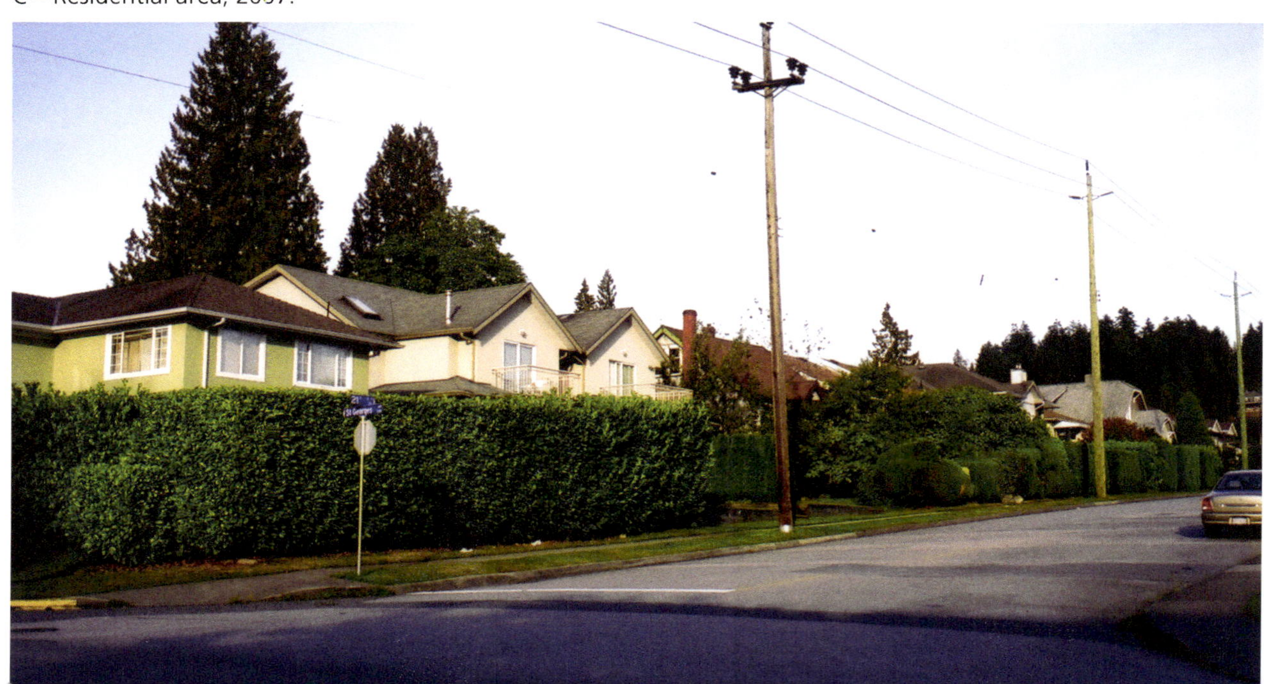

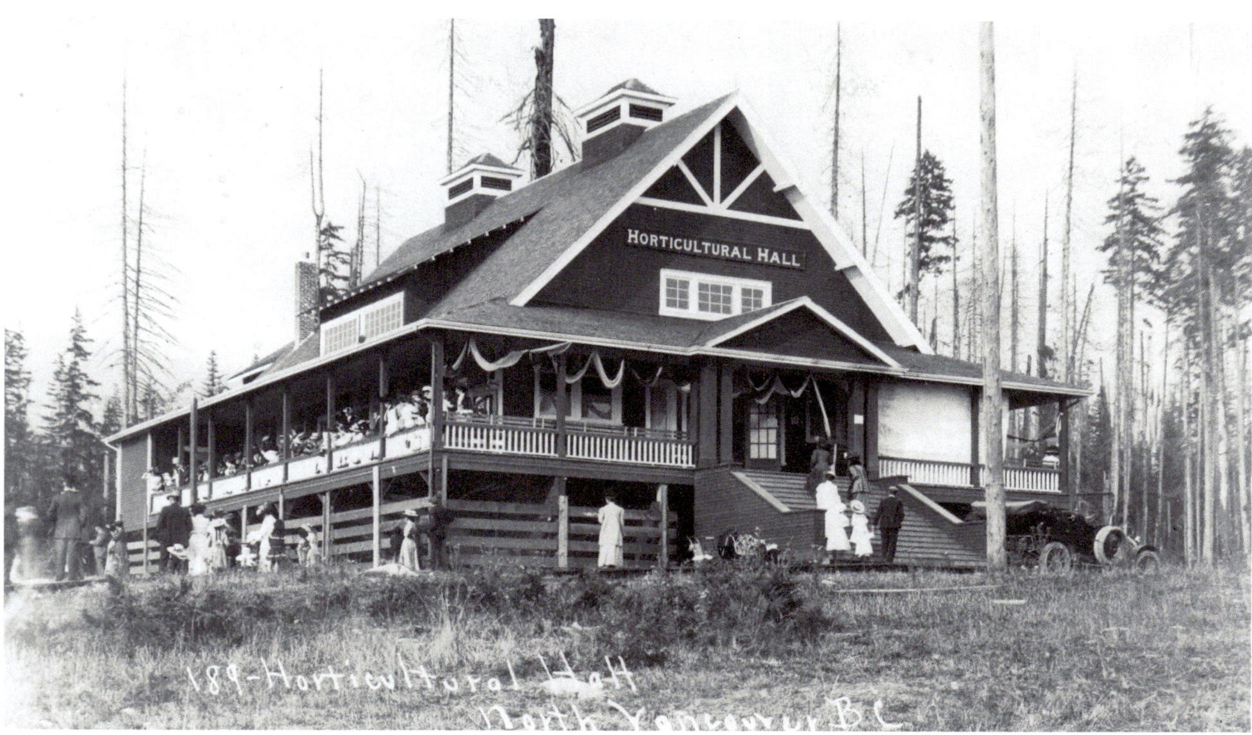

A – Horticultural Hall, 1910.

Horticultural Hall

In 1904 a group of residents formed the North Vancouver Horticultural Association & Farmers' Institute. They raised funds, purchased five acres on the east side of Lonsdale, between 21st and 23rd, and created a park. In 1908 they opened the Horticultural Hall on 23rd Street, shown in this 1910 photo (A). The hall was for many years an important venue, not only for the association's annual horticultural shows (flowers, fruits, vegetables, and ornamental plants), but also for stage productions, club meetings, banquets, dances, political gatherings, special exhibits, and events put on by other groups. At present, the Harry Jerome Recreation Centre sits on the former Horticultural Hall site (B). It and other recreation venues, in fact, now cover the whole five acres purchased in 1908.

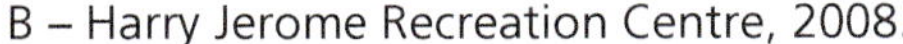
B – Harry Jerome Recreation Centre, 2008.

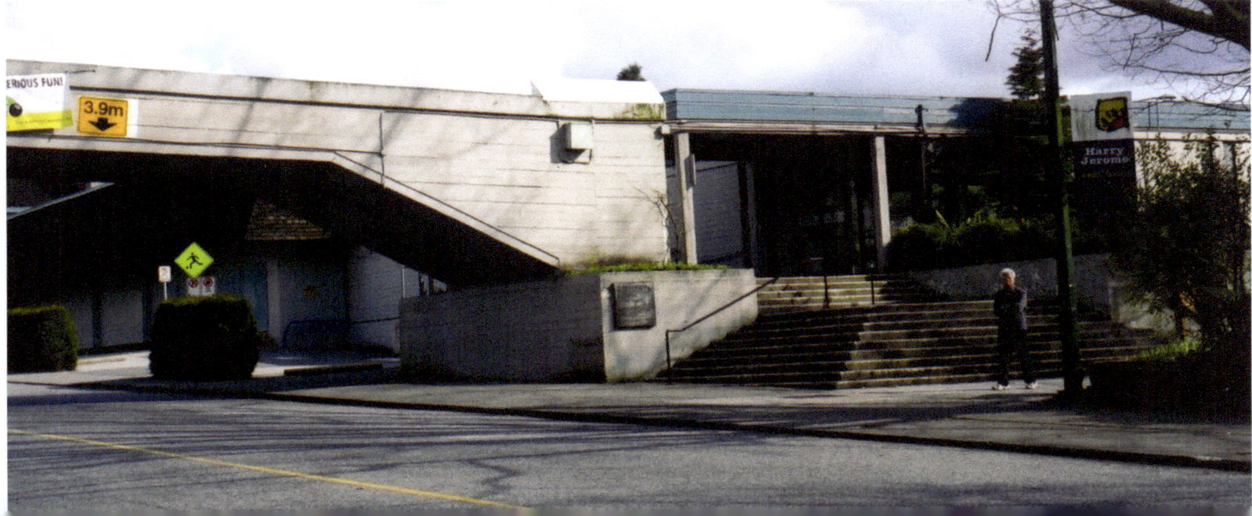

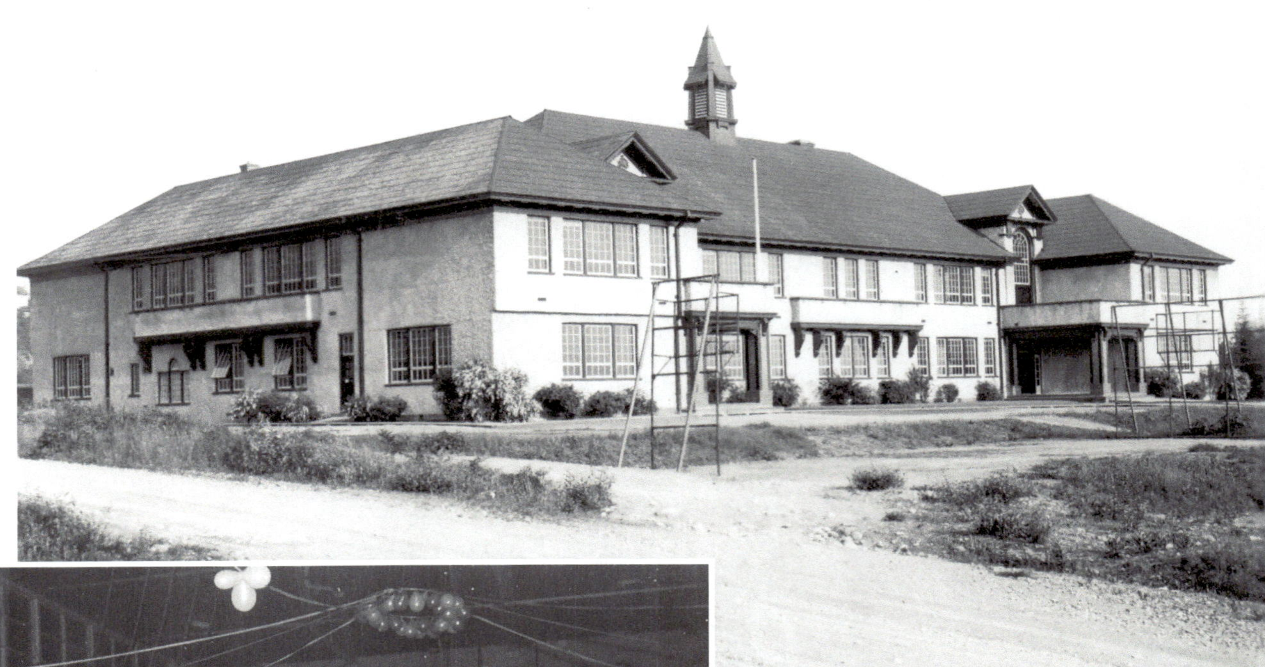

A – North Vancouver High School, 1938.

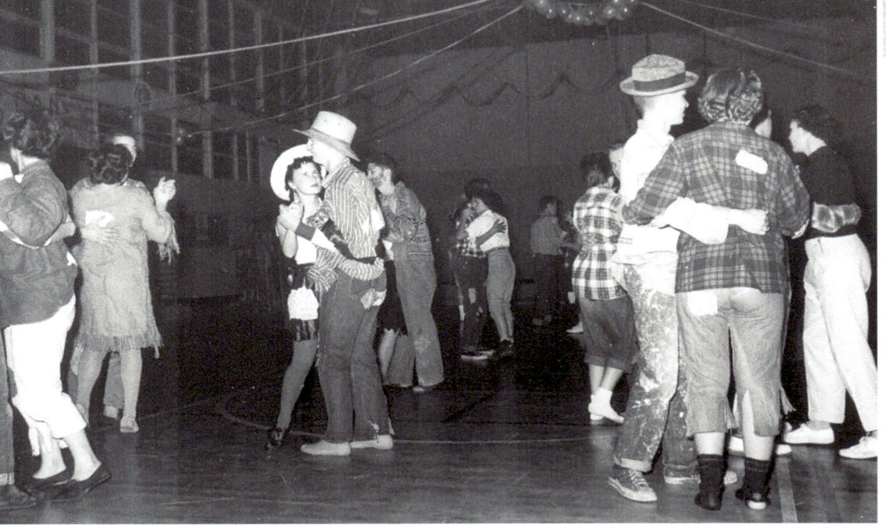

B – Sadie Hawkins Day dance, c.1960.

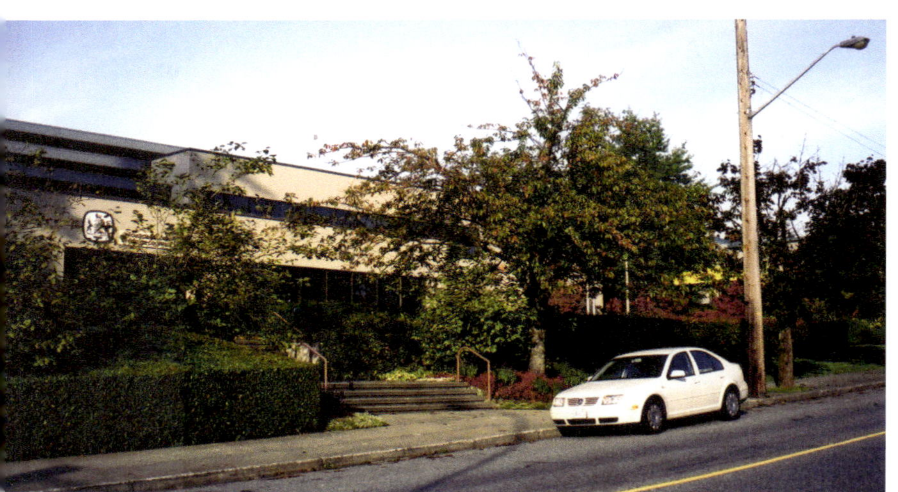

C – Provincial Courthouse, 2007.

North Vancouver High School

Nearly everyone over the age of 70, who grew up here, went to North Vancouver High School on East 23rd Street. Here it is in 1938 (A). From 1924 to 1957 this was North Vancouver's only secondary school. After that, schools were built in other neighbourhoods. North Van High closed in 1979 and was demolished in 1980. Fortunately, school loyalty can be fierce. Class reunions are keeping alive memories of the many excellent teachers, the student dances (B), the clubs, and sports events — and the "smokers union," a place off campus (in the bush) where boys could "sneak" a cigarette! A Provincial Courthouse at 200 East 23rd covers the school site today (C).

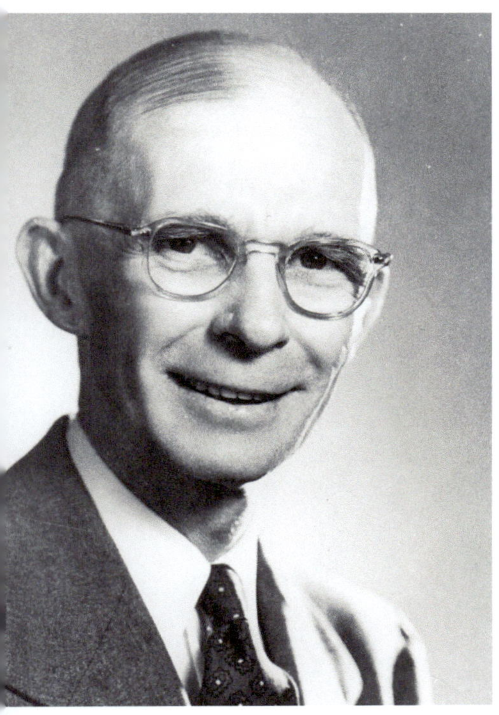

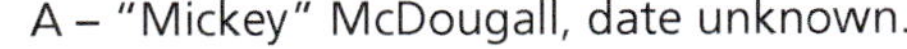

A – "Mickey" McDougall, date unknown.

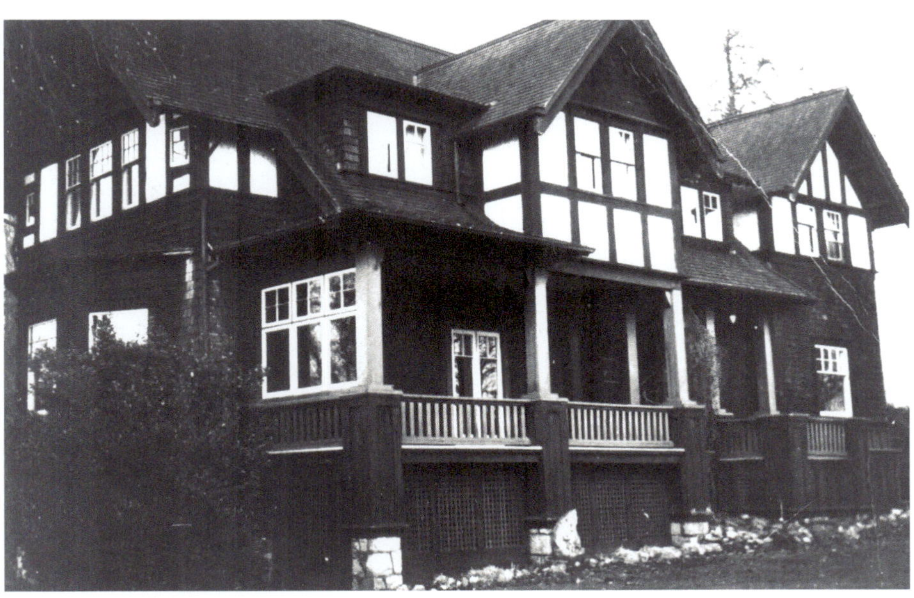

B – McDougall home, c.1945.

"Mickey" McDougall's Former Home

Ex-students of North Vancouver High School will remember W.R. "Mickey" McDougall (A), the school's principal from 1936 to 1961. From 1938 to 1946, he and his family lived in a 1911 two-storey house at 116 West 23rd, seen here around 1945 (B). They'd purchased it from the original owner, H.D. Green-Armytage. It remained a private home until the 1960s. Then it was a rest home — first named "Laburnum Cottage Rest Home," later "Barony Lodge," and finally "United Lodge." At some point, a front wing was added. Here it is in 2007, after United Lodge had moved out (C). In early 2016 (D) we find the house relocated to the corner of the property, now part of a condominium complex.

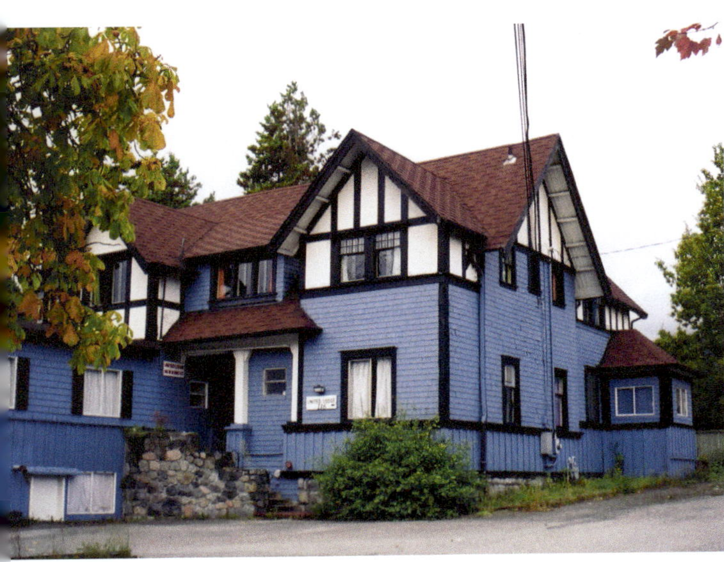

C – Empty United Lodge Rest Home, 2007.

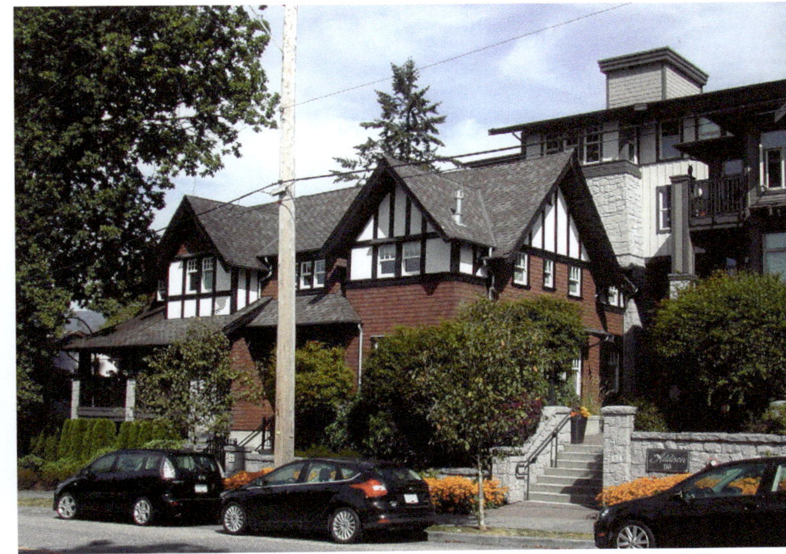

D – Part of condo complex, 2016.

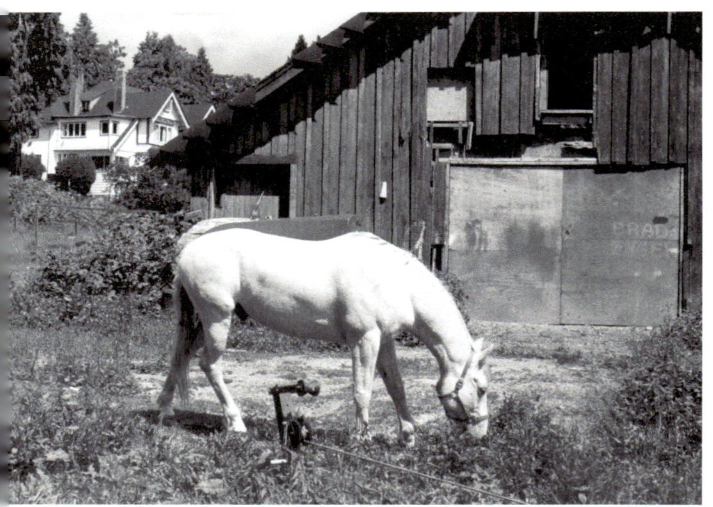

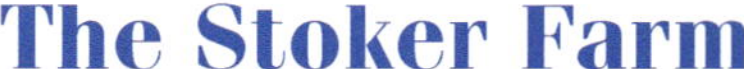

A – Barn and house, 1979.

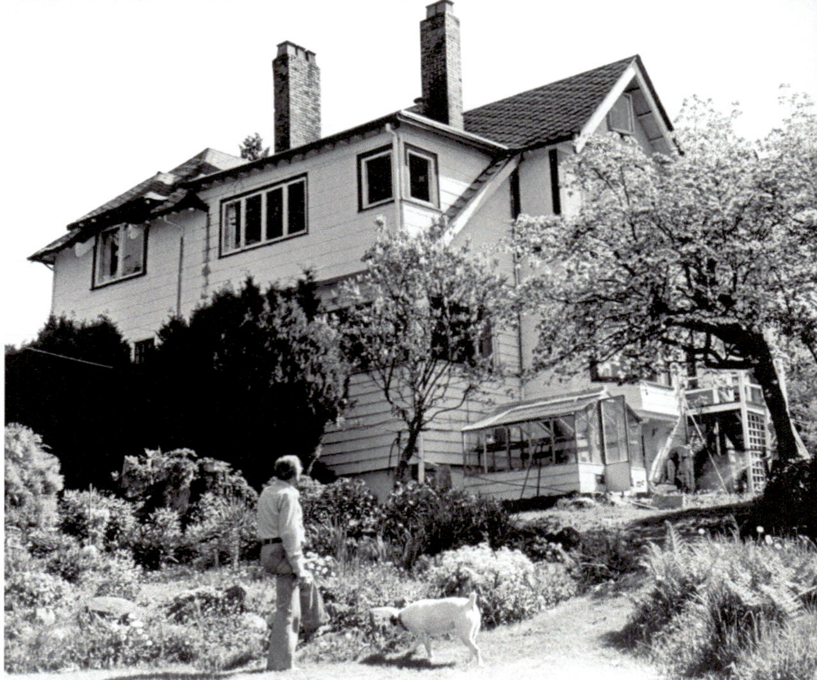

B – Stoker house, 1980.

The Stoker Farm

"Save the Stoker Farm!!!" The vociferous 1980 public campaign failed, and the one remaining farm in the City of North Vancouver disappeared. Among the last photos taken were a 1979 view of the barn and house (A), and one in 1980 of the house alone (B). Situated at the southwest corner of Lonsdale and 29th, the property was originally purchased in 1905 by Rupert Archibald. It was he who built the house, which had 28 rooms. Here's an early view of it showing the front side (C). When Archibald's daughter, Marie, and her husband, Howard Stoker, acquired the property around 1920, they set up a dairy farm. "Dearne Dairies" continued until 1951, after which the farm produced chickens and eggs. It's all condominiums now (D).

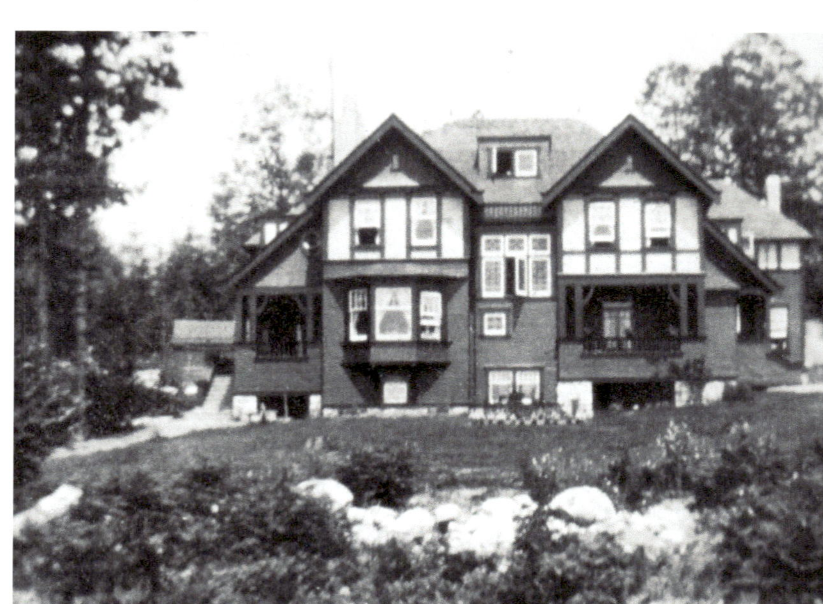

C – Early front-view of house, date unknown.

D – Condominiums, 2016.

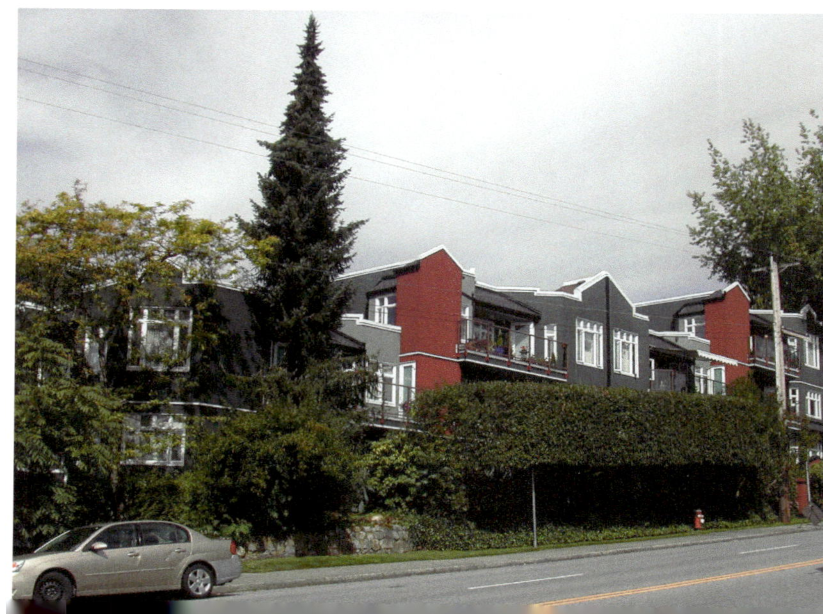

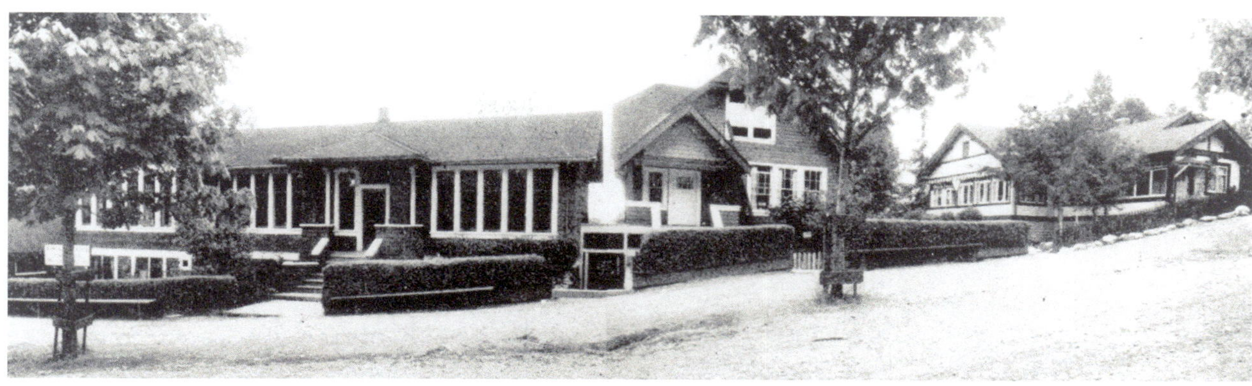

A – Kingsley School, c.1935.

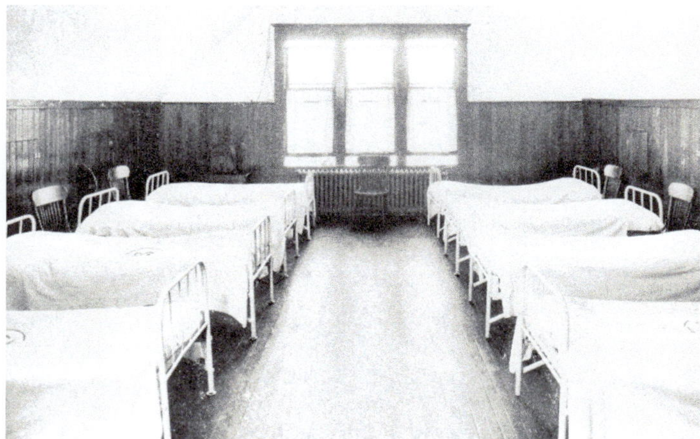

B – Dormitory, c.1935.

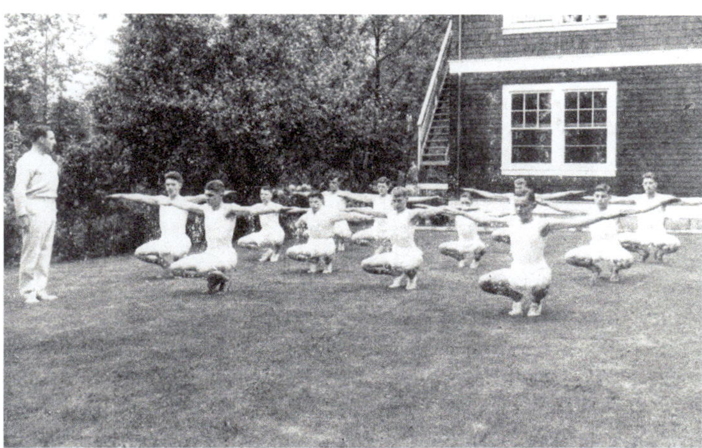

C – Physical training, c.1935.

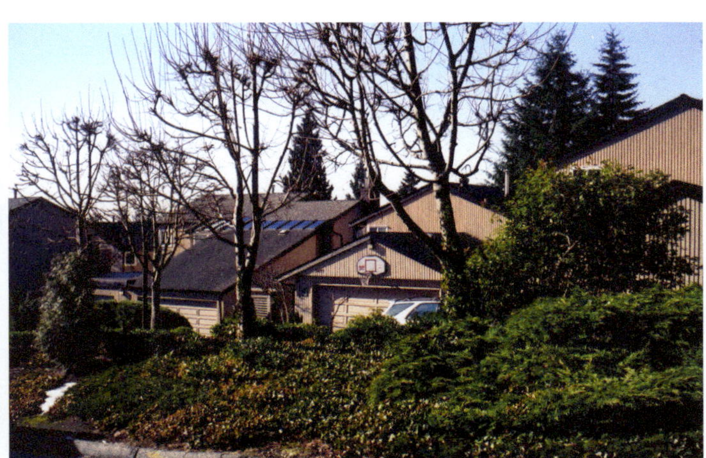

D – Residential complex, 2008.

Kingsley School for Boys

There used to be several English-style private schools here in North Vancouver. One was Kingsley School for Boys, seen in these mid-1930s photos (A, B, & C). Founded in 1920, it covered grades 1–12 and occupied ten acres along St. Marys Avenue. Kingsley had classrooms, a science laboratory, library, gymnasium, dormitories, tennis court, basketball court, and fields for football, soccer, cricket, and other sports. It was a rigorous school, backed by strict discipline. Among other things, boys studied English literature, composition, grammar, history, geometry, physics, chemistry, Latin, French, and geography. They did a one-mile run before breakfast. After school they swam, did field sports, or played tennis. Kingsley closed around 1950. There's a residential complex there now, at 3431–3439 St. Marys (D).

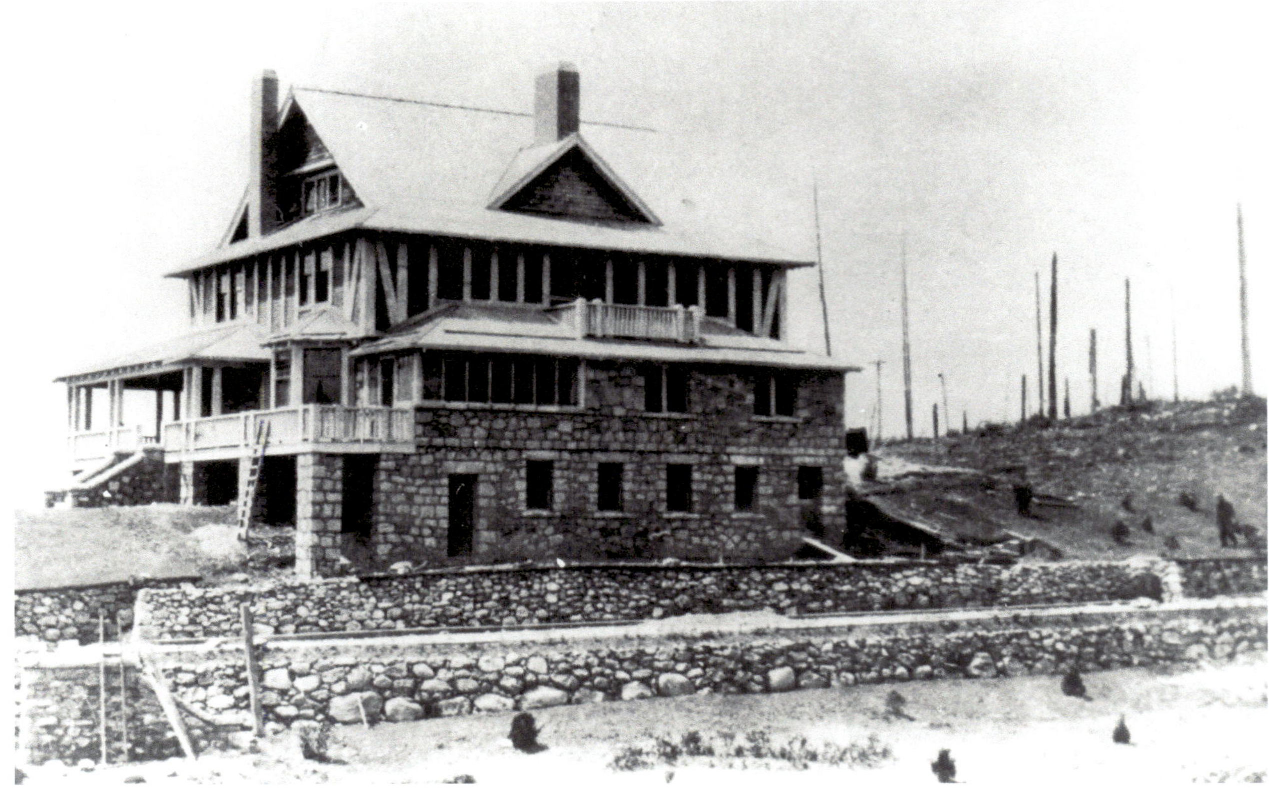

A – The Nye mansion, 1912.

Thomas Nye Home

In 1902, as a reward for serving in the Boer War, longshoreman Thomas Nye was given 160 acres in the Upper Lonsdale area. Lonsdale in those days was a rough trail and this acreage was "out in the middle of nowhere." The good news is there was a real estate boom and Nye made a lot of money subdividing his land and selling residential lots. So, in 1912 he built this huge mansion on the property for himself and his wife (A). The bad news is he was deeply affected by the depression of 1913. The Nyes moved out of the house and left North Vancouver in 1916. Today their old home is part of a Tudor-style residential development (B). You'll find it at 3545 Dowsley Court.

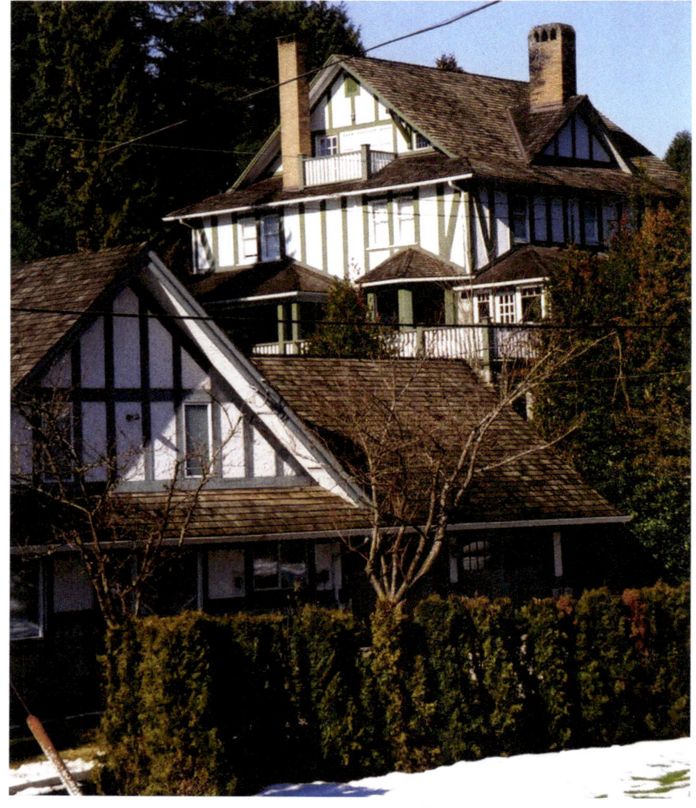

B – Part of residential development, 2008.

2 West to the Capilano River

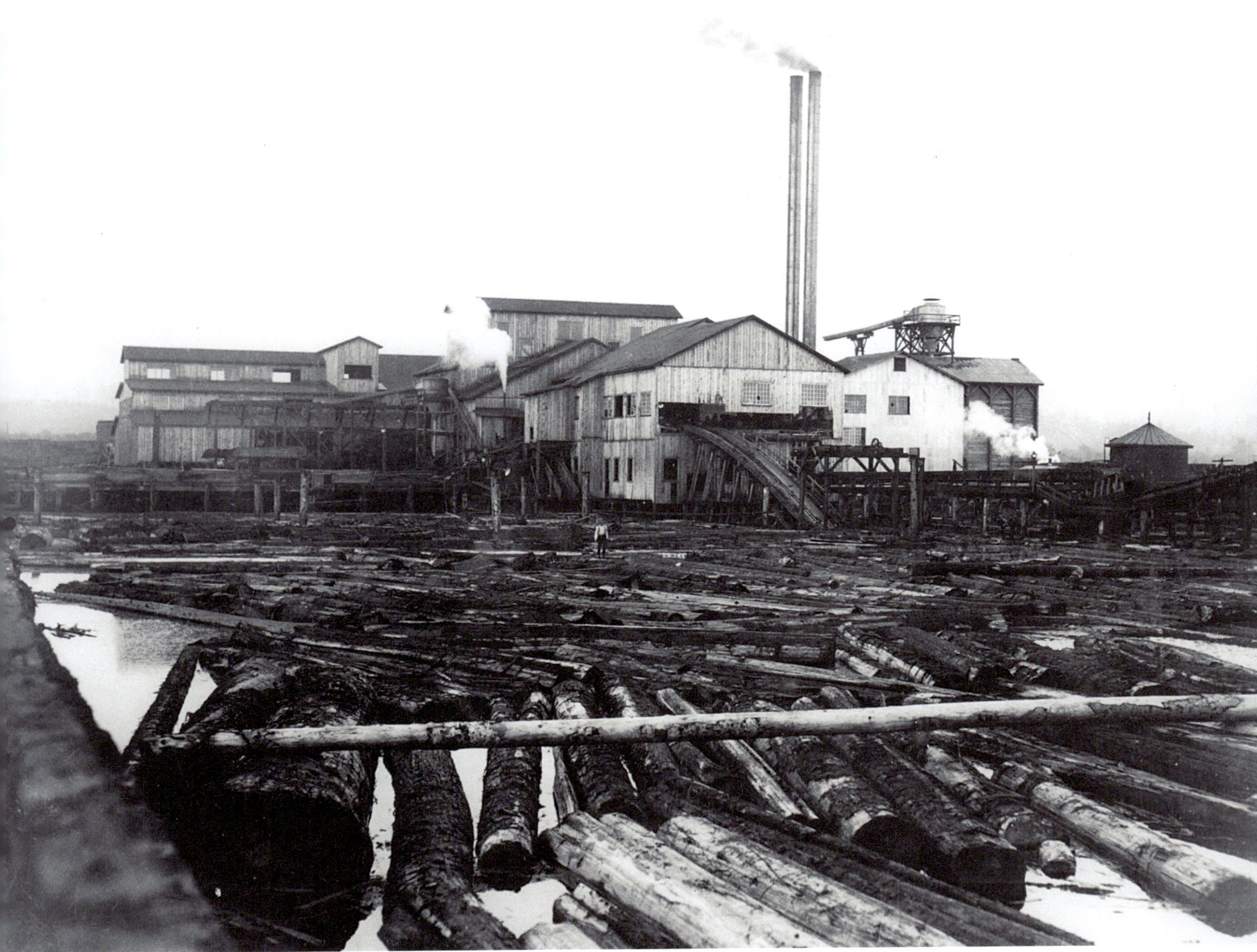

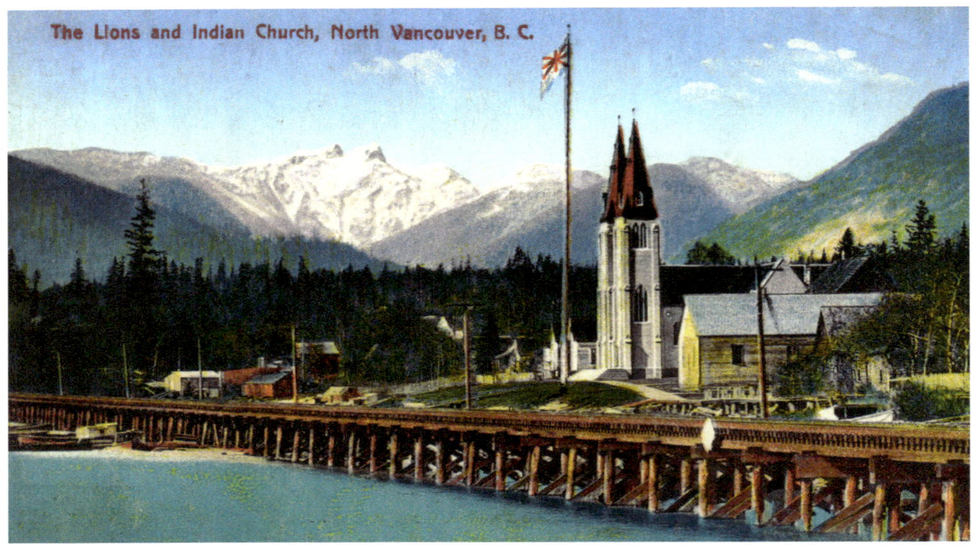

A – St.Paul's Church, 1920s.

St. Paul's Catholic Church

Historic St. Paul's Church, which dates back to the 1800s, is located on the Mission Reserve at 424 West Esplanade. In the 1920s there was not yet a street in front of it, and it sat right by the water's edge (A). Notice the railroad trestle running in front, parallel to the shore. In the 2007 photo, we still see railroad tracks running in front of St. Paul's, but they now sit on solid ground (B). This is because the near-shore area has been filled in, producing a new shoreline further out. Today there's a street, railway tracks, and a parking lot between the Church and the water, and a marina at the water's edge.

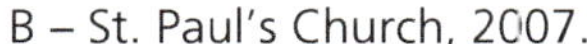
B – St. Paul's Church, 2007.

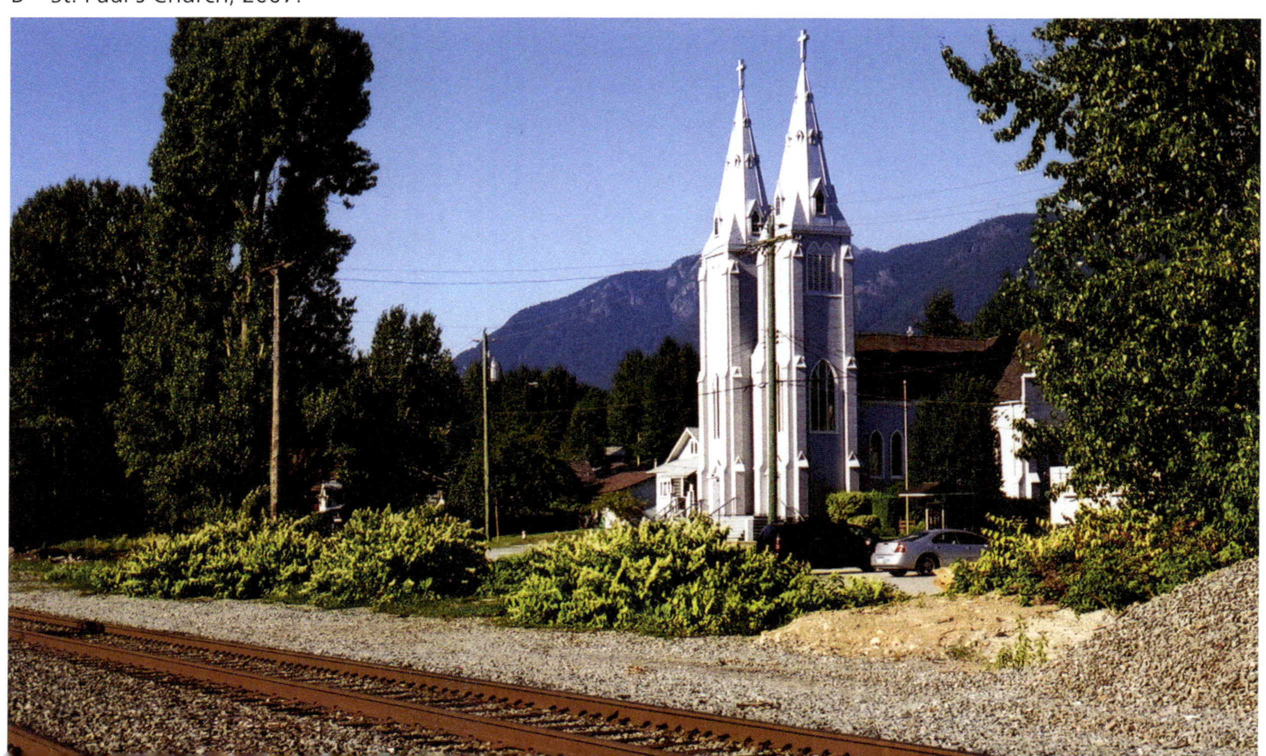

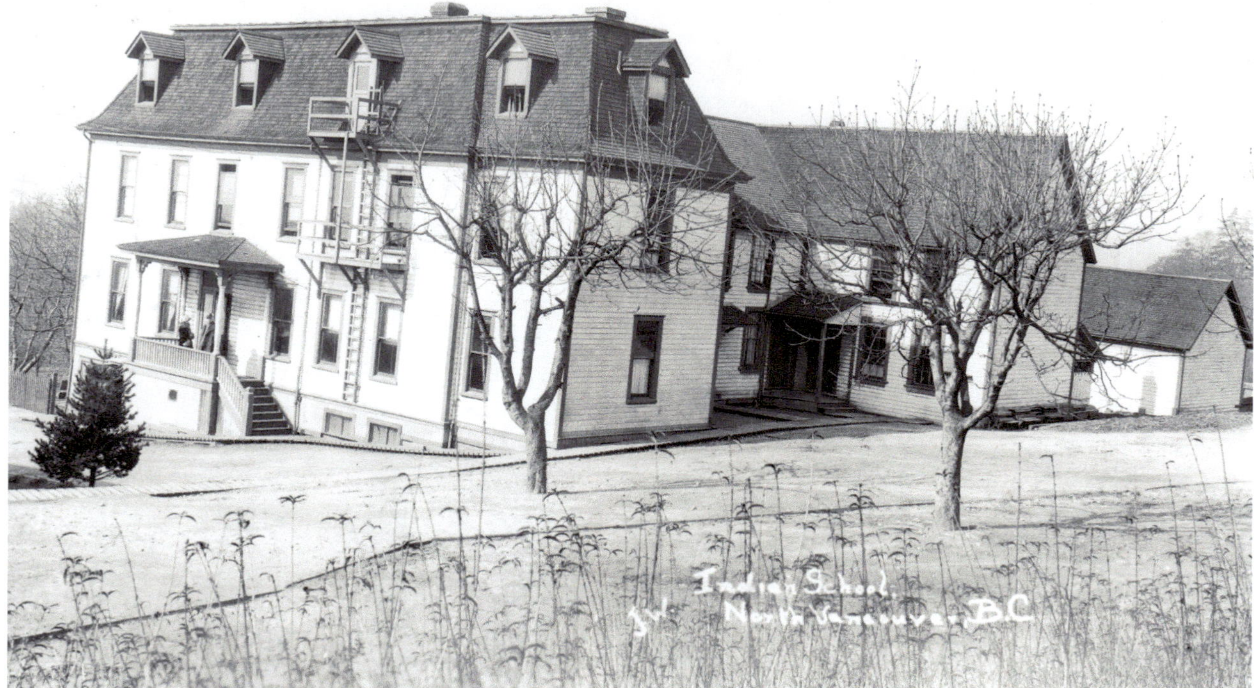

A – St.Paul's Indian Residential School, 1920s.

St. Paul's Indian Residential School

"I stand before you today to offer an apology to former students of Indian residential schools. The treatment of children in these schools is a sad chapter in our history." Prime Minister Stephen Harper spoke these words in June 2008. One such school, photographed in the 1920s (A), was St. Paul's Indian School at 541 West Keith Road. Founded in the late 1890s, it operated in this location from around 1907 to 1959. Its purpose: to purge local First Nations children of their traditions, culture, and language, so they'd fit into the dominant Canadian culture. Sadly, as in residential schools across Canada, a number of students died here. Today St. Thomas Aquinas High School sits on the site (B) — an independent Catholic school open to students of all religions.

B – St.Thomas Aquinas High School, 2008.

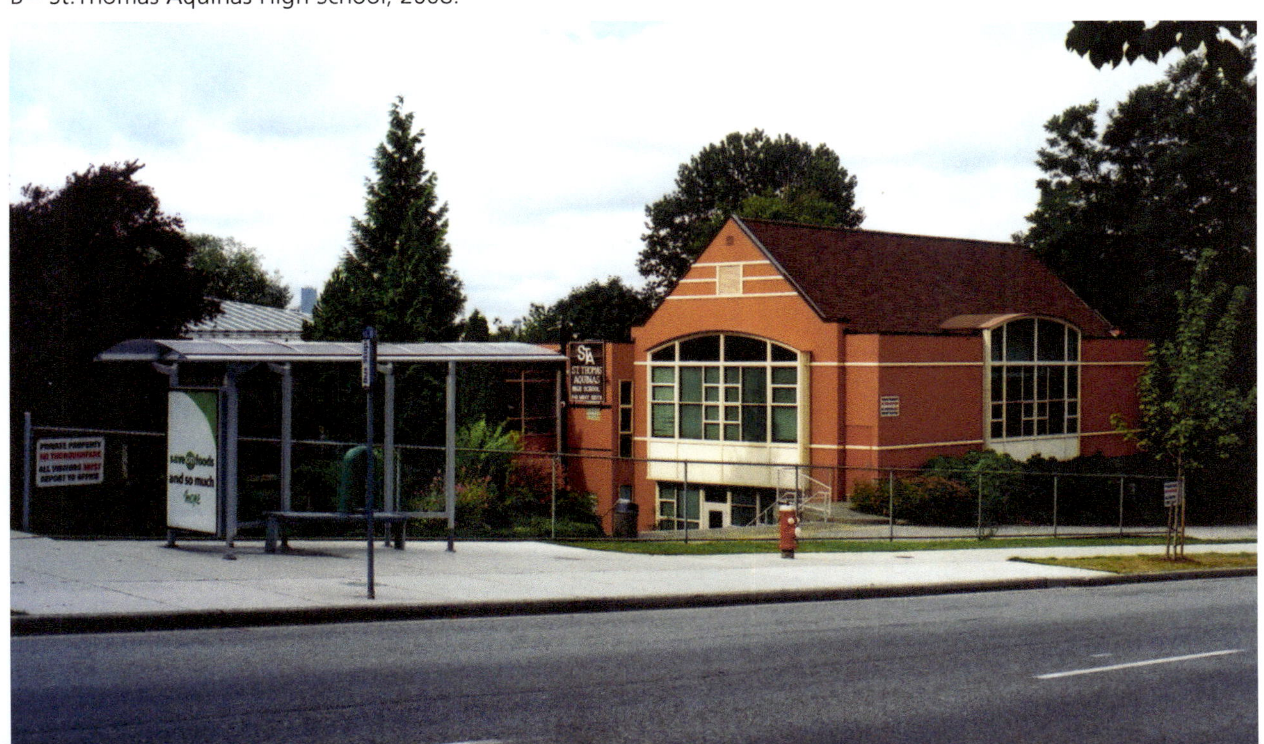

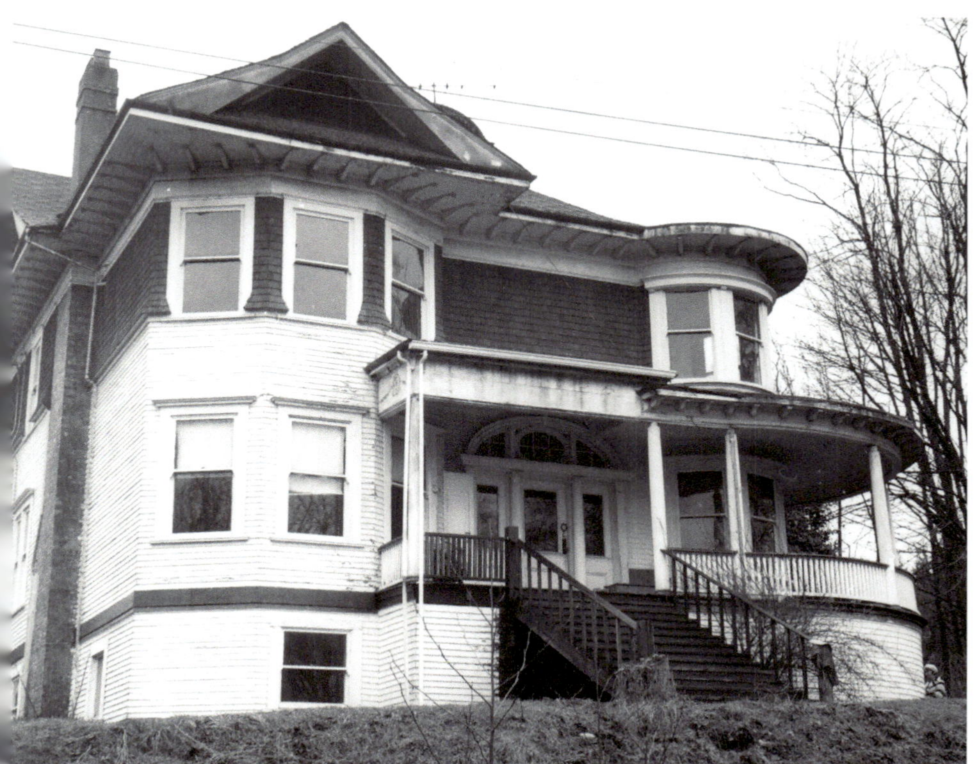

A – Empty McNeish house, 1982.

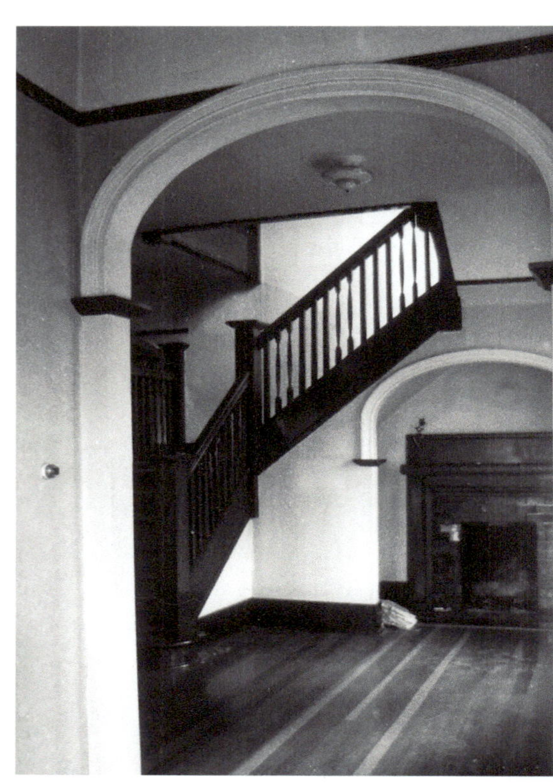

B – Interior, 1982.

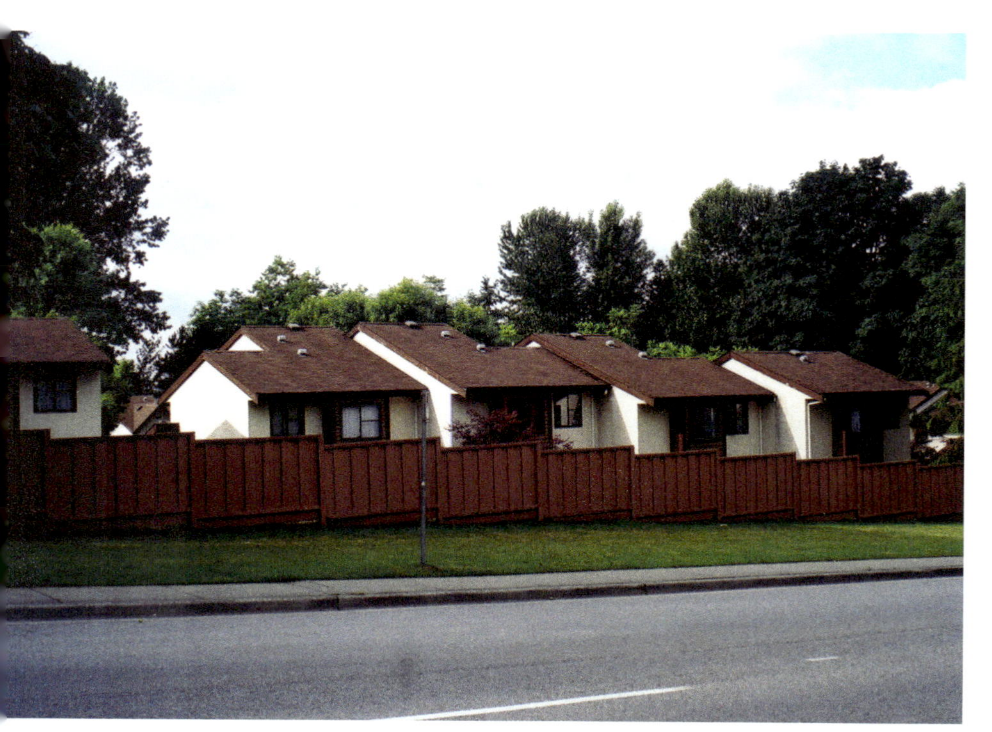

C – Townhouses, 2008.

The McNeish Home

Among the many beautiful mansions that were built in North Vancouver in the early 1900s was the McNeish home at 613 West Keith Road. Here it is in 1982, before its demolition (A). It was an architectural "gem," owned by William McNeish and his family. McNeish was a city alderman in 1909–1910 and mayor in 1911–1912. In the early 1980s there was a brief effort to save the house, with its beautiful interior (B) and solid structure. But progress prevailed. The site was cleared to allow construction of the Walnut Gardens townhouse complex, at 601 West Keith (C). Not *everything* was lost, however. Someone removed a few tiles from the house's fireplace. Over a century old, they reside in the North Vancouver Museum's collection.

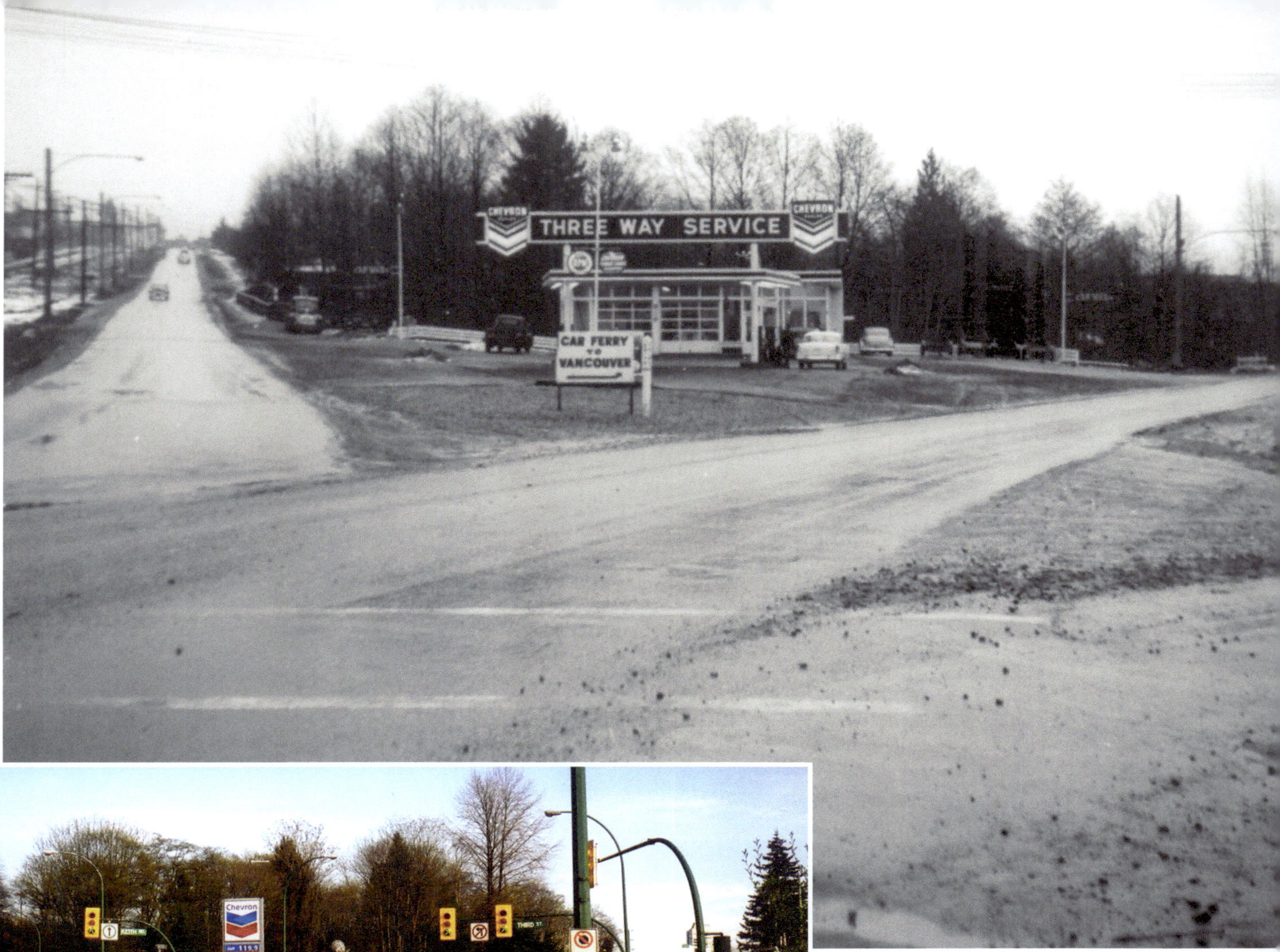

A – Three streets converge, 1957.

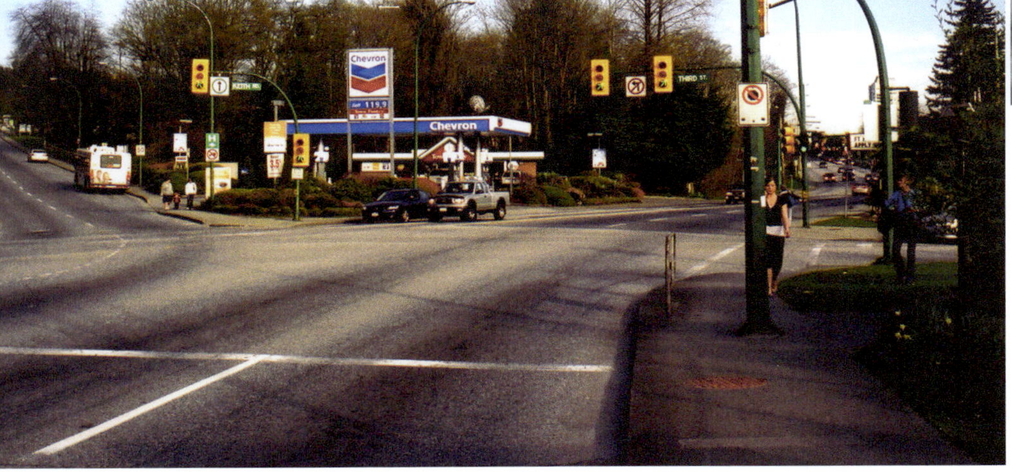

B – Same intersection, 2008.

"Three Way" Intersection

Recognize this junction? It's where Marine Drive, Keith Road, 3rd Street, and Bewicke Avenue converge at the bottom of the Keith Road hill. The 1957 photo (A) looks east from Marine Drive and shows three unpaved streets approaching the intersection. That's Keith on the left, 3rd in the middle, and Bewicke on the right. The "Three Way Service" Chevron station you see between Keith and 3rd was built after World War II, around 1946. Now look at the 2008 photo taken from the same angle (B). The streets are paved, and a modern Chevron station has replaced the original structure. In 2016, you'll find the station still here at 660 West 3rd.

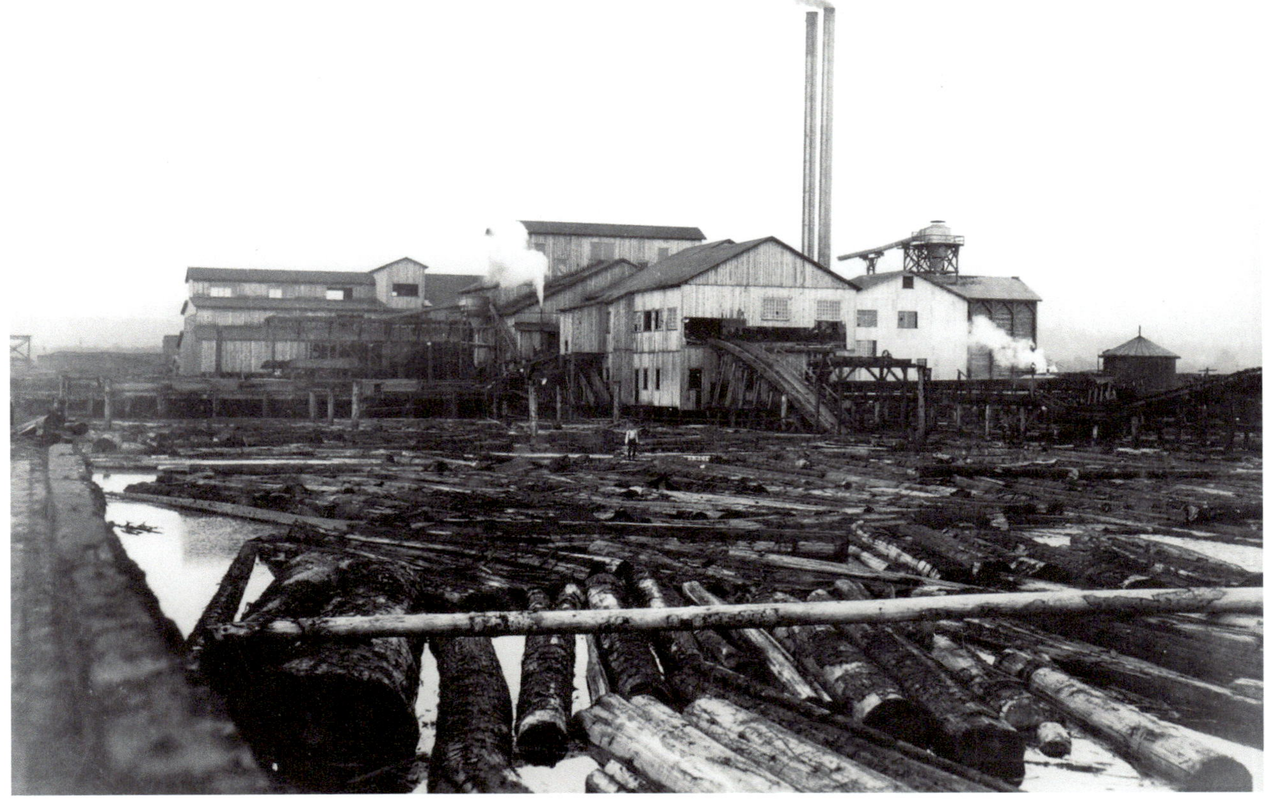

A – Sawmill, 1928.

Capilano Timber Company Sawmill

The 1928 photograph shows the Capilano Timber Company Sawmill that used to be located along the shore between Pemberton and Lloyd Avenues (A). In those days Lloyd wasn't a true public street. It was the railroad right-of-way for the Capilano Timber Company train that brought huge cedar and hemlock logs down to the mill on flat cars, shown here in a 1920 photo (B), logs harvested up in the Capilano Valley. The mill burned down in the early 1930s and the company ceased operation soon after. Today, the ship-building firm, Seaspan International Ltd., covers the old lumber mill site (C).

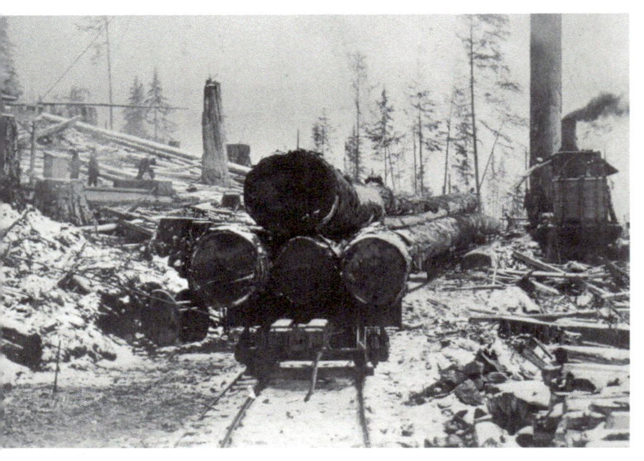

B – Hauling logs to the mill, 1920.

C – Seaspan, 2014.

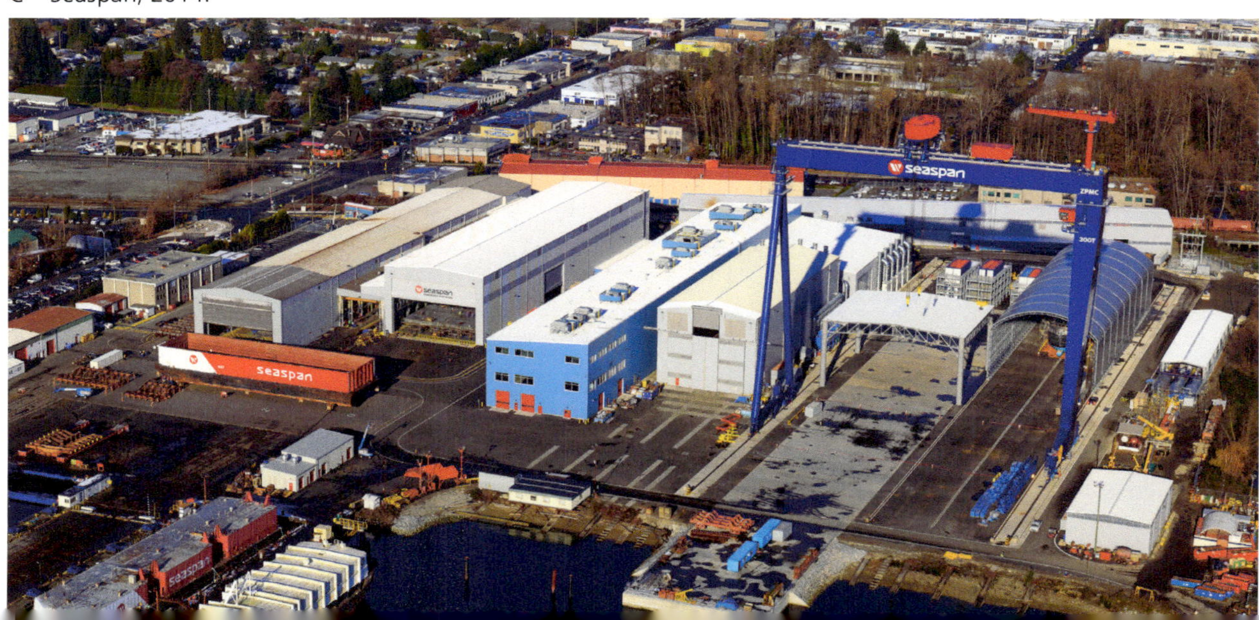

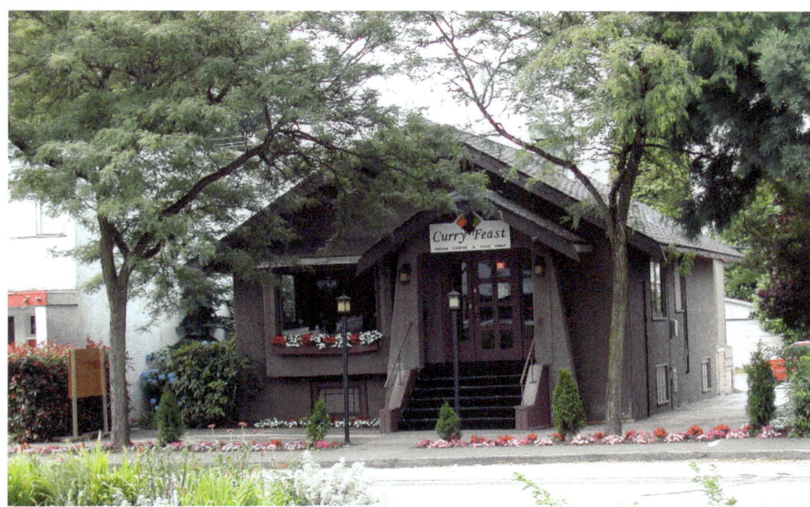

A – Curry Feast restaurant, 2008.

Pemberton Gardens

In recent years, you may have noticed a restaurant located in an old house at 1265 Marine Drive. It was the "Moustache Café" for a long time. Then it became the "Curry Feast." Not only was this once a private home, but it was part of a subdivision conceived and promoted in the mid to late 1920s. Pemberton Gardens was the brainchild of Vancouver real estate guru R.P. Whitaker. His plan was to develop several blocks around Marine Drive and Pemberton, which he mapped out in his 1925 promotional brochure (B). Unfortunately the 1929 crash killed the scheme, and fewer than two dozen houses were built. In 2016 the Marine Drive house is gone, but there's still one at 1381 West 17th (C).

B – Promotional brochure, 1925.

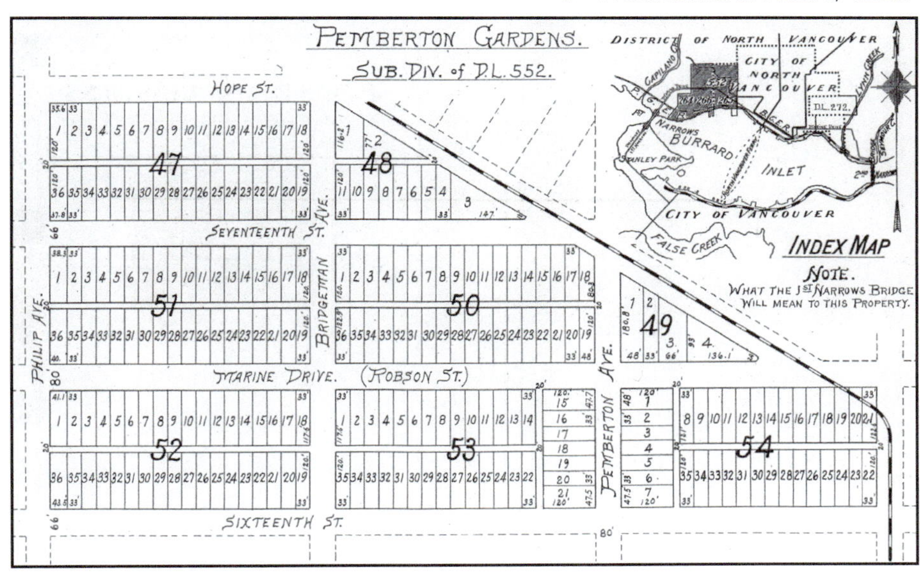

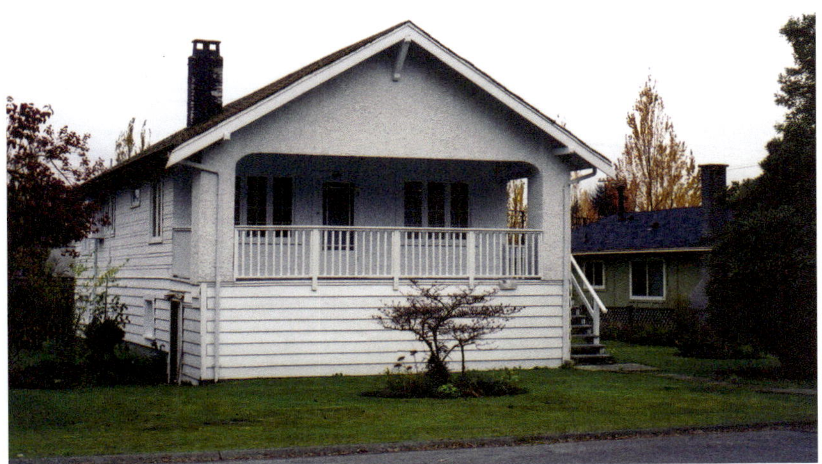

C – House on West 17th, 2007.

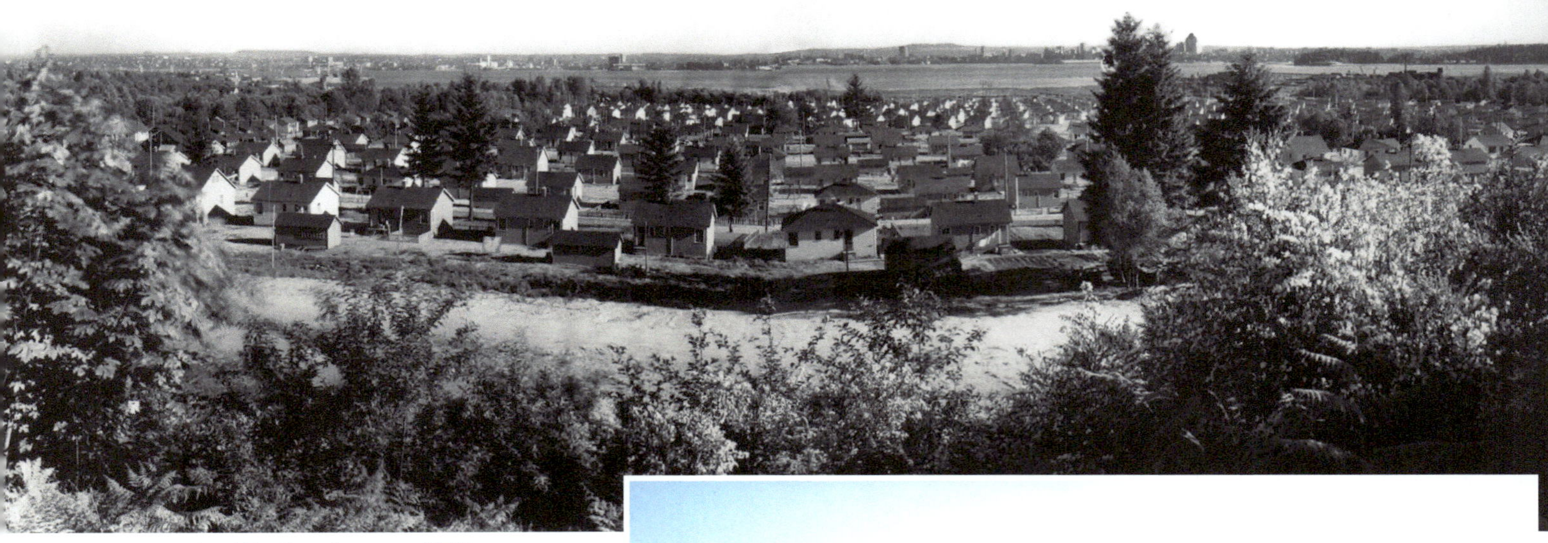

A – Wartime houses, 1943.

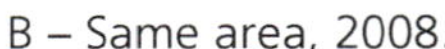

B – Same area, 2008.

Wartime Housing & Westview School

When thousands of defence workers moved to North Vancouver during World War II to staff our shipbuilding industry, they and their families needed places to live. So the federally created Wartime Housing Ltd. built hundreds of small homes for them. One subdivision was located above and below Marine Drive, between Mosquito Creek and Lloyd Avenue. Here it is in 1943 (A). Today, the whole area is filled with condos, commercial buildings, and malls (B). For the children in these homes, Wartime Housing built Westview Elementary School at 1660 Bewicke Avenue, seen in this 1980 picture (C). The original school lasted until 2005, when it was torn down and a new one built. The site of the old school is the new Westview School's playing field (D).

C – Original Westview Elementary School, 1980.

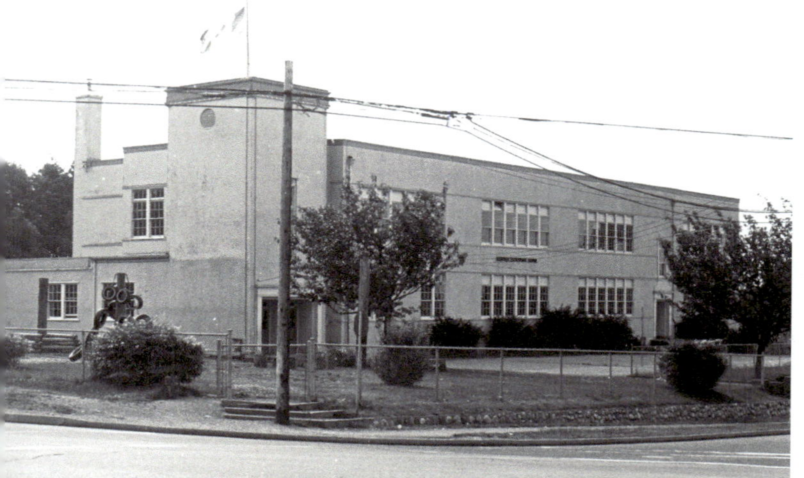

D – Playing field, 2008.

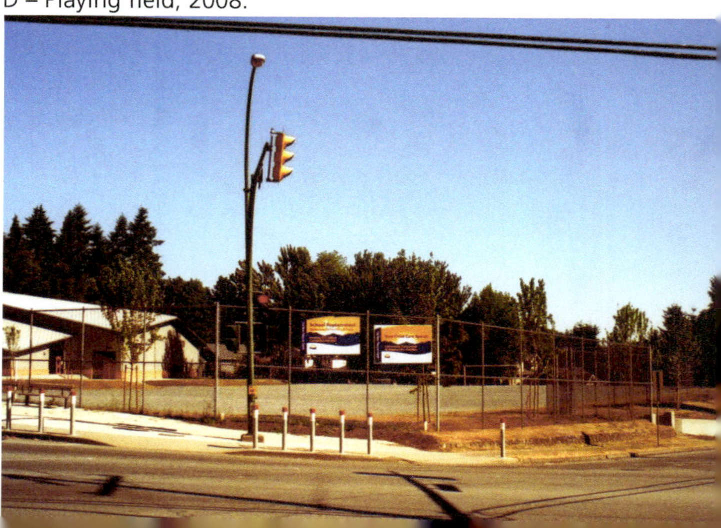

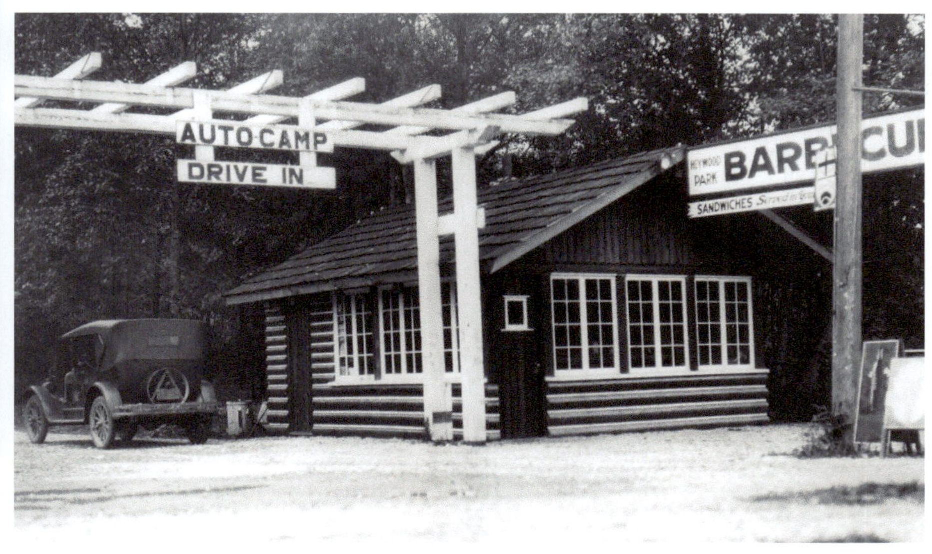

A – Entrance to auto camp, 1928.

Tourist Camp on Marine Drive

The Upper Capilano area and West Vancouver were tourist attractions in the 1920s. The result was increased visitor traffic along Marine Drive. So in 1924 the City of North Vancouver opened an auto camp in Heywood Park, on the north side of Marine Drive. It provided overnight campers with water, showers, kitchens, electric lighting, dressing rooms, a refreshment booth, and other amenities. By 1928 it had evolved into the Heywood Park Barbecue & Auto Camp (A), with a proper restaurant and several log cabins (B). Though the restaurant was enlarged in the 1930s, the Heywood Camp as a whole eventually became a problem for the city. It was demolished 1943. Today the site is grass and trees, plus a children's play area (C).

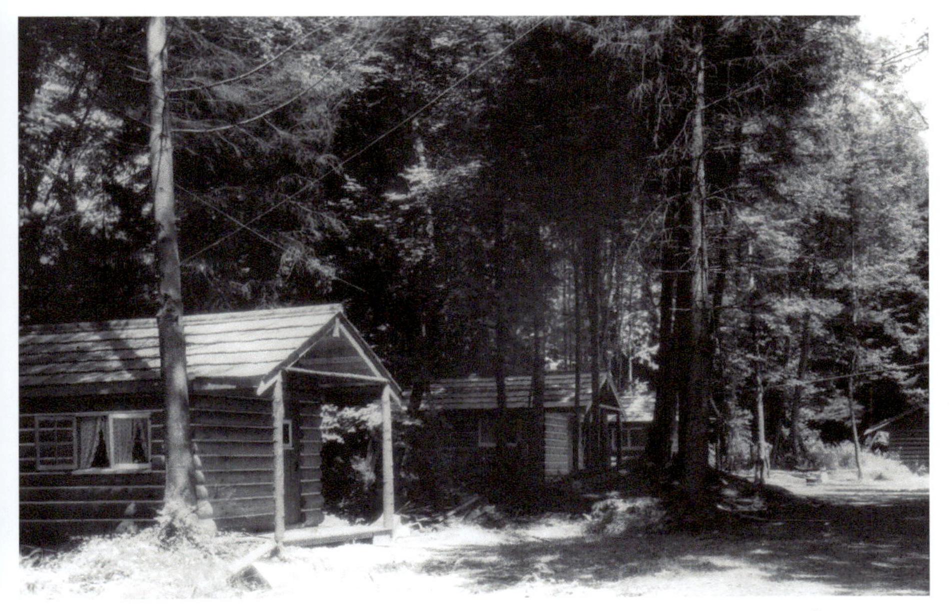

B – Log cabins, 1928.

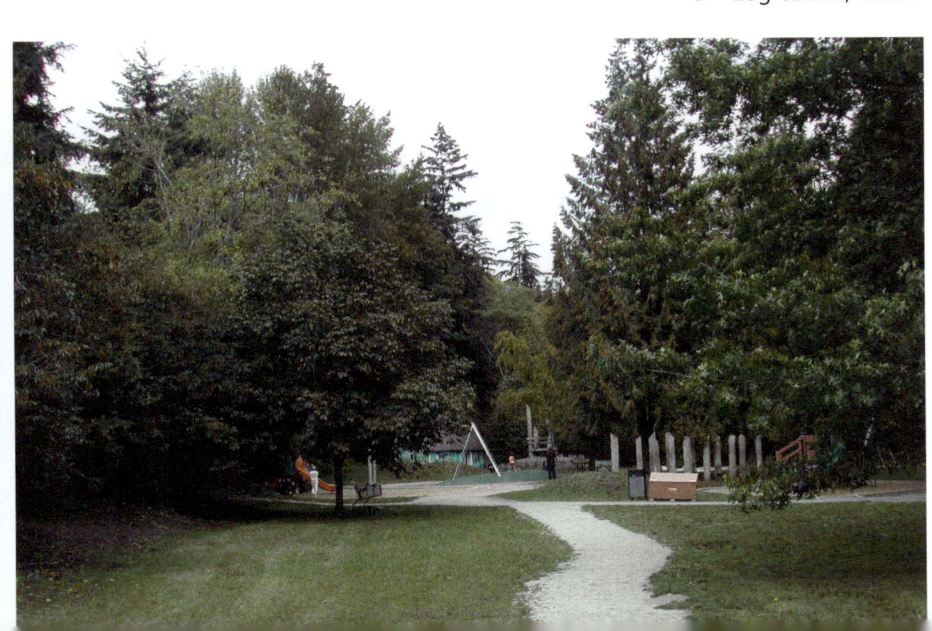

C – Site of auto camp, 2016.

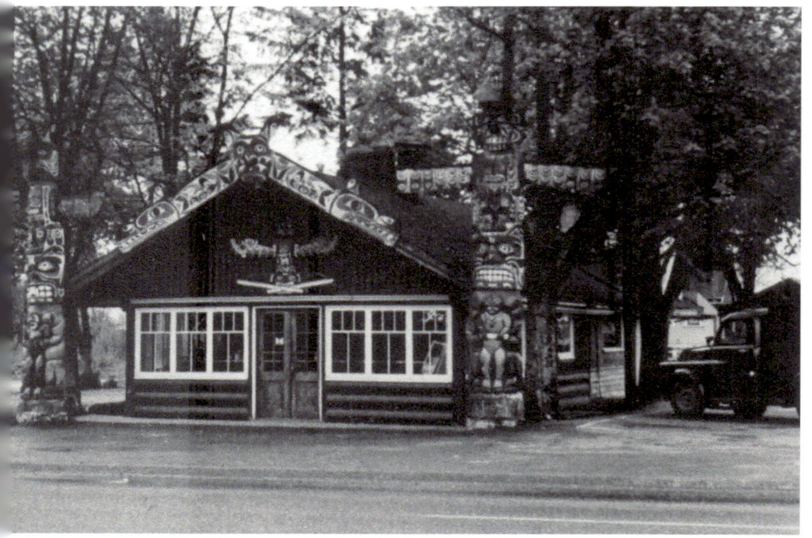

A – Original Tomahawk Barbecue, c.1957.

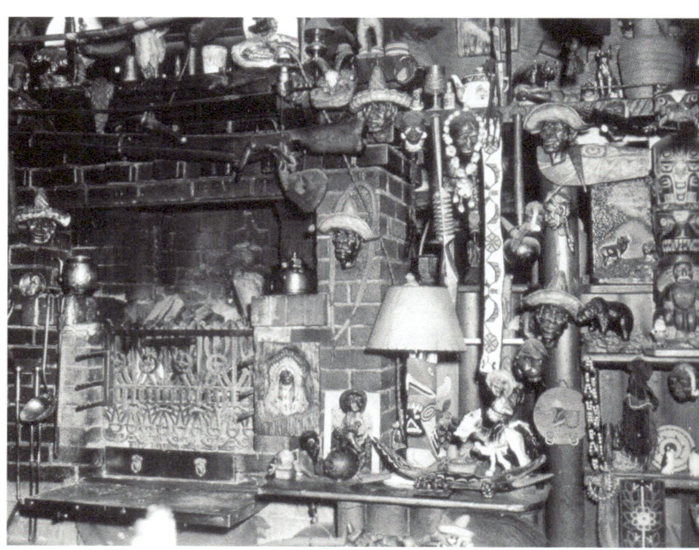

B – Early indoor decorations, date unknown.

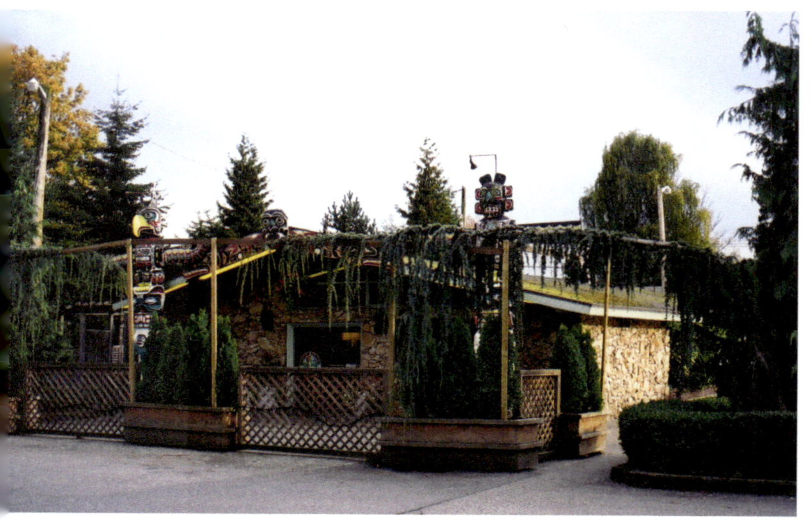

C – Present-day restaurant, 2007.

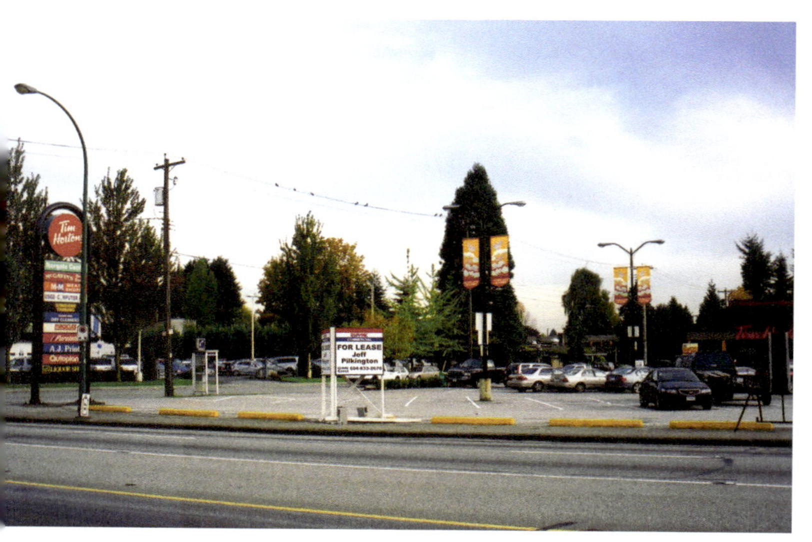

D – Parking lot, 2007.

The Tomahawk Barbecue

Around 1930, Charles "Chick" Chamberlain built his original "Tomahawk Barbecue" restaurant at 1405 Marine. This photo shows it around 1957 (A). Notice how it resembles the Heywood Park Barbecue on the outside (see previous page). This was no coincidence. Before he established the Tomahawk, Chamberlain helped manage the Heywood facility. He liked the log-cabin look. As for the inside of the Tomahawk, Chamberlain decorated it with handcrafted West Coast Native artefacts and other collectibles (B), creating a unique ambiance for diners. This décor, plus the "down-home meals" and fresh-baked pies, made the Tomahawk Barbecue immensely popular with both locals and celebrities. In 1960 it moved to its present location at 1550 Philip (C). The original Tomahawk site became a parking lot (D).

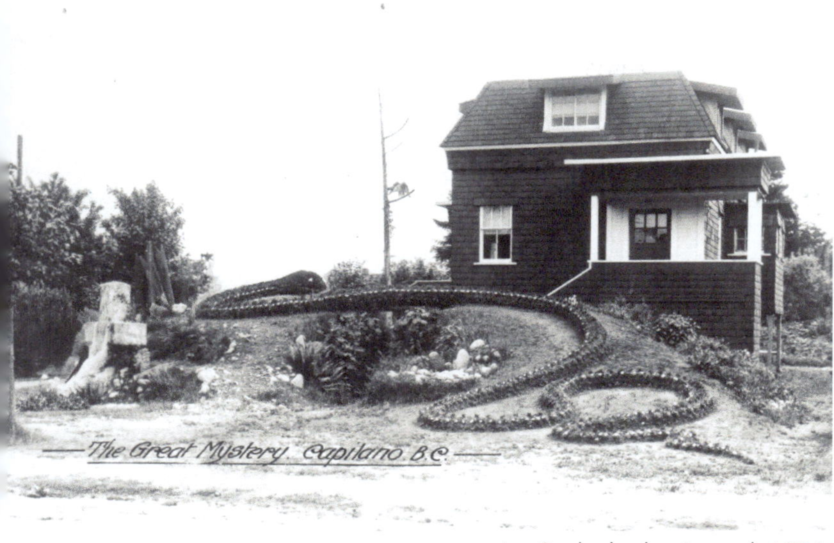

A – Snake hedge in yard, 1934.

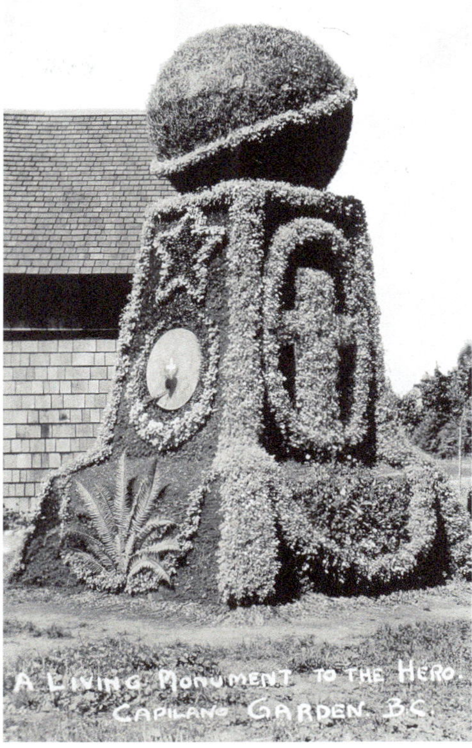

B – "Monument to the Hero," date unknown.

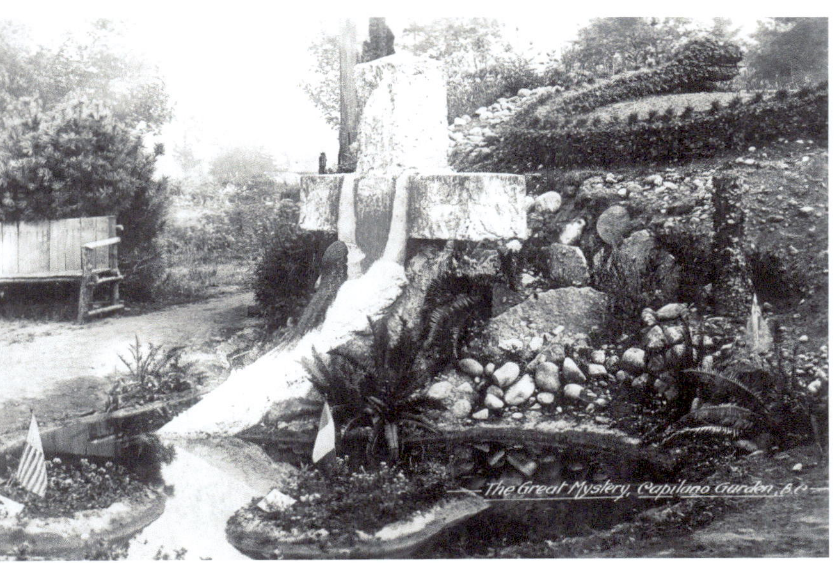

C – Garden with woman and cross, date unknown.

D – La Cucina, 2016.

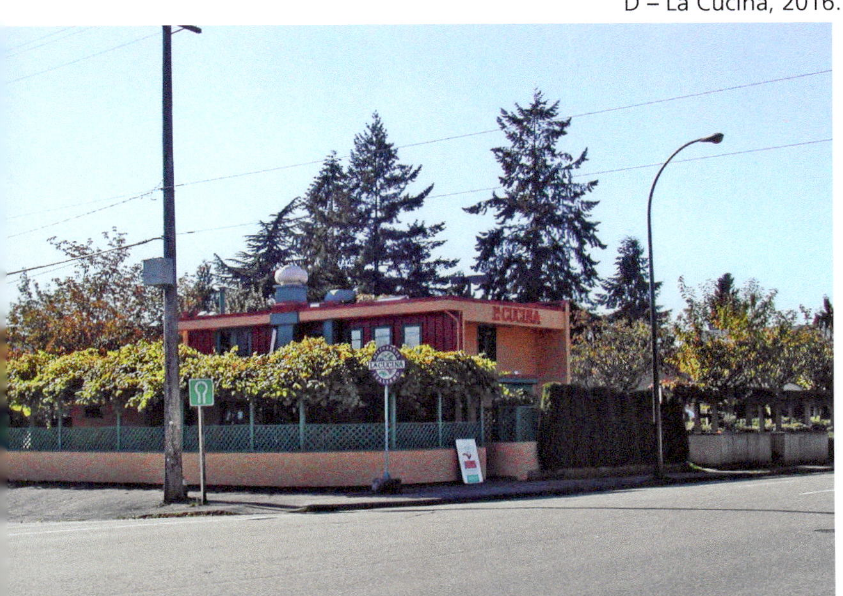

Napoleon St. Pierre's "Capilano Gardens"

Napoleon St. Pierre lived on the southwest corner of Marine Drive and McGowan. He became famous in the 1920s after he started landscaping his yard with decorated plants, cement sculptures, and bushes pruned and shaped into three-dimensional figures. Visitors from all over came by to see his floral displays. Best known was the snake hedge shown in this 1934 photo (A). Visitors also enjoyed his cenotaph-shaped "Monument to the Hero" (B) and the small garden with a woman's figure leaning on a cross (C). When St. Pierre died in 1937, North Vancouver lost one of its most popular "characters." La Cucina Italiana Restaurant sits there now (D).

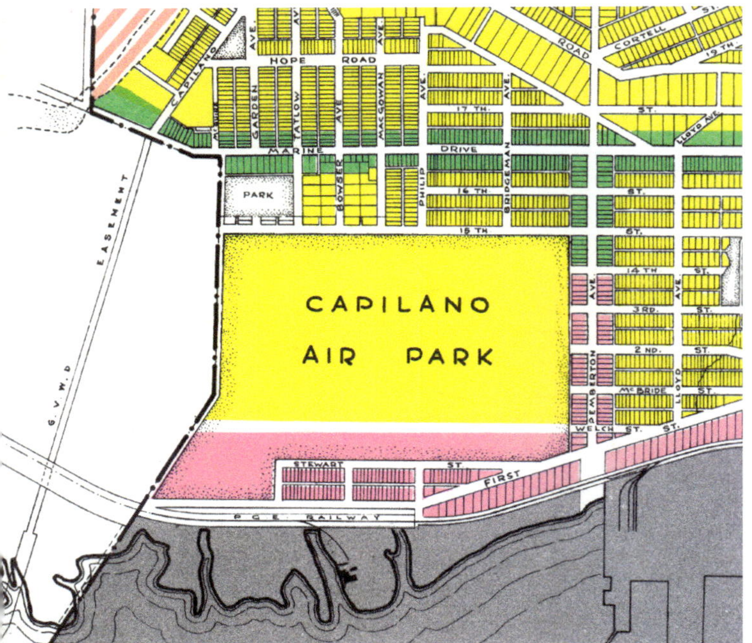

A – Proposed airfield, 1947.

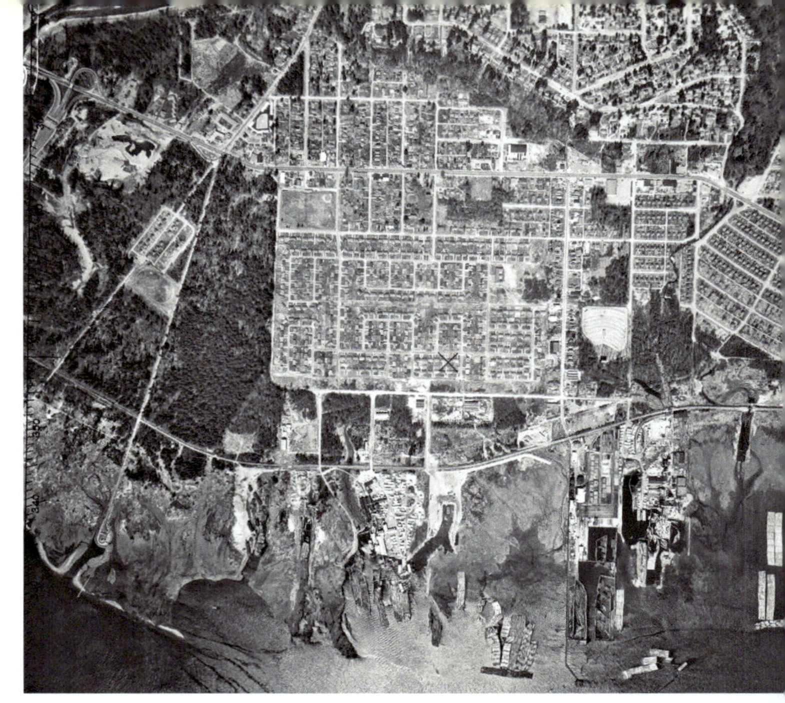

B – Aerial view of Norgate, 1954.

Norgate

The land that Norgate subdivision sits on was supposed to be an airfield — the one indicated on the 1947 map (A). In 1945 a group of businessmen decided the North Shore needed an airport for visitors arriving in private planes. They secured the land, cleared it, and marked where a runway would be. The scheme fell through in 1947. Enter Norman Hullah, of Hullah Construction Company. In 1948 he offered to purchase the airfield site and build houses on it; the offer was accepted. In the 1954 aerial photo (B), you can see Norgate over the airfield footprint. The 1950s photo shows newly constructed homes on Sowden Street (C). The homes are still there, surrounded by thick foliage (D).

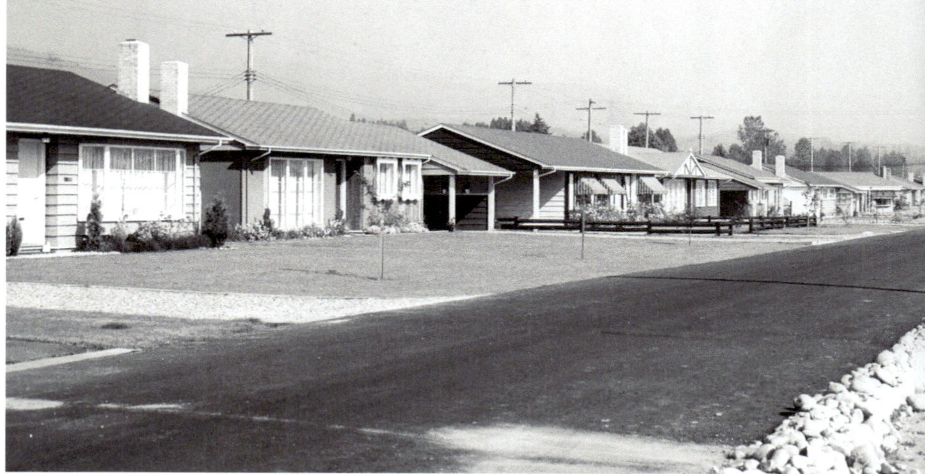

C – Homes on Sowden Street, 1950s.

D – Same view, 2007.

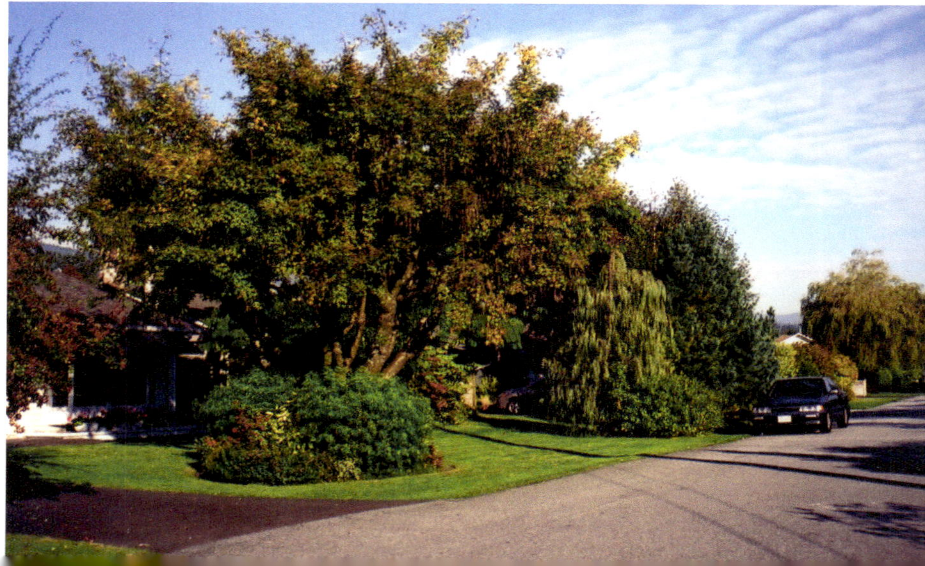

3 Upper Capilano

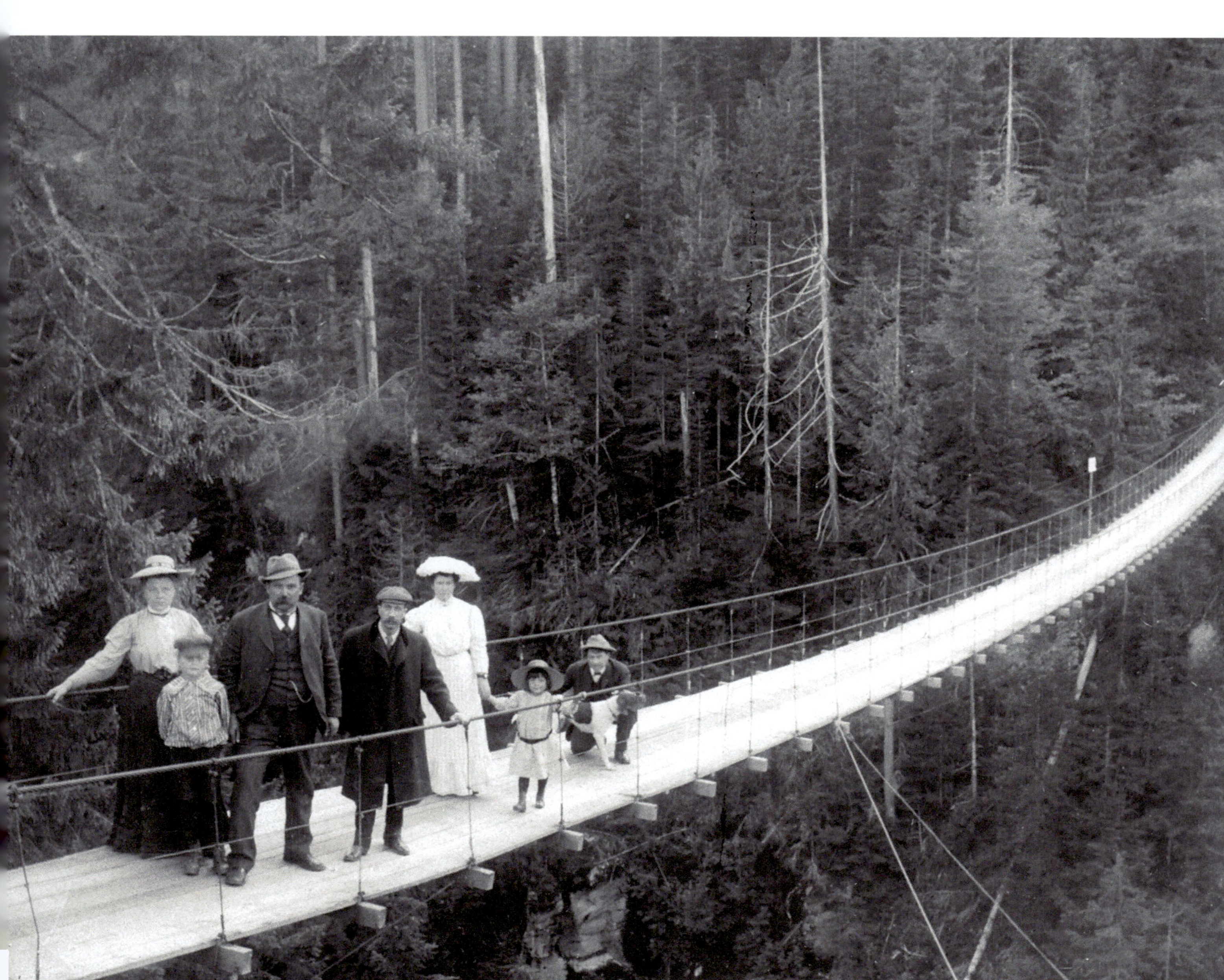

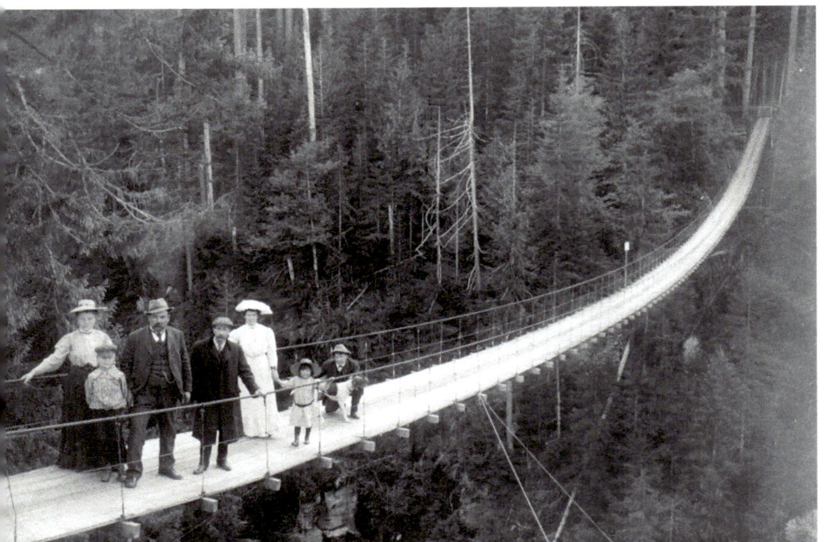

A – Capilano Suspension Bridge, 1905.

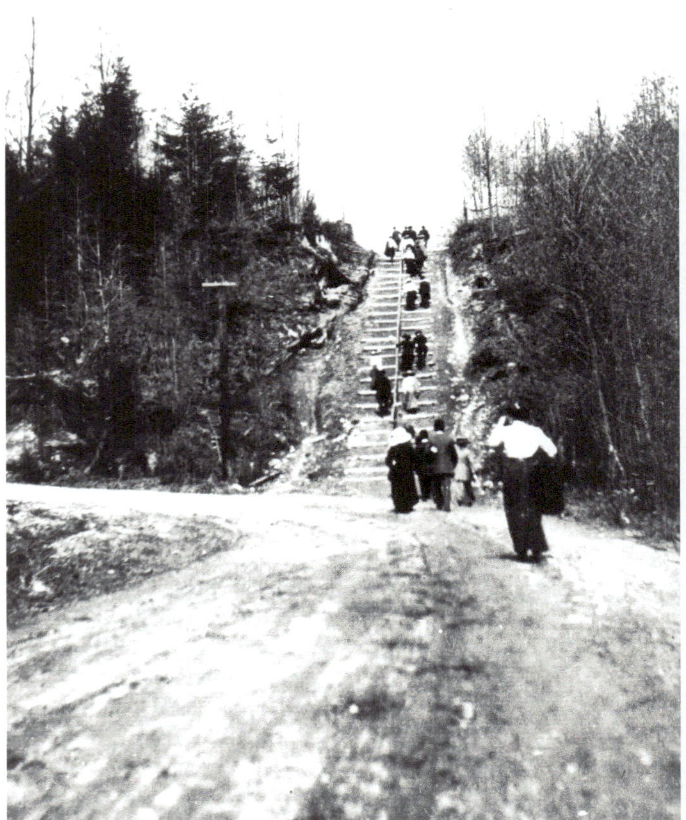

B – Stairs to the top, date unknown.

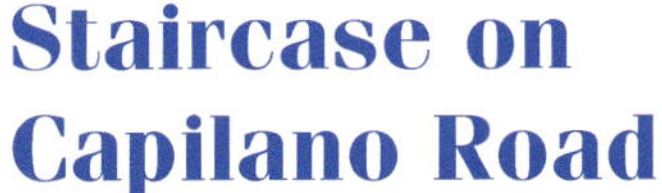

Staircase on Capilano Road

In 1905 the newly built Capilano Suspension Bridge (3735 Capilano Road) was quickly becoming popular (A), despite the fact that Capilano was a rugged dirt road. But that was okay with visitors — especially after the Capilano streetcar was built in 1910. They could get to the "swinging bridge" by taking the streetcar to its terminus (see page 70), then heading north on foot. There was one spot where a rocky bluff forced Capilano Road to veer west and loop around precariously to the other side, before heading north again (the loop is now "Capilano Crescent"). However, when pedestrians reached the bluff, they simply climbed a set of stairs to the top and continued on (B). Author Eleanore Dempster called it "The Golden Staircase." Both the stairs and much of the bluff were removed long ago (C).

C – The staircase site, 2007.

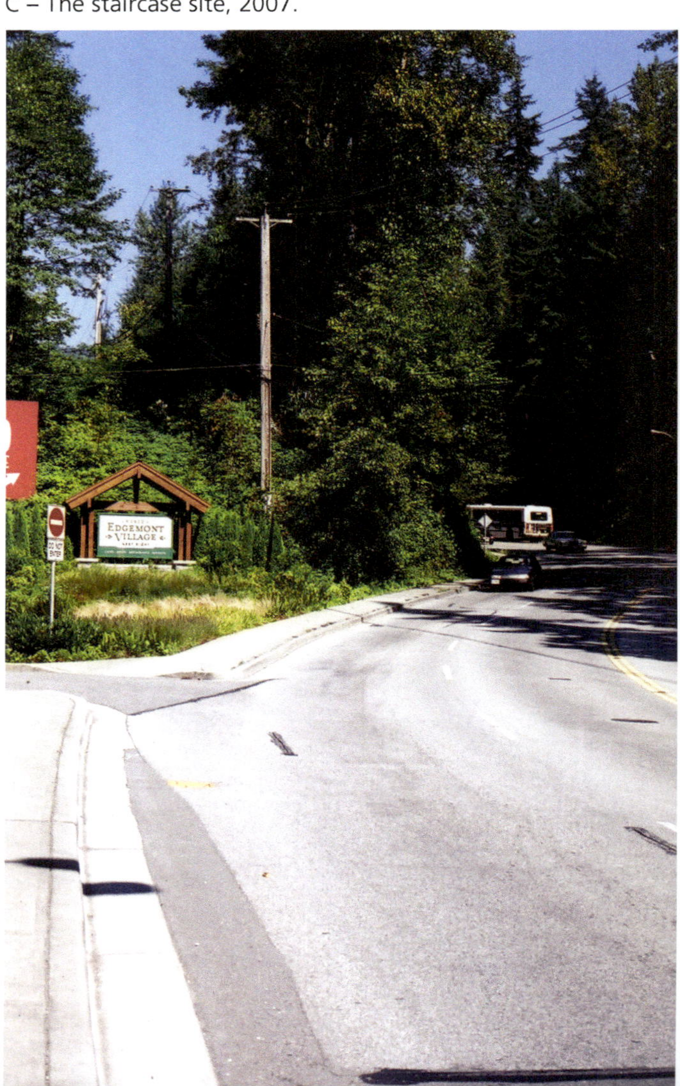

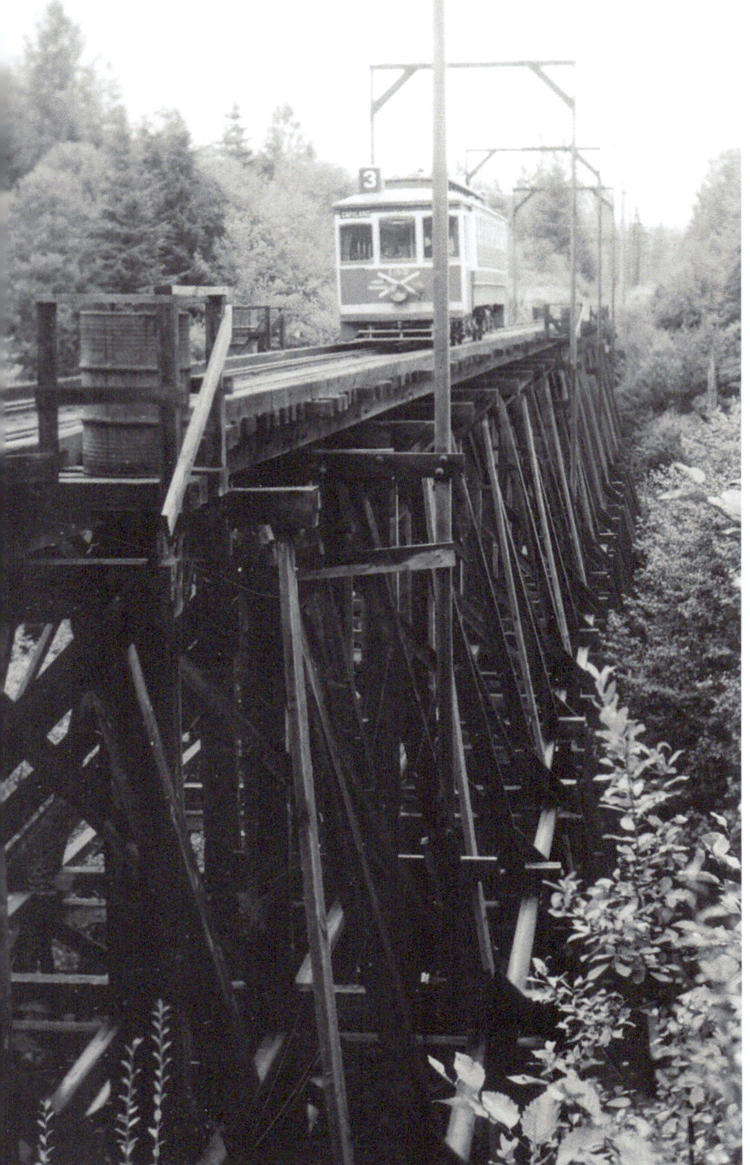

A – Streetcar trestle, 1943.

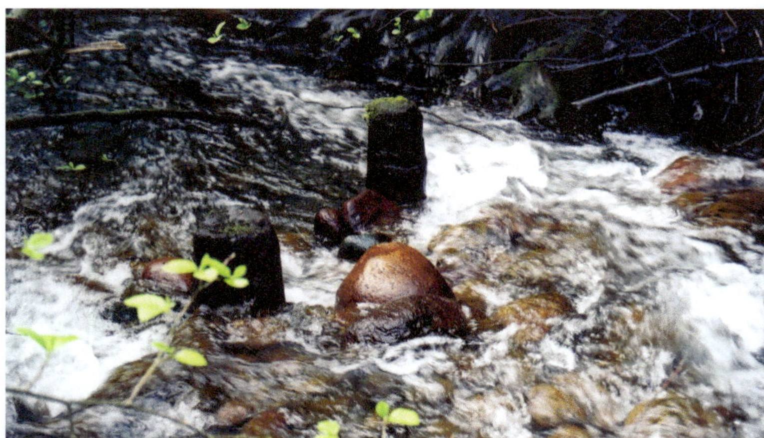

B – Trestle remnants, 2008.

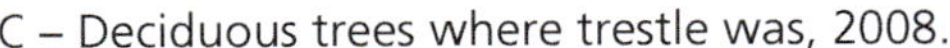

C – Deciduous trees where trestle was, 2008.

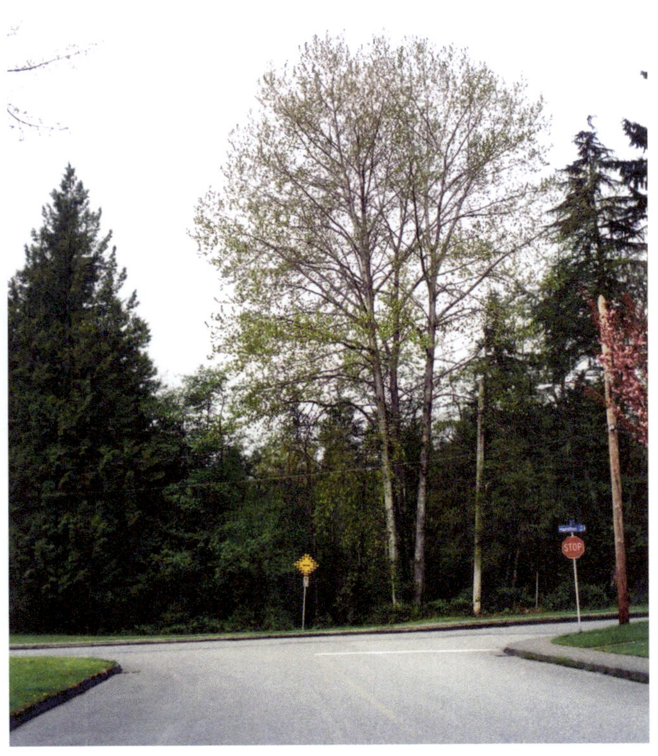

Mackay Creek Trestle

From 1910 to 1943 an elaborate wooden streetcar trestle spanned the Mackay Creek ravine at West 20th Street. Here it is in the 1940s (A). The trestle was 30 metres (98 feet) high and 137 metres (450 feet) long. The Capilano streetcar crossed the ravine here on its way to and from the streetcar terminus at School Road and Bowser Avenue (now under the Upper Levels Highway). Sadly, in 1943 the trestle was deemed unsafe and thus removed. For many years there were still signs of it — a few cut-off trestle footings in the creek bed (B). On the other hand, if you stand at 20th and Hamilton and look west, you'll see deciduous trees growing where the trestle once stood (C), instead of the ravine's normal evergreen trees.

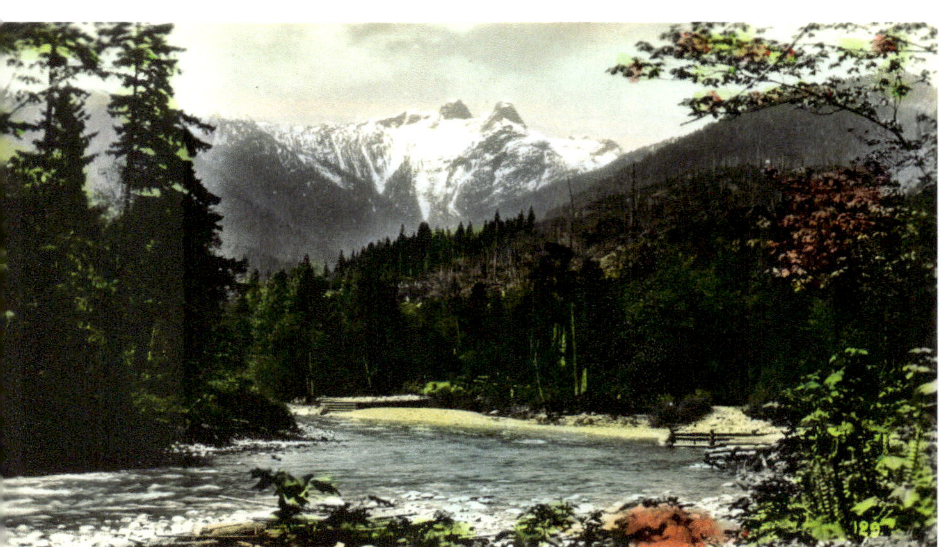

A – Capilano Valley, date unknown.

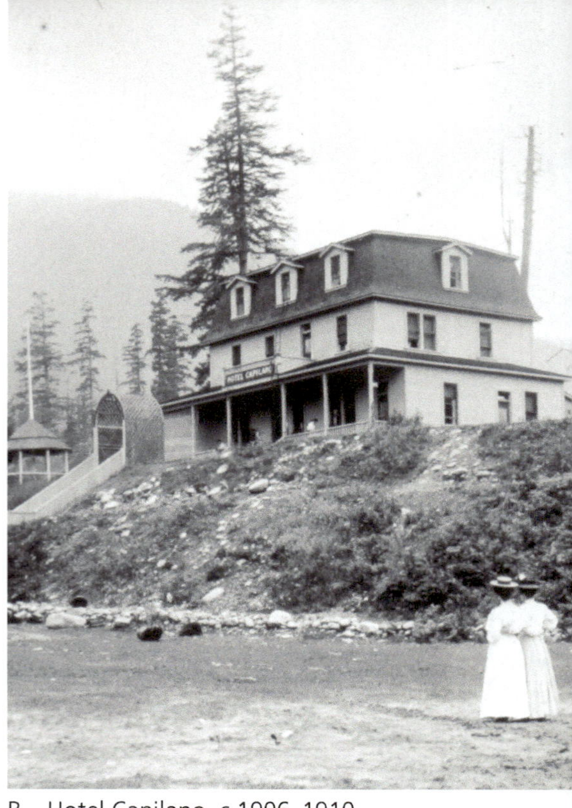

B – Hotel Capilano, c.1906–1910.

The Capilano Valley

One of North Vancouver's early tourist attractions was the Capilano River Valley (A). Rich in wildlife, forests, and mountain scenery, it attracted hunters, fishermen, hikers, and businessmen who wanted to "get away from it all." Far up the valley was the Hotel Capilano, seen in the photo taken between 1906 and 1910 (B). It had 15 bedrooms, several sitting rooms, and a large dining room. The hotel closed in 1921 due to prohibition. The valley itself disappeared when the Cleveland Dam was built across its entrance. At one point in the mid 1950s you could stand on the new dam and still see the empty valley (C). Standing there today, you see only a lake (D).

C – View from new dam, c.1954.

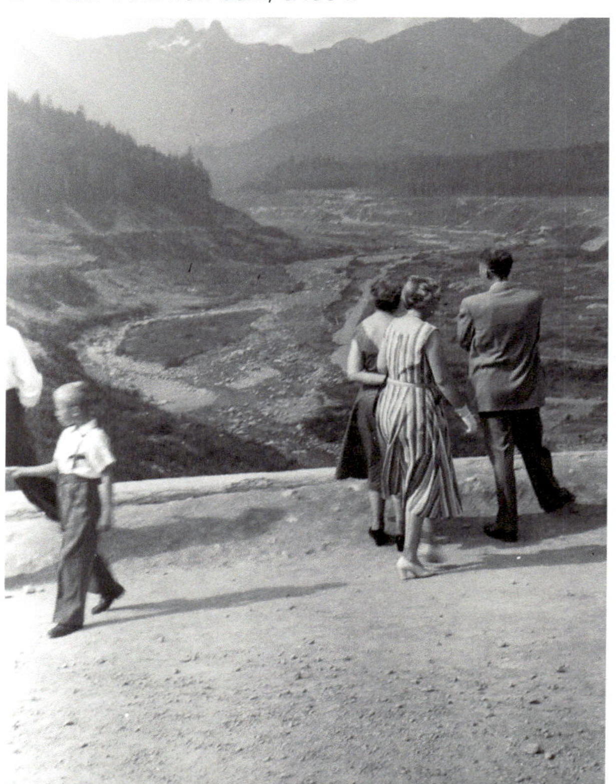

D – Same view, 2007.

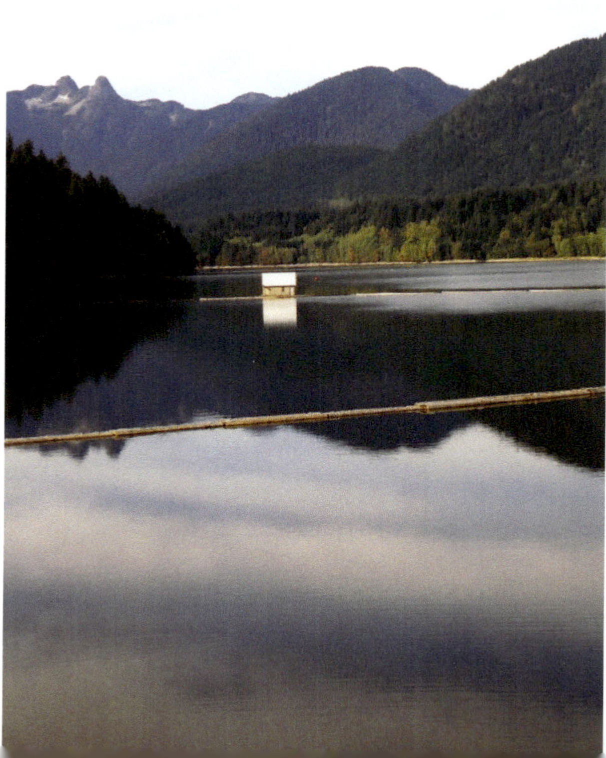

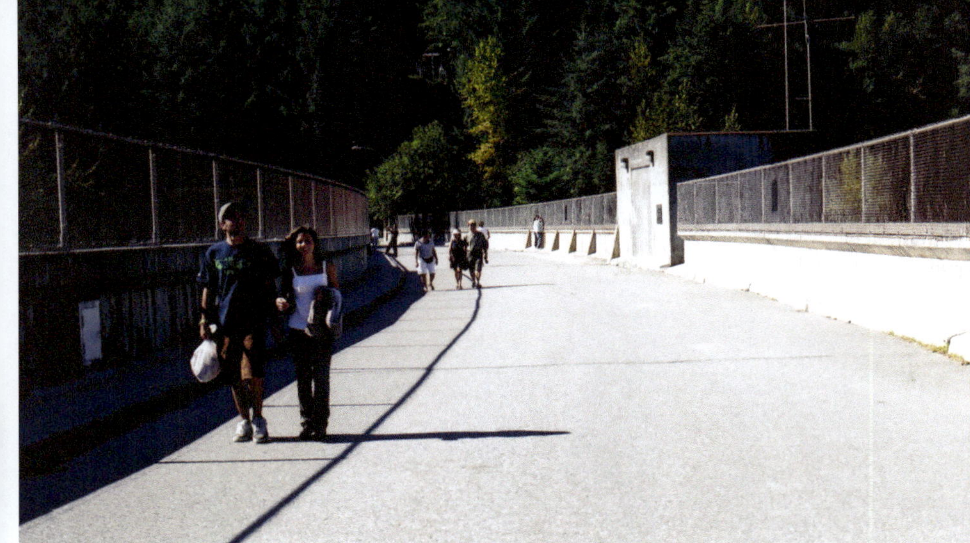

A – On Cleveland Dam, 2007.

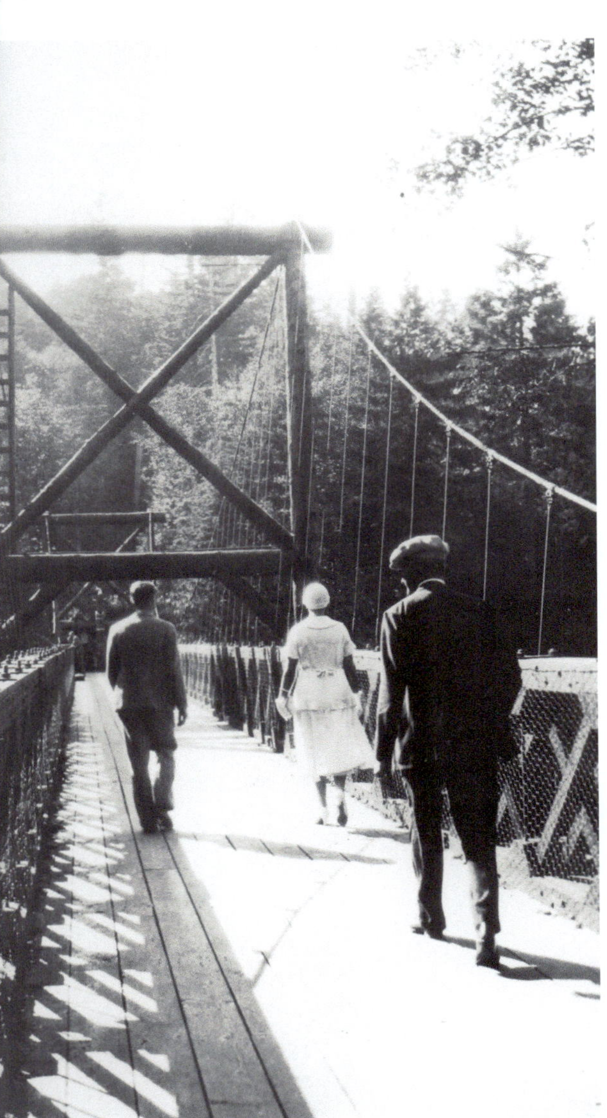

Grand Canyon Suspension Bridge

If you get a chance, drive to the Cleveland Dam and walk across the top (A). The view north — of the lake and mountains — is spectacular. In the 1930s and 1940s this same walk would have taken you over the Grand Canyon Suspension Bridge, shown in this 1931 photo (B), and you'd have looked north at the Capilano River Valley (C). The bridge was built in 1928 by the owners of the nearby Grand Canyon Hotel. Anchored 3.7 metres (12 feet) into the canyon wall, it was 130 metres (425 feet) high and 76 metres (250 feet) long. It was removed in 1951 when the dam was built.

B – On suspension bridge, 1931.

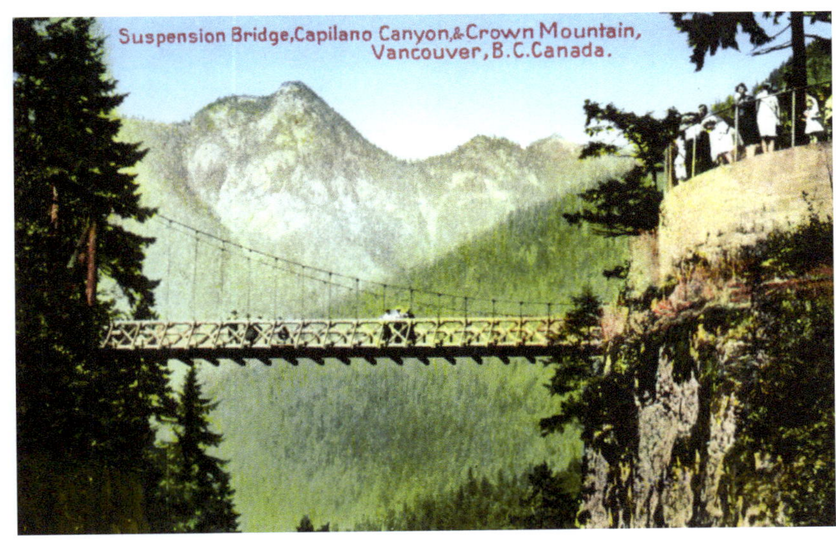

C – Bridge and Capilano Valley, date unknown.

Hotel at the Valley Entrance

The Canyon View Hotel (A) once overlooked the entrance to the Capilano Valley. Opened in 1909, it catered to visitors seeking both scenery and *luxury*. It had 30 bedrooms, three suites, a dining room, sitting room, mirrored bar, even a ladies' parlour. When owner Pete Larson retired in 1928, he sold it to investors. They renovated it, re-named it Grand Canyon Hotel, and built the Grand Canyon Suspension Bridge in front. Then came the Great Depression in 1929. The hotel struggled for years, then closed in 1939. It became Taunton House School, seen here in 1942 (B). Later it was Taunton House Apartments and finally a bunkhouse for the Cleveland Dam construction workers. It was torn down in 1952. Today, the site is a grassy knoll by the dam (C).

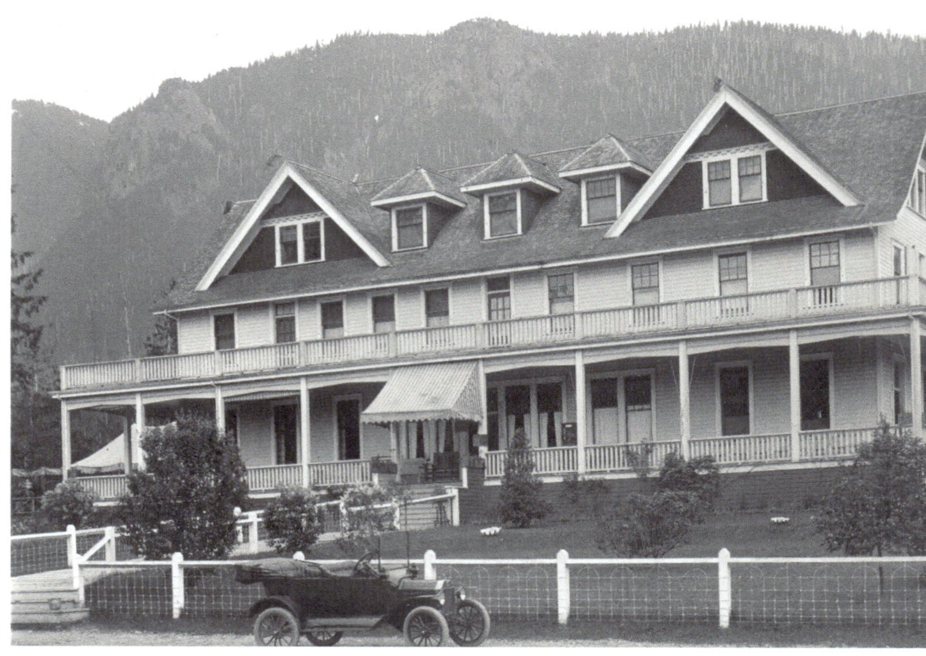

A – Canyon View Hotel, date unknown.

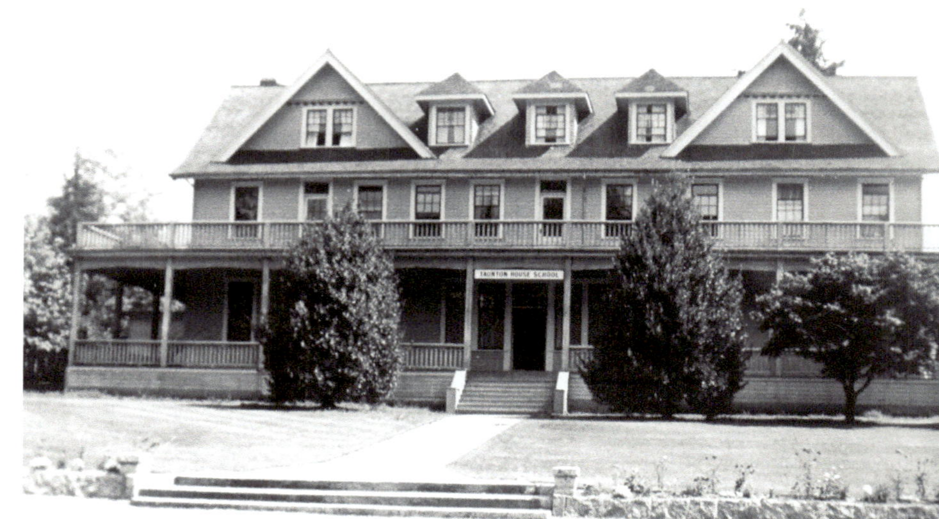

B – Taunton House School, 1942.

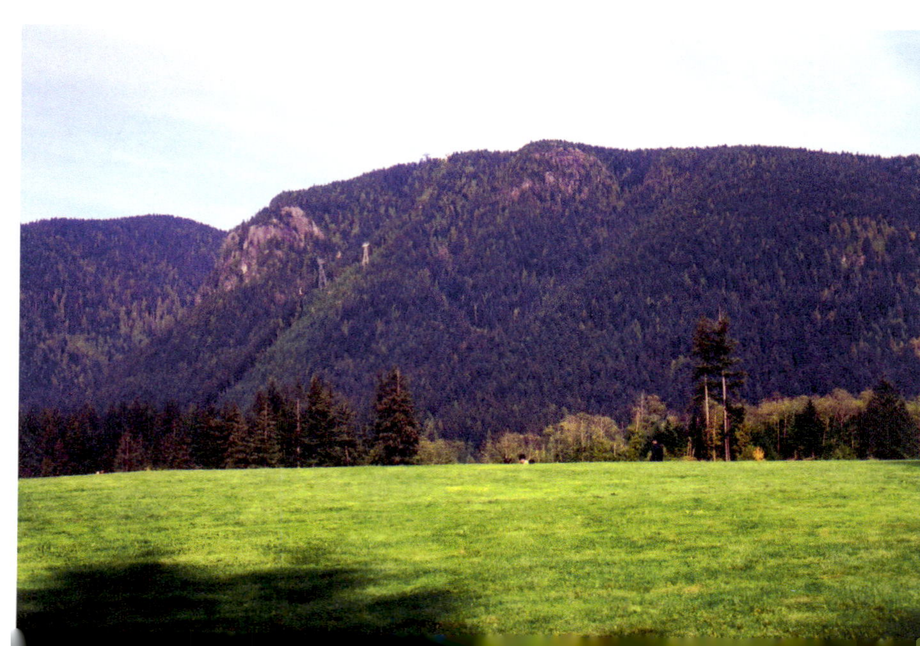

C – Grassy knoll, 2007.

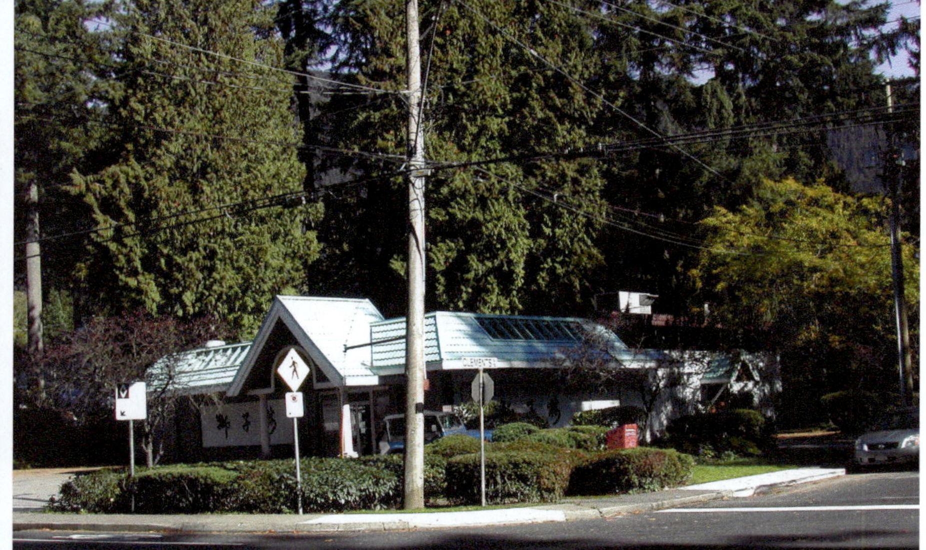

A – Chinese restaurant, 2016.

Tipperary Tea Gardens

The Capilano Heights Chinese Restaurant (A) is located at 5020 Capilano Road. It stands on the site once occupied by Charlie Anderson's "Tipperary Tea Gardens," a popular North Vancouver attraction in the 1920s, 30s and early 40s (B). The Tea Gardens consisted of a tearoom, a tower, and a small zoo. The tower offered visitors a fabulous view of the Capilano Valley, shown in this photo taken from the tower around 1929 (C). The zoo displayed several kinds of animals, but its most popular resident was a black bear named "Grunty" (D). Mr. Anderson had found it as an orphaned cub and raised it in a cage beneath the tower.

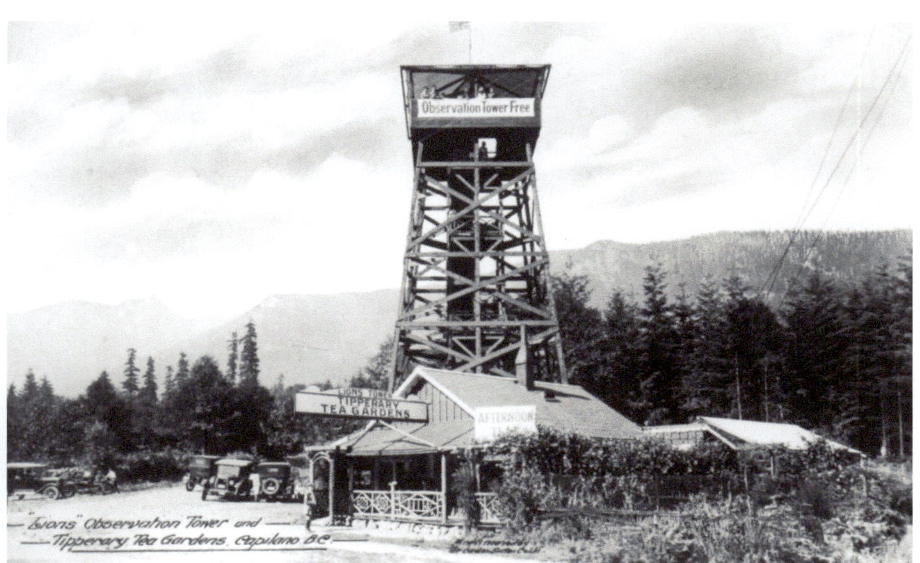

B – Tipperary Tea Gardens, date unknown.

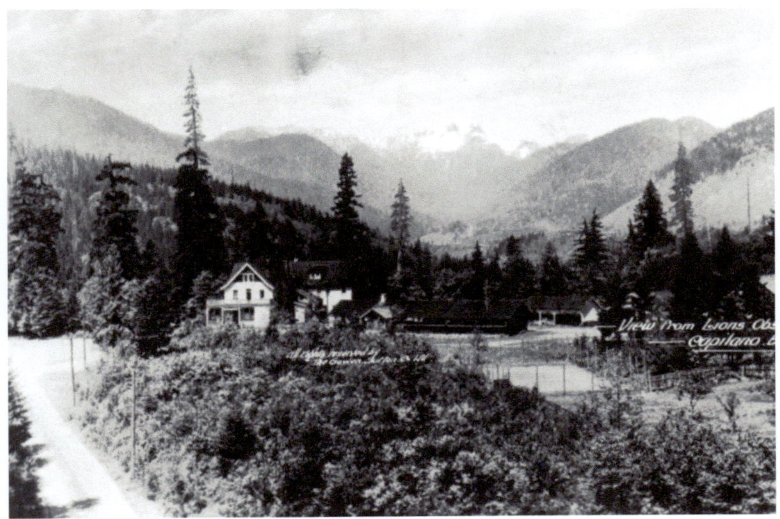

C – View from tower, c.1929.

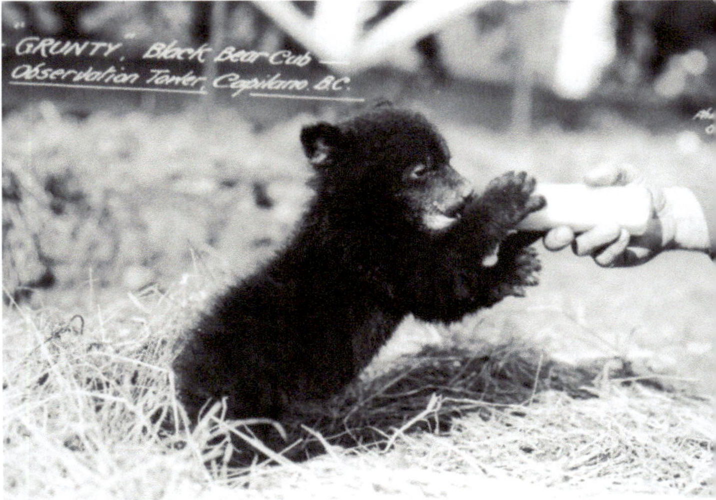

D – "Grunty," date unknown.

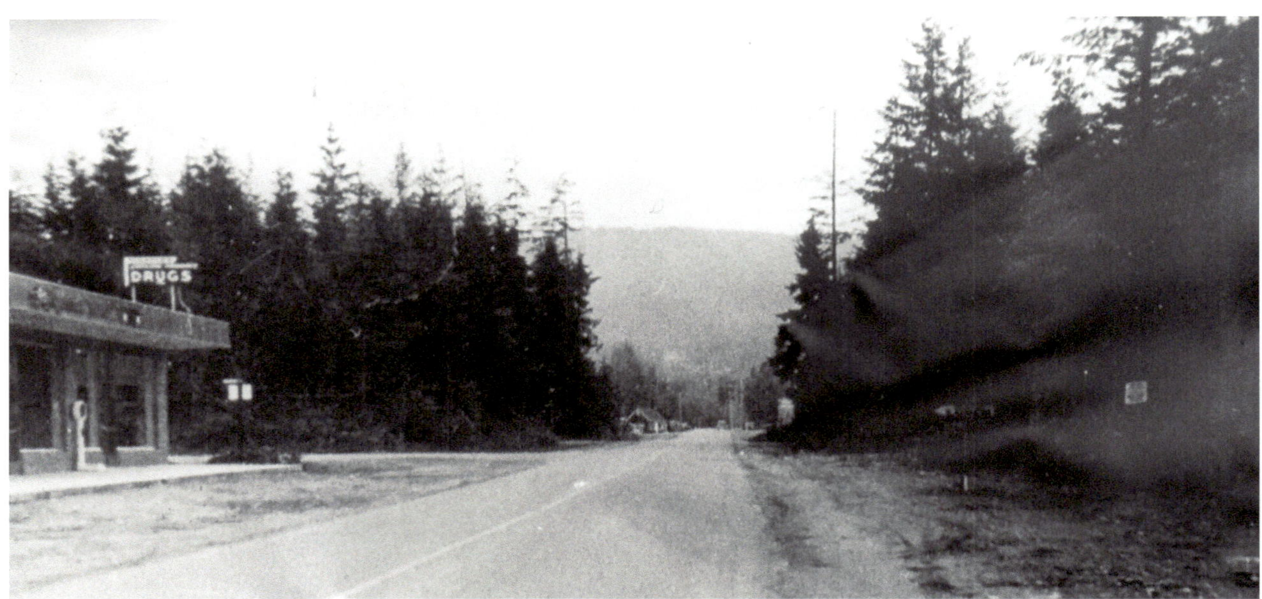

A – Edgemont Boulevard, 1948.

Edgemont Village

Edgemont Village is a charming alpine village located below Grouse Mountain in the heart of Capilano Highlands. This North Vancouver shopping destination has come a long way since its modest beginning in the late 1940s. It sits on several acres set aside by the original developer of Capilano Highlands for the business core of the new sub-division. In the 1948 photo (A) you can see what the heart of Edgemont Village originally looked like. The view looks north along the 3100 block of Edgemont Boulevard. The modern photo (B) was shot from further back. It shows the whole 3100 block today, an attractive "main street" lined with colourful and interesting shops, restaurants, cafes, and other establishments.

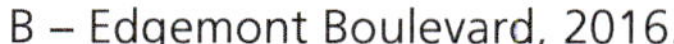

B – Edgemont Boulevard, 2016.

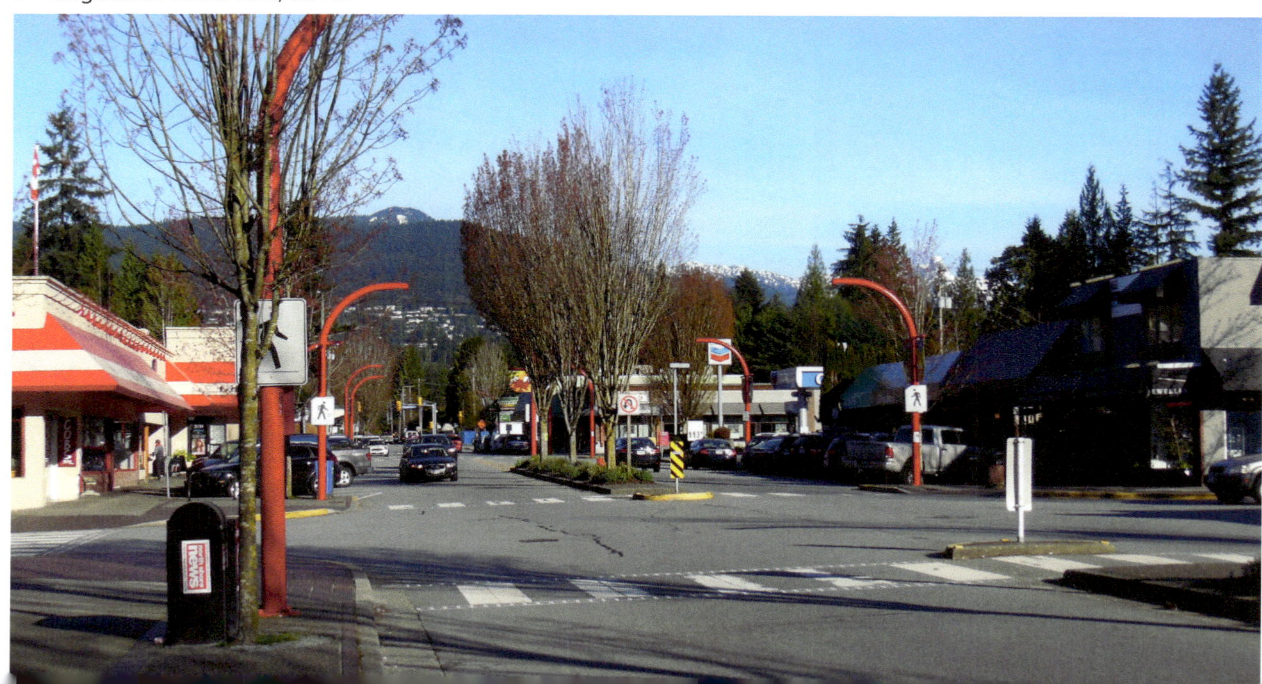

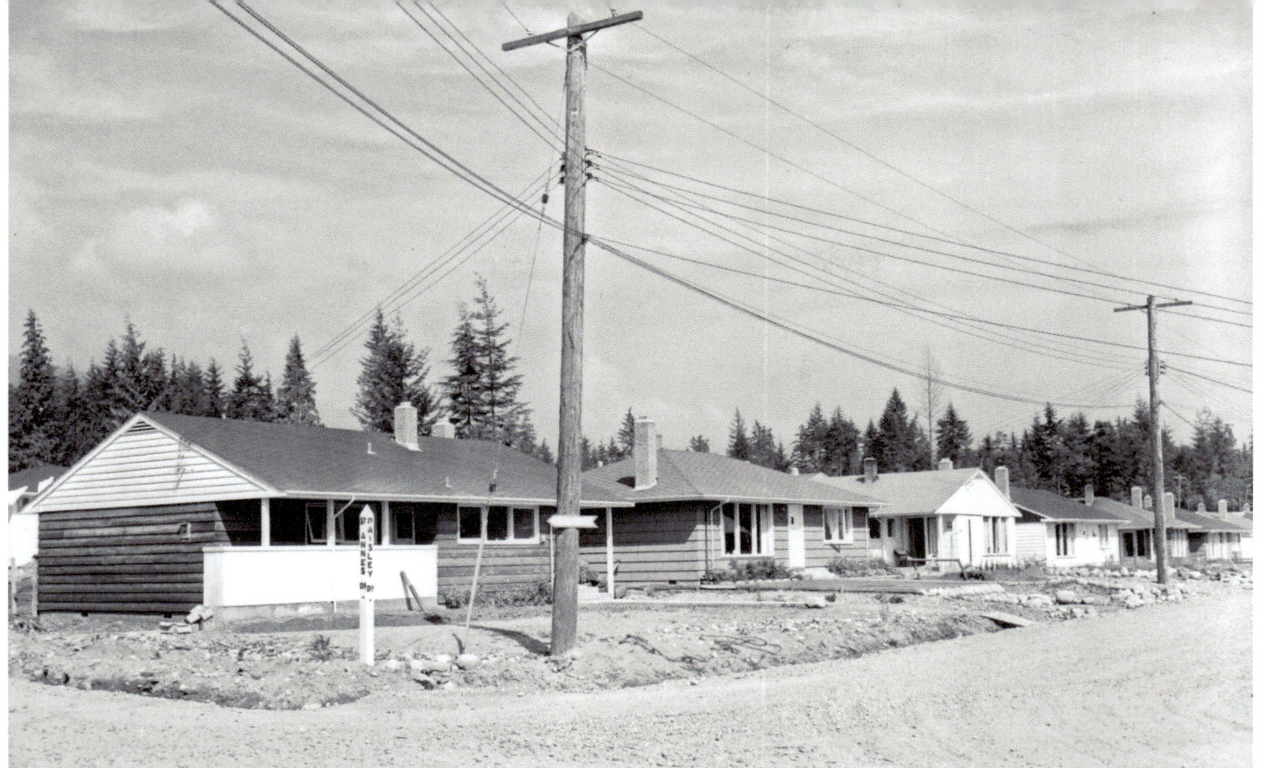

A – Ranchers on Paisley Road, 1949.

Capilano Ranchers

Just northeast of where Capilano Road and Upper Levels Highway intersect, lies a tiny enclave called "Capilano." Often thought of as part of the adjacent Capilano Highlands, it's actually a separate subdivision dating back to just after World War II. You can see what it originally looked like in the 1949 photo (A), which looks east on Paisley Road from St. Annes Drive. The houses were one-storey, rectangular "ranchers," built to appeal to returning servicemen who wanted to settle down and raise families. Today the view from the corner of Paisley and St. Annes is of lush foliage and mature homes (B). While several original houses remain, they are very much modified, and one or two have been torn down and replaced by larger, more modern structures.

B – Same view, 2016.

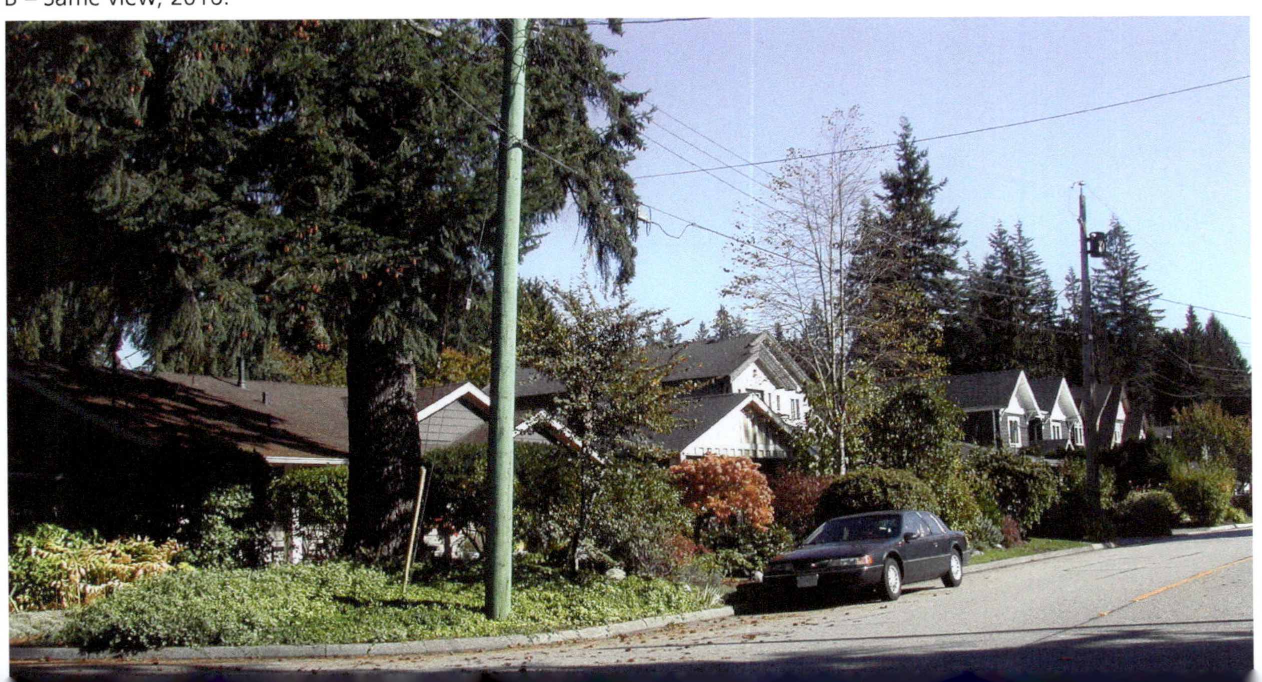

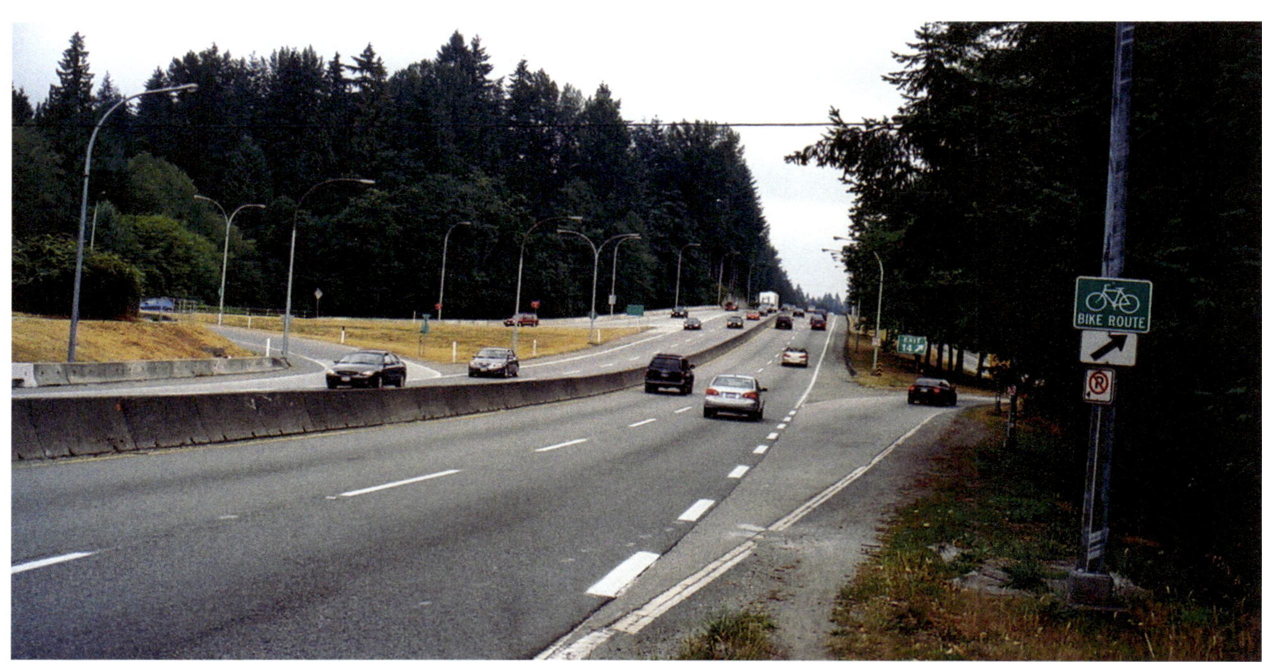

A - Highway above site of streetcar terminus, 2009.

End of the Capilano Streetcar Line

Imagine heading east on Upper Levels Highway, crossing over Capilano Road, and stopping after a few yards (A). You're directly above what once was the Capilano streetcar terminus on School Street (B). For many years this was the business and social centre for "Capilano, BC," a neighbourhood that ran along the river to the inlet. There was Norman McLeod's general store & post office, Wood's Red & White Store (C), a community hall, and a small fire station. People came for mail, groceries, supplies, bingo, dances, concerts, and to "hang-out." Meanwhile, the streetcar (1910 to 1943) brought tourists heading for the suspension bridge and Capilano Valley. They'd disembark, buy provisions, then walk or catch a taxi. The little neighbourhood centre was demolished in the late1950s to make way for the highway.

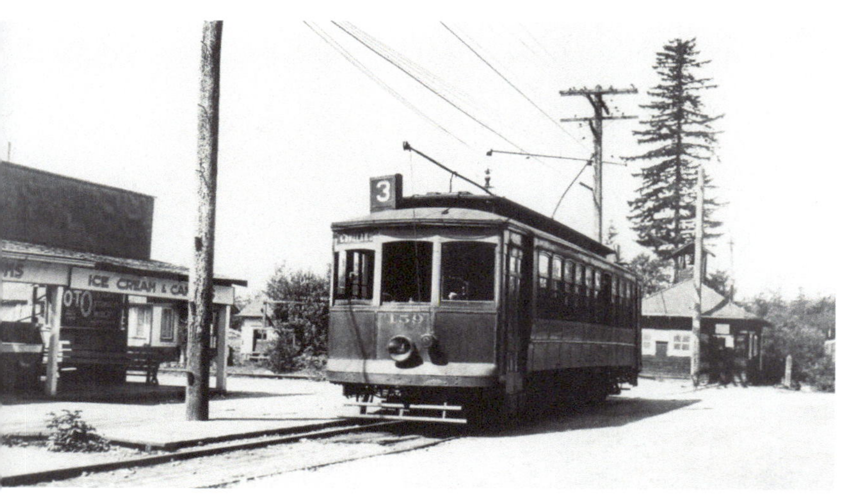

B - Streetcar by McLeod's (left) and fire station (right), 1925.

C - Red & White Store, 1950s.

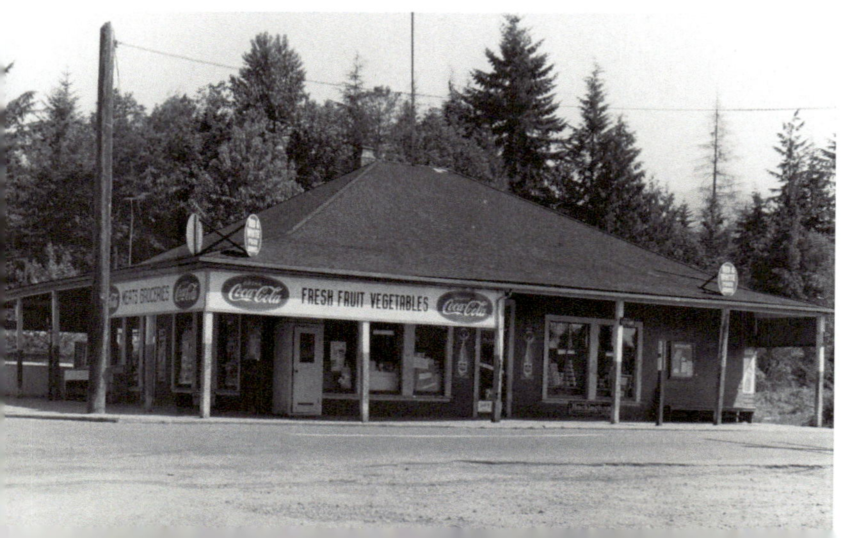

4 East to Deep Cove

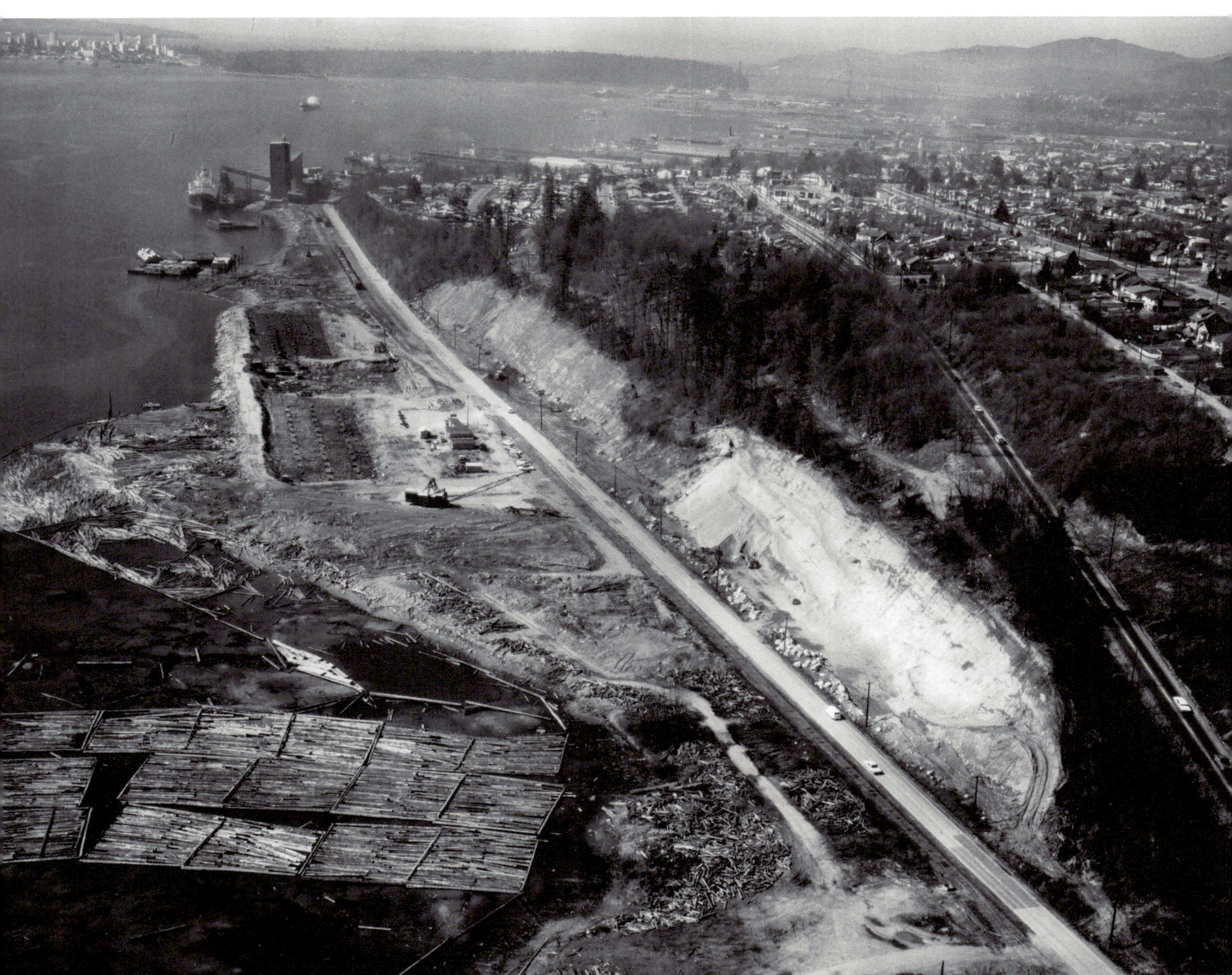

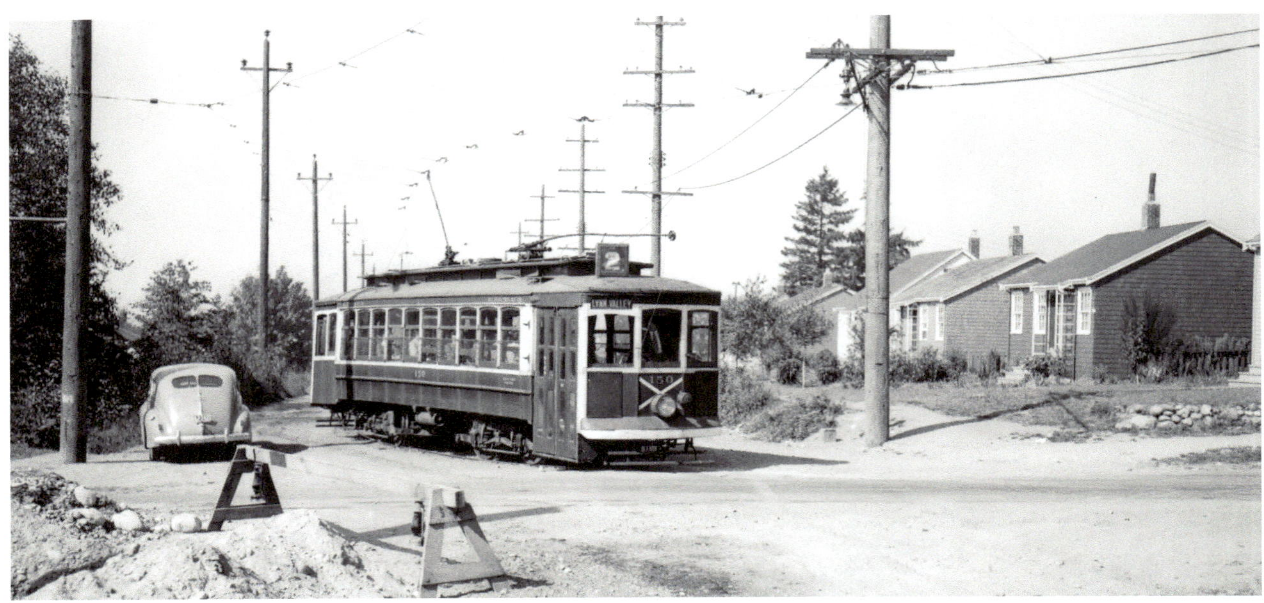

A – Streetcar turning onto Queensbury, 1946.

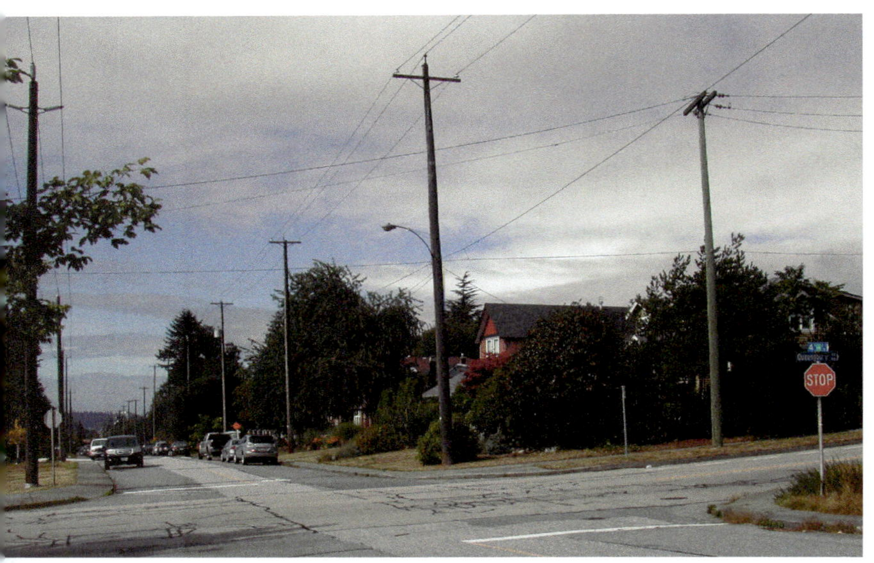

B – The same corner, 2016.

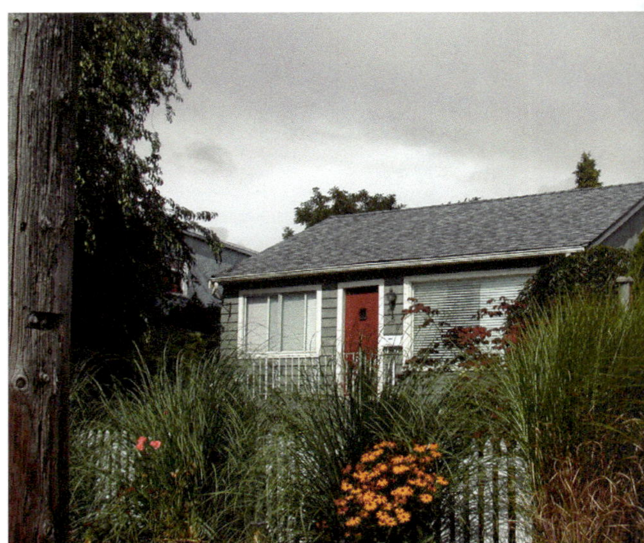

C – Wartime house, 2016.

Corner of 4th & Queensbury

In the 1940s the Lynn Valley streetcar ran east on 4th Street as far as Queensbury, where it then turned north and headed toward Grand Boulevard. The 1946 photo (A) shows it making the turn onto Queensbury. Notice the small bungalows on the right. They're wartime houses, built in 1941–42 for shipyard workers employed by Burrard Dry Dock and North Van Ship Repairs at the foot of Lonsdale. Today, the trolley tracks are long gone, as you can see in the 2016 photo (B). But a few of the wartime houses remain, including the second one from the right in the early photo. Here it is in 2016 (C) at 652 East 4th. Though altered, it's still recognizable.

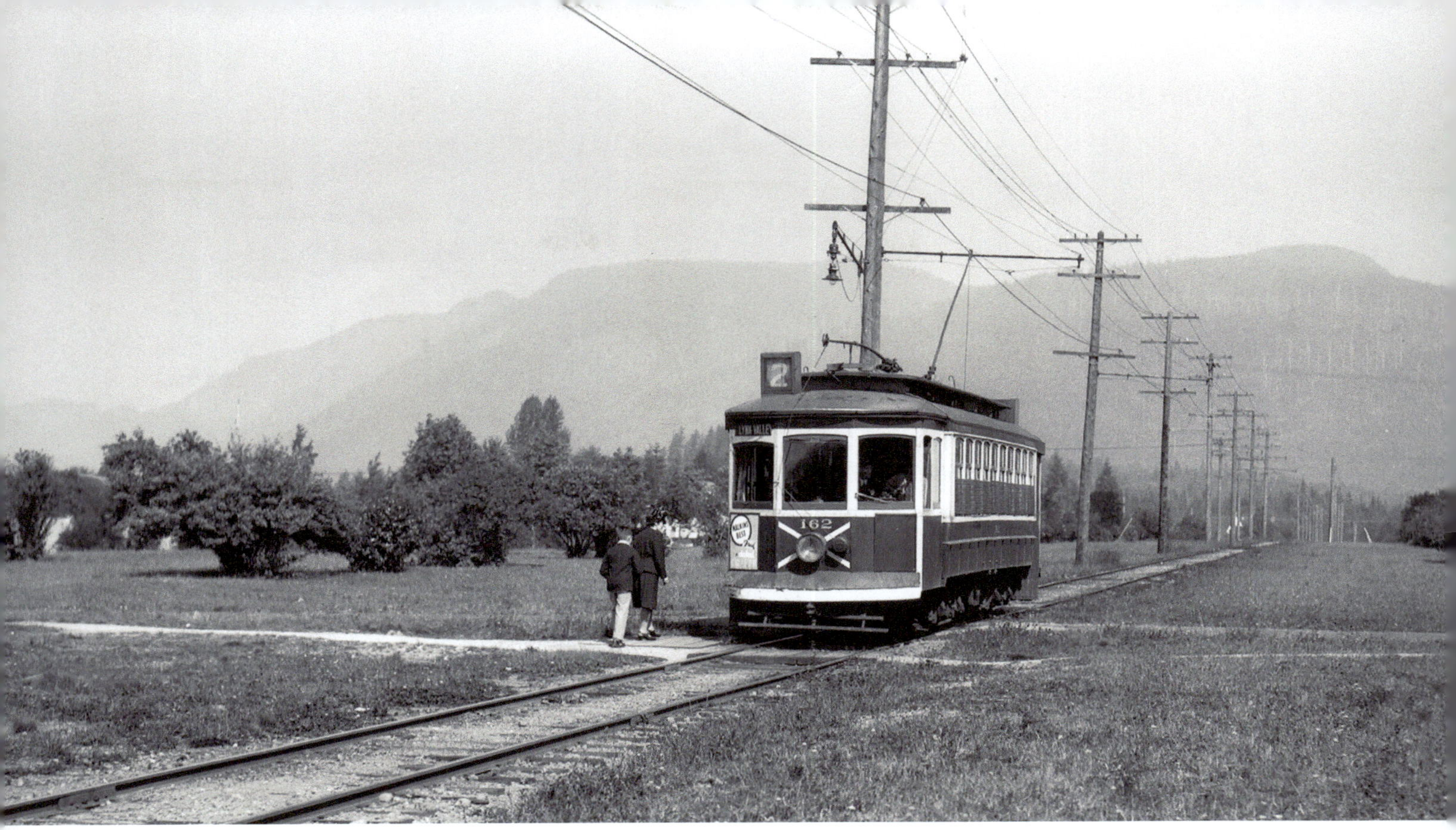

A – Streetcar stop, 1946.

B – Same view, 2007.

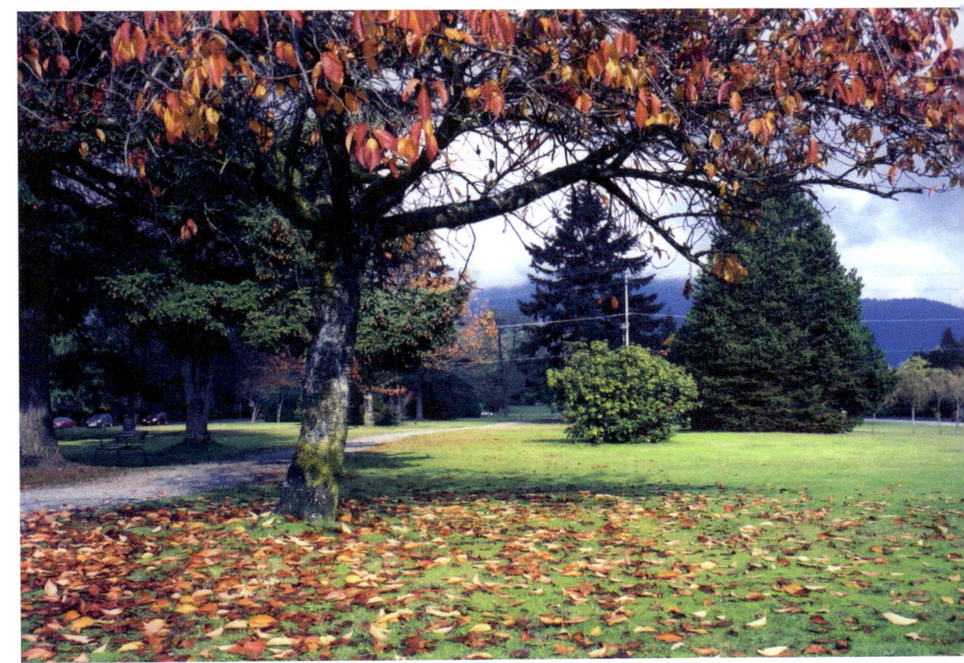

Streetcars on Grand Boulevard

Grand Boulevard dates back to 1906 when a real estate developer created a 12-block-long park to be surrounded by luxury homes. Almost from the beginning there were streetcar tracks running up the centre. The Lynn Valley streetcar, in fact, passed along here on its way to and from the ferry wharf at the foot of Lonsdale. It stopped near 15th and Grand Boulevard to take on and let off passengers, as you can see in this 1946 view (A). When North Vancouver's streetcar service ended a year later, the tracks were removed. The next photo (B) shows the former streetcar stop in recent years. A footpath replaced the tracks.

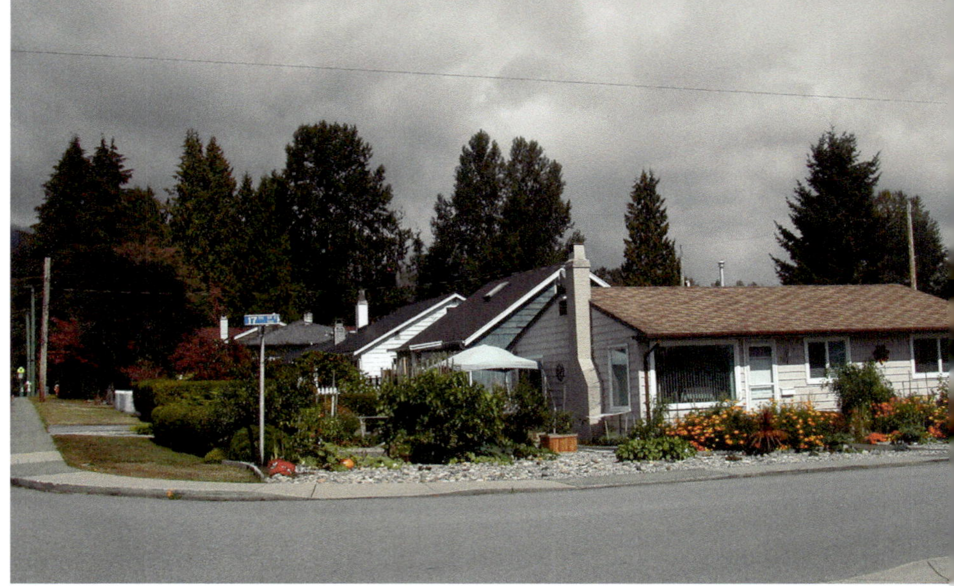
A – Modern homes, 2016.

B – Seymour Lumber Co. sawmill, 1906.

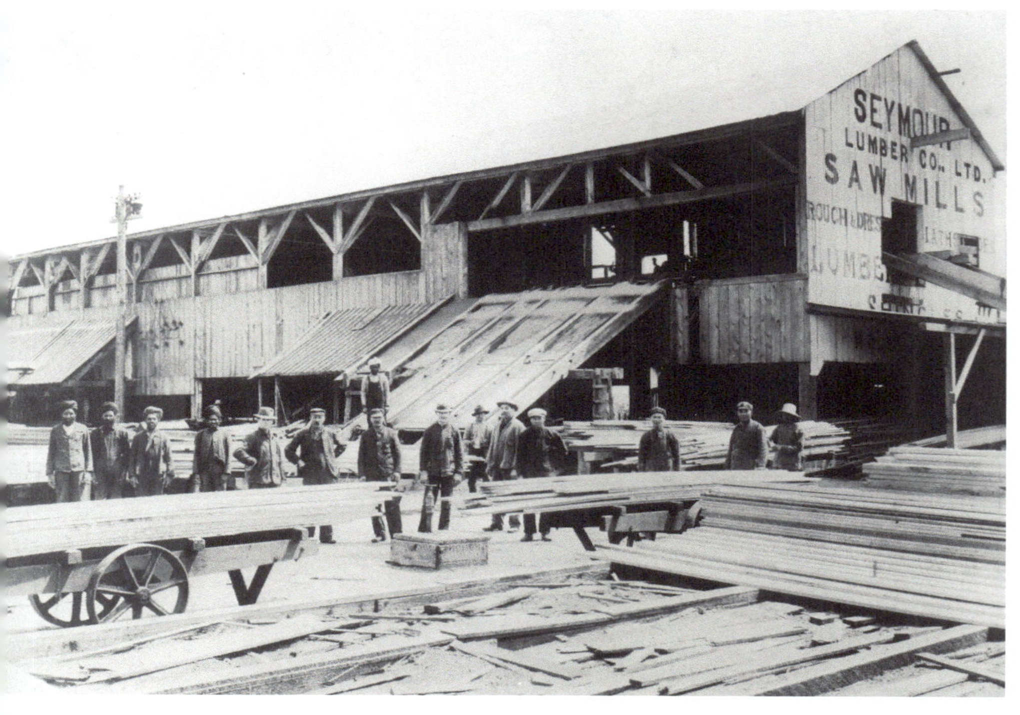

C – Log headed for sawmill, c.1906–10.

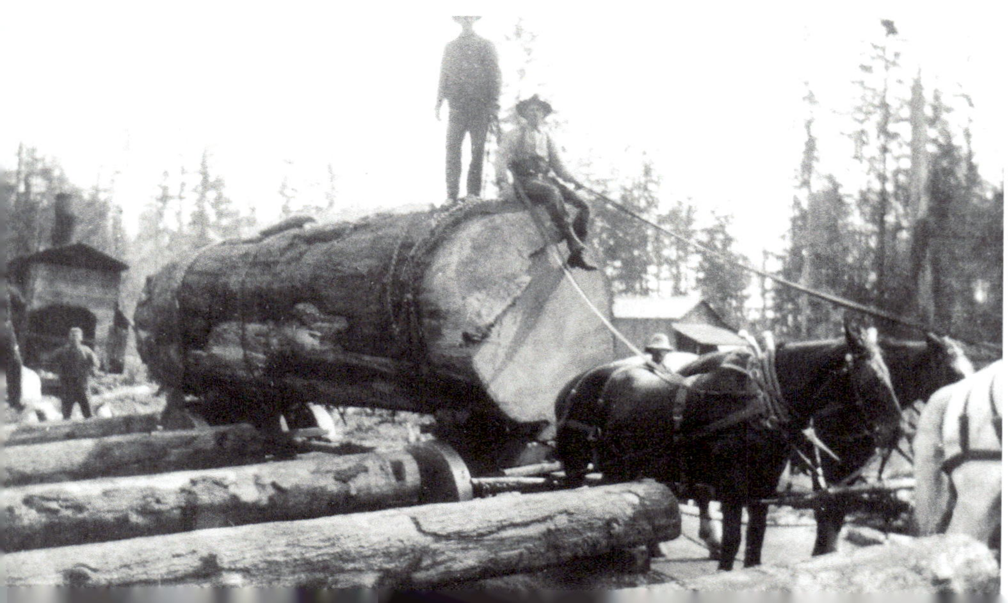

Sawmill at 17th & Sutherland

The homes in the modern photo (A) are located at 17th and Sutherland. Today they sit in a quiet, family-friendly neighbourhood. A century ago this was a totally different scene. The Seymour Lumber Company sawmill had an active lumber mill in the 1600 block (B). It was part of a large, messy, noisy operation spread over two blocks of Sutherland's east side, from 16th to 18th. From 1906 to 1910 large tree trunks were processed in the sawmill (B), having been cut from the nearby forest to the north and hauled here by horses (C). When the closest trees were gone, the Company moved the operation further north to improve its access to the remaining forest.

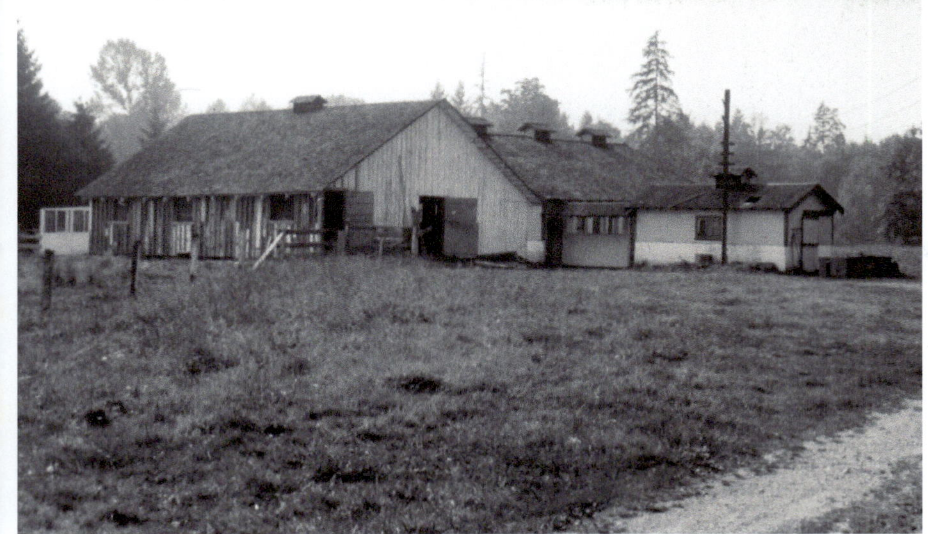

A – Cow barn and small shed (at right), 1940s.

Maplewood Farm

In the early 1900s there were farms all around North Vancouver. They supplied local residents with most of their food and dairy products. But after World War II the old farms were replaced by subdivisions, condominiums, and shopping malls. One, however, managed to survive. Maplewood Farm, the popular children's zoo at 405 Seymour River Place, was originally the Ellis Dairy farm, then the Smyth Dairy. In fact, Maplewood Farm still uses some of the old dairy buildings *in their original locations*. For instance, the old cow barn and shed in the 1940s photo (A) are still there (B). Likewise, the shed and family home in the 1950s photo (C) were still by the Farm's entrance in 2007 (D).

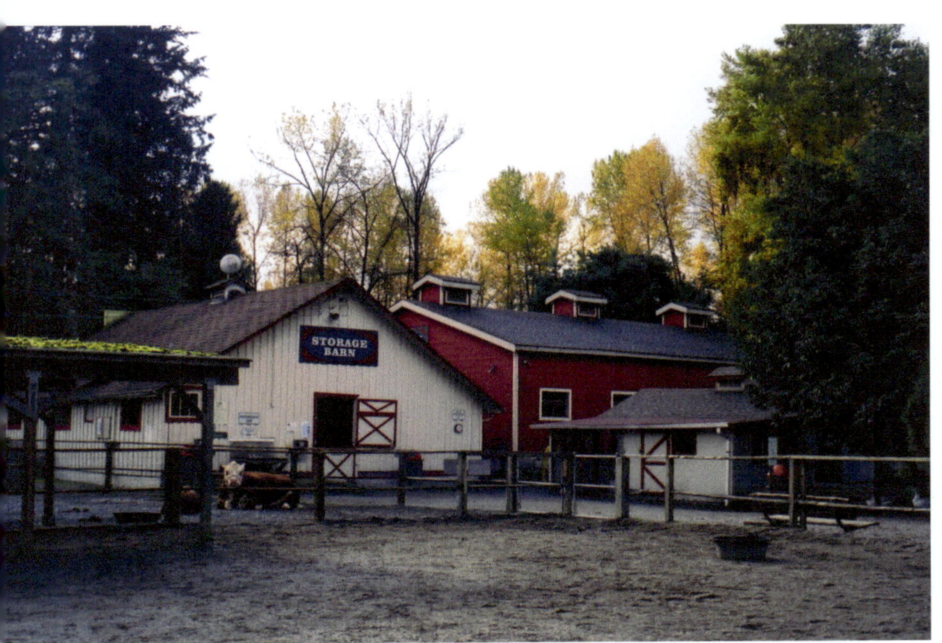

B – Cow barn and shed, 2007.

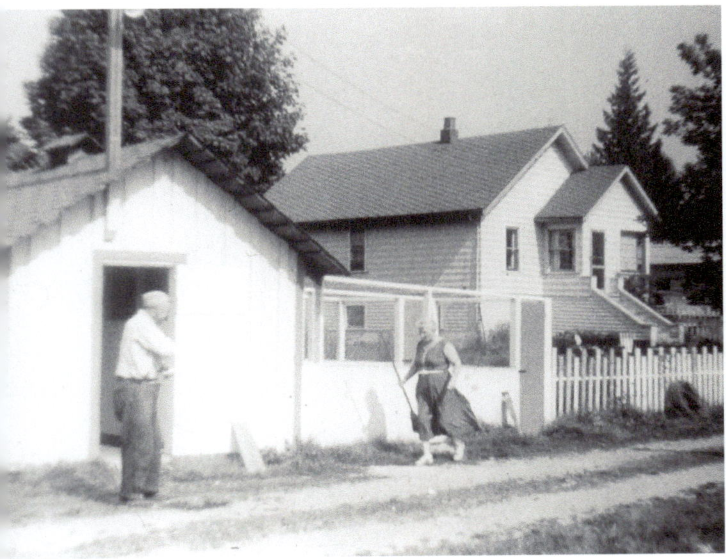

C – Shed and family home, 1950s.

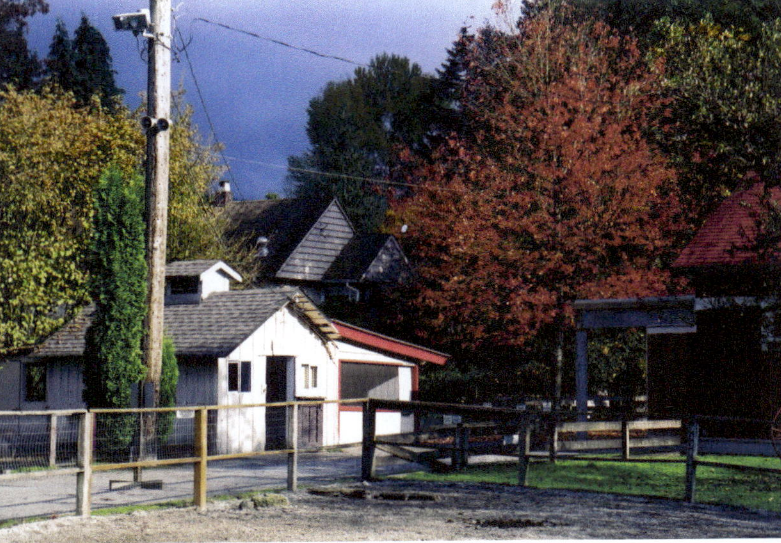

D – Shed and house, 2007.

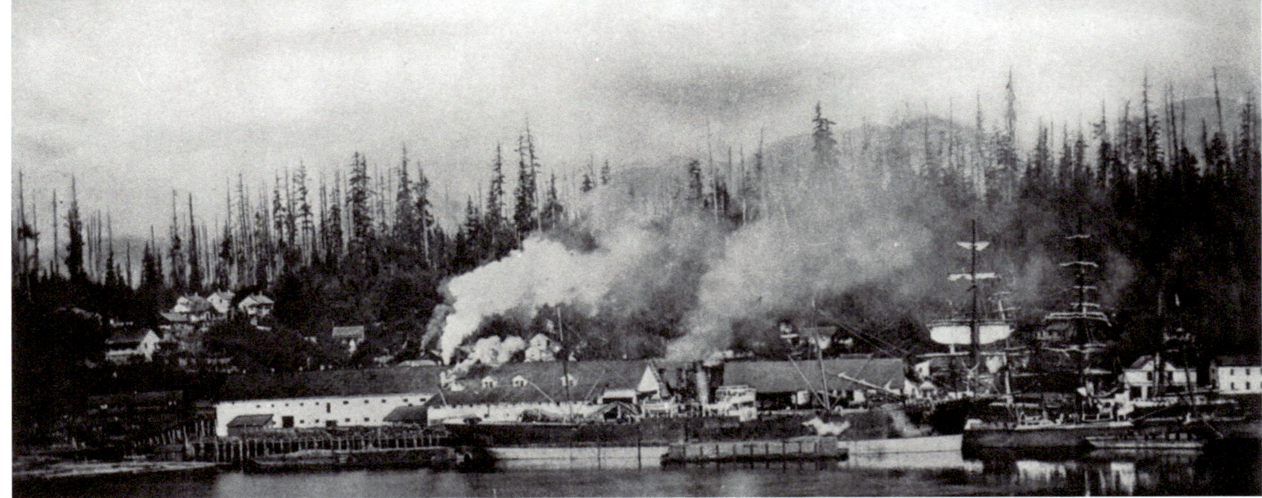

A – Moodyville at its peak, 1898.

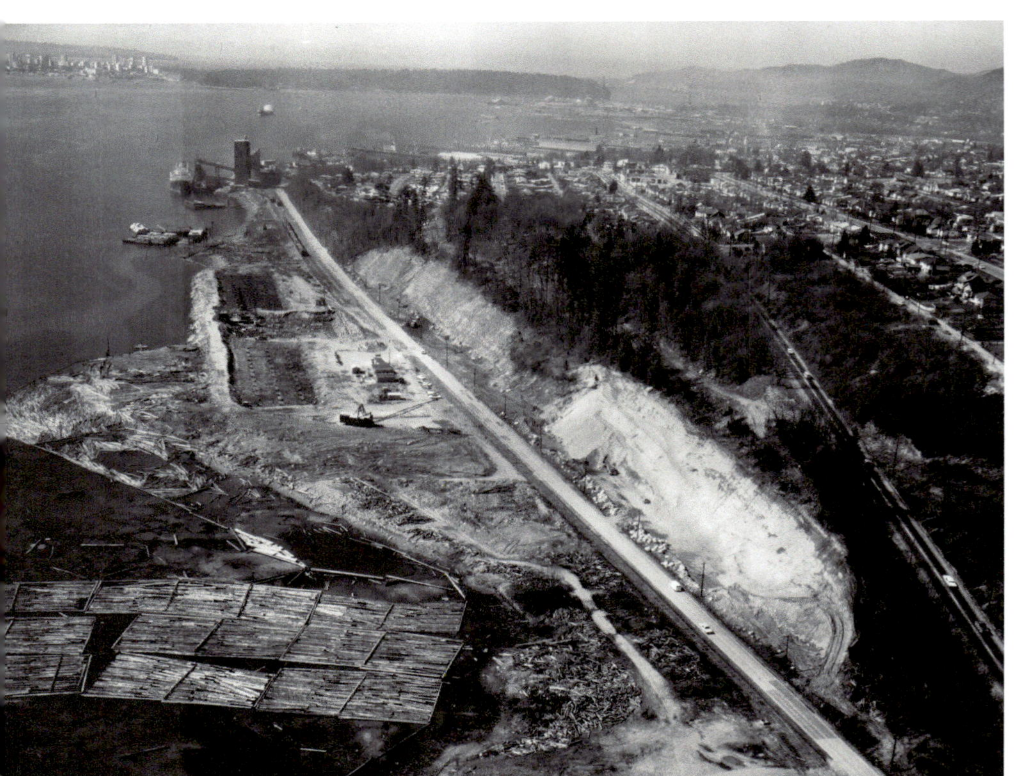

B – Carved-out hillside, 1966.

Moodyville

Moodyville, seen here in 1898 (A), was a thriving company-owned lumber town, set up in the 1860s on the flats below today's Moodyville Park. It boasted a large mill, worker housing, hotel, library, school, Masonic Lodge, its own ferry service, and other amenities. The more affluent residents lived on the hill above. Independent of North Vancouver and operating under provincial law, Moodyville resisted attempts to join it to the municipality. The town peaked in 1898, and then declined. Eventually its lands were annexed to the City of North Vancouver. In 1929, part of the hillside was removed to make way for the Low Level Road (B). Railway tracks and grain elevators now cover the flats (C).

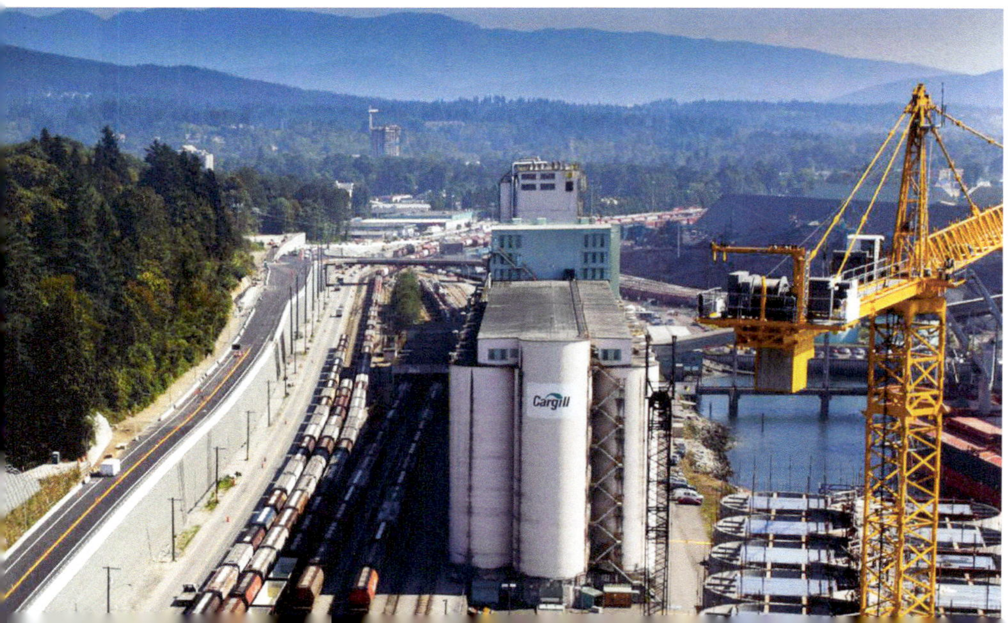

C – Moodyville site, 2016.

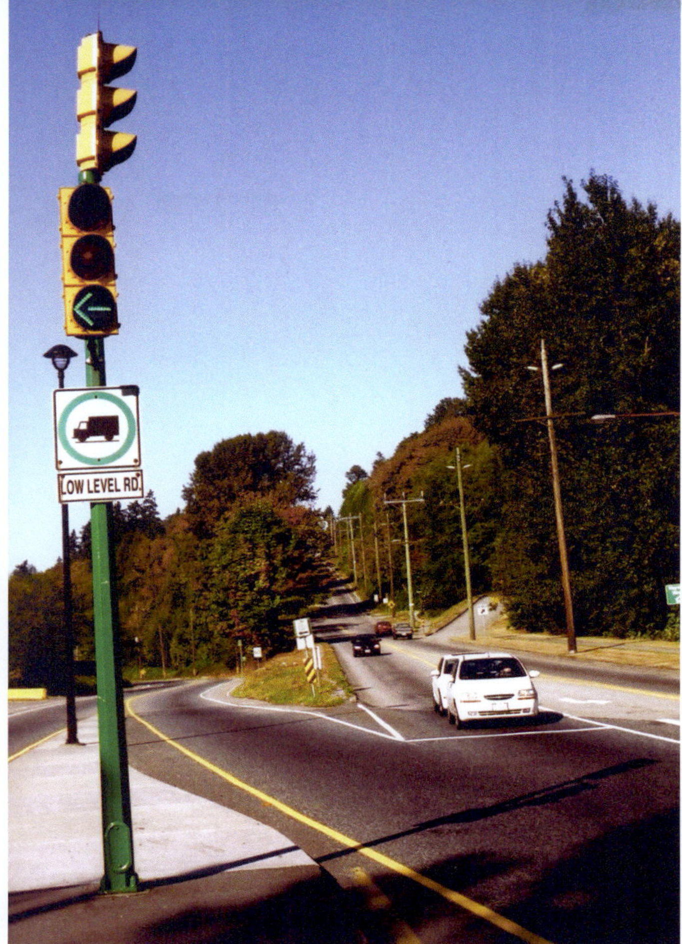

A – Low Level Road & East 3rd, 2007.

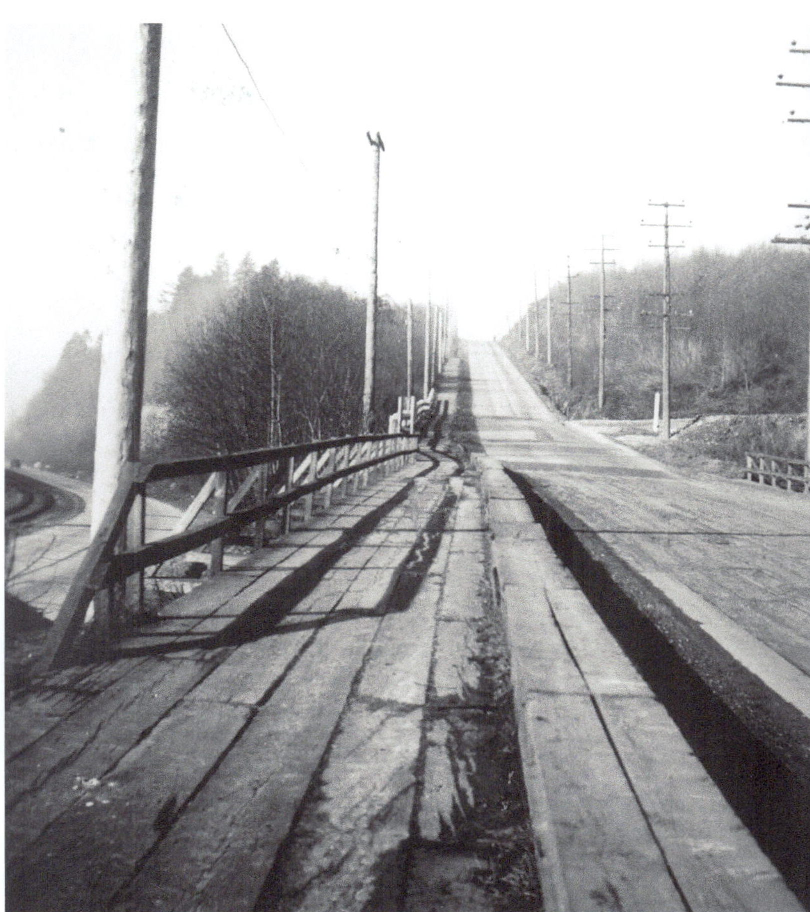
B – Same view, 1938.

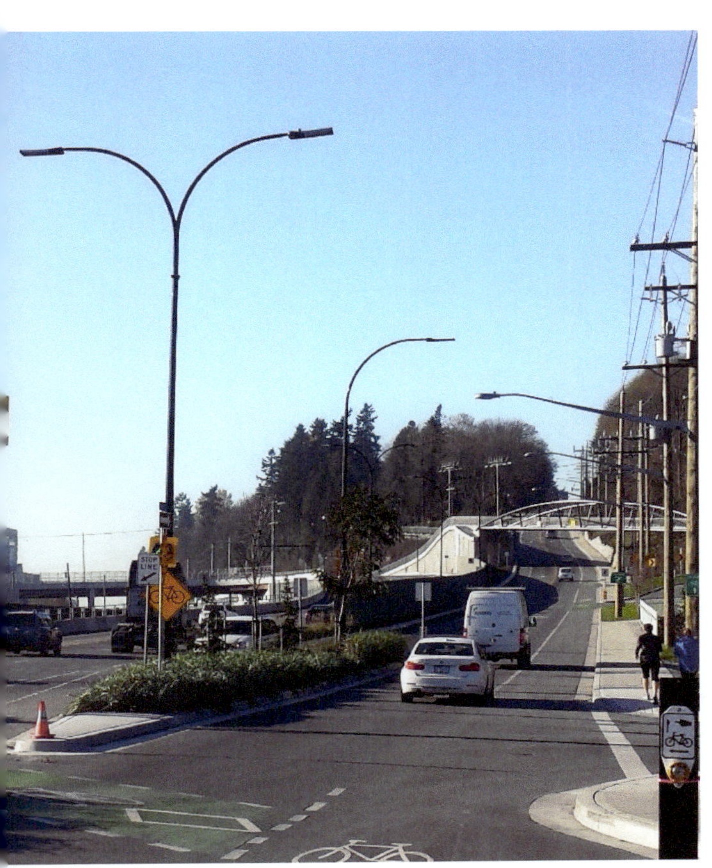
C – Low Level Road & East 3rd, 2016.

Where East 3rd and the Low Level Road Merge

East of the grain elevators the Low Level Road merges with East 3rd Street. The 2007 photo looks back from this junction, toward Moodyville and the 3rd Street Hill (A). (The lower road is on the left.) In 1938 the scene was totally different (B). The Low Level Road didn't merge with 3rd, but continued east on its own. Moreover, there was a creek here — and a wooden bridge for East 3rd and its wooden sidewalk. When the bridge was condemned in the mid 1940s, it was not replaced. A large reinforced-concrete pipe was installed in the streambed, and the bed filled-in with boulders and dirt. Now on solid ground, East 3rd was free to merge with the road below. Today we find the intersection greatly modernized (C).

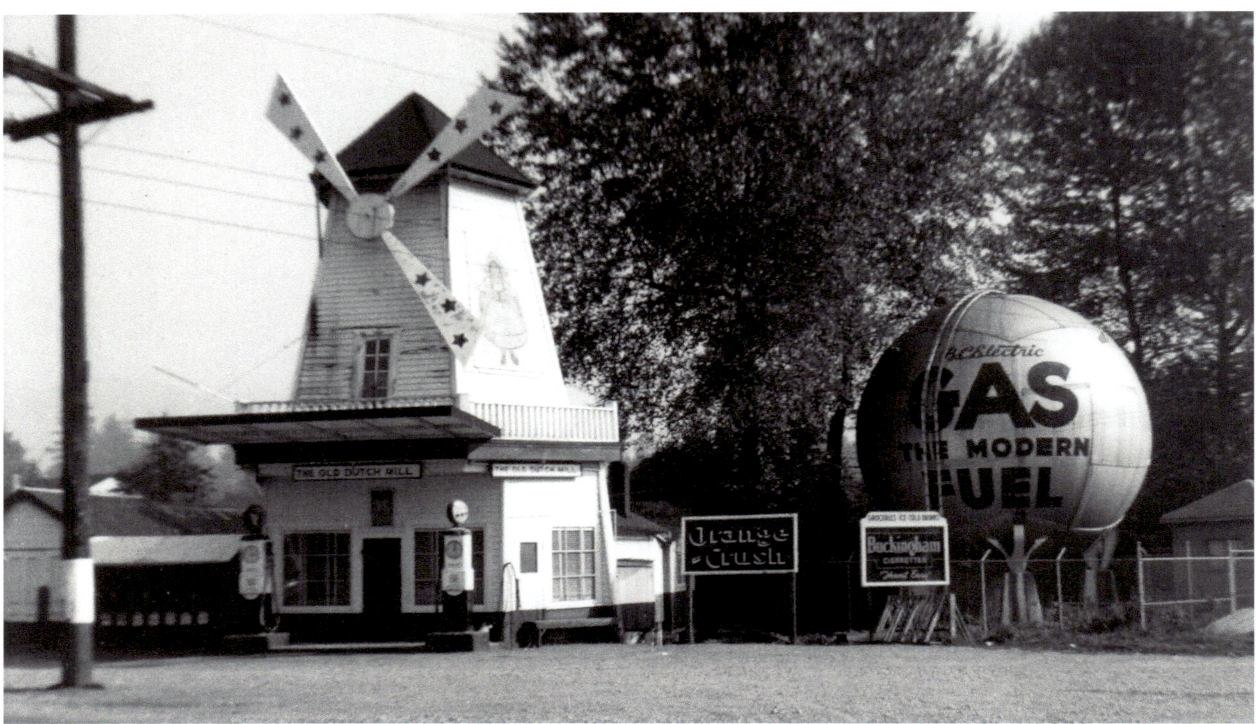

A – Old Dutch Mill service station, 1940s.

Old Dutch Mill Service Station

Ever hear of "fantastic architecture"? (Yes, that's what it's called.) It was an early twentieth century design fad in North America. It arose when the automobile became popular. As a result, numerous roadside restaurants, motels, service stations, and other businesses were built to look like pyramids, tepees, windmills, castles, or other fantasies to make them "stand out in a crowd." A North Vancouver example was the Old Dutch Mill service station, shown in this 1940s photo (A). Built in the late 1920s on the northeast corner of Main Street and Mountain Highway, it was designed to catch the eye of drivers entering North Vancouver from the Second Narrows Bridge. Today an A&W restaurant occupies the corner (B).

B – A&W on corner, 2016.

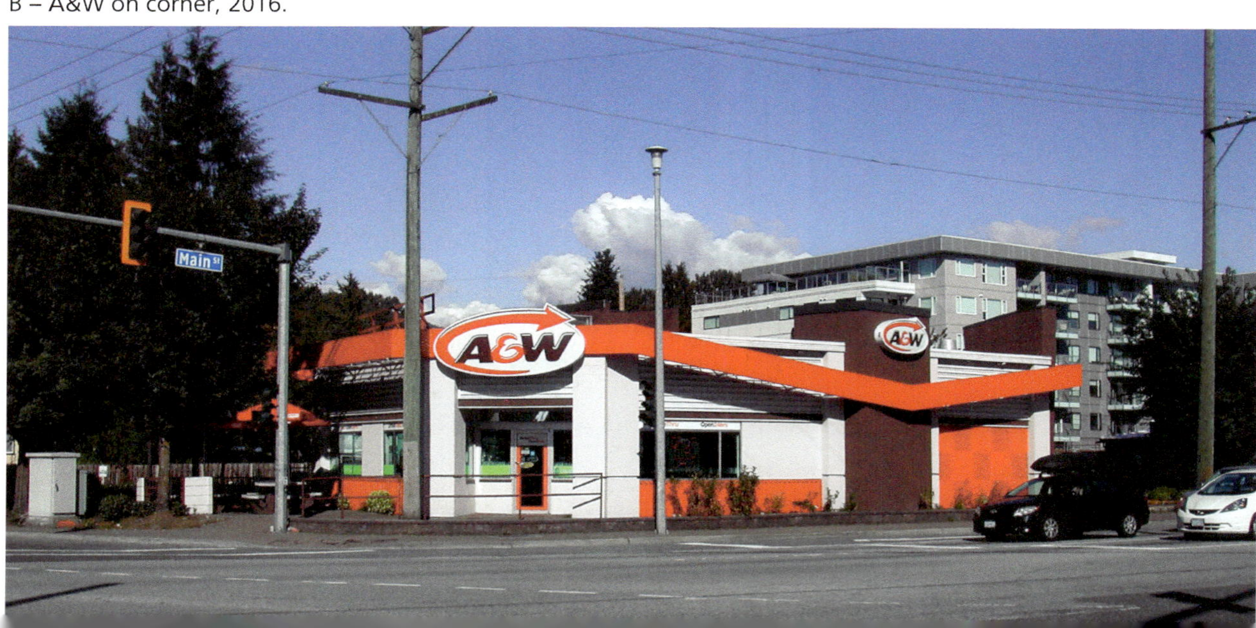

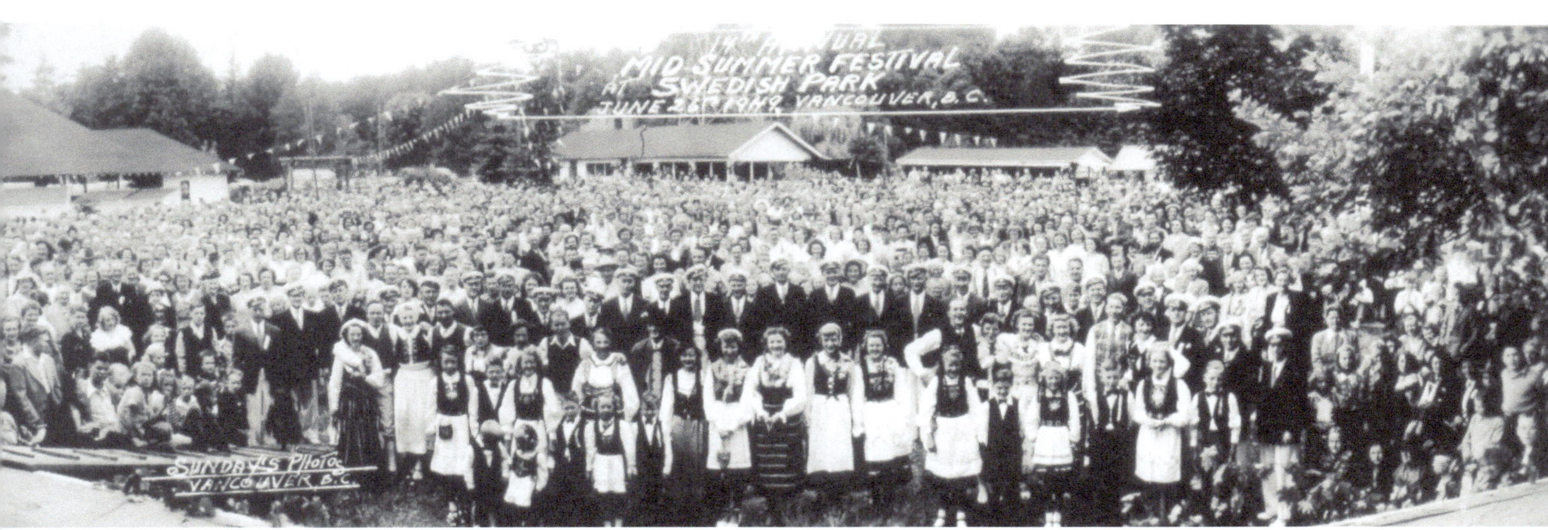

A – Midsummer Festival (pavilion at left), 1949.

Swedish Park

The two "crowd scenes" on this page were captured at Swedish Park, which once sat on the south side of Main Street beside the Seymour River. In the 1940s North Vancouverites came here in droves for summer picnics, cultural celebrations, special camps, music performances, and dances. It was essentially a grass-covered space surrounded by five small buildings. One of these was a dance pavilion with walls that folded down for air circulation, seen here on the left during the 1949 Scandinavian "Midsummer Festival" (A). Another structure was the Lind Bowl, shown in the 1946 photo (B). This was a stage where groups performed for outdoor audiences. Today, Swedish Park is just a memory. Large "Public Storage" buildings (1775 Main Street) were built on the site (C) and are still there in 2016.

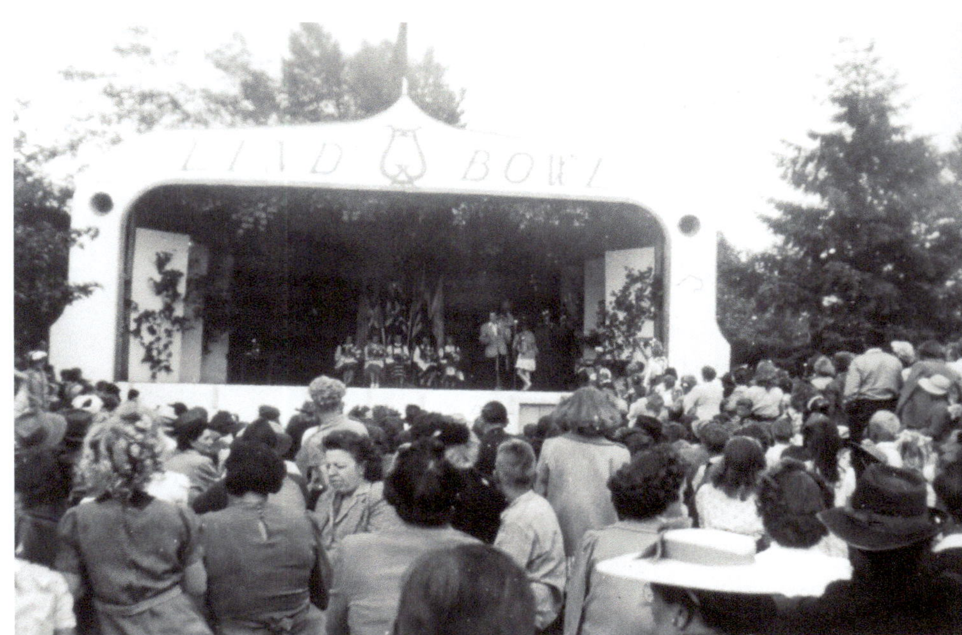
B – Lind Bowl, 1946.

C – Public Storage, 2008.

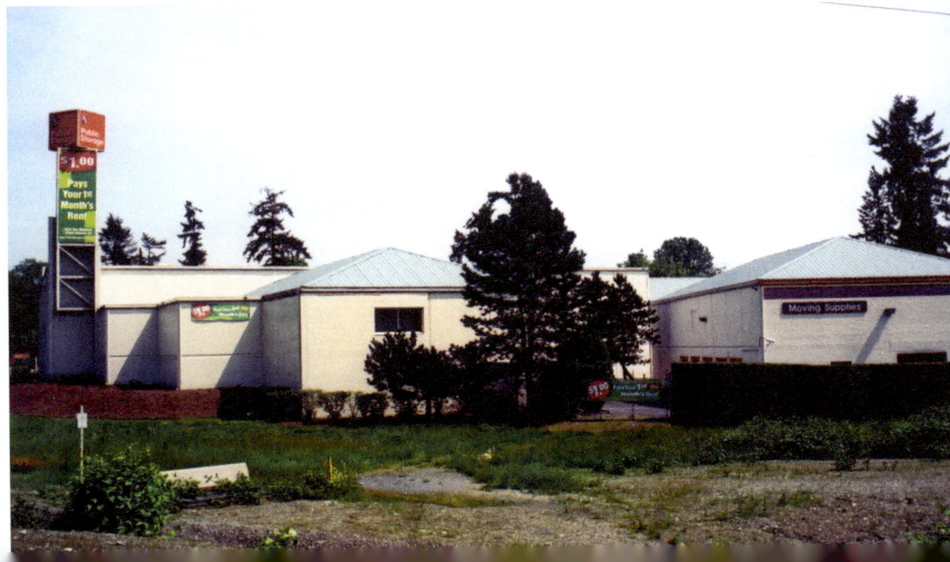

Capilano University

The North Shore was one of Metro Vancouver's fastest growing areas in the 1960s. Local students, however, had little access to post-secondary institutions, the closest being many miles away. So, through a 1968 referendum, the school boards and residents of North Vancouver, West Vancouver, and Howe Sound founded Capilano Community College. At first, classes were held in high schools, churches, and other locations. Then, in 1973, a small permanent campus opened at 2055 Purcell Way (A), nestled in a 34-acre forest. Thirty-five years later, the much-expanded "college" became Capilano University, seen here in 2008 (B). Now there are also regional campuses in Squamish and Sechelt. What happened to the 1973 structure? It was years ago incorporated into a new library building, which looked like this in 2008 (C).

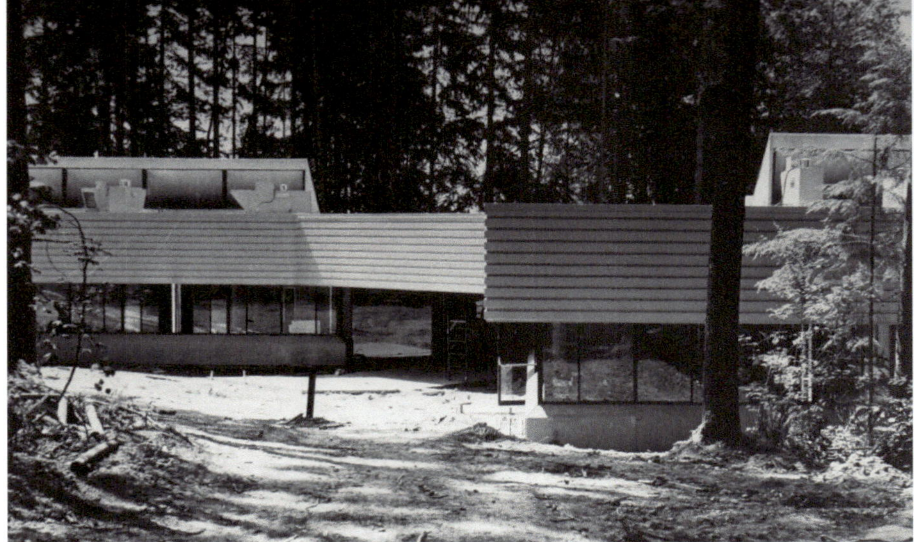

A – New campus, 1973.

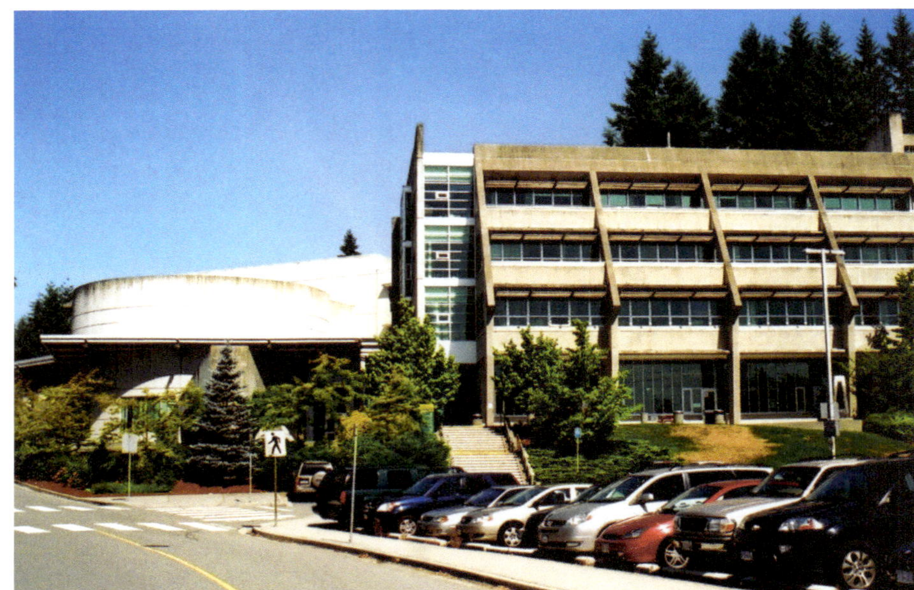

B – Capilano University, 2008.

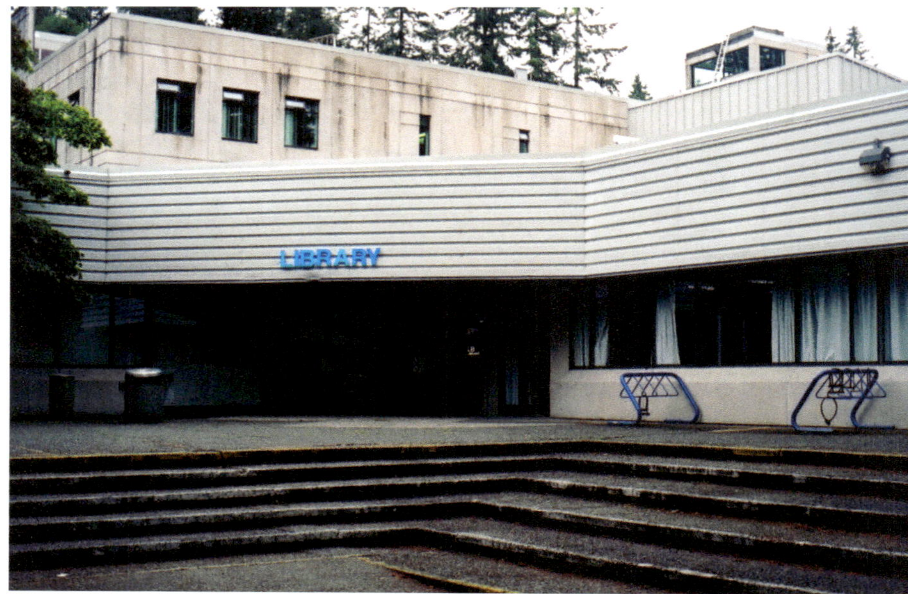

C – Library building, 2008.

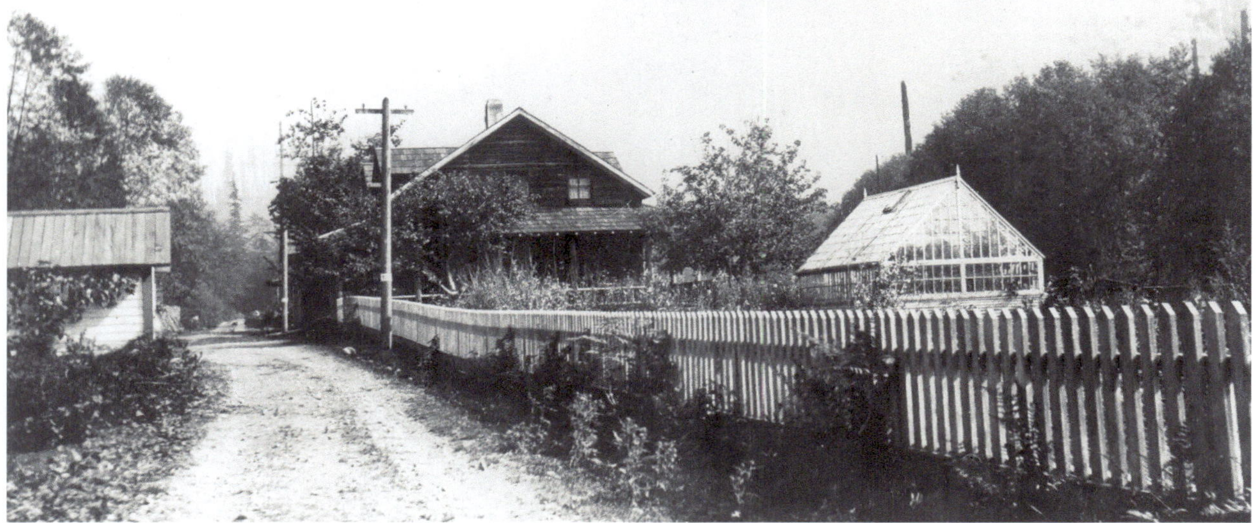

A – Community on Pipeline Road, date unknown.

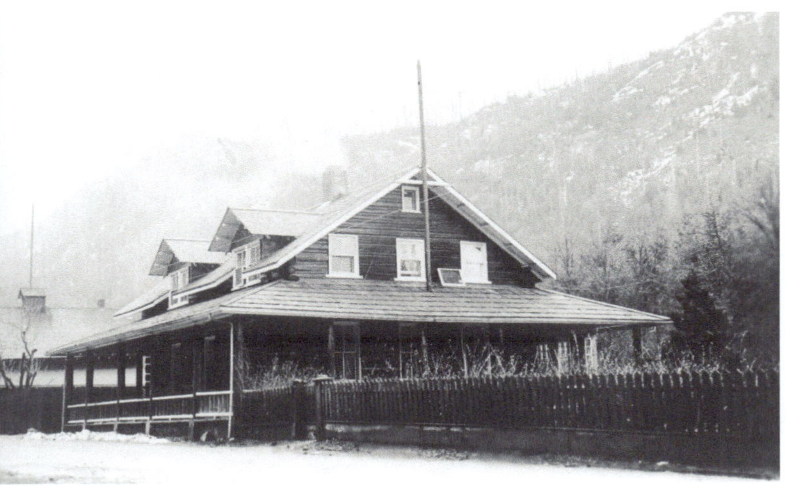

B – The Log House, date unknown.

The Log House

There was once a thriving community in the Lower Seymour Conservation Reserve. It straddled Pipeline Road (A), which ran parallel to the Seymour River's west bank. It boasted ranches, houses, cabins, barns, grocery stores, and even a tearoom. One house stood out — the "Log House" (B). It belonged to the City of Vancouver, owner of the Seymour water intake to the north. The Log House had ten rooms, a veranda, and walls of thick cedar logs. For decades water board staff lived here. In 1948, to protect the watershed, all properties were expropriated and buildings destroyed. Today the scene in the first photo is "Fishermen's Trail" flanked by thick forest (C). The Log House's cedar walls, meanwhile, were used to build the house at 171 East St. James (D).

C – Scene in first photo, 2008.

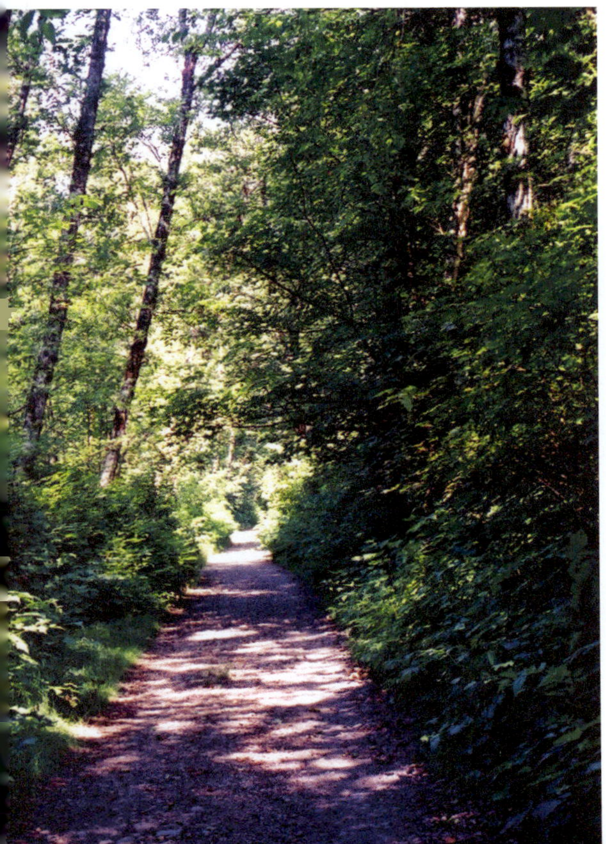

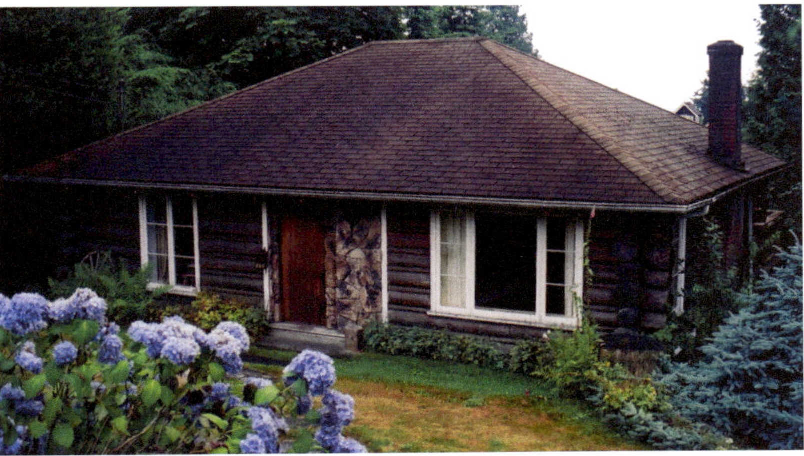

D – House on St. James, 2008

Squatters on the Maplewood Mudflats

The Maplewood mudflats east of Second Narrows Bridge are submerged at high tide, exposed at low tide. Before 1969 there were only a few squatters living here. Their numbers increased with the influx of (mostly) hippies in 1969–1970. Environmentalists, artists, musicians, sculptors, writers, idealists, non-conformists — squatters loved this wild place, its isolation and tidal rhythms. They built their houses (A & B) here out of driftwood, flotsam, jetsam, scraps, salvage, whatever they could find. And they lived without electricity, running water, telephones, plumbing, sewers (the tides washed away wastes), building codes or taxes. Soon North Vancouver taxpayers were complaining about the "slums," pot-smoking, and raw sewage. Many shacks were removed in 1971, more in 1973. The "flats" then became part of the Maplewood Conservation Area (C).

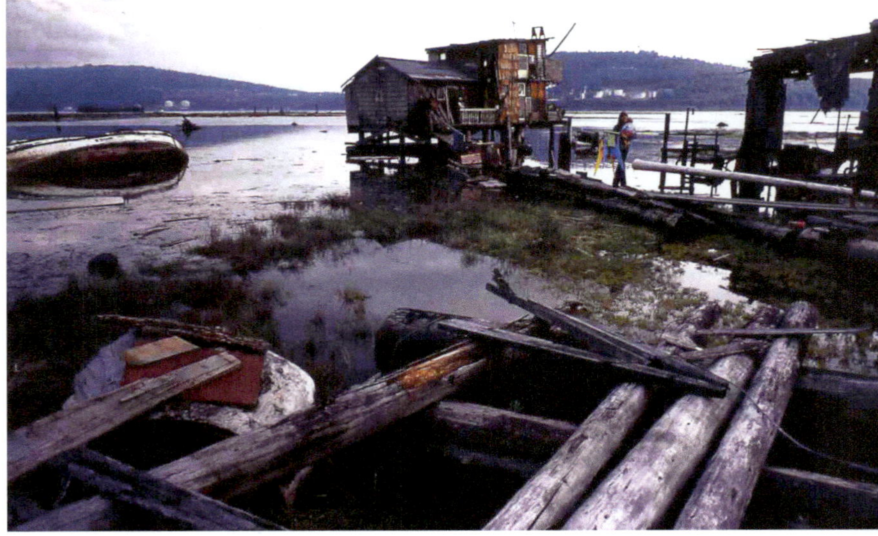

A – Shacks at the outer edge, 1971.

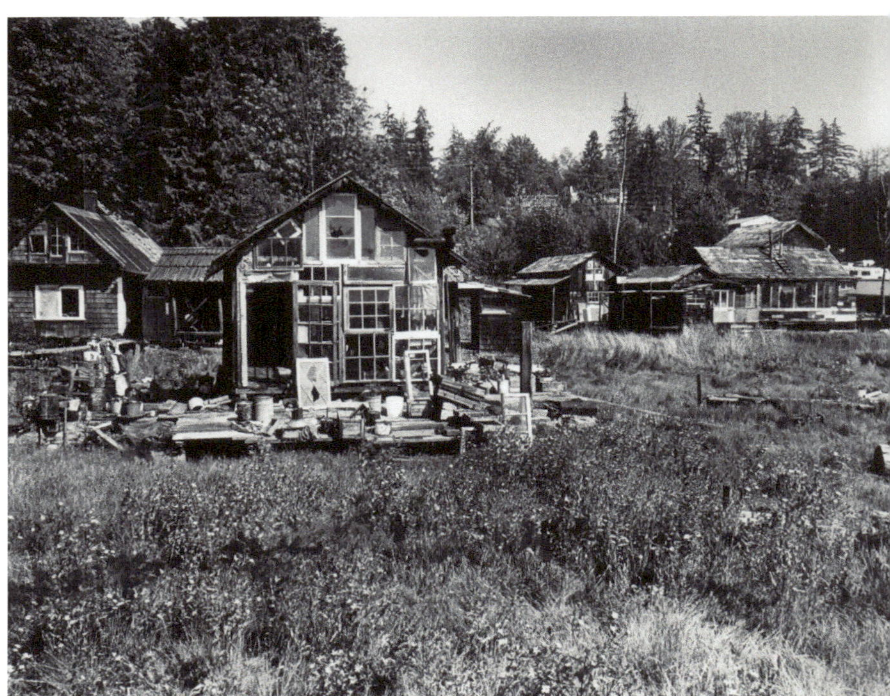

B – Shacks close to shore, 1972.

C – Maplewood mudflats, 2009.

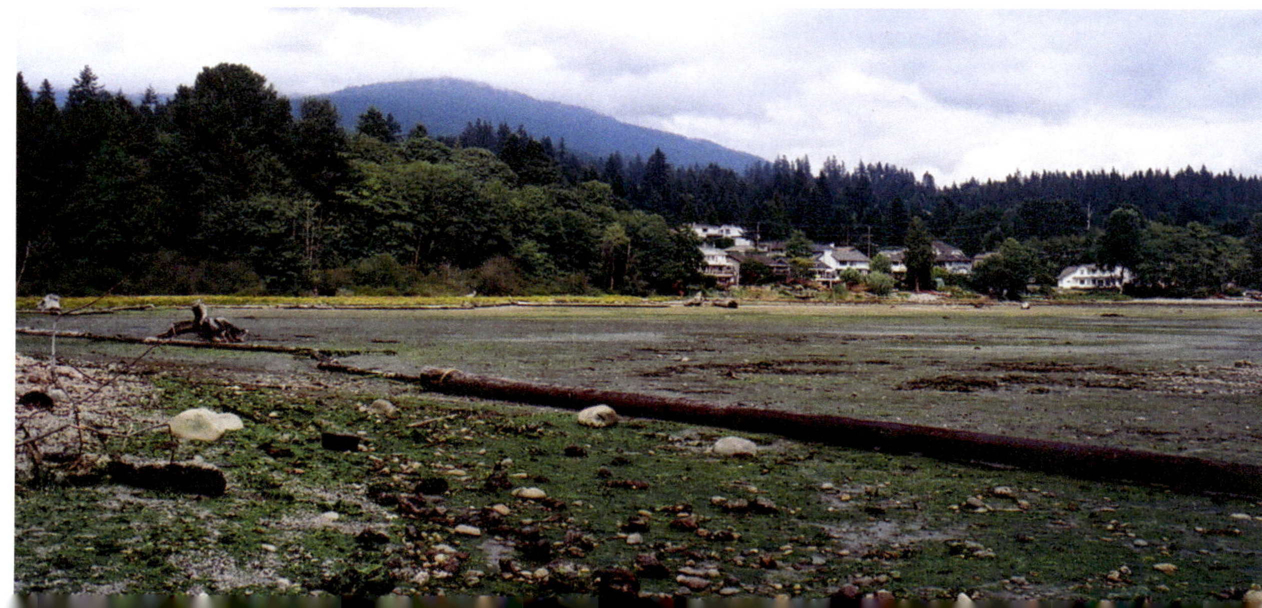

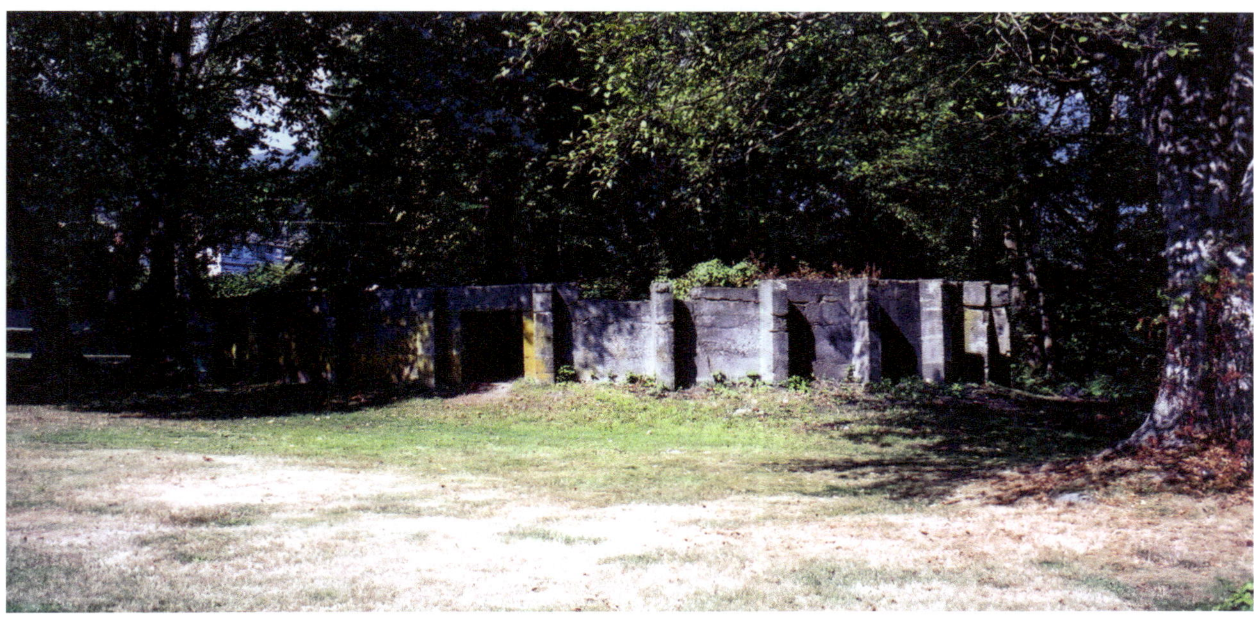

A – Concrete circle, 2007.

Vancouver Cedar Mill

Cates Park has something for everyone — grassy open spaces, forest trails, children's playground, squirrels, birds, picnic tables, and a boat launch. There's even a treat for the history buff. It's an old concrete circle located at the eastern end of the park (in "Little Cates Park"), seen in this 2007 photo (A). In near perfect condition, this is the base of the wood-waste burner used by the Vancouver Cedar Mills sawmill that operated here in the 1920s. You can see the cone-shaped burner to the left of the sawmill buildings in the 1926 view from the water side (B). While the burner-base sits in a public park, private homes and beach presently occupy the rest of the mill site.

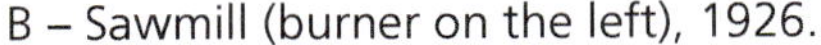
B – Sawmill (burner on the left), 1926.

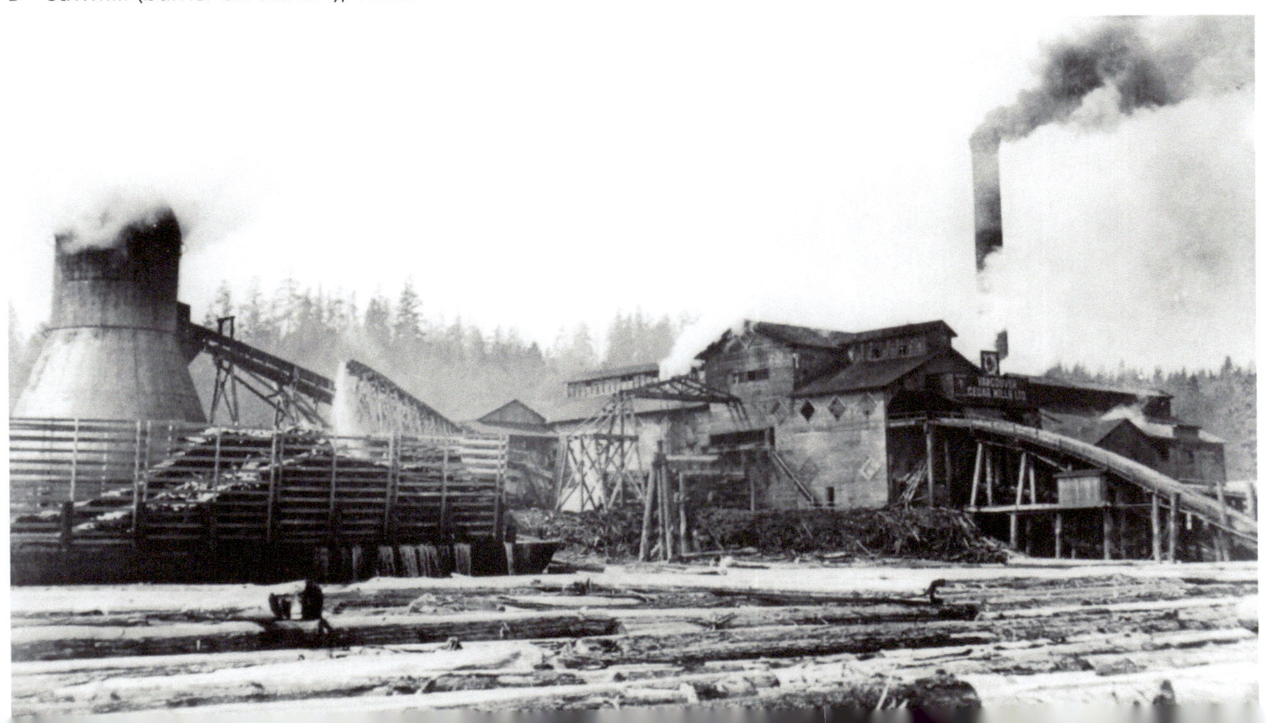

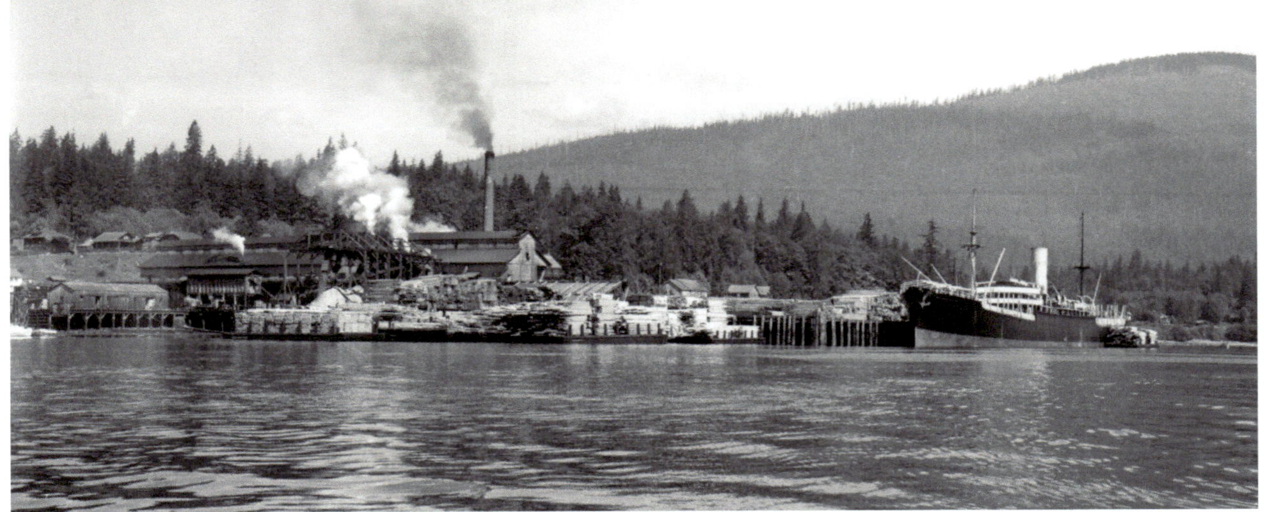

A – Robert Dollar Mill, 1939.

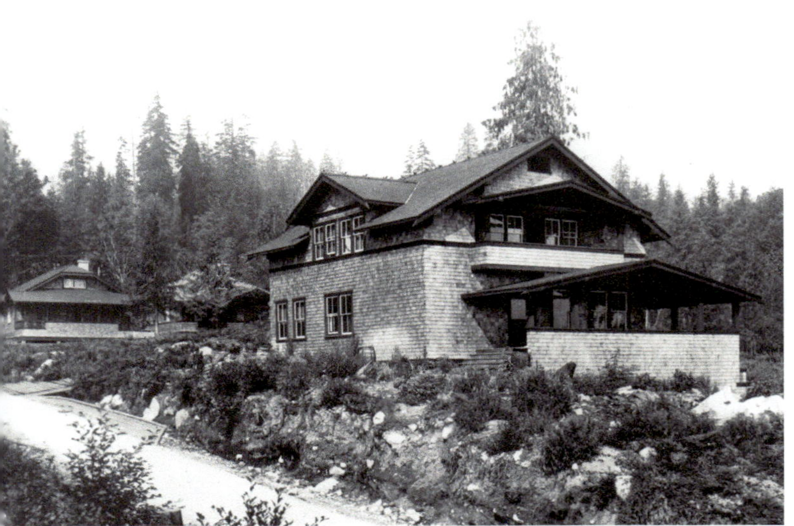

B – Manager's office, 1918.

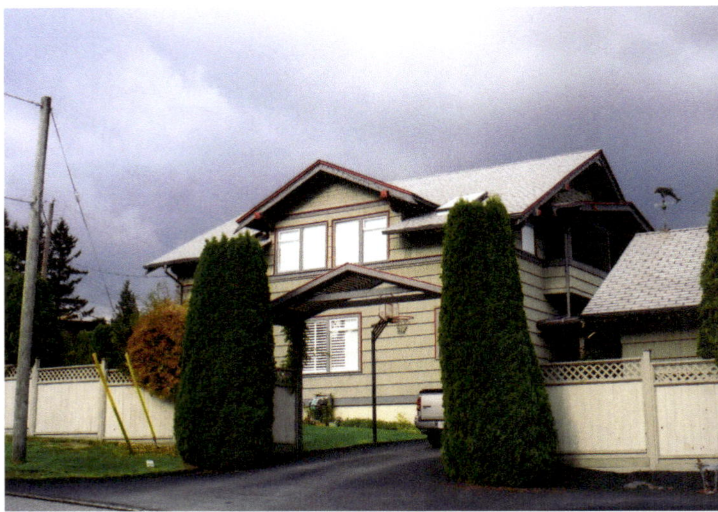

C – Private home, 2007.

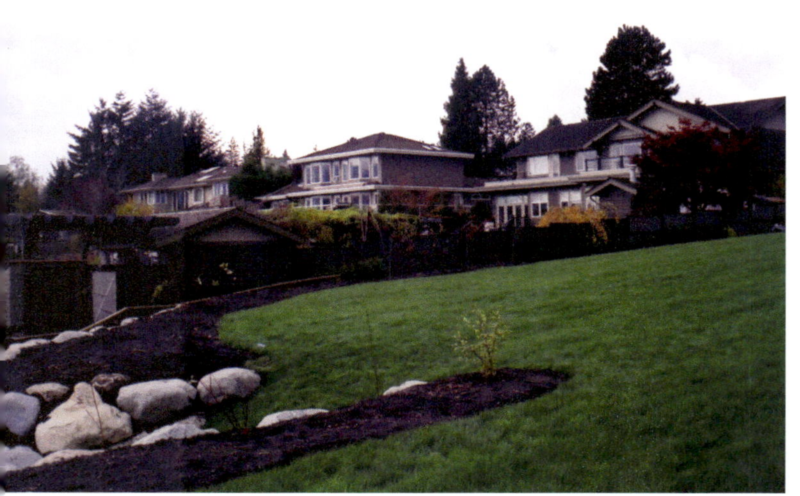

D – Homes on mill site, 2007.

Robert Dollar Mill

East of the Cedar Mills sawmill was a larger mill owned by California shipping magnate and lumber baron Robert Dollar. It was the Robert Dollar Mill, photographed in 1939 (A). The company had purchased 100 acres of land on which it built a well-equipped sawmill, a dock for large ships, and a community called "Dollarton." In addition to the mill manager's office, seen here in 1918 (B), Dollarton had homes for key staff, several bunkhouses for labourers, a post office, community hall, a country store, school, church, tennis court, and ferry service. The mill closed in late 1942. The mill manager's office became a private home, at 518 Beachview (C), and modern homes cover the mill site (D).

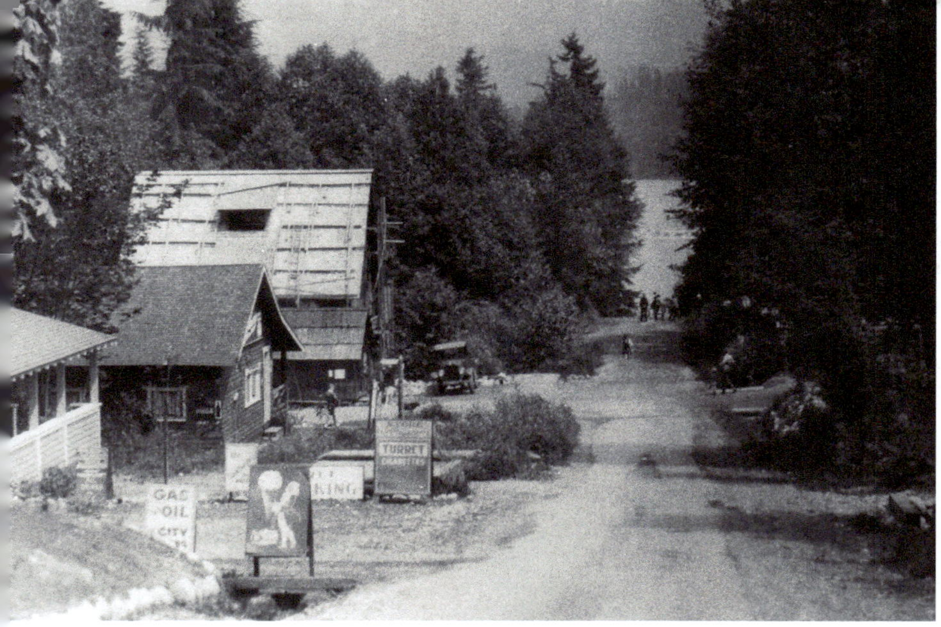

A – Gallant Avenue, 1920s.

Gallant Avenue in Deep Cove

It was a short dirt road in the 1920s, running down to the water and a pier (A), and it was flanked by a few small houses and stores. The exception was the large structure seen on the left, halfway down to the water. This 14-room house was built by the Moore family, early settlers who lived in it for many years. It was located on the northeast corner of Gallant and Panorama Drive, until it burned down in the 1950s. Today, the Deep Cove Cultural Centre sits on the site (B). As for Gallant Avenue itself, it was an idyllic little "main street" in 2008 (C), lined with small shops, an art gallery, the cultural centre, a yacht club, a park, and a restaurant or two. It's still "idyllic" in 2016, dispite some modern development.

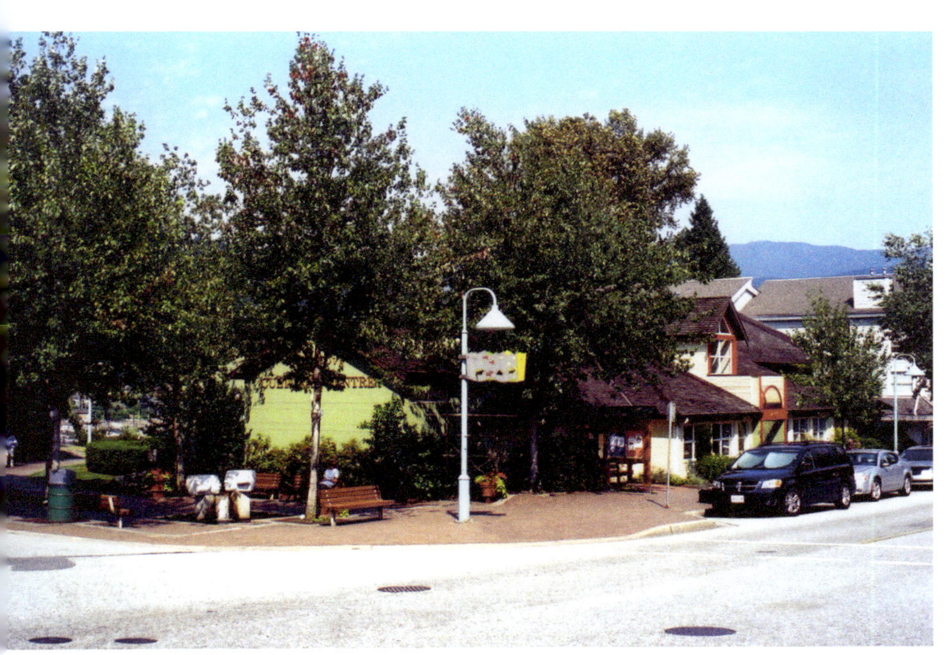

B – Deep Cove Cultural Centre, 2008

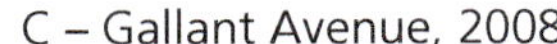

C – Gallant Avenue, 2008.

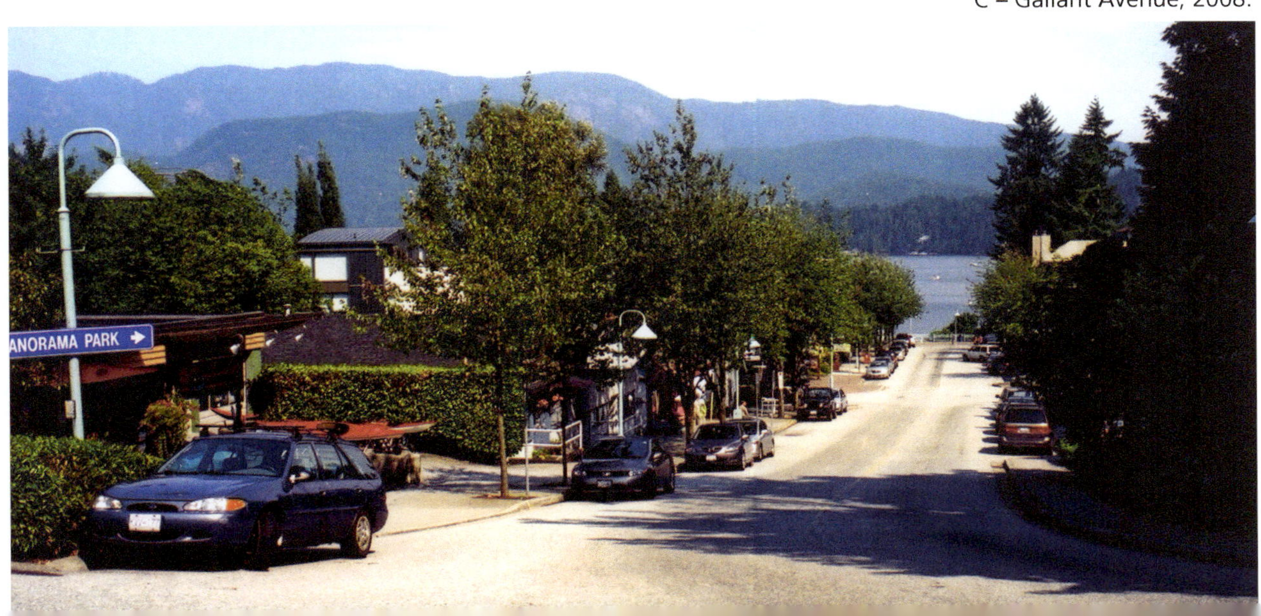

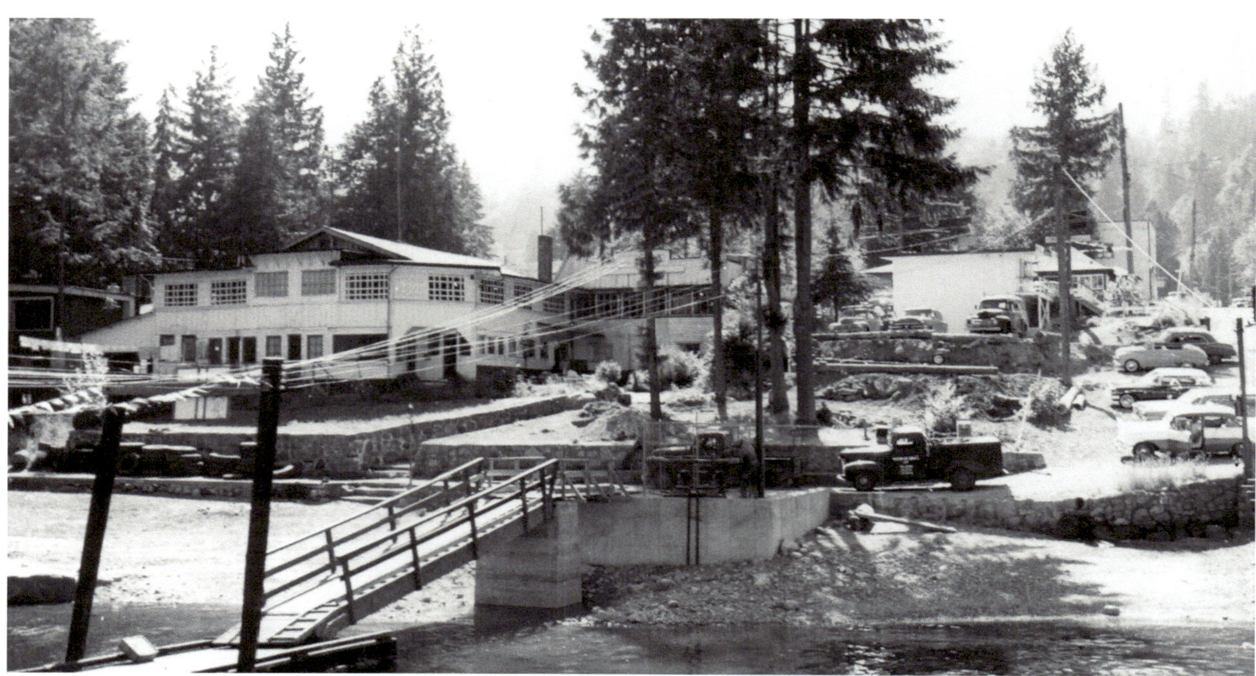

A – Deep Cove Pavilion, 1958.

Deep Cove Pavilion

For several decades the Deep Cove Pavilion, shown in this 1958 photo (A), was a popular social centre for Deep Cove residents, especially on Saturday nights. Built in the late 1920s at the foot of Gallant Avenue, it featured a large dance floor and at different times boasted a tea garden, general store, boat-rental business, gas station, and restaurant. Notice the stone wall and pier in the early photo. While the pavilion and pier are gone, the old stone wall and the pier supports were still there in 2007 (B). The site is now part of Deep Cove Park.

B – Same view, 2007.

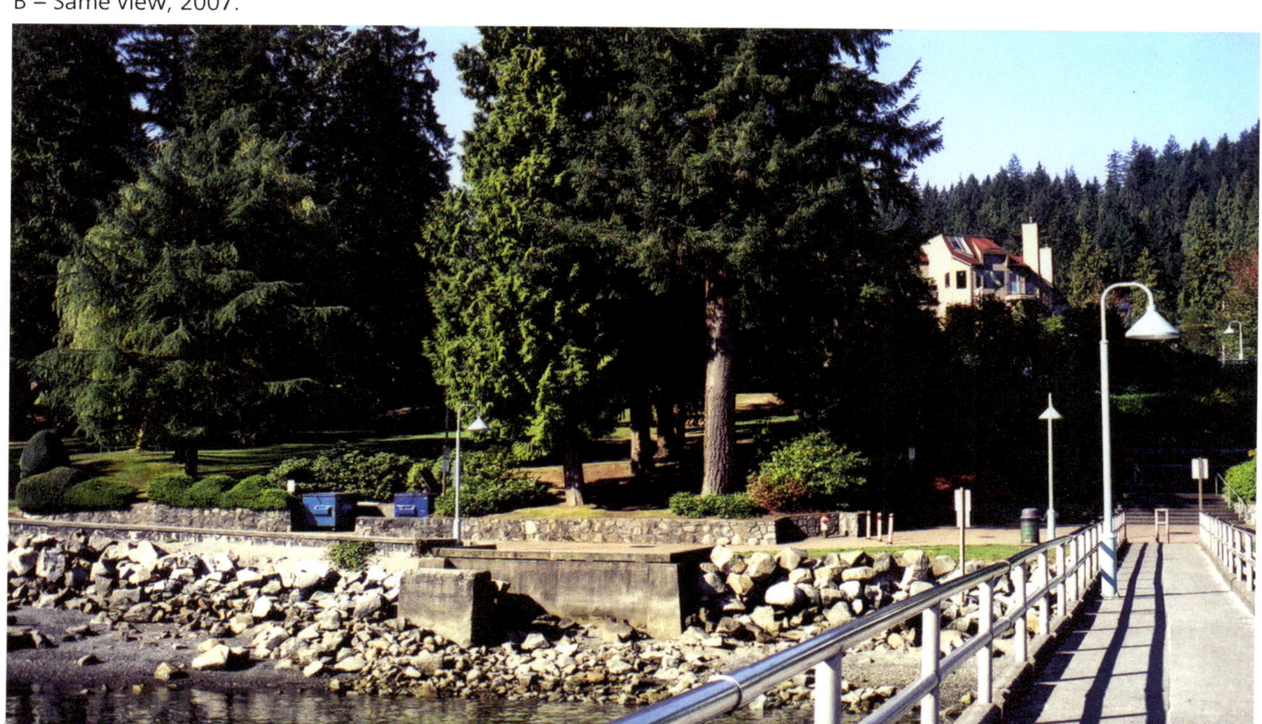

5 Lynn Valley

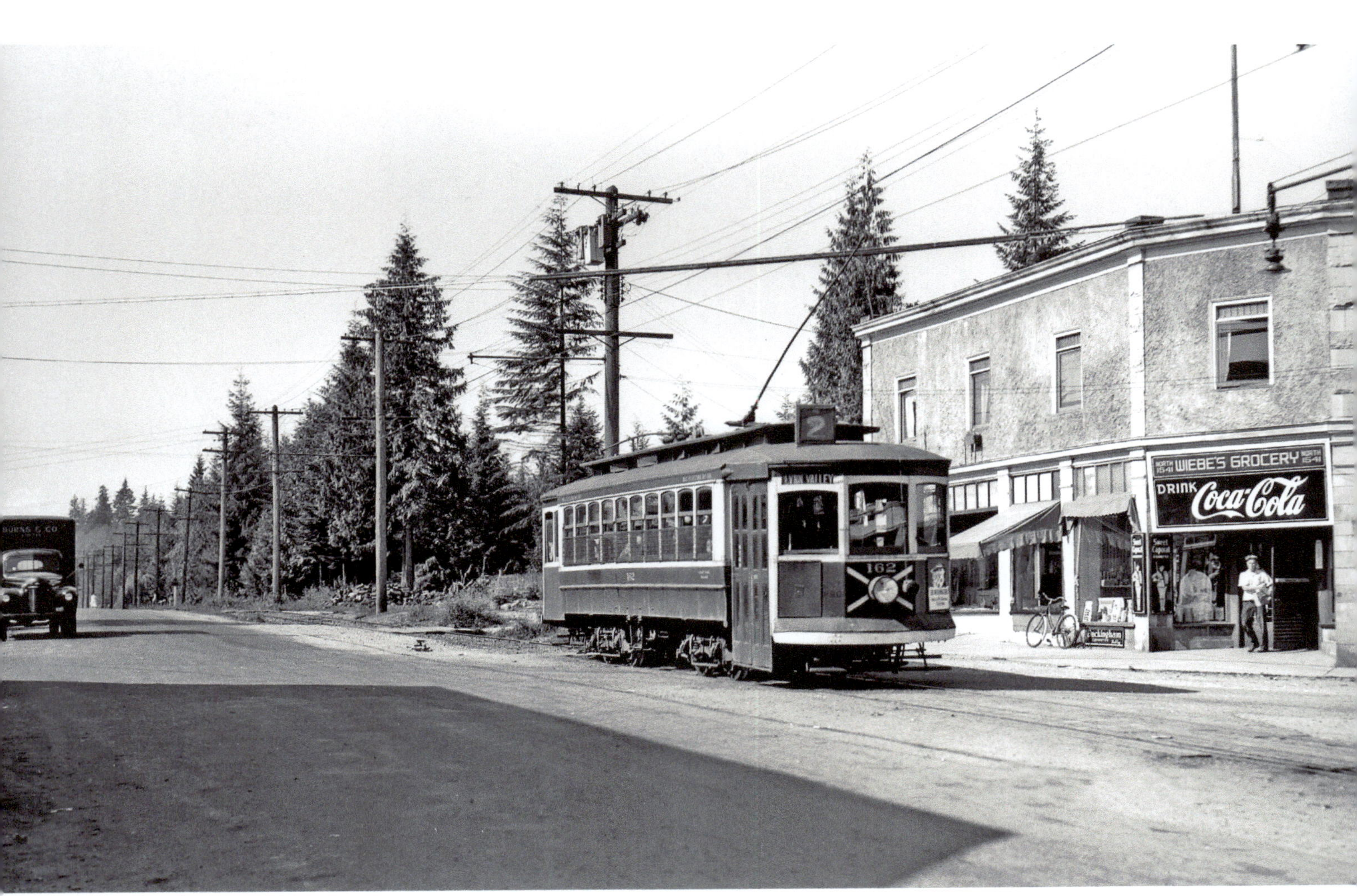

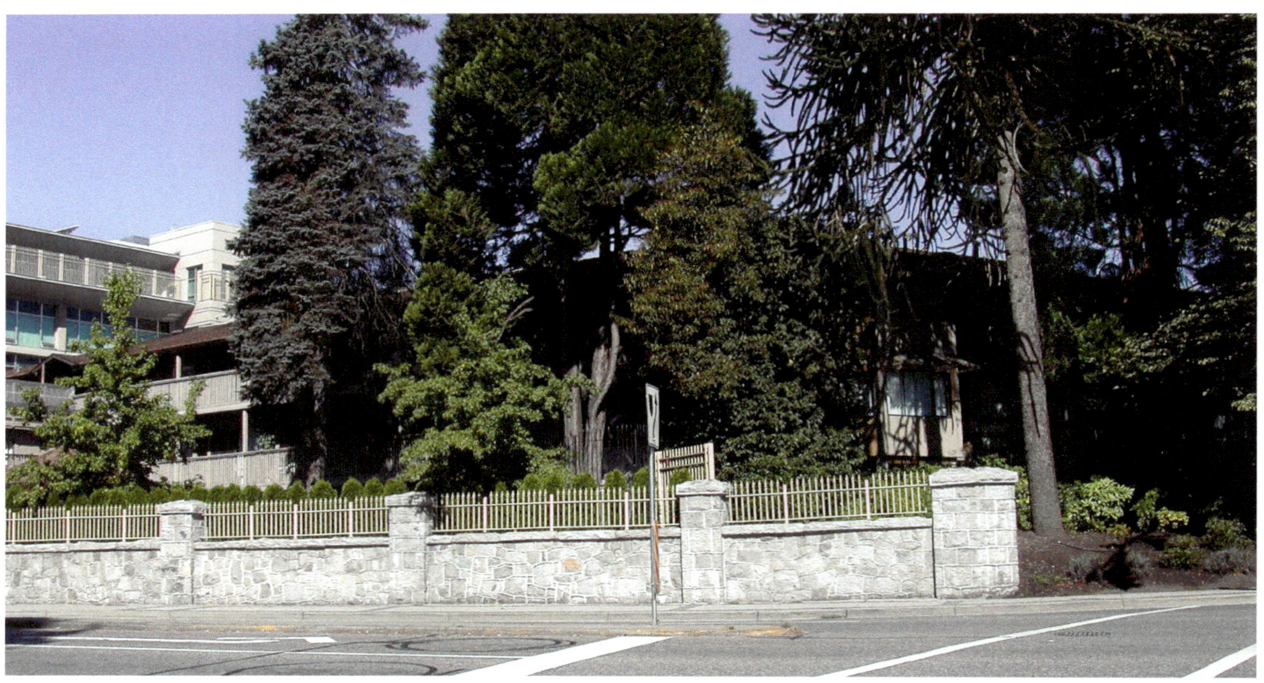

A – Rebuilt stone wall, 2016.

Old District Hall

The stone wall in this 2016 photo (A) is in front of a care centre at Lynn Valley and Fromme Roads. In 1920 (B) we see a wall in the same spot, but in front of the District of North Vancouver Municipal Hall. When there was one North Vancouver municipality extending from Deep Cove to Howe Sound, its municipal hall was at 1st and Lonsdale. Then the City split off in 1907, and the District built this new hall a few years later. Erecting the wall in front followed an ancient tradition of having a symbolic boundary separate those who govern from those who *are governed.* In the 1950s a new district hall was built on Queens (no wall this time). The old hall was demolished in 1972. And in 2009 the wall in the 1920 photo was taken apart and rebuilt.

B – District Hall, 1920.

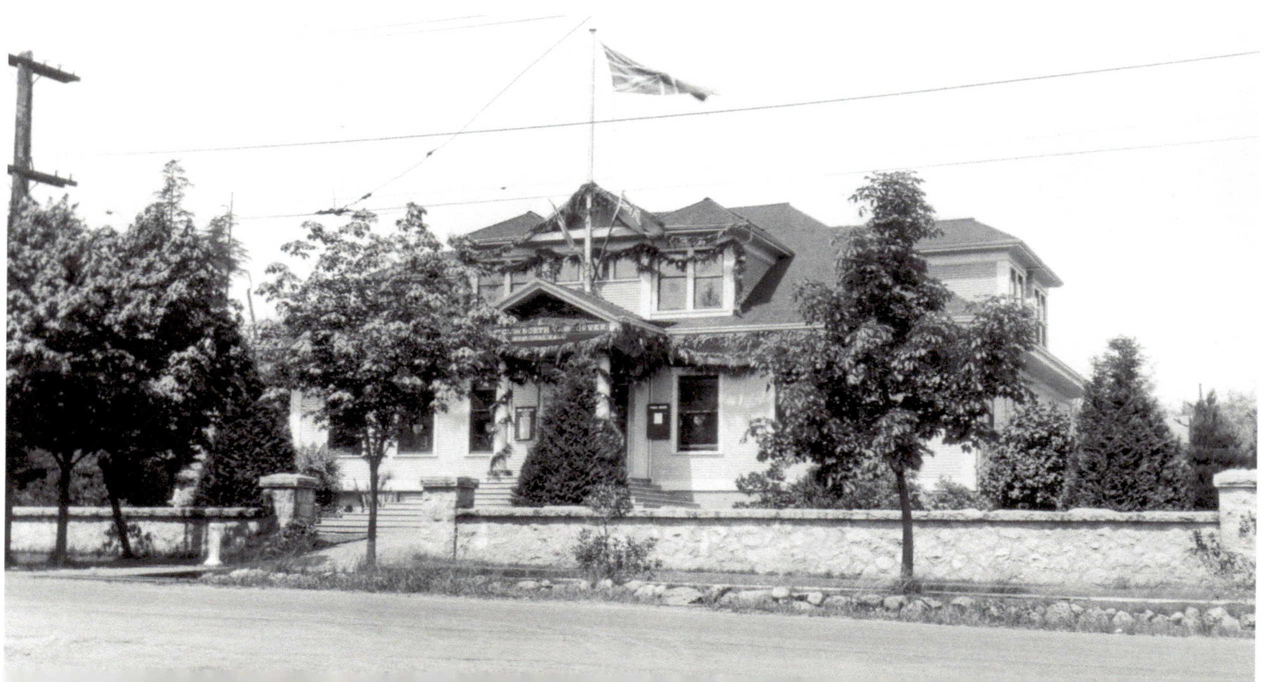

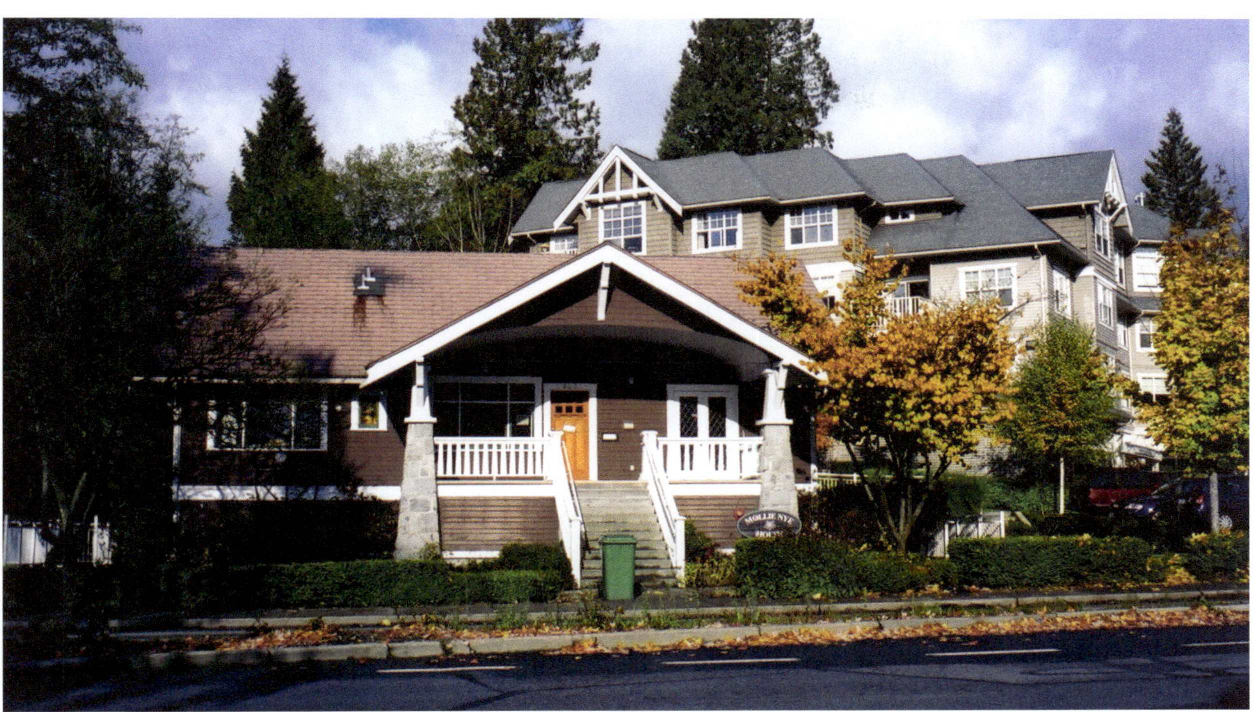

A – Mollie Nye House, 2007.

Mollie Nye House

"Mollie Nye House" (A), at 940 Lynn Valley Road, is a neighbourhood activity centre that sits beside a seniors' condominium complex. It was once the home of Alfred J. Nye and his wife Olive. They built it in 1913 on 160 acres of land Nye received for serving in the Boer War. The vintage photos were taken around 1914 (B & C). Alas, during World War I the property was heavily taxed and the Nyes lost all but the house and 2½ acres. The Nyes raised two daughters here, one of whom was Mollie, who lived here into the 1990s. When modern condos were built on the 2½ acres, the developer moved the house to the corner of the property and restored it.

B – Nye home, c.1914.

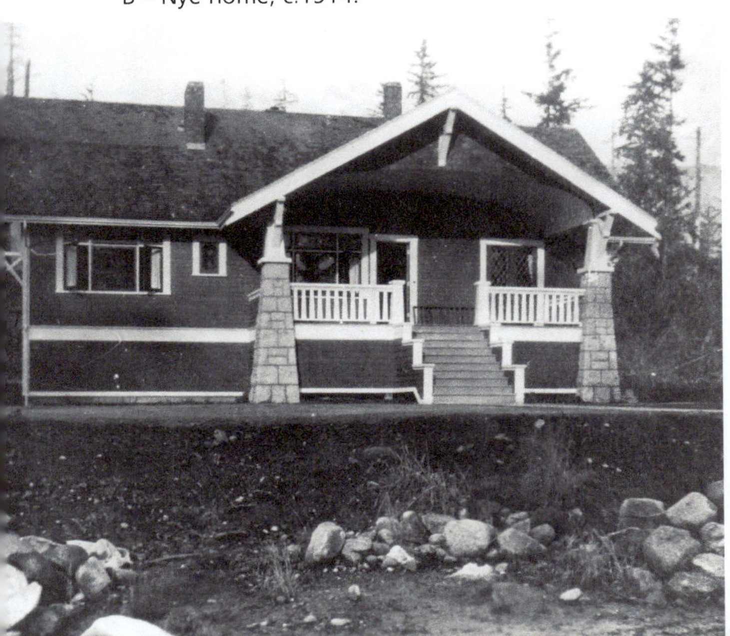

C – Sitting room, c.1914.

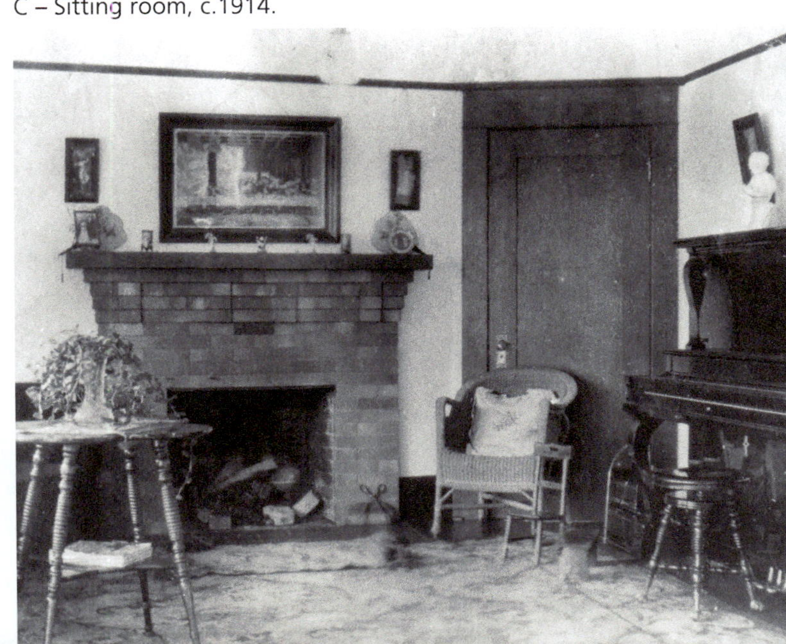

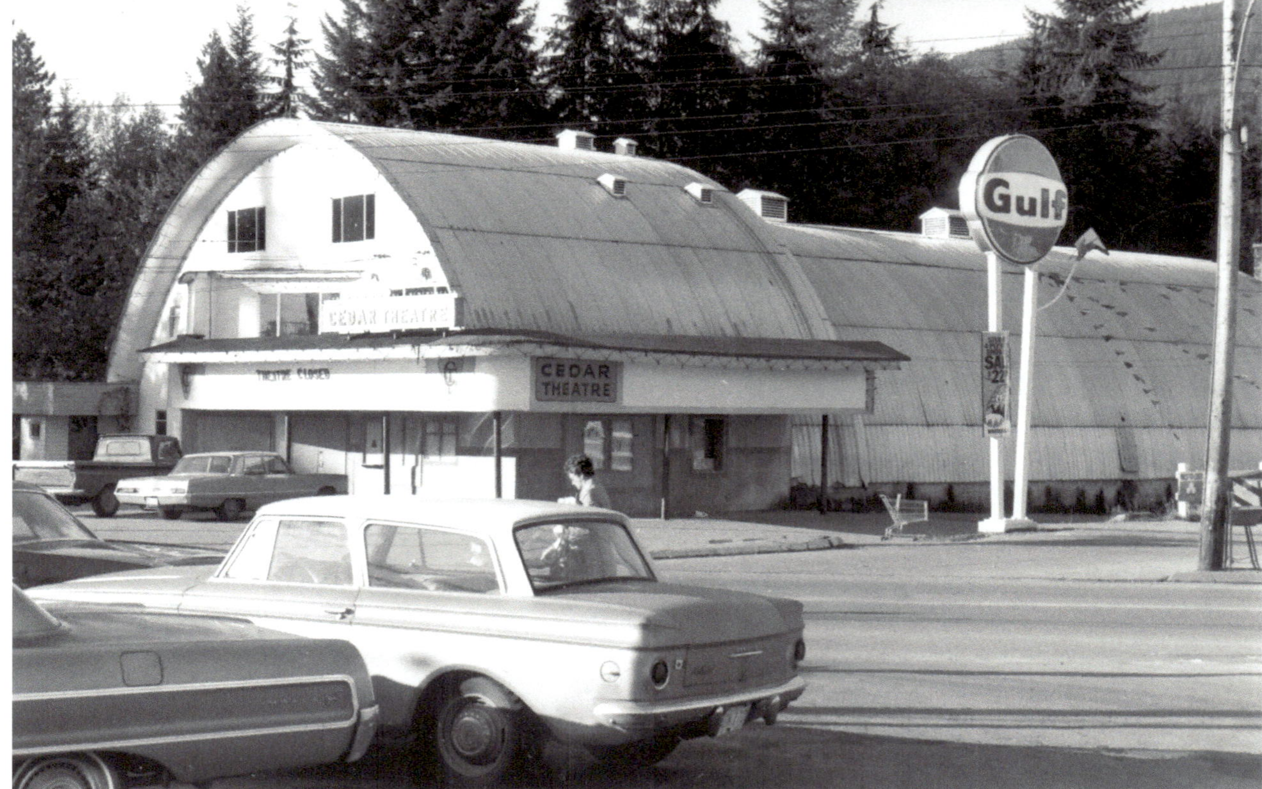

A – Cedar Theatre, 1971.

Cedar Theatre

A "Quonset-hut" style movie theatre once stood in the 1200 block of Lynn Valley Road. Here it is in 1971, after it closed (A). Shaped like a half cylinder, the Cedar Theatre (originally called "Cedar V Theatre") opened in 1953. Arched, pre-fabricated steel structures like this were popular after World War II, for they were portable, cheap to assemble, and easily adapted for use as theatres, housing, churches, garages, barns, and other functions. The Cedar showed popular Hollywood movies, and on Saturdays its double-feature matinees attracted hoards of local children who screamed, cheered, threw popcorn, spilled their soft drinks, and otherwise had a fabulous time. The Cedar ceased operation around 1970. Today a Scotiabank (1246 Lynn Valley Road) and a few adjacent businesses occupy the site (B).

B – Theatre site, 2007.

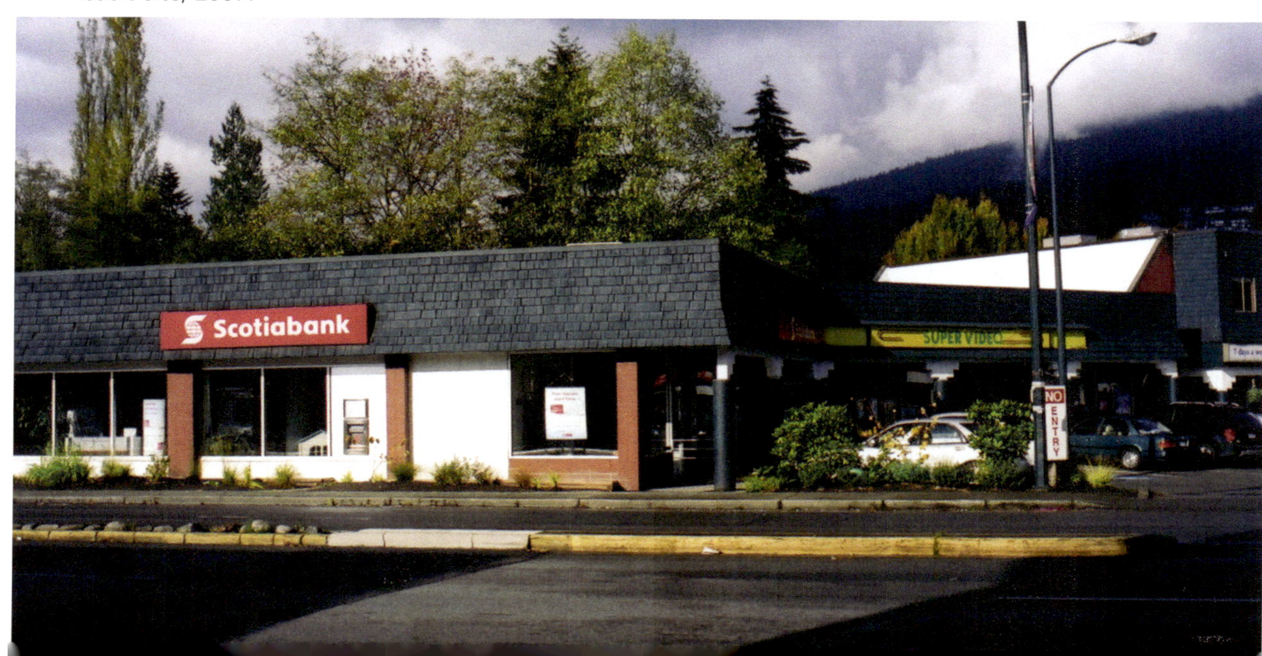

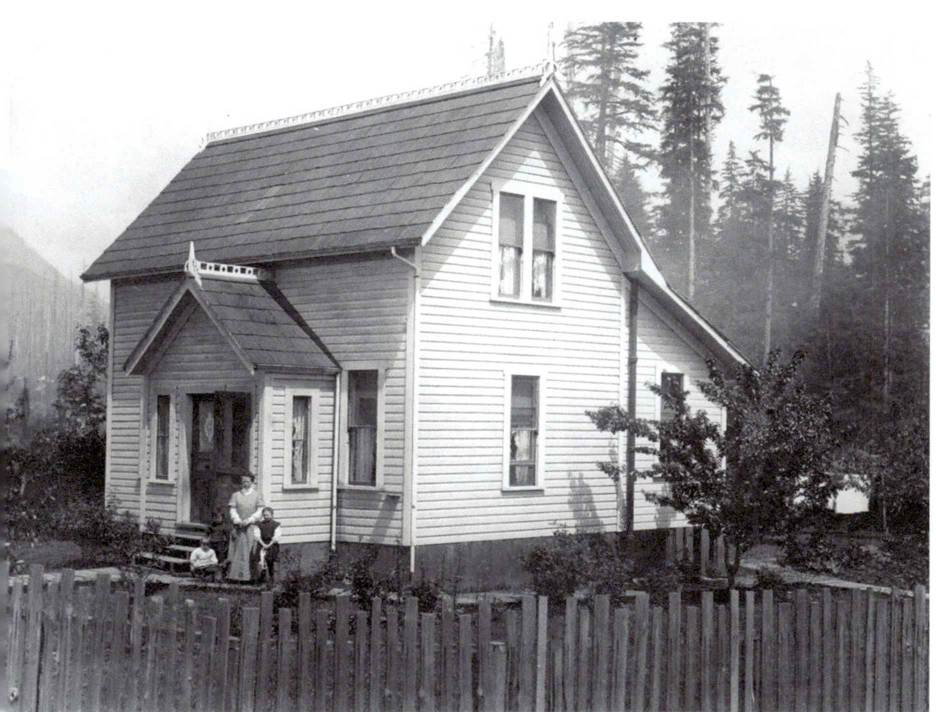

A – Fromme house, c.1910.

The Fromme Home

Julius Fromme, owner of the Lynn Valley Lumber Company, was a driving force behind Lynn Valley's development in the first decades of the twentieth century. He'd homesteaded a large chunk of land in 1899 and the following year built a house on it. You can see it in the photo taken around 1910 (A). Originally the house faced a "skid road" (a road made of logs, for dragging fresh-cut timber to a mill), and it had a fruit orchard and a garden. The Fromme children, in fact, used to have "tea" in the garden, as shown in this 1911 photo (B). The house is still there today (1466 Ross Road), little changed from this 2007 photo (C).

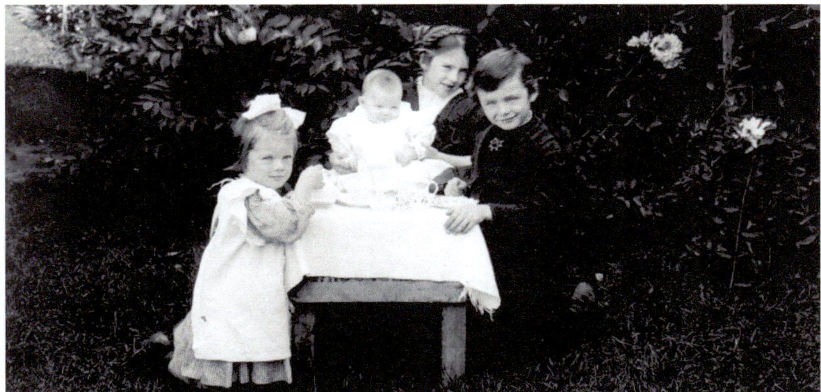

B – Children in garden, 1911.

C – Fromme house, 2007.

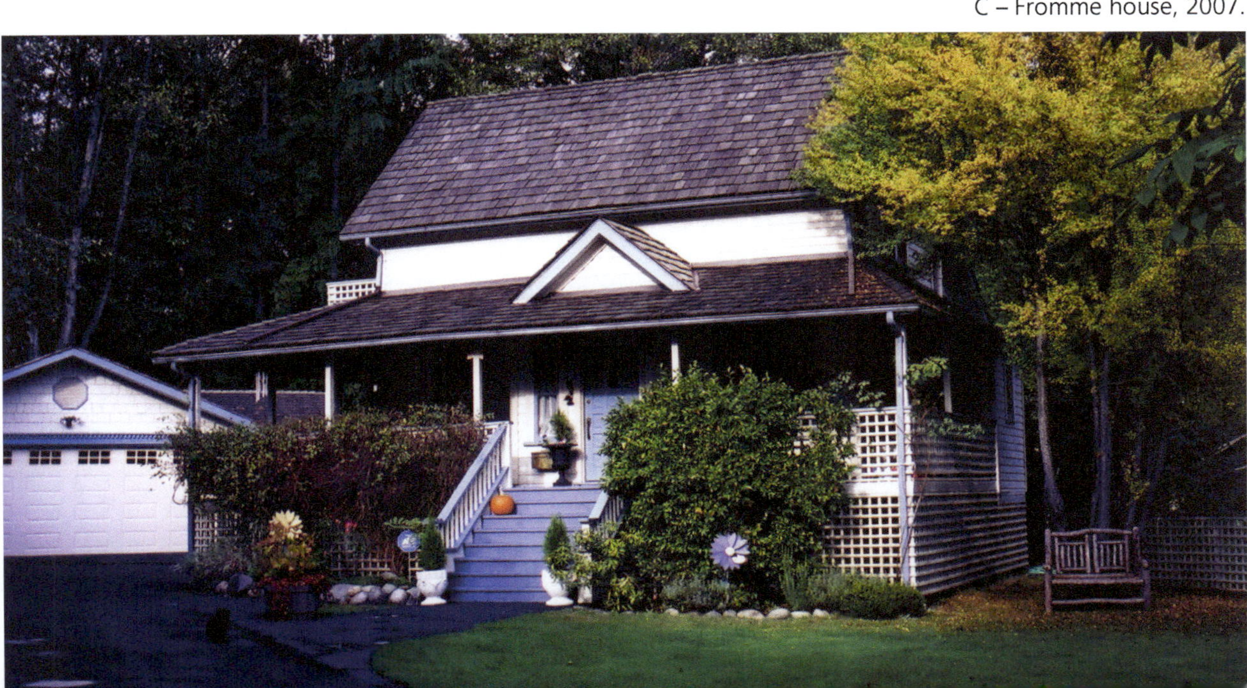

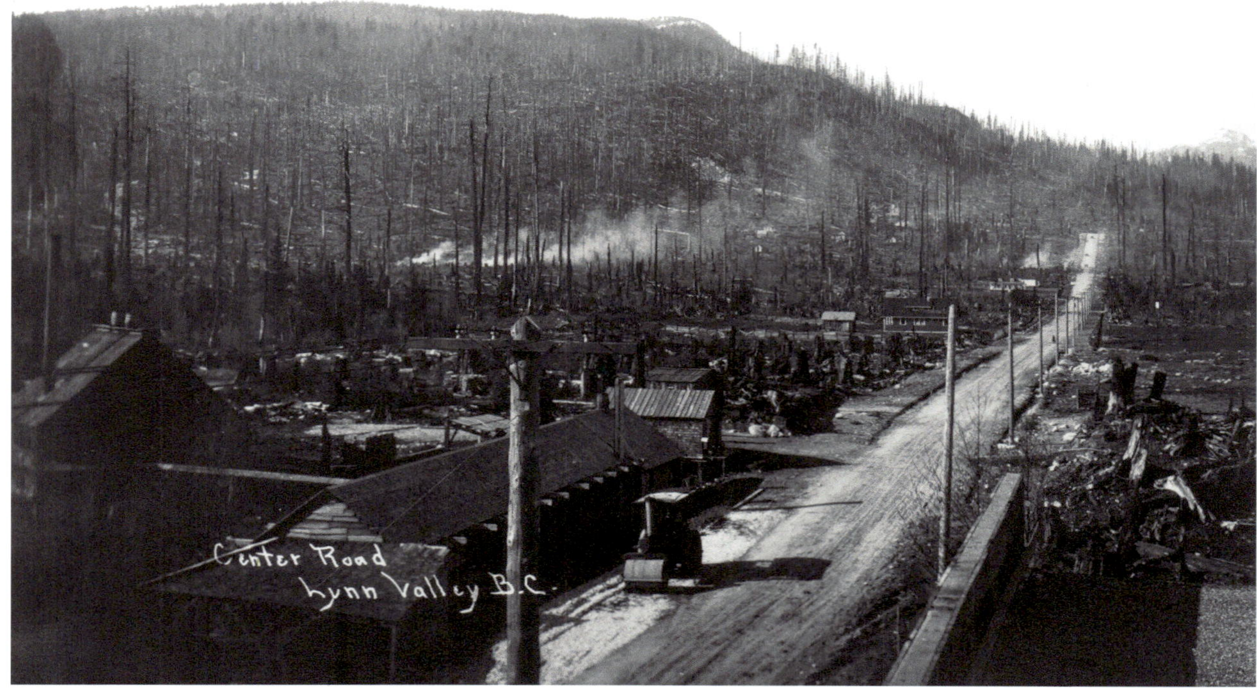

A – Mountain Highway, c.1912.

Looking North on Mountain Highway

The top photo (A) was taken around 1912 and, as you can see, it captured a scene of blackened tree trunks — the result of a fire that ravaged Lynn Valley in 1910. That's Mountain Highway running north from Lynn Valley Road. Despite the destruction, there was a new real estate boom here and people were clearing land to build homes. (Notice the smoke). David Cook's Shingle Mill sits in the left foreground. The 2018 view (B) shows a paved street running through a sea of trees. And among all those trees were homes, condos, a school, a church and other community facilities.

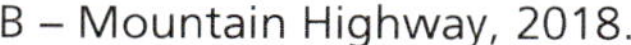

B – Mountain Highway, 2018.

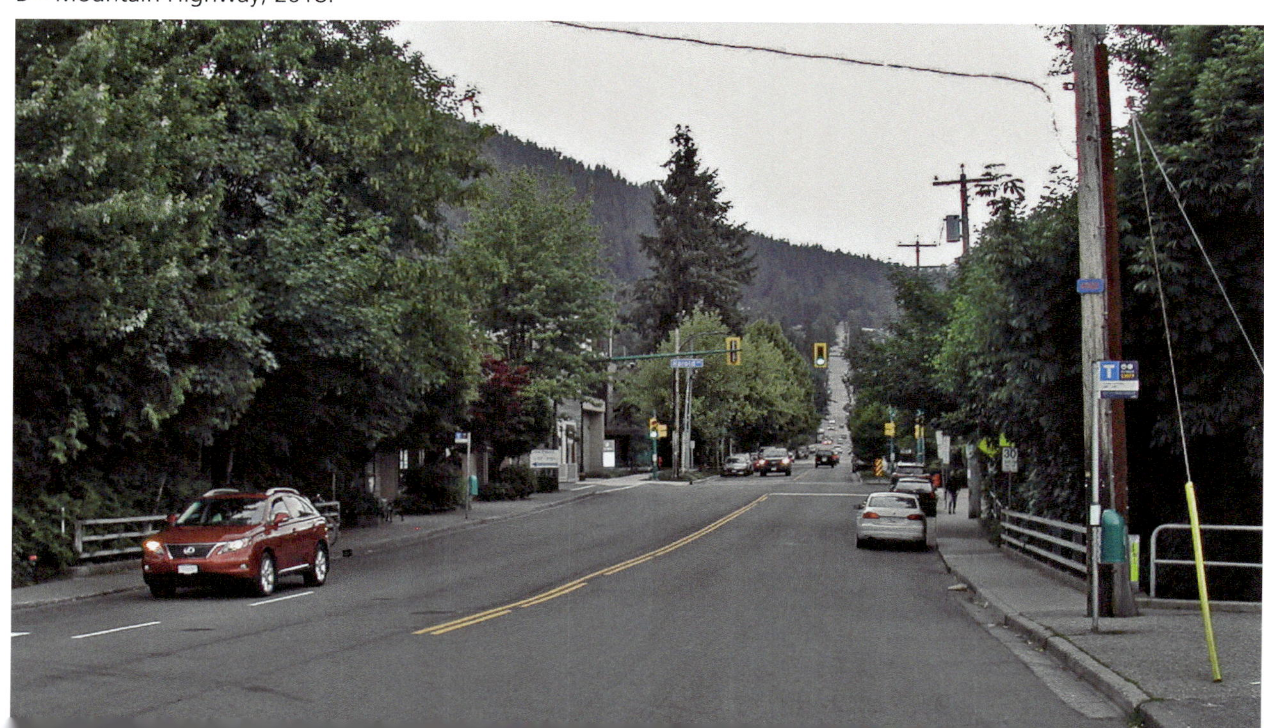

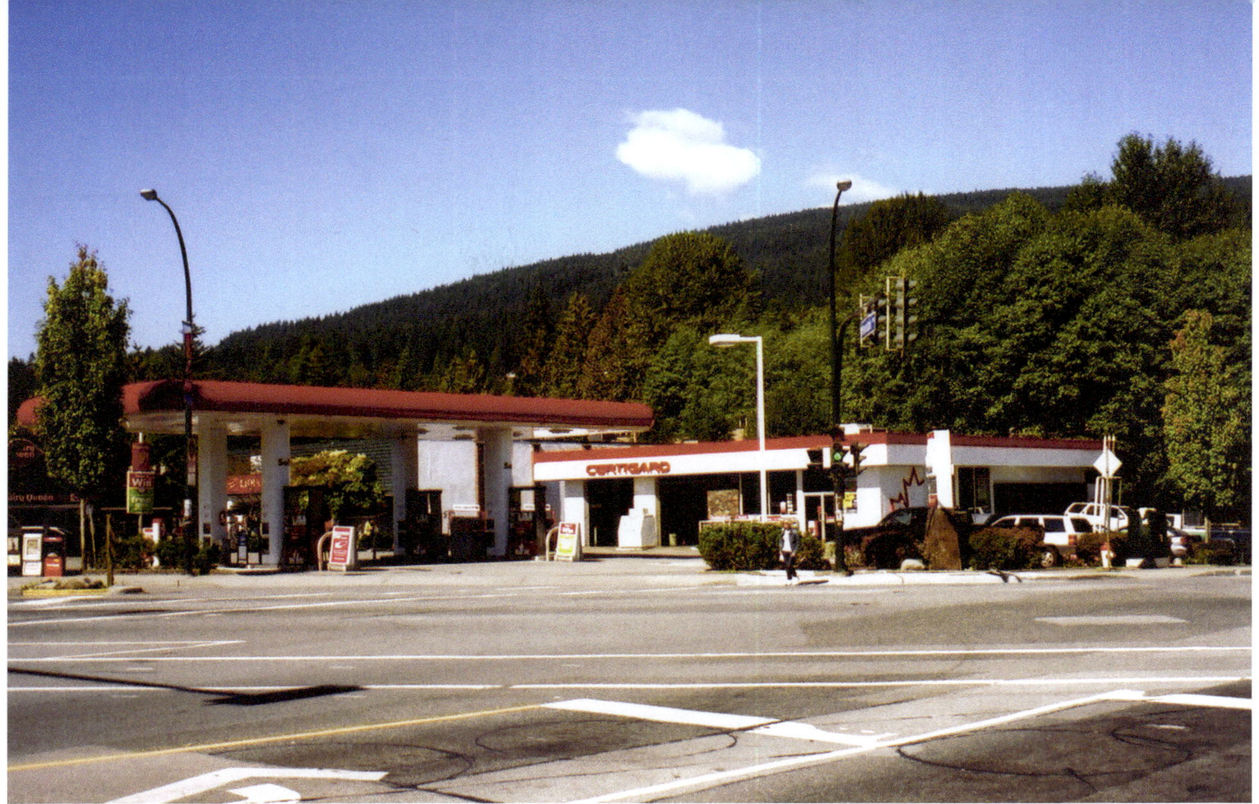

A – Gas station, 2007.

Brier Block

There's a Petro Canada service station on the northwest corner of Lynn Valley Road and Mountain Highway (A). In 1946 the Brier Block stood here (B). The Brier Block was built in 1926 by Louis Brier, who made a fortune in the late 1890s selling supplies to miners in the Yukon gold fields. Like many small commercial buildings, this one was constructed to house merchants and other businesses on the street level, and apartments for rent above. As you can see in the 1946 photo, the building's tenants at the time had the pleasure of hearing the *whrrrrrrr* and clang-clang of streetcars passing close by several times a day. The Brier Block was demolished in 1972.

B – Brier Block, 1946.

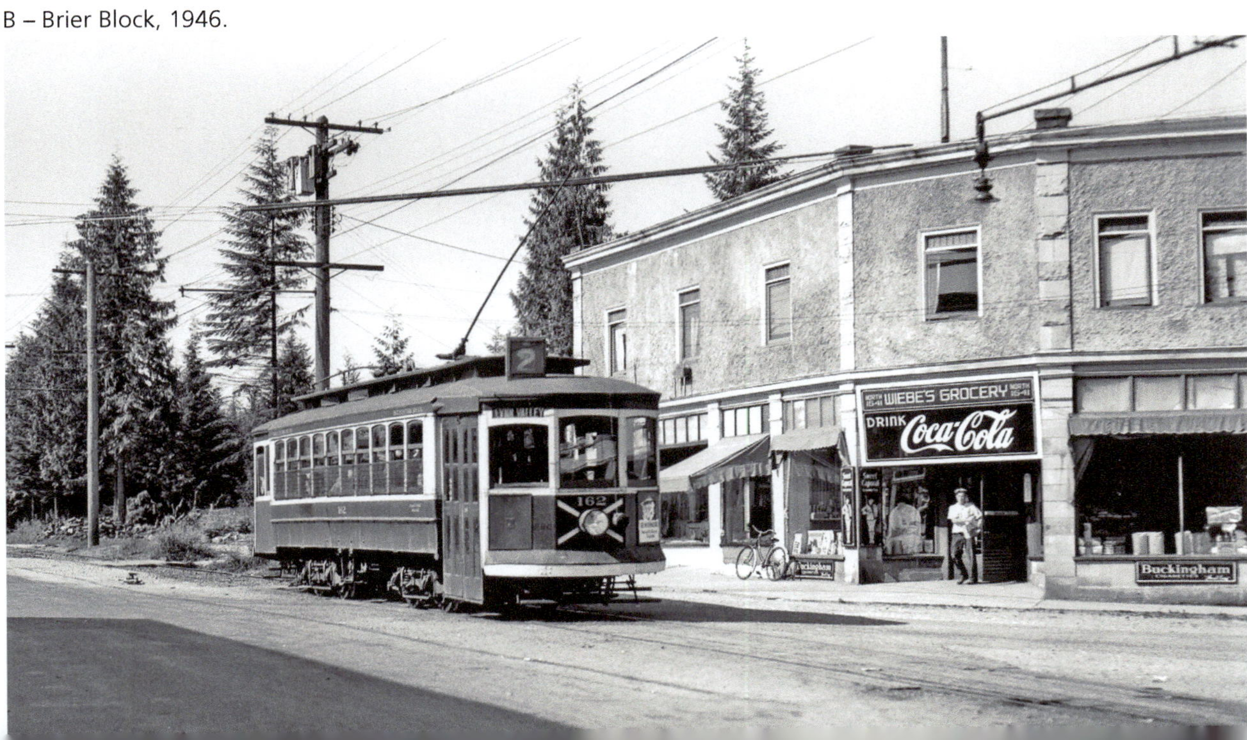

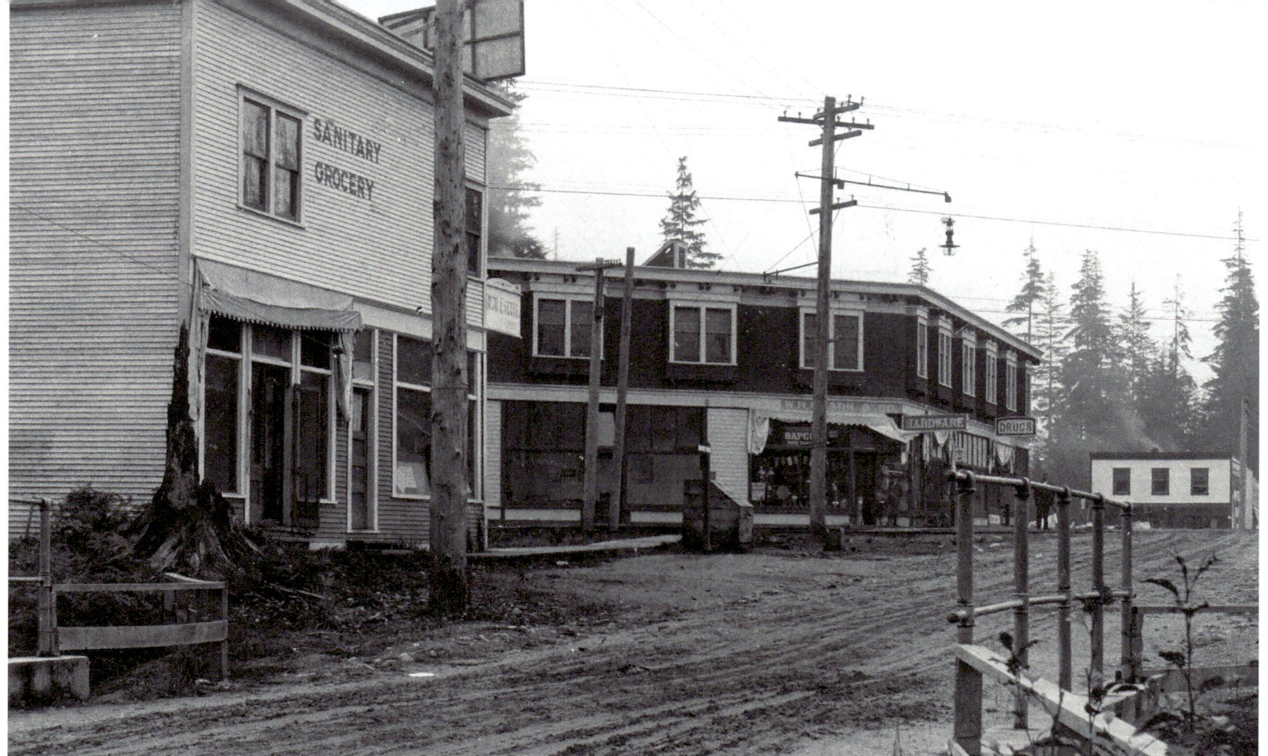

A – Triangle and Fromme Blocks, c.1913.

Triangle and Fromme Blocks

Before there were malls, people went "downtown" to shop. In Lynn Valley around 1913, "downtown" was the intersection of Lynn Valley Road and Mountain Highway (A). The vintage photo looks south along Mountain. You can see the Triangle Block at the left, with a grocery store on its ground floor. On the right is the Fromme Block, built by Julius Fromme. It has a hardware store and other businesses on the ground floor and apartments above. In the foreground is a bridge over Hastings Creek. The 2007 view (B) shows a small public plaza where the Triangle Block once stood. And behind we see the Fromme Block, restored and with a bank on the ground floor. Across the street, on the southeast corner of this intersection, is the new Lynn Valley Library and Town Centre. All are still there today.

B – Same view, 2007.

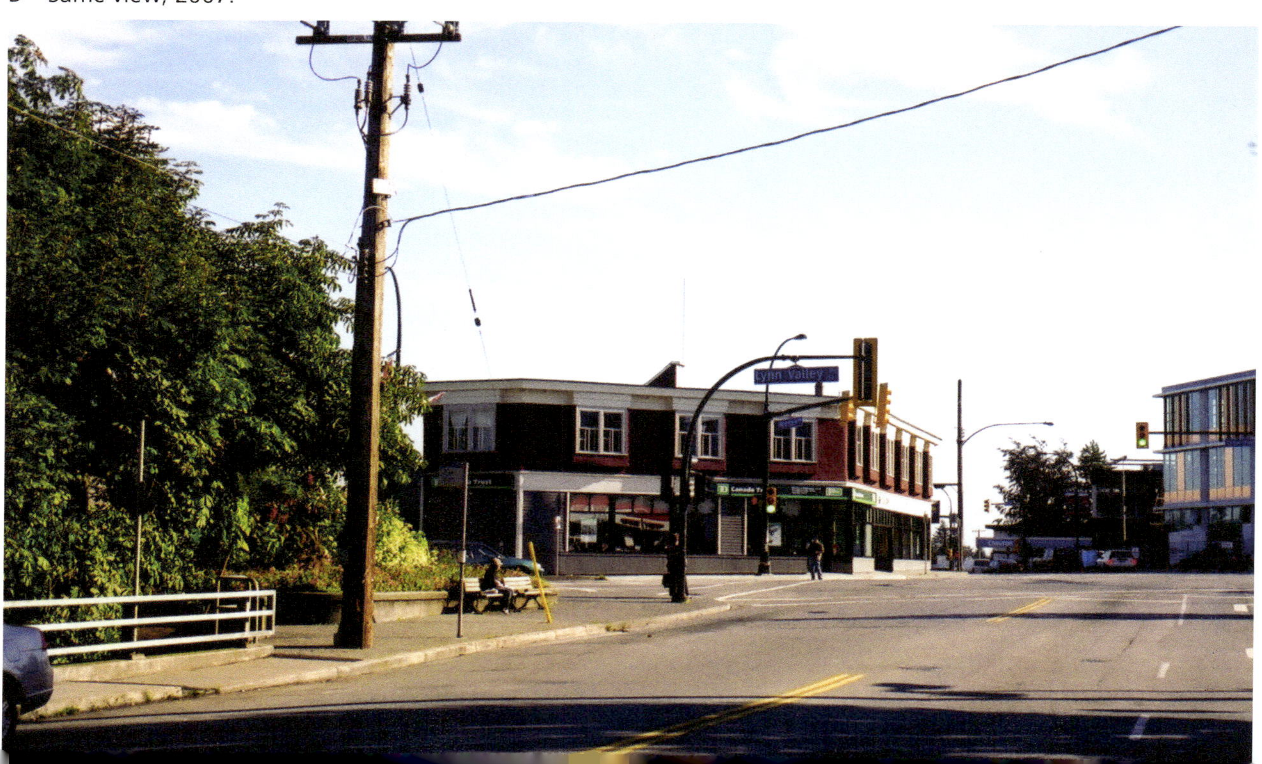

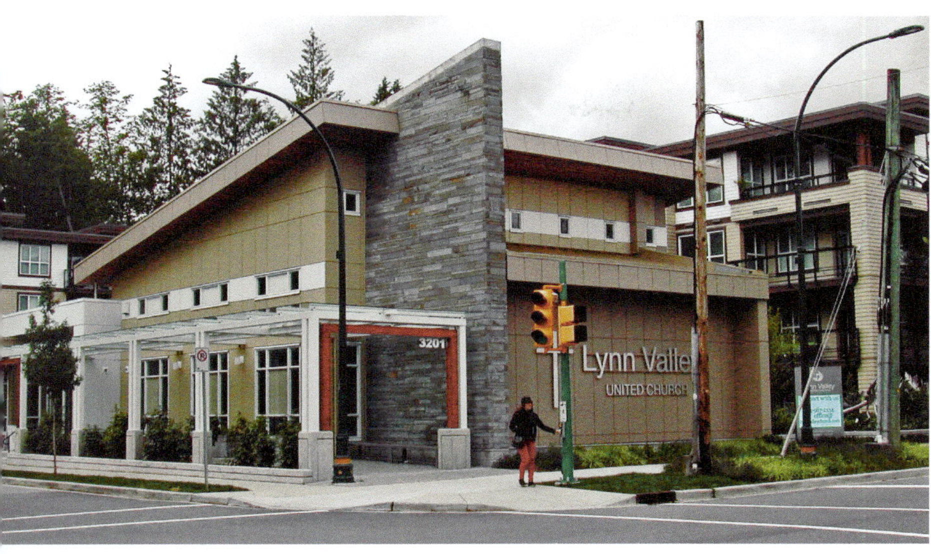

A – New Church, 2018.

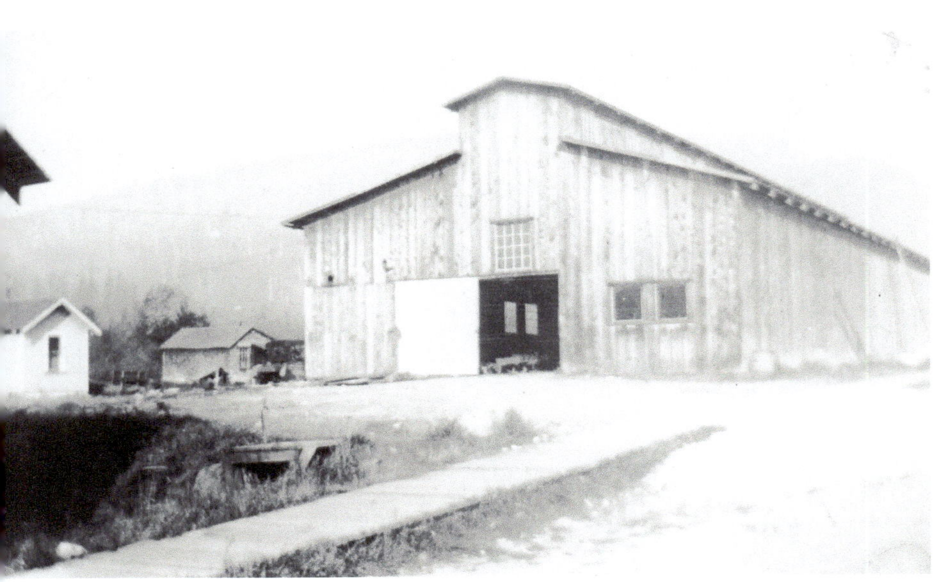

B – Lumber-storage shed, c.1925.

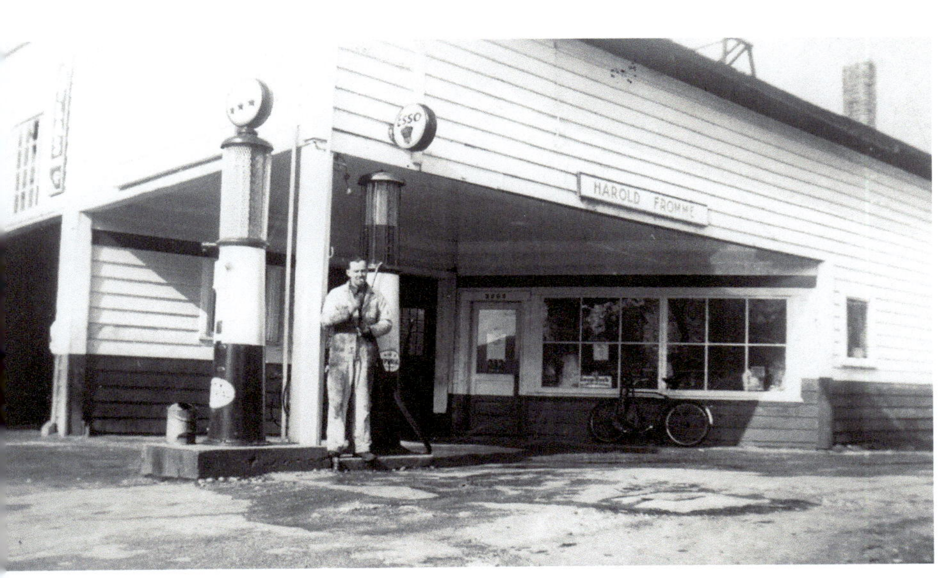

C – Auto-repair garage, late 1930s.

Lynn Valley Lumber Co. Shingle Mill

For many years, the northwest corner of Mountain Highway and Harold Road has been occupied by the Lynn Valley United Church (3201 Mountain Highway). The building was recently demolished and, in 2016, was being replaced with a new building (A) as part of a modern condo development. It's hard to believe there was once a noisy shingle mill here. In fact, the mill's lumber-storage shed, pictured in the 1925 photo (B), was located right where the church has always sat, and will continue to sit. Julius Fromme's Lynn Valley Lumber Company owned this shingle operation, which extended along both sides of Harold Road and included a large shingle-bolt pond. After the mill closed in 1924, Fromme's son Harold converted the lumber shed into an auto-repair garage and gas station, pictured here in the late 1930s (C).

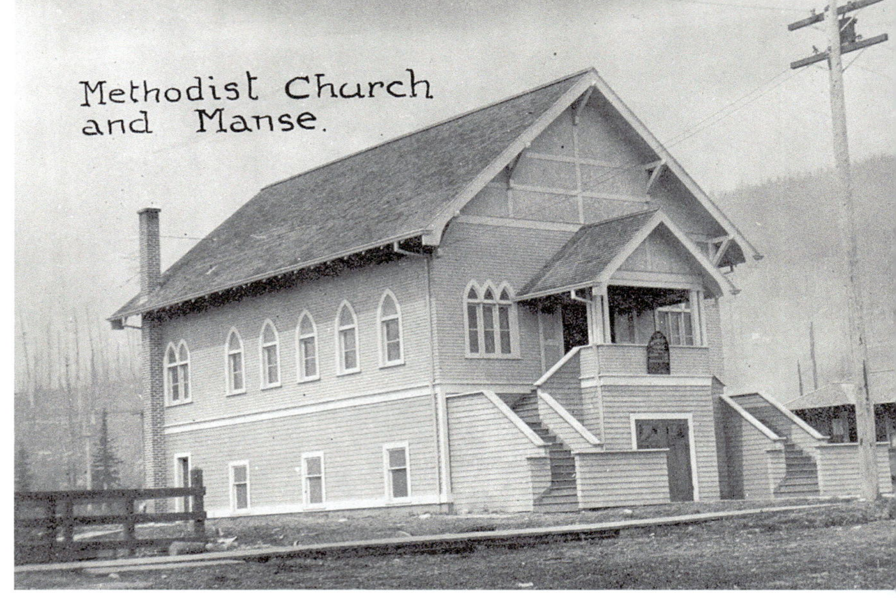

A – Lynn Valley Methodist Church, c.1920.

Old Methodist Church Building

The Lynn Valley Methodist Church, seen here around 1920 (A), once sat on Institute Road where the Lynn Valley School playground is now. Built in 1912, the building was sold to the school board in 1925 when the congregation merged with the Knox Presbyterian Church congregation (see page 98). For years it hosted manual-training classes, dances, concerts, a playschool, and a gymnasium. Then, in 1963, the Lynn Valley Arts Guild purchased the structure from the school board. They moved the top half to a nearby site where it remains today. It's part of the RNB Dance & Theatre Arts Society's studio at 3355 Mountain Highway (B & C). You can see the original church windows in this 2008 photo (D).

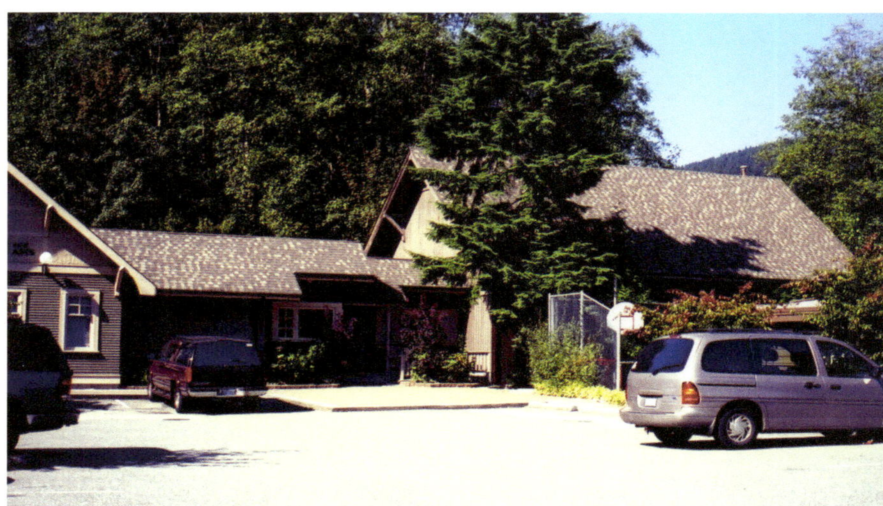
B – Dance-and-theatre studio, 2007.

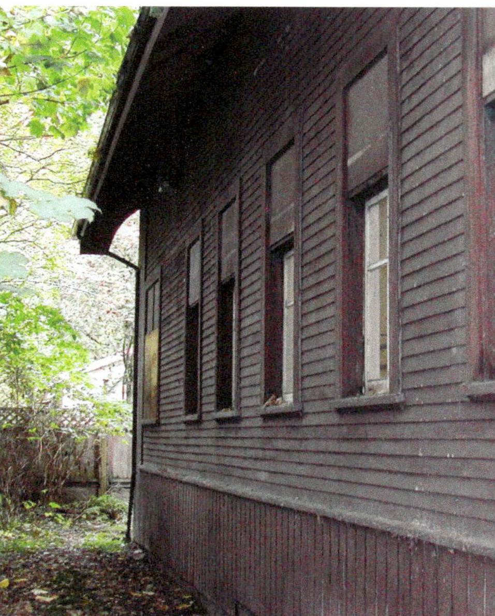
D – Windows, 2008.

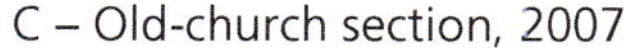

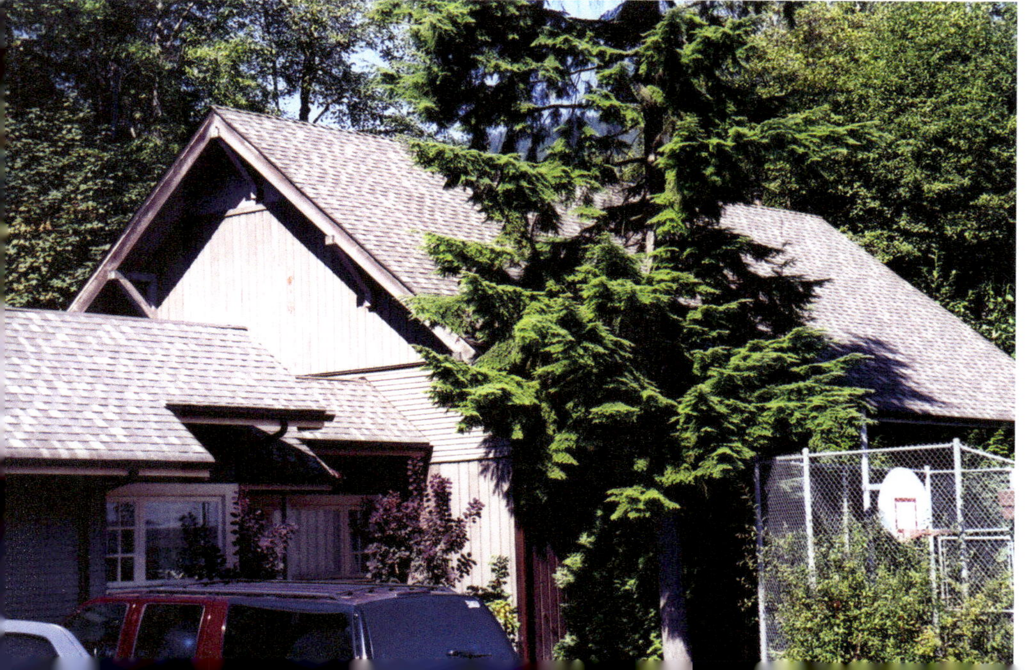
C – Old-church section, 2007.

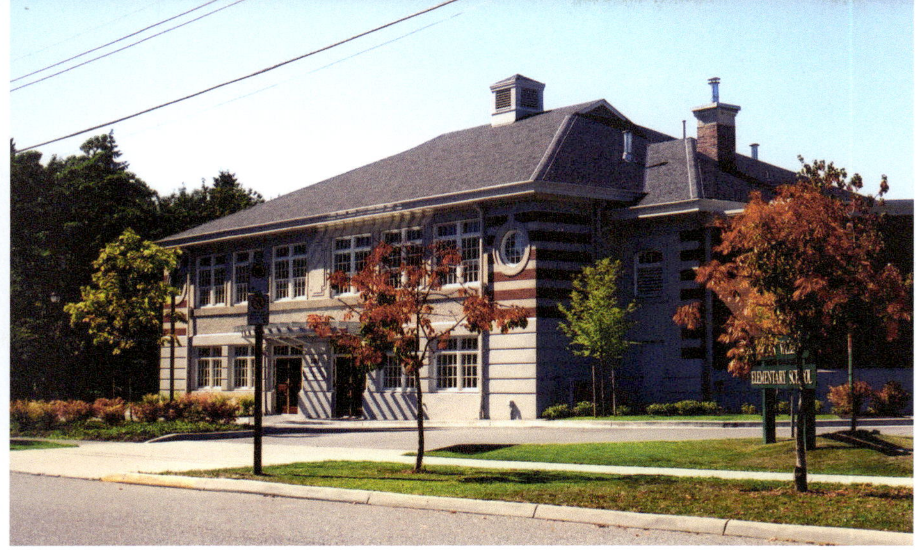

A – Community History Centre, 2007.

The Fourth Lynn Valley School

The Community History Centre, photographed in 2007 (A), is a beautiful, freestanding, brick and sandstone building located at 3203 Institute Road. Now home to the North Vancouver Archives, it was originally the fourth Lynn Valley School. Built in 1920, it was converted to its present use in 2005–2006. For over 80 years, however, it didn't stand alone. It was attached to the *third* Lynn Valley School — the 1911 building it was supposed to replace. The school board had to keep using the older structure due to increasing student enrolment. Here are the two buildings in 2002 (B), viewed from the same angle as in the first photo. Here they are around 1954, seen from the other side (C). The 1911 building was demolished in 2005.

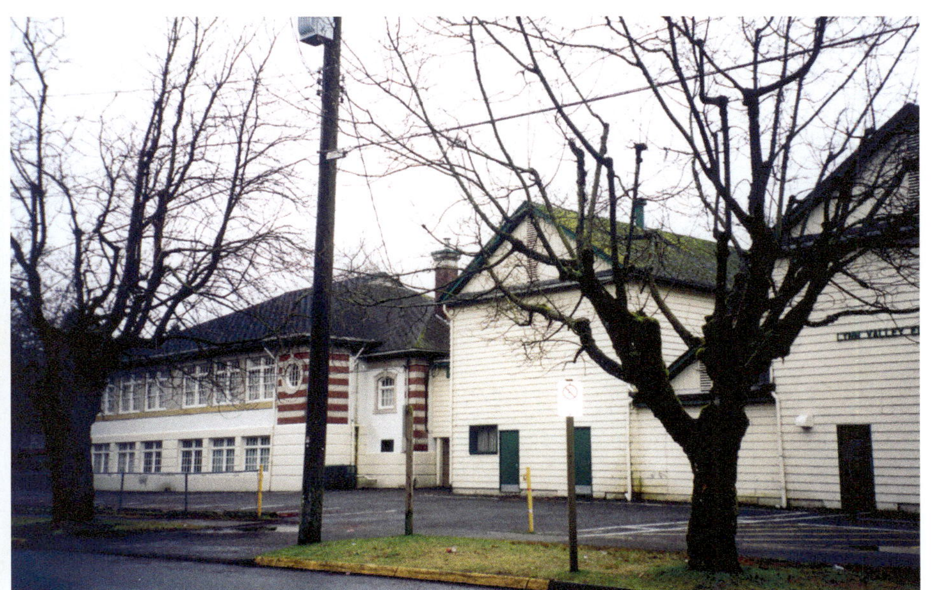

B – Fourth and third schools, 2002.

C – Other side, c.1954.

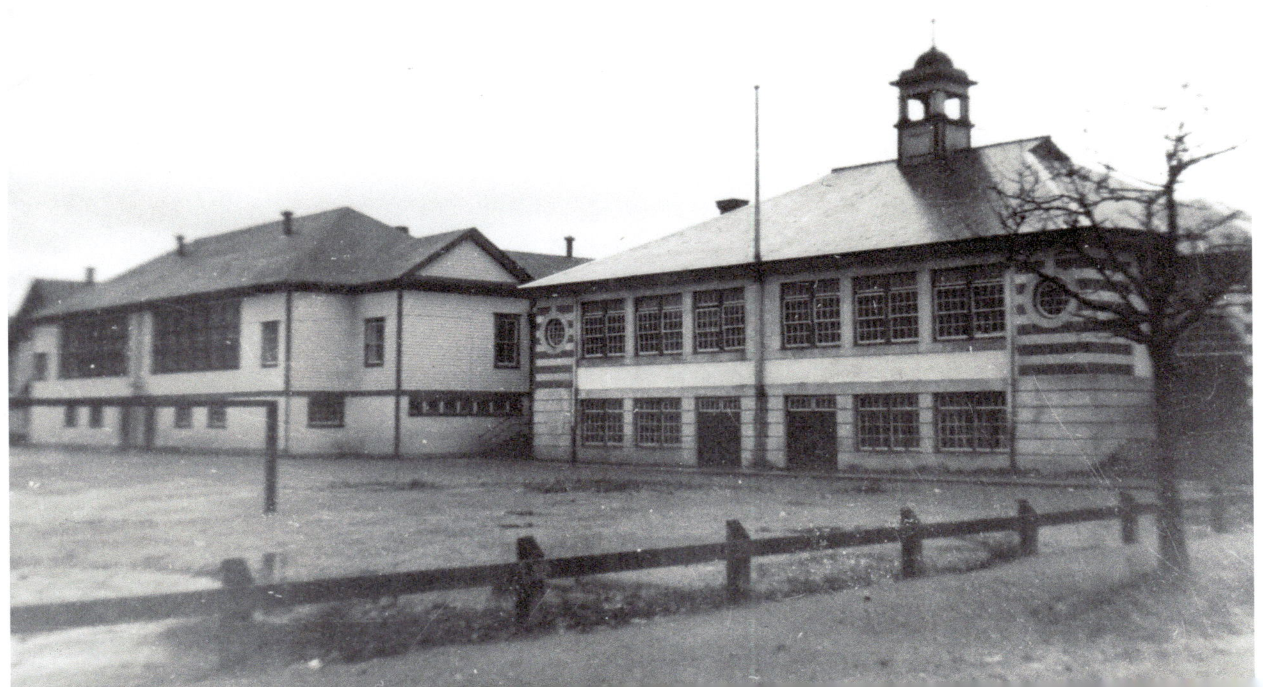

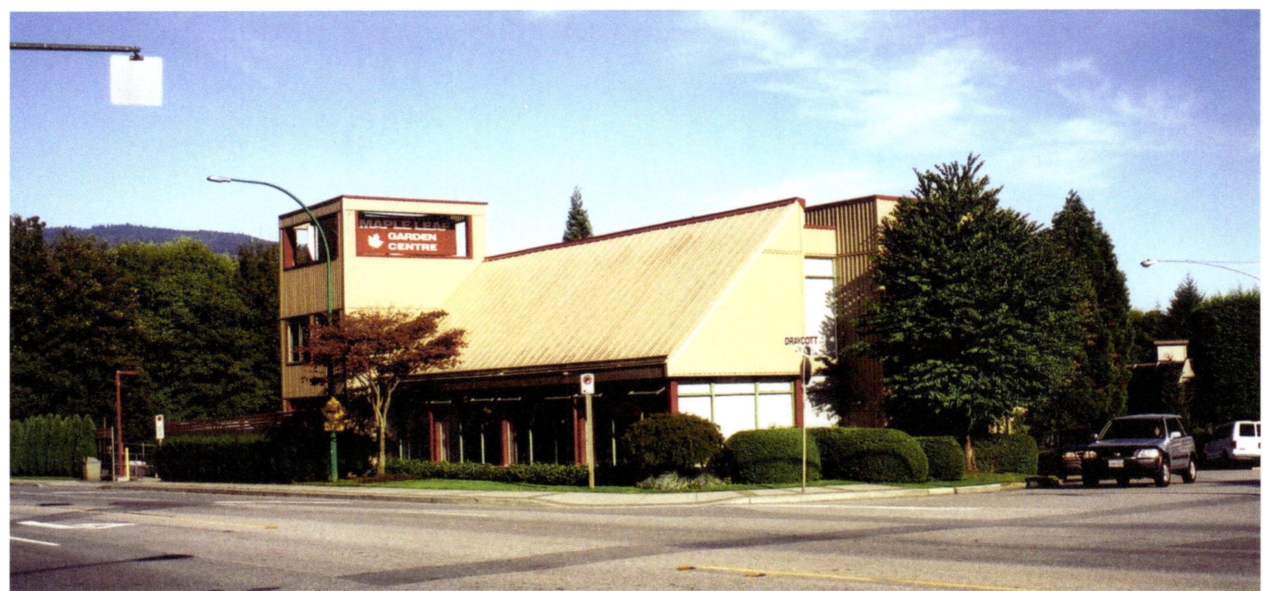

A – Maple Leaf Garden Centre, 2007.

Knox Presbyterian Church

Driving northeast on Lynn Valley Road, you can't miss the imposing façade of the Maple Leaf Garden Centre (A). It's located at the corner of Lynn Valley and Draycott Roads. Upon entering, you'll find that the outdoor plant-displays are below street level, and you have to walk down a ramp to view them. The anomaly is due to there having once been a church complex here — the Knox Presbyterian Church and its minister's house (manse), seen here in 1911 (B). The present-day nursery's below-ground display area grew out of the original hole left by the church basement, when the church was demolished in 1967. The minister's house actually survived into recent times as the nursery owner's home. But it too is gone now.

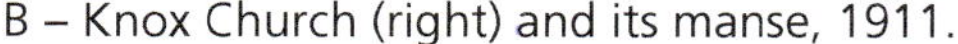

B – Knox Church (right) and its manse, 1911.

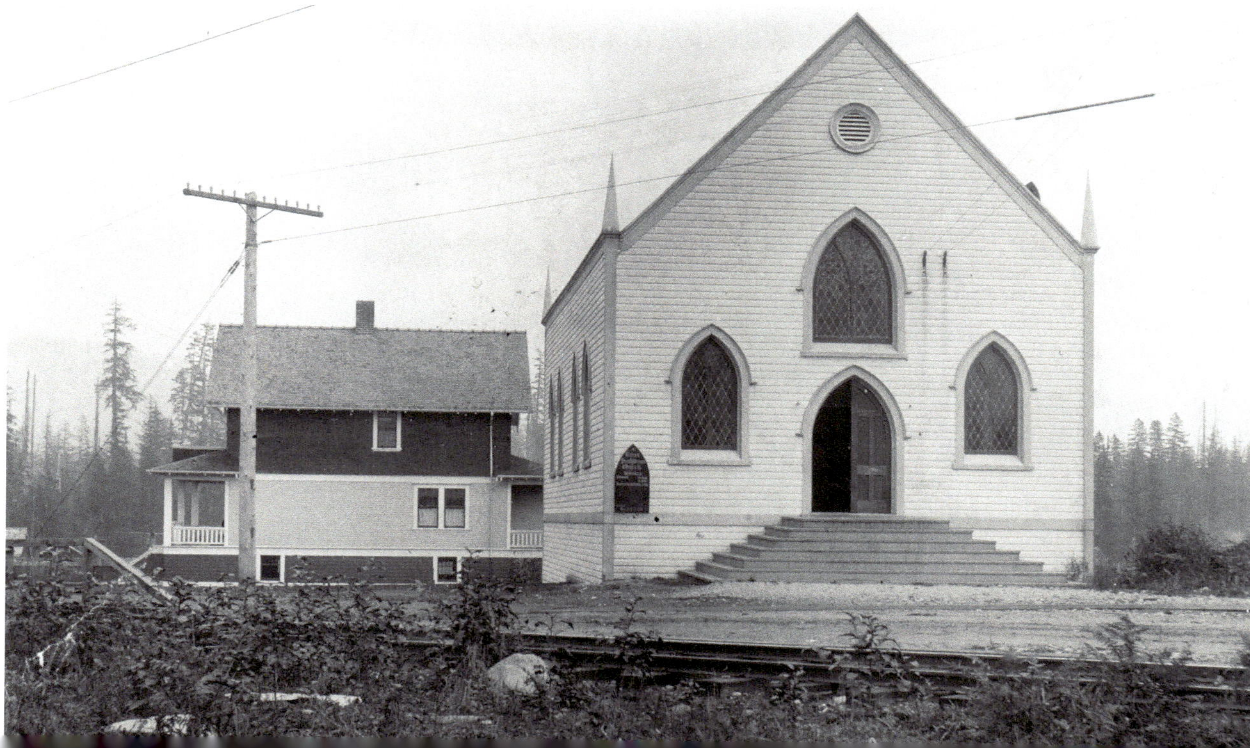

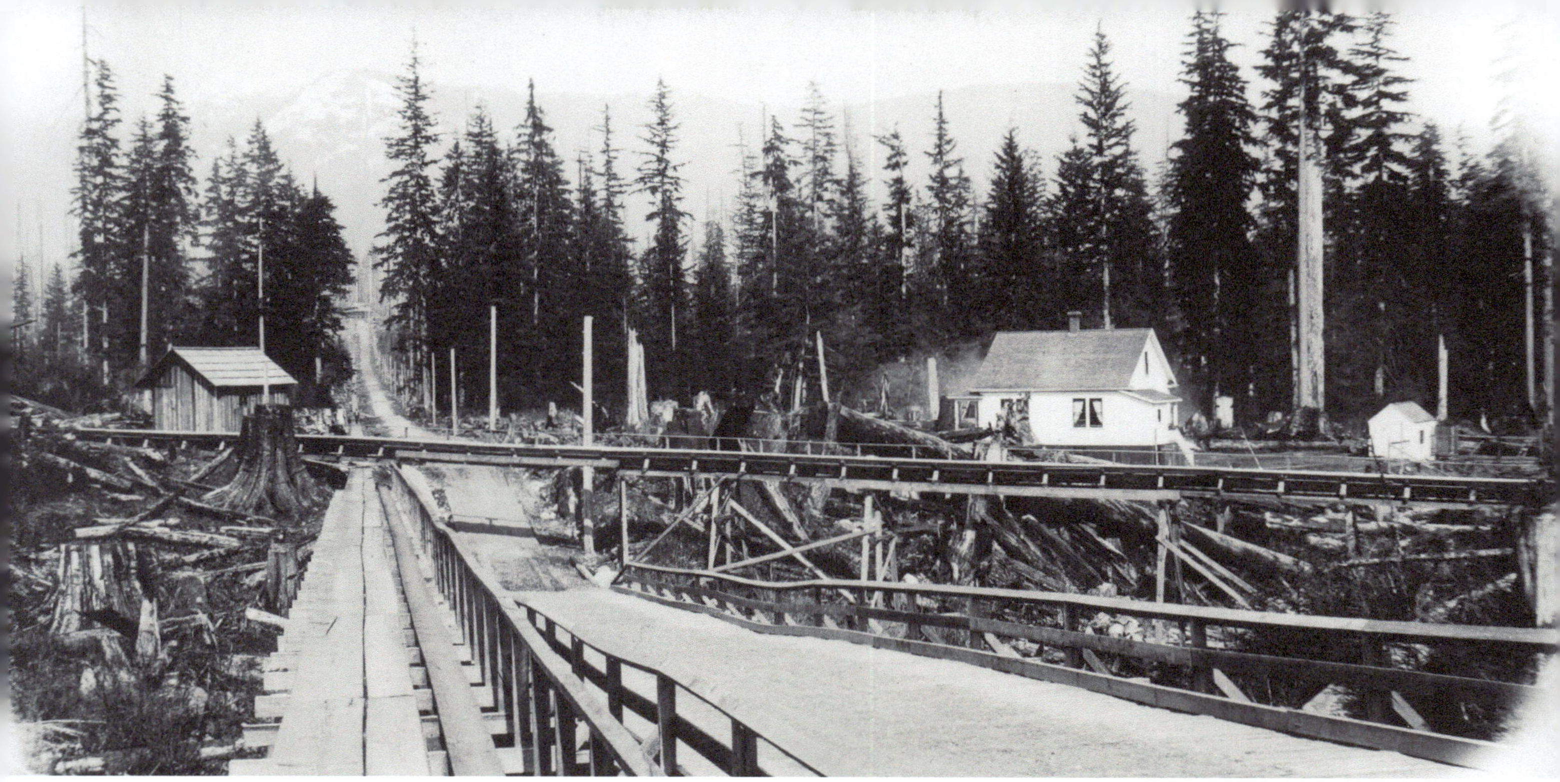

A – Bridge and waste timber, 1909.

Lynn Valley Road, Crossing Hastings Creek

Just northeast of where it intersects with Mountain Highway, Lynn Valley Road crosses Hastings Creek. There used to be a wooden bridge here. In the 1909 view (A), we see this bridge and a messy scene of waste timber. Notice the wooden flume crossing the photo from left to right. This was a trough filled with flowing water. Like a conveyor belt, it carried newly cut shingle bolts down from upper Lynn Valley to the Inlet and a mill. The main part of the bridge dipped under the flume, because in those days flumes had the right of way. That's a separate foot and water-pipe bridge on the left. The 2007 view (B) of Lynn Valley Road shows a modern thoroughfare. It's the same in 2016. You're hardly aware of crossing Hastings Creek.

B – Modern thoroughfare, 2007.

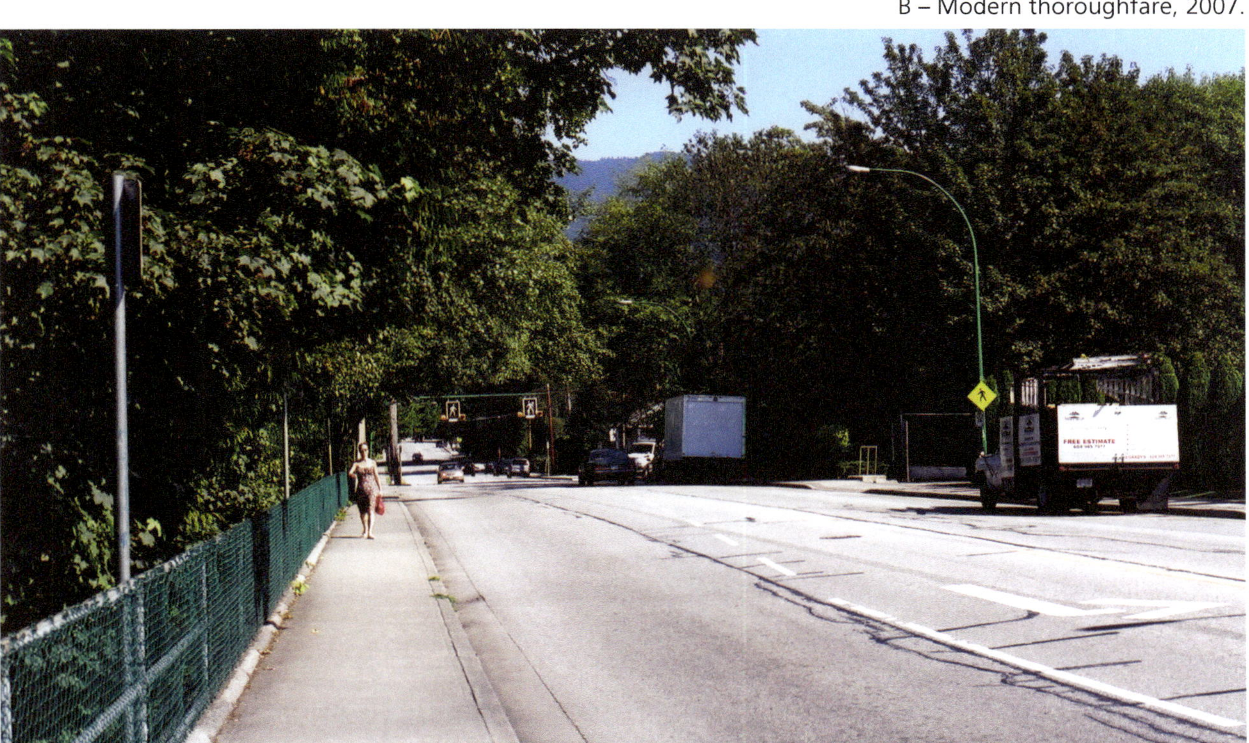

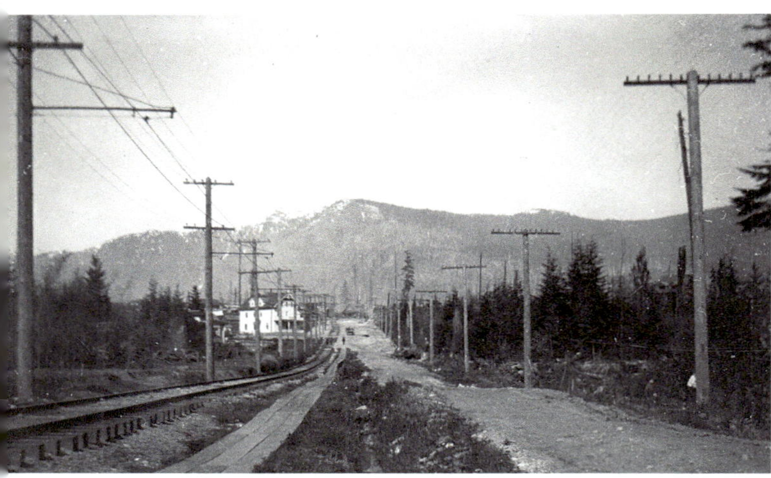

A – Lynn Valley Road, 1914.

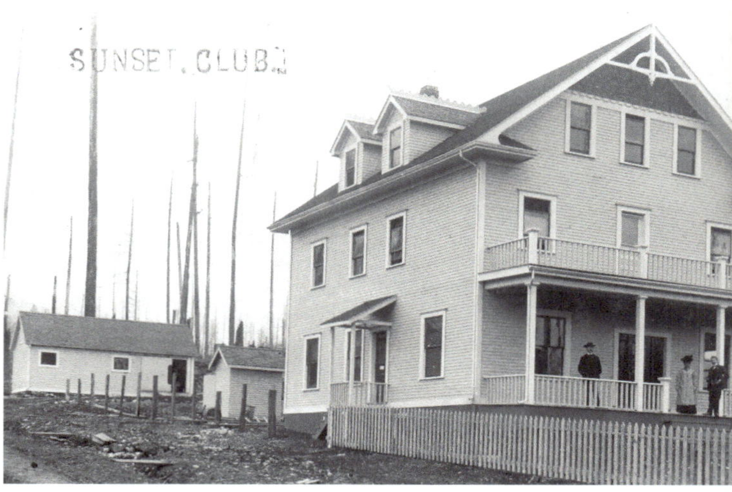

B – Lynn Valley Hotel, c.1913.

The Lynn Valley Hotel

The 1914 photo (A) shows the upper end of Lynn Valley Road. That white building in the distance is the Lynn Valley Hotel, shown here around 1913 (B). Built in 1908, it catered to visitors who came by streetcar to relax in pleasant indoor surroundings and explore the nearby Lynn Canyon Park and suspension bridge (C). It also housed workers employed by the municipality and lumber companies. From the early 1940s on, however, it was a rest home — first "Dovercourt Rest Home," then decades later "Dovercourt Lodge." Today (D) it houses a residential recovery program (1606 Lynn Valley Road).

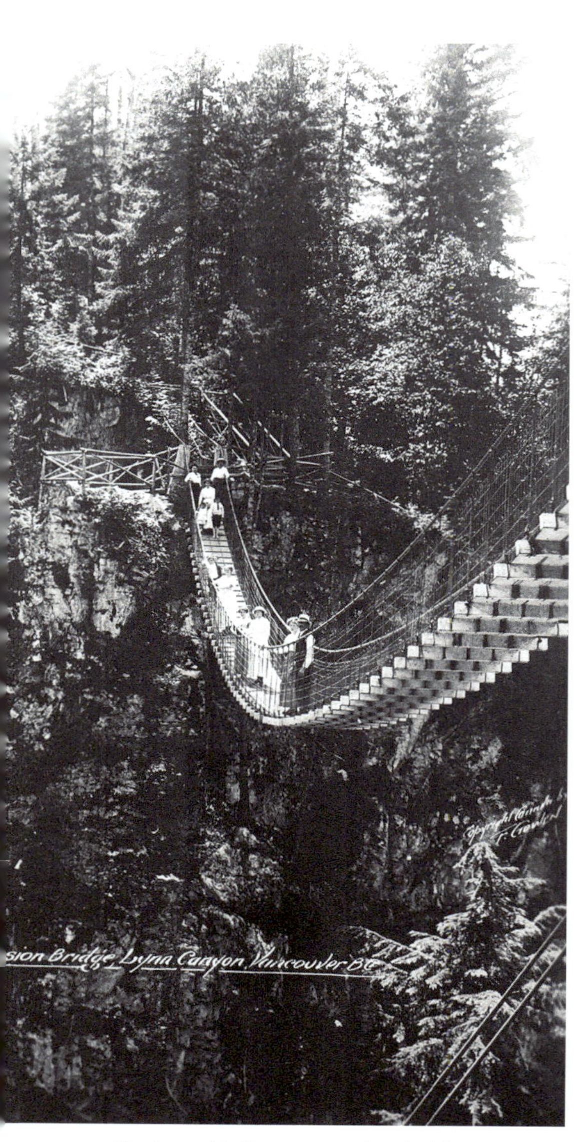

C – Lynn Valley suspension bridge, c.1915.

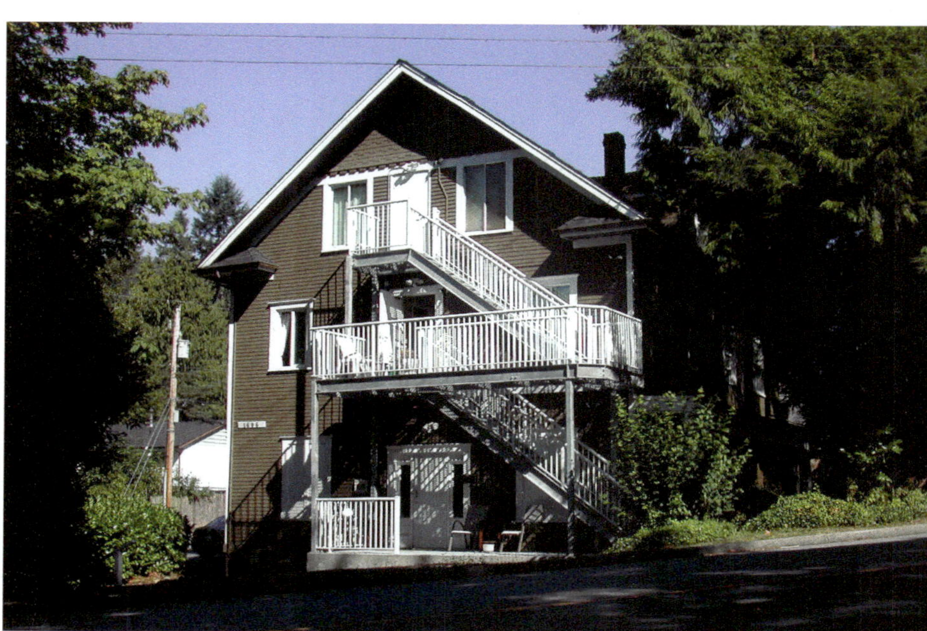

D – Dovercourt, 2016.

6 Mountains

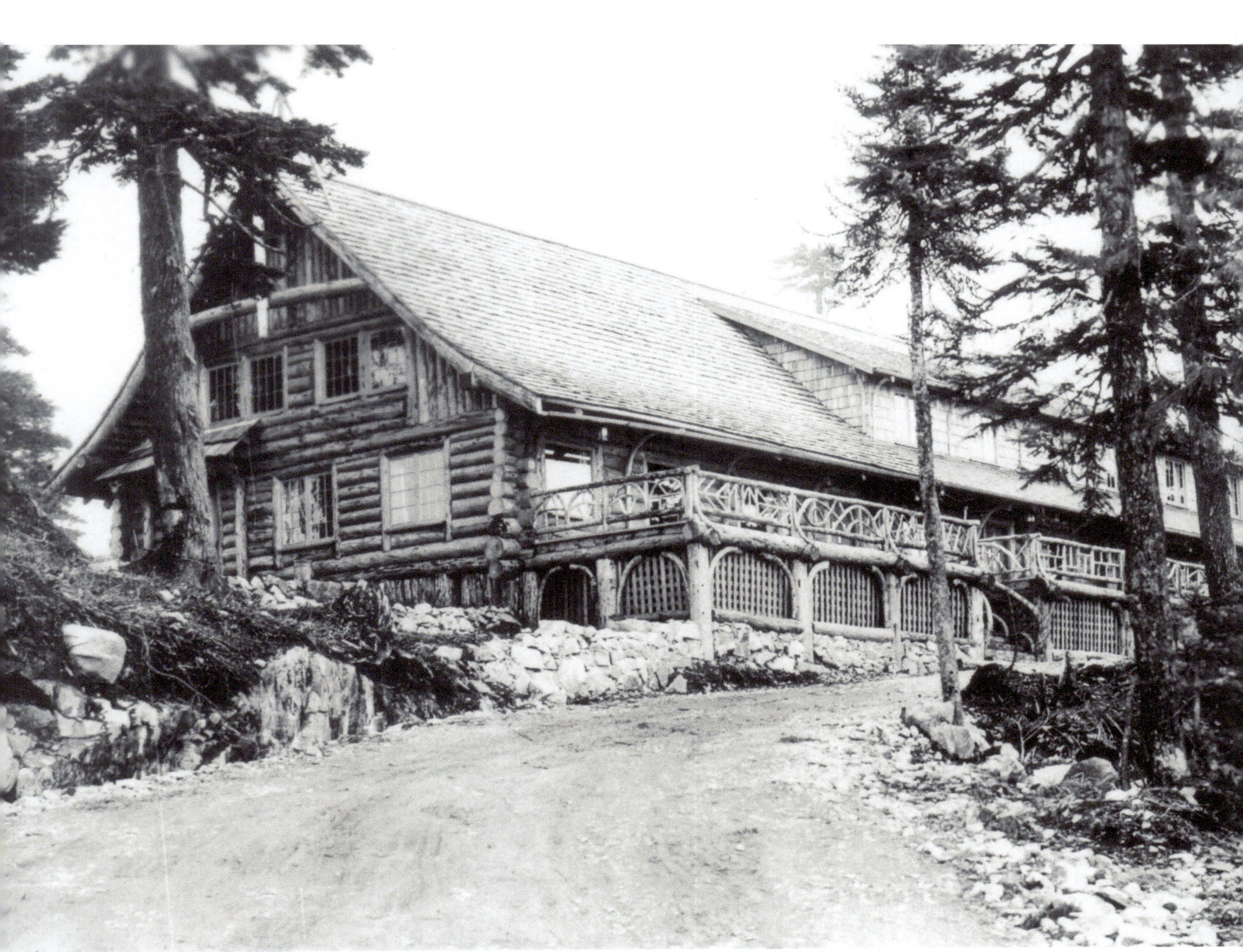

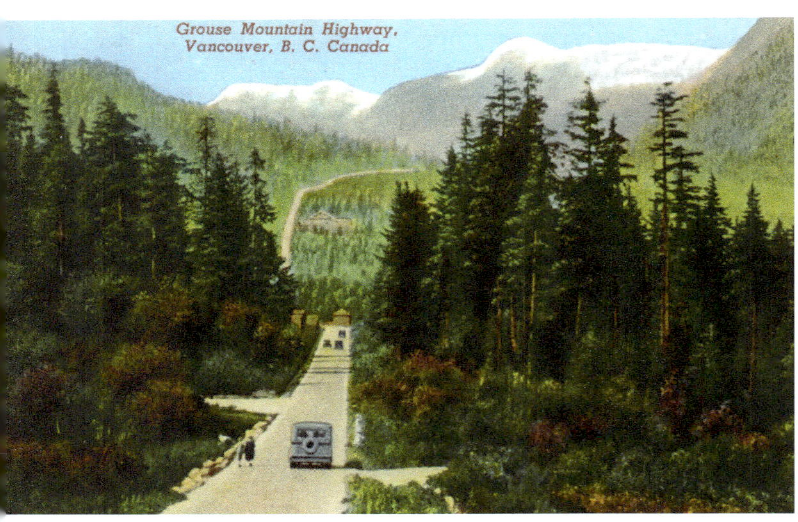

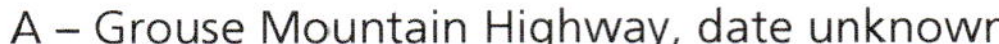
A – Grouse Mountain Highway, date unknown.

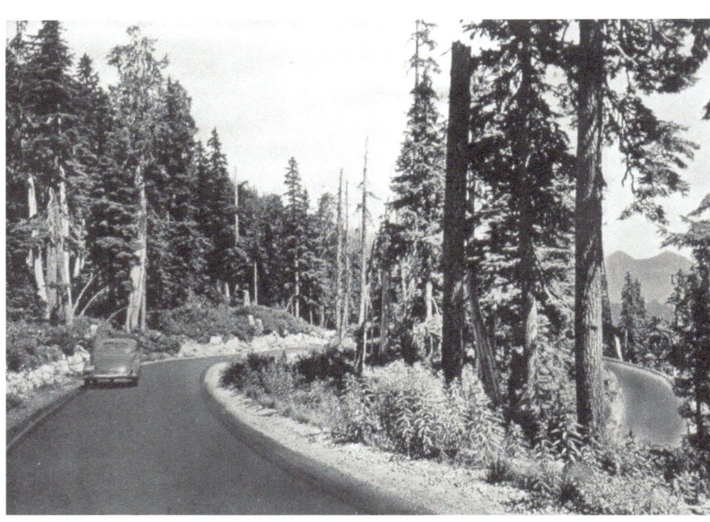
B – Switchback on Grouse, date unknown.

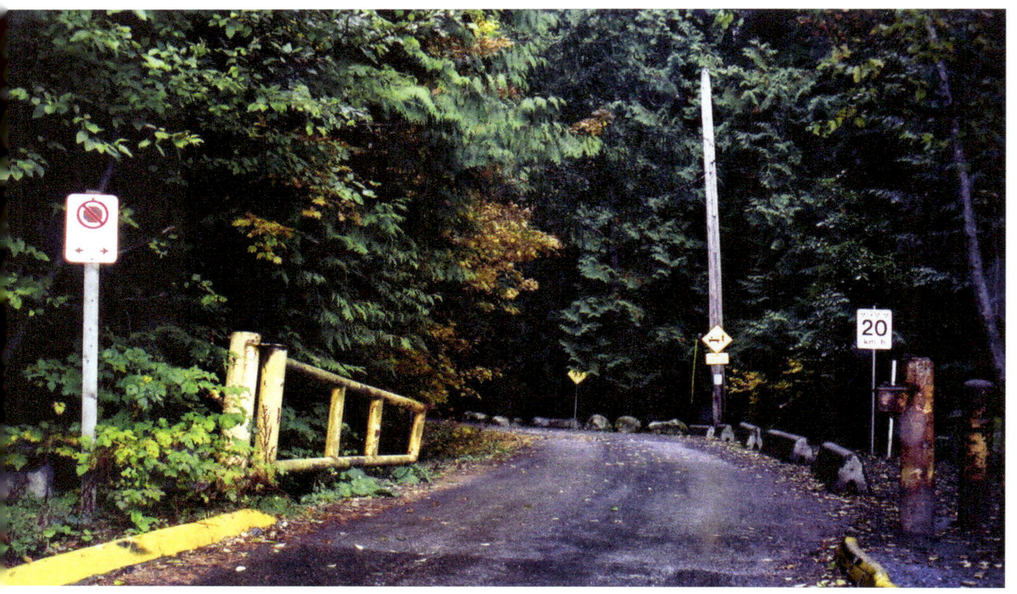

C – Gate at Borthwick Road, 2007.

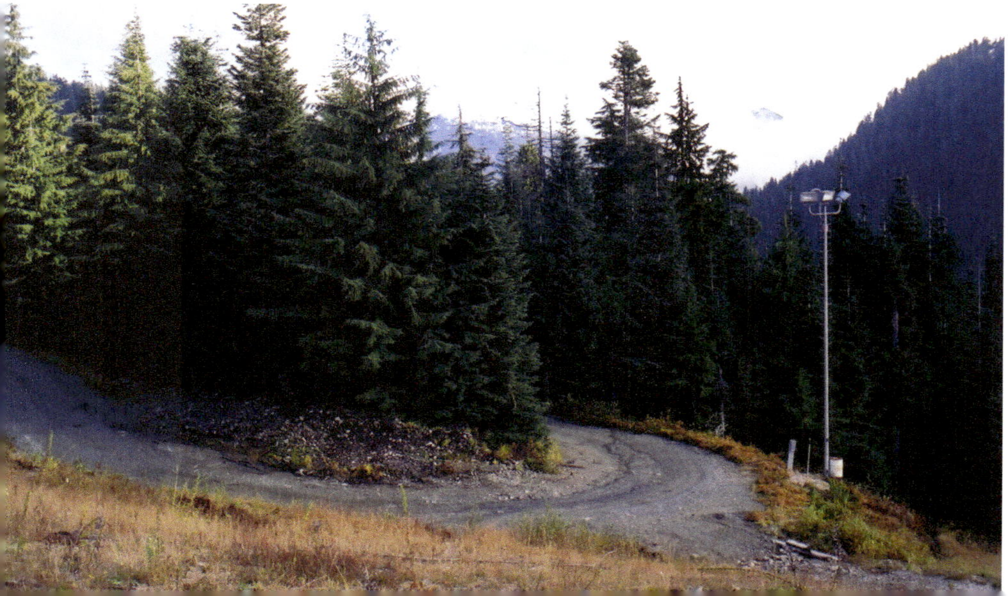
D – Private dirt road, 2007.

Grouse Mountain Highway

Mountain Highway didn't always end abruptly at Borthwick Road like it does now. In the 1940s, 50s and 60s you could drive this paved highway all the way to the top of Grouse Mountain (A). It was called "Grouse Mountain Highway" then. It continued up Fromme Mountain, proceeded across to Grouse, then up to the Grouse Mountain Chalet on top. To get there you had to navigate eight dramatic twists and switchbacks (B). Today there's a gate at Borthwick, seen here in 2007(C). The road beyond (D) is a rough, *unpaved*, private service-road that attracts mountain bikers from around the world!

Grouse Mountain Chairlift

One of the first "double chairlifts" ever built was installed on Grouse Mountain in 1949. The chairlift's Lower Terminal, seen here in the 1950s (A), was located at the top of Skyline Drive. Skiers and others rode up here by car or bus, and then took the chairlift up the mountain to "The Cut" (main ski area) in two stages, seen in this other 1950s view (B). Years later the chairlift and its terminals were removed, replaced by the Skyride and Gondola located further west. The deserted Lower Terminal site was eventually swallowed up by forest, as you can see in the 2007 photo (C) taken from an angle similar to that of the first photo.

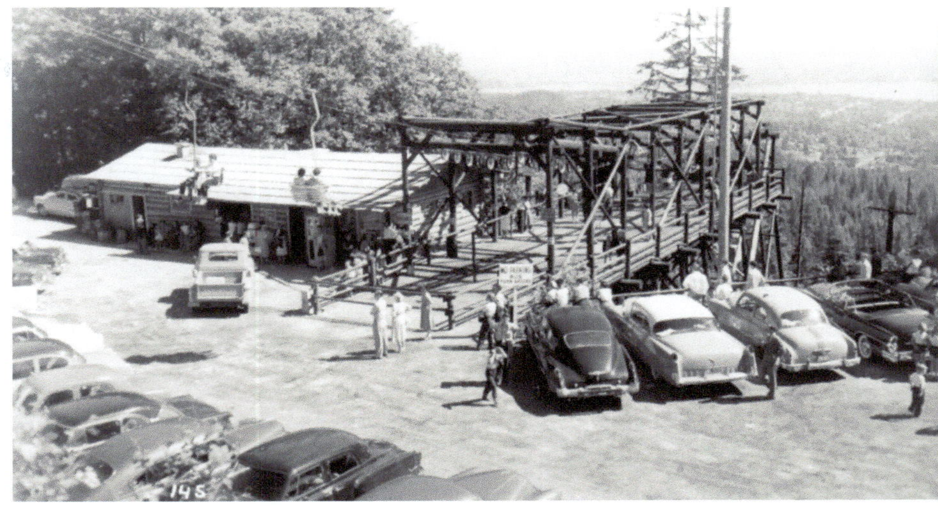

A – Lower Terminal, 1950s.

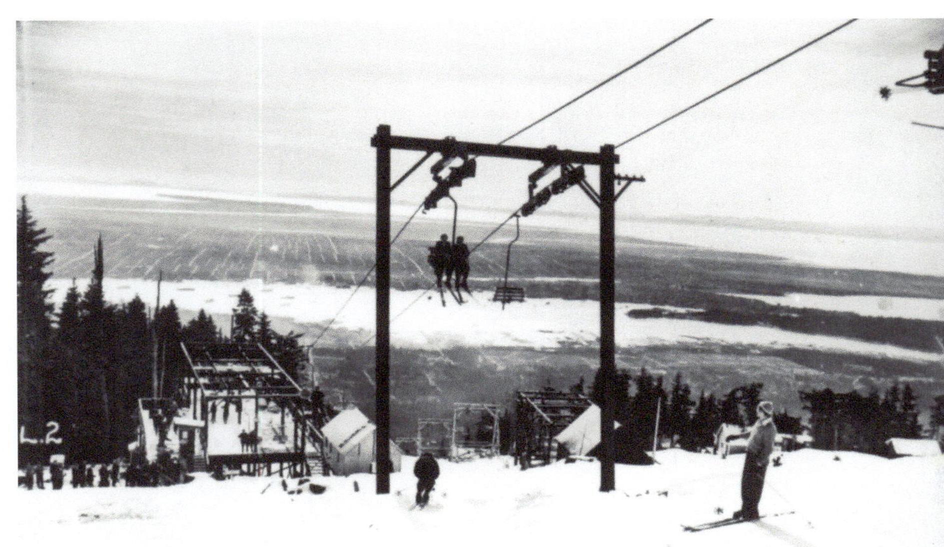

B – Two chairlift stages, 1950s.

C – Lower Terminal site, 2007.

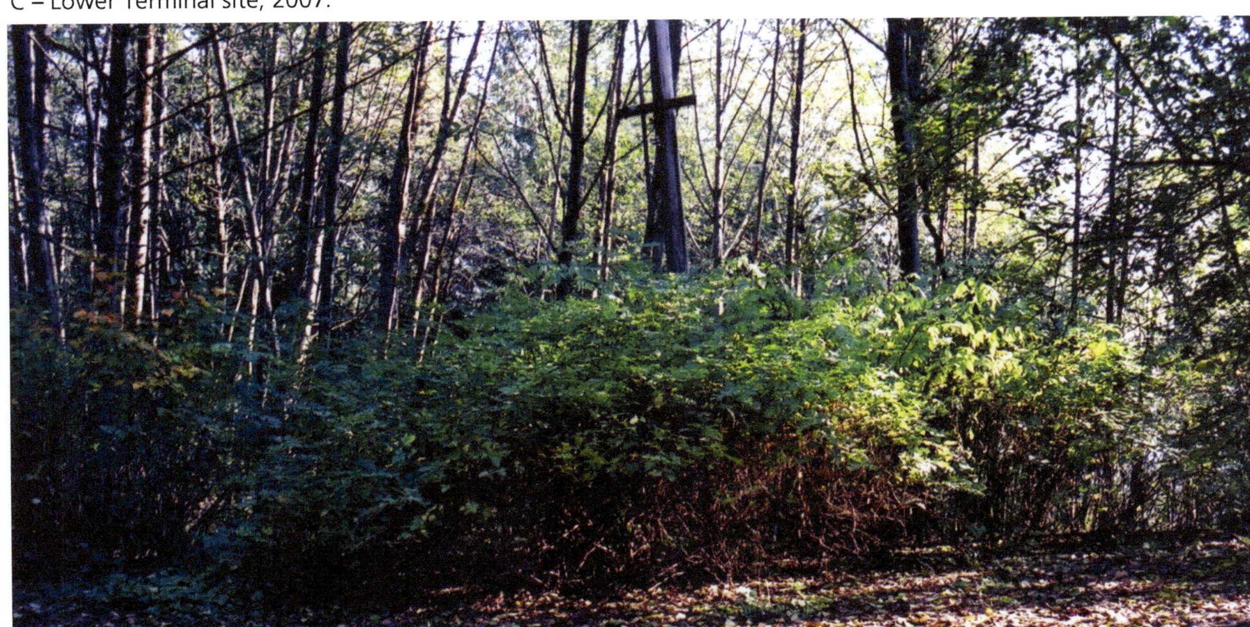

Grouse Mountain Chalet

The Grouse Mountain Chalet opened in 1926. Perched 4,000 feet above sea level, it was by the 1930s a popular destination for skiers, hikers, mountain climbers, horseback riders, vacationers, and sightseers. The original building (more were added later) was constructed of natural logs, as you can see in this early view (A). It had eleven bedrooms upstairs, and a kitchen, dining room, ballroom, and lounge downstairs. The lounge, seen here around 1926 (B), featured a large stone fireplace, rustic décor, and a log staircase to the second floor. Unfortunately the chalet burned down in 1962. The site, seen here in 2008 (C), is now covered with carved wooden statues and a centre for equipment-rentals & zipline-tours.

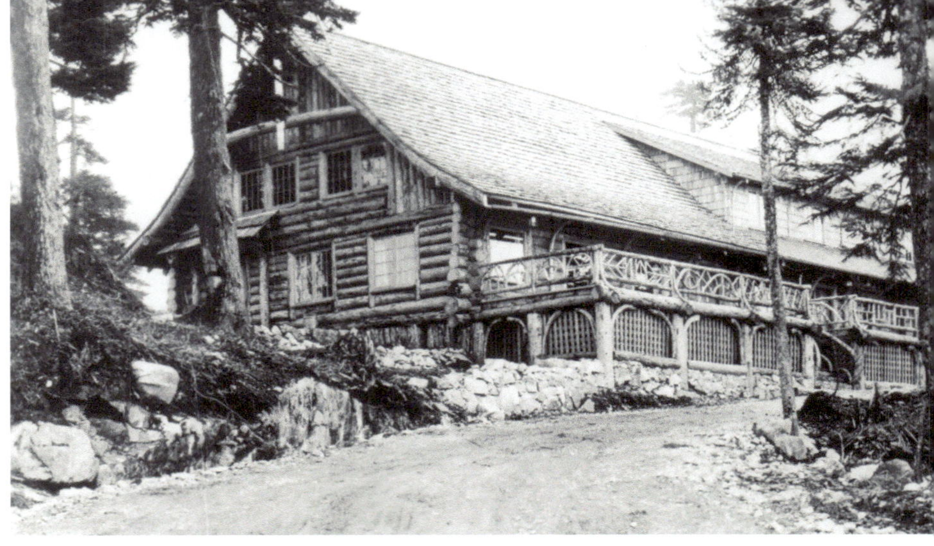

A – Early photo of chalet, date unknown.

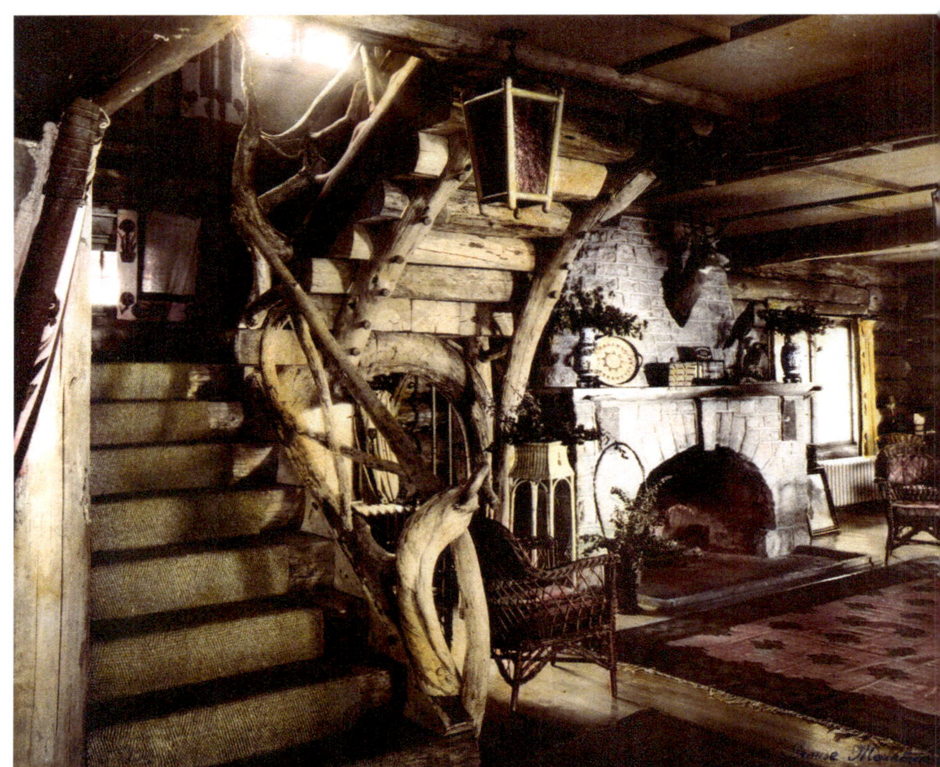

B – Chalet lounge, c.1926.

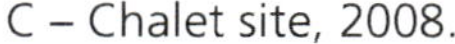

C – Chalet site, 2008.

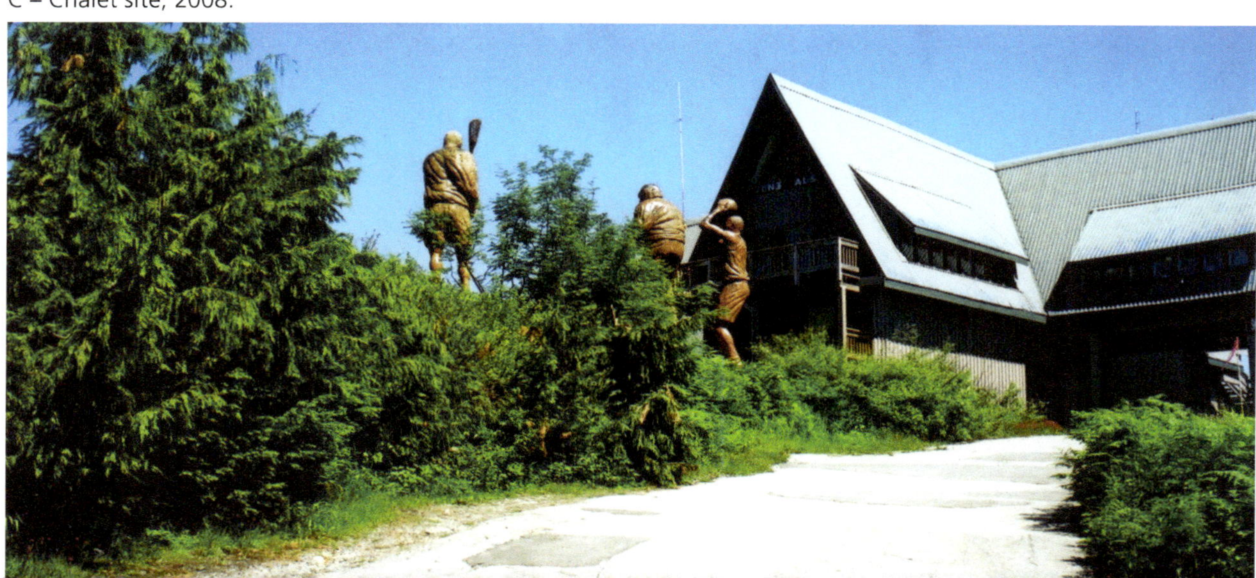

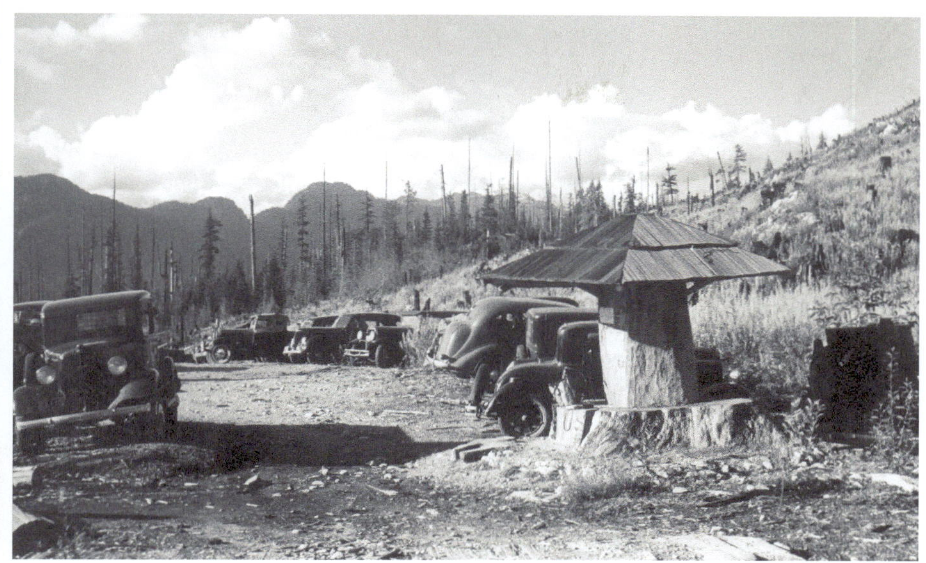

A – Parking lot, 1935.

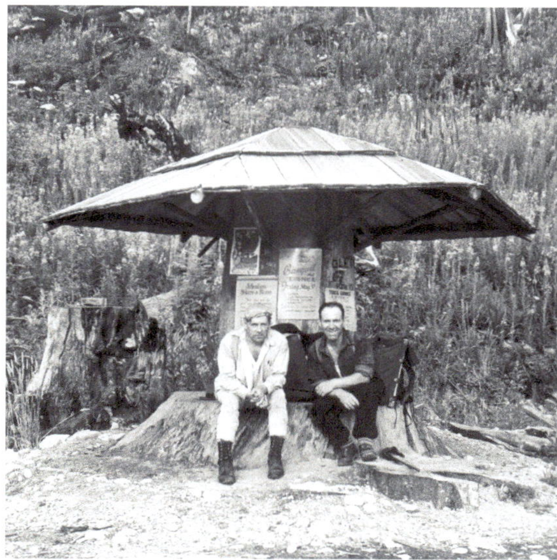

B – Mushroom shelter, 1935.

Mushroom Shelter on Seymour Mountain

In the 1920s and 30s many hikers and skiers had cabins on Seymour Mountain. They'd drive their cars partway up on an old logging road, leave them in a parking lot, and then proceed on foot to their cabins for a few days' recreation. Here's a 1935 photo of the parking lot (A). Notice the mushroom-shaped shelter at the right. You can see it better in another 1935 photo (B). Carved from a cedar stump, this was the community bulletin board where people left messages for each other. A 2007 view of the parking lot reveals a regenerating forest and a fenced-in, decaying shelter (C). No one needs a cabin now. You just drive to the top, ski or hike, then drive home the same day.

C – Forest and shelter remnant (brown), 2007.

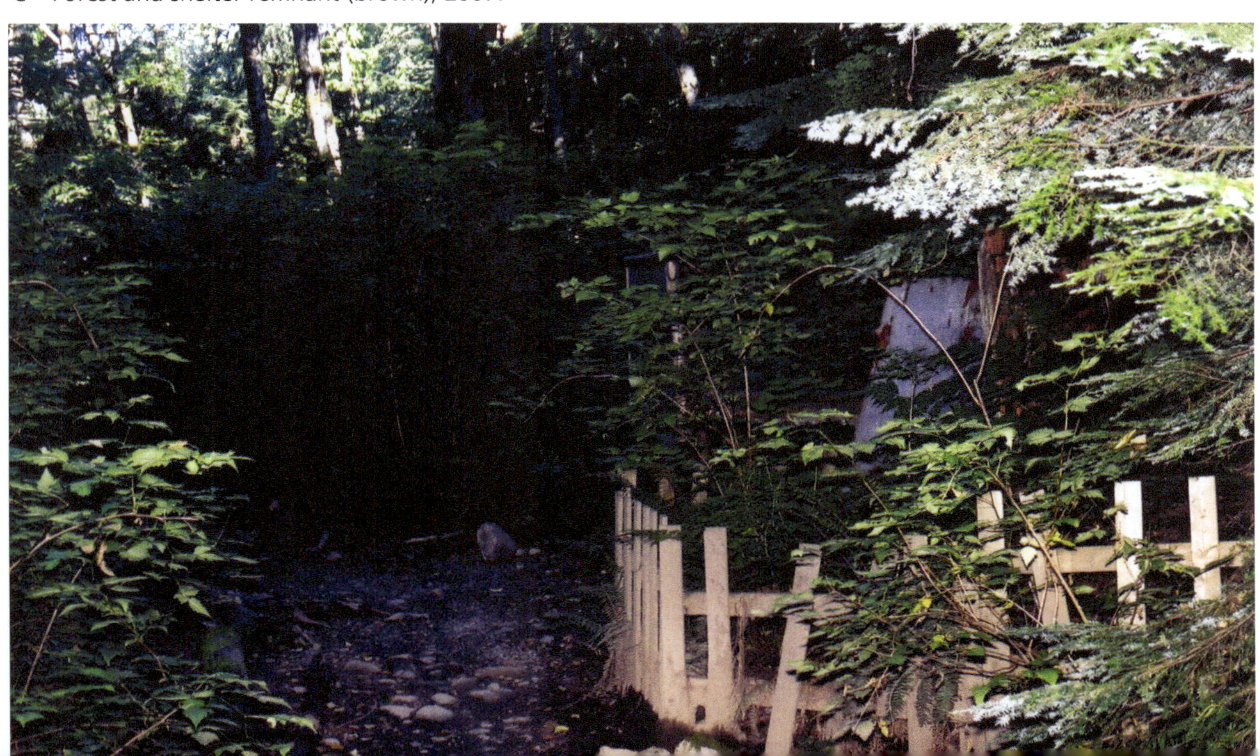

Picture Credits

Introduction

A – Clear-cut, 1911. City of Vancouver Archives, CVA Dist. N83.2

B – Residential area, 2007. Sharon J. Proctor

1. Lonsdale

Esplanade

A – Esplanade, 1907. North Vancouver Museum & Archives 5704

B – View from Chesterfield, 1907. North Vancouver Museum & Archives 5705

C – Same view, 2016. Sharon J. Proctor

Hotel North Vancouver

A – Modern buildings, 2016. Sharon J. Proctor

B – Hotel North Vancouver, c. 1912. North Vancouver Museum & Archives 15805

C – View from the water, 1908. Philip Timms photo, Vancouver Public Library, VPL 5498

Lower Lonsdale

A – Lower Lonsdale, 1905. City of Vancouver Archives, CVA 677-702

B – Lower Lonsdale (southbound lane), 2016. Sharon J. Proctor

Horne Bros. Shingle Mill

A – Concrete circle, 2016. Sharon J. Proctor

B – Aerial view of mill, 1927. North Vancouver Museum & Archives 5560

Ferry No. 5

A – Ferry approaching wharf, 1958. North Vancouver Museum & Archives 2061

B – Floating restaurant, date unknown. North Vancouver Museum & Archives 15806. Reproduced under a non-exclusive licence issued by the Copyright Board of Canada in cooperation with the Canadian Artists' Representation Copyright Collective.

C – Former berth, 2016. Sharon J. Proctor

Burrard Dry Dock

A – Burrard Dry Dock, 1944. North Vancouver Museum & Archives 27-8H

B – Quitting time, 1944. North Vancouver Museum & Archives 27-678

C – Ships under construction, 1945. North Vancouver Museum & Archives 27-2289

D – Two saved buildings & company crane, 2016. Sharon J. Proctor

Burrard Dry Dock Pier

A – Restored pier, 2007. Sharon J. Proctor

B – Aerial view, 1963. North Vancouver Museum & Archives 27-8M

C – Stationary crane, 1953. North Vancouver Museum & Archives 27-30

D – Base piece, 2007. Sharon J. Proctor

The Machine Shop

A – Machine Shop skeleton, 2007. Sharon J. Proctor

B – Interior, 1945. North Vancouver Museum & Archives 27-86

C – Exterior, 1991. North Vancouver Museum & Archives 15010

D – Machine Shop site, 2016. Sharon J. Proctor

East 1st Street

A – Looking east, c. 1905. City of Vancouver Archives, CVA 677-831

B – Same view, 2016. Sharon J. Proctor

Lonsdale & 1st: northeast corner

A – Northeast corner, 1906. North Vancouver Museum & Archives 14683

B – Modern view, 2016. Sharon J. Proctor

C – Friendly Grocery, 2016. Sharon J. Proctor

Lonsdale & 1st: northwest corner

A – Northwest corner, 1936. North Vancouver Museum & Archives 5710

B – Same corner, 2016. Sharon J. Proctor

C – Food Warehouse entrance, 2016. Sharon J. Proctor

St. Alice Hotel

A – St. Alice Hotel, 1970. North Vancouver Museum & Archives 15085

B – Condominium tower, 2007. Sharon J. Proctor

Palace Hotel
A – Palace Hotel, c. 1909. North Vancouver Museum & Archives 8155
B – Central courtyard, date unknown. North Vancouver Museum & Archives 8166
C – Ladies reception room, date unknown. North Vancouver Museum & Archives 8167
D – "Olympic" high-rise, 2007. Sharon J. Proctor

Lonsdale & 3rd: northwest corner
A – Morden home, c. 1907. North Vancouver Museum & Archives 8179
B – Everett Motors, 1950s. North Vancouver Museum & Archives 11004
C – Condominium complex, 2007. Sharon J. Proctor

John Brind's Blacksmith Shop
A – Blacksmith shop, 1913. North Vancouver Museum & Archives 2767
B – Interior, 1920. North Vancouver Museum & Archives 2772
C – NIKI, 2007. Sharon J. Proctor

100 Block of East 3rd
A – East 3rd, c. 1910. North Vancouver Museum & Archives 9822
B – Same view, 2008. Sharon J. Proctor

Funeral Chapel
A – Funeral Chapel, c. 1950. North Vancouver Museum & Archives 14087
B – Chapel, early 1960s. North Vancouver Museum & Archives 14096
C – High-rise & parking, 2007. Sharon J. Proctor

The McNair Home
A – McNair family home, 1907. North Vancouver Museum & Archives 2842
B – Part of a condo complex, 2007. Sharon J. Proctor

The Cenotaph
A – North Vancouver Cenotaph, c. 1925. North Vancouver Museum & Archives 3446
B – Close-up of base, c. 1923. North Vancouver Museum & Archives 8933
C – Added plaque: Boer War, World Wars I & II, 2007. Sharon J. Proctor
D – Korea & Afghanistan, 2016. Sharon J. Proctor

Morden Hall
A – Morden Hall, c. 1907. North Vancouver Museum & Archives 1867
B – Apartment building, 2008. Sharon J. Proctor

Corner of Lonsdale & 8th
A – The Burnes home, 1906. North Vancouver Museum & Archives p86
B – Drug store, early 1950s. North Vancouver Museum & Archives 10491
C – Office building, 2007. Sharon J. Proctor

Vintage Buildings at 10th & St. Georges
A – Five buildings, 1920s. North Vancouver Museum & Archives 11422
B – Four buildings, 2007. Sharon J. Proctor
C – "The Colonial" apartments, 2008. Sharon J. Proctor
D – The houses, 2008. Sharon J. Proctor

Fire Hall
A – Fire hall, 1921. North Vancouver Museum & Archives 7644
B – Fire hall, 1950s. North Vancouver Museum & Archives 2659
C – Modern fire hall, 2007. Sharon J. Proctor

The First Hospital
A – North Vancouver Hospital, c. 1908-1910. North Vancouver Museum & Archives p42
B – Apartment complex, 2007. Sharon J. Proctor

The Second Hospital
A – North Vancouver General Hospital, date unknown. North Vancouver Museum & Archives 10402
B – Lonsdale Private Hospital, 1983. North Vancouver Museum & Archives 4969
C – Condominiums, 2007. Sharon J. Proctor

The Curtis Home
A – Petro Canada station, 2007. Sharon J. Proctor
B – Curtis home, date unknown. North Vancouver Museum & Archives 4217
C – Bridge over stream, date unknown. North Vancouver Museum & Archives 4221
D – Flowerbeds, date unknown. North Vancouver Museum & Archives 4218

Looking North on Lonsdale from 13th
A – Central Lonsdale, mid 1940s. North Vancouver Museum & Archives 4661
B – Central Lonsdale, 2016. Sharon J. Proctor

The Shakespeare Home
A – Psychiatric Services, 2007. Sharon J. Proctor
B – Shakespeare home, c. 1912. North Vancouver Museum & Archives 7717

Harbottle's Jersey Products
A – Harbottle's store, c. 1950. North Vancouver Museum & Archives 8791
B – Commercial building, 2008. Sharon J. Proctor

The Irwin Home
A – High-rise on East 15th, 2016. Sharon J. Proctor
B – Parking in the rear, 2016. Sharon J. Proctor

C – Irwin house, 1910. North Vancouver Museum & Archives p15

D – Irwin family on grounds, 1910. North Vancouver Museum & Archives 2572

Lonsdale Theatre

A – Lonsdale Theatre, 1920s. North Vancouver Museum & Archives 6344

B – Opening audience, 1911. North Vancouver Museum & Archives 2427

C – HSBC bank, 2008. Sharon J. Proctor

The Jackson Home

A – Jackson home, date unknown. North Vancouver Museum & Archives 8326

B – Shipyard staff at work, 1945. Picture copied from article in Wallace Shipbuilder, Vol. 3, No. 8, July 1945; Versatile Pacific Shipyards Inc. Fonds No. 27; North Vancouver Museum & Archives

C – Hospital parking lot, 2008. Sharon J. Proctor

Japanese Tea Gardens

A – Teahouse, 1911. North Vancouver Museum & Archives 9819

B – Tower, date unknown. North Vancouver Museum & Archives 4360

C – Residential area, 2007. Sharon J. Proctor

Horticultural Hall

A – Horticultural Hall, 1910. North Vancouver Museum & Archives 26-3-2

B – Harry Jerome Recreation Centre, 2008. Sharon J. Proctor

North Vancouver High School

A – North Vancouver High School, 1938. North Vancouver Museum & Archives 5339

B – Sadie Hawkins Day dance, c. 1960. North Vancouver Museum & Archives 10528

C – Provincial Courthouse, 2007. Sharon J. Proctor

"Mickey" McDougall's Former Home

A – "Mickey" McDougall, date unknown. North Vancouver Museum & Archives 4243

B – McDougall home, c. 1945. North Vancouver Museum & Archives 7723

C – Empty United Lodge Rest Home, 2007. Sharon J. Proctor

D – Part of condo complex, 2016. Sharon J. Proctor

The Stoker Farm

A – Barn and house, 1979. North Vancouver Museum & Archives 4407

B – Stoker house, 1980. North Vancouver Museum & Archives 6745

C – Early front-view of house, date unknown. North Vancouver Museum & Archives 8605

D – Condominiums, 2016. Sharon J. Proctor

Kingsley School for Boys

A – Kingsley School, c. 1935. North Vancouver Museum & Archives 5260

B – Dormitory, c. 1935. North Vancouver Museum & Archives 5268

C – Physical training, c. 1935. North Vancouver Museum & Archives 5267

D – Residential complex, 2008. Sharon J. Proctor

Thomas Nye Home

A – The Nye mansion, 1912. North Vancouver Museum & Archives 3900

B – Part of residential development, 2008. Sharon J. Proctor

2. West to the Capilano River

St. Paul's Catholic Church

A – St. Paul's Church, 1920s. North Vancouver Museum & Archives 15804

B – St. Paul's Church, 2007. Sharon J. Proctor

St. Paul's Indian Residential School

A – St. Paul's Indian Residential School, 1920s. North Vancouver Museum & Archives 11417

B – St. Thomas Aquinas High School, 2008. Sharon J. Proctor

The McNeish Home

A – Empty McNeish house, 1982. North Vancouver Museum & Archives 6041

B – Interior, 1982. North Vancouver Museum & Archives 6049

C – Townhouses, 2008. Sharon J. Proctor

"Three Way" Intersection

A – Three streets converge, 1957. North Vancouver Museum & Archives 13730

B – Same intersection, 2008. Sharon J. Proctor

Capilano Timber Company Sawmill

A – Sawmill, 1928. Leonard Frank photo, Vancouver Public Library, VPL 5954

B – Hauling logs to the mill, 1920. North Vancouver Museum & Archives 1174

C – Seaspan, 2014. Courtesy of Seaspan International Ltd.

Pemberton Gardens

A – Curry Feast restaurant, 2008. Sharon J. Proctor

B – Promotional brochure, 1925. North Vancouver Museum & Archives [c 1925]-15

C – House on West 17th, 2007. Sharon J. Proctor

Wartime Housing & Westview School

A – Wartime houses, 1943. Images NA-41450 & NA-41451 courtesy of Royal BC Museum, BC Archives

B – Same area, 2008. Sharon J. Proctor

C – Original Westview Elementary School, 1980. North Vancouver Museum & Archives 3421

D – Playing field, 2008. Sharon J. Proctor

Tourist Camp on Marine Drive

A – Entrance to auto camp, 1928. Leonard Frank photo, Vancouver Public Library, VPL 6287

B – Log cabins, 1928. Leonard Frank photo, Vancouver Public Library, VPL 6290

C – Site of auto camp, 2016. Sharon J. Proctor

The Tomahawk Barbecue

A – Original Tomahawk Barbecue, c. 1957. North Vancouver Museum & Archives 7011

B – Early indoor decorations, date unknown. North Vancouver Museum & Archives10627

C – Present-day restaurant, 2007. Sharon J. Proctor

D – Parking lot, 2007. Sharon J. Proctor

Napoleon St. Pierre's "Capilano Gardens"

A – Snake hedge in yard, 1934. North Vancouver Museum & Archives 3297

B – "Monument to the Hero," date unknown. North Vancouver Museum & Archives 10624

C – Garden with woman and cross, date unknown. North Vancouver Museum & Archives 1417

D – La Cucina, 2016. Sharon J. Proctor

Norgate

A – Proposed airfield, 1947. North Vancouver Museum & Archives, Map 120

B – Aerial view of Norgate, 1954. BC Provincial Government aerial photo BC 1673:58; reprinted with permission of the Province of British Columbia, GeoBC, Integrated Land Management Bureau.

C – Homes on Sowden Street, 1950s. North Vancouver Museum & Archives 572

D – Same view, 2007. Sharon J. Proctor

3. Upper Capilano

Staircase on Capilano Road

A – Capilano Suspension Bridge, 1905. North Vancouver Museum & Archives 2904

B – Stairs to the top, date unknown. North Vancouver Museum & Archives 3992

C – The staircase site, 2007. Sharon J. Proctor

Mackay Creek Trestle

A – Streetcar trestle, 1943. Victor L. Sharman photo. Printed with permission.

B – Trestle remnants, 2008. Sharon J. Proctor

C – Deciduous trees where trestle was, 2008. Sharon J. Proctor

The Capilano Valley

A – Capilano Valley, date unknown. North Vancouver Museum & Archives 15807

B – Hotel Capilano c. 1906–1910. North Vancouver Museum & Archives 8255

C – View from new dam, c. 1954. North Vancouver Museum & Archives 13330

D – Same view, 2007. Sharon J. Proctor

Grand Canyon Suspension Bridge

A – On Cleveland Dam, 2007. Sharon J. Proctor

B – On suspension bridge, 1931. North Vancouver Museum & Archives 15795

C – Bridge and Capilano Valley, date unknown. North Vancouver Museum & Archives 15808

Hotel at the Valley Entrance

A – Canyon View Hotel, date unknown. North Vancouver Museum & Archives 11349

B – Taunton House School, 1942. North Vancouver Museum & Archives 5506

C – Grassy knoll, 2007. Sharon J. Proctor

Tipperary Tea Gardens

A – Chinese restaurant, 2016. Sharon J. Proctor

B – Tipperary Tea Gardens, date unknown. North Vancouver Museum & Archives 15809

C – View from tower, c. 1929. North Vancouver Museum & Archives 15810

D – "Grunty," date unknown. North Vancouver Museum & Archives 15811

Edgemont Village

A – Edgemont Boulevard, 1948. North Vancouver Museum & Archives 11340

B – Edgemont Boulevard, 2016. Nancy Kirkpatrick

Capilano Ranchers

A – Ranchers on Paisley Road, 1949. Tom Christopherson photo, Vancouver Public Library, VPL 80991

B – Same view, 2016. Sharon J. Proctor

End of the Capilano Streetcar Line

A - Highway above site of streetcar terminus, 2009. Sharon J. Proctor

B - Streetcar by McLeod's (left) & fire station (right), 1925. North Vancouver Museum & Archives 4587

C - Red & White Store, 1950s. North Vancouver Museum & Archives 4853

4. East to Deep Cove

Corner of 4th & Queensbury

A – Streetcar turning onto Queensbury, 1946. Photo by Robert Loewing, John F. Bromley Collection, North Vancouver Museum & Archives 1119-28

B – The same corner, 2016. Sharon J. Proctor

C – Wartime house, 2016. Sharon J. Proctor

Streetcars on Grand Boulevard

A – Streetcar stop, 1946. Photo by Robert Loewing, John F. Bromley Collection, North Vancouver Museum & Archives 1119-32

B – Same view, 2007. Sharon J. Proctor

Sawmill at 17th & Sutherland

A – Modern Homes, 2016. Sharon J. Proctor

B – Seymour Lumber Co. sawmill, 1906. North Vancouver Museum & Archives 257

C – Log headed for sawmill, c. 1906–10. North Vancouver Museum & Archives p400

Maplewood Farm

A – Cow barn and small shed (at right), 1940s. North Vancouver Museum & Archives 15424

B – Cow barn and shed, 2007. Sharon J. Proctor

C – Shed and family home, 1950s. North Vancouver Museum & Archives 15421

D – Shed and house, 2007. Sharon J. Proctor

Moodyville

A – Moodyville at its peak, 1898. Image D-04134 courtesy of Royal BC Museum, BC Archives

B – Carved-out hillside, 1966. Kenne Allen Collection, aerial photograph 012182, Department of Geography, University of British Columbia

C – Moodyville site, 2016. William Jans

Where East 3rd and the Low Level Road Merge

A – Low Level Road & East 3rd, 2007. Sharon J. Proctor

B – Same view, 1938. North Vancouver Museum & Archives 11157

C – Low Level Road & East 3rd, 2016. City of North Vancouver

Old Dutch Mill Service Station

A – Old Dutch Mill service station, 1940s. North Vancouver Museum & Archives 7026

B – A&W on corner, 2016. Sharon J. Proctor

Swedish Park

A – Midsummer Festival (pavilion at left), 1949. North Vancouver Museum & Archives 8431

B – Lind Bowl, 1946. North Vancouver Museum & Archives 14646

C – Public Storage, 2008. Sharon J. Proctor

Capilano University

A – New campus, 1973. Photo courtesy of Capilano University

B – Capilano University, 2008. Sharon J. Proctor

C – Library building, 2008. Sharon J. Proctor

The Log House

A – Community on Pipeline Road, date unknown. North Vancouver Museum & Archives Fonds 26, Album 3, p. 34

B – The Log House, date unknown. North Vancouver Museum & Archives 4759

C – Scene in first photo, 2008. Sharon J. Proctor

D – House on St. James, 2008. Sharon J. Proctor

Squatters on the Maplewood Mudflats

A - Shacks at the outer edge, 1971. Tony Westman photo, North Vancouver Museum & Archives 15825

B - Shacks close to shore, 1972. Vlad Keremidschieff / Vancouver Sun

C - Maplewood mudflats, 2009. Sharon J. Proctor

Vancouver Cedar Mill

A – Concrete circle, 2007. Sharon J. Proctor

B – Sawmill (burner on the left), 1926. Vancouver Public Library, Special Collections, VPL 2460

Robert Dollar Mill

A – Robert Dollar Mill, 1939. Leonard Frank photo, Vancouver Public Library, Special Collections, VPL 6507

B – Manager's office, 1918. North Vancouver Museum & Archives 3329

C – Private home, 2007. Sharon J. Proctor

D – Homes on mill site, 2007. Sharon J. Proctor

Gallant Avenue in Deep Cove

A – Gallant Avenue, 1920s. Deep Cove Heritage Society 399

B – Deep Cove Cultural Centre, 2008. Sharon J. Proctor

C – Gallant Avenue, 2008. Sharon J. Proctor

Deep Cove Pavilion

A – Deep Cove Pavilion, 1958. North Vancouver Museum & Archives 106-1-16

B – Same view, 2007. Sharon J. Proctor

5. Lynn Valley

Old District Hall

A – Rebuilt stone wall, 2016. Sharon J. Proctor

B – District Hall, 1920. North Vancouver Museum & Archives 26-19A-21

Mollie Nye House

A – Mollie Nye House, 2007. Sharon J. Proctor

B – Nye home, c. 1914. North Vancouver Museum & Archives 4699

C – Sitting room, c. 1914. North Vancouver Museum & Archives 3269

Cedar Theatre

A – Cedar Theatre, 1971. North Vancouver Museum & Archives 106-6-16

B – Theatre site, 2007. Sharon J. Proctor

The Fromme Home

A – Fromme house, c. 1910. North Vancouver Museum & Archives 6627

B – Children in garden, 1911. North Vancouver Museum & Archives 6969

C – Fromme house, 2007. Sharon J. Proctor

Looking North on Mountain Highway

A – Mountain Highway, c. 1912. North Vancouver Museum & Archives 26-19H-44

B – Mountain Highway, 2018. Sharon J. Proctor

Brier Block

A – Gas station, 2007. Sharon J. Proctor

B – Brier Block, 1946. Photo by Robert Loewing, John F. Bromley Collection, North Vancouver Museum & Archives 1119-30

Triangle and Fromme Blocks

A – Triangle and Fromme Blocks, c. 1913. North Vancouver Museum & Archives 2929

B – Same view, 2007. Sharon J. Proctor

Lynn Valley Lumber Co. Shingle Mill

A – Rendering of new church, 2016. Marcon Developments Ltd.

B – Lumber-storage shed, c. 1925. North Vancouver Museum & Archives 6657

C – Auto-repair garage, late 1930s. North Vancouver Museum & Archives 6662

Old Methodist Church building

A – Lynn Valley Methodist Church, c. 1920. North Vancouver Museum & Archives 26-19B-1

B – Dance-and-theatre studio, 2007. Sharon J. Proctor

C – Old-church section, 2007. Sharon J. Proctor

D – Windows, 2008. Sharon J. Proctor

Fourth Lynn Valley School

A – Community History Centre, 2007. Sharon J. Proctor

B – Fourth and third schools, 2002. North Vancouver Museum & Archives 13624

C – Other side, c. 1954. North Vancouver Museum & Archives 12328

Knox Presbyterian Church

A – Maple Leaf Garden Centre, 2007. Sharon J. Proctor

B – Knox Church (right) and its manse, 1911. North Vancouver Museum & Archives 6651

Lynn Valley Road, Crossing Hastings Creek

A – Bridge and waste timber, 1909. North Vancouver Museum & Archives 191

B – Modern thoroughfare, 2007. Sharon J. Proctor

The Lynn Valley Hotel

A – Lynn Valley Road, 1914. North Vancouver Museum & Archives 11892

B – Lynn Valley Hotel, c. 1913. North Vancouver Museum & Archives p60

C – Lynn Valley suspension bridge, c. 1915. North Vancouver Museum & Archives 7744

D – Dovercourt, 2016. Sharon J. Proctor

6. Mountains

Grouse Mountain Highway

A – Grouse Mountain Highway, date unknown. North Vancouver Museum & Archives 8854

B – Switchback on Grouse, date unknown. North Vancouver Museum & Archives 7090

C – Gate at Borthwick Road, 2007. Sharon J. Proctor

D – Private dirt road, 2007. Sharon J. Proctor

Grouse Mountain Chairlift

A – Lower Terminal, 1950s. North Vancouver Museum & Archives 15793

B – Two chairlift stages, 1950s. North Vancouver Museum & Archives 15794

C – Lower Terminal site, 2007. Sharon J. Proctor

Grouse Mountain Chalet

A – Early photo of chalet, date unknown. North Vancouver Museum & Archives 4397

B – Chalet lounge, c. 1926. City of Vancouver Archives, CVA Out P230

C – Chalet site, 2008. Sharon J. Proctor

Mushroom Shelter on Seymour Mountain

A – Parking lot, 1935. North Vancouver Museum & Archives 4646

B – Mushroom shelter, 1935. North Vancouver Museum & Archives 4644

C – Forest and shelter remnant (brown), 2007. Sharon J. Proctor

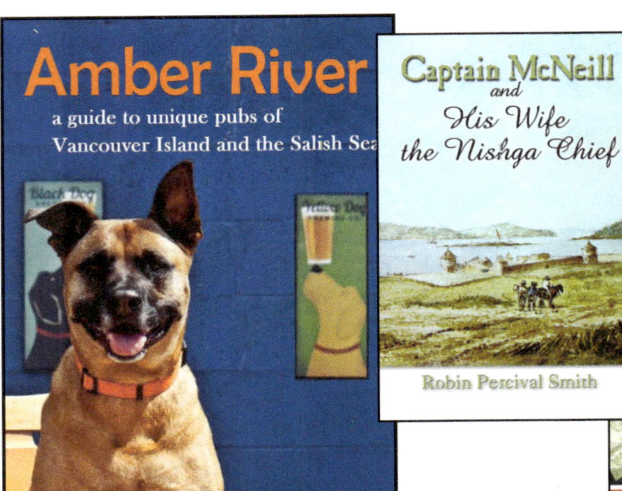

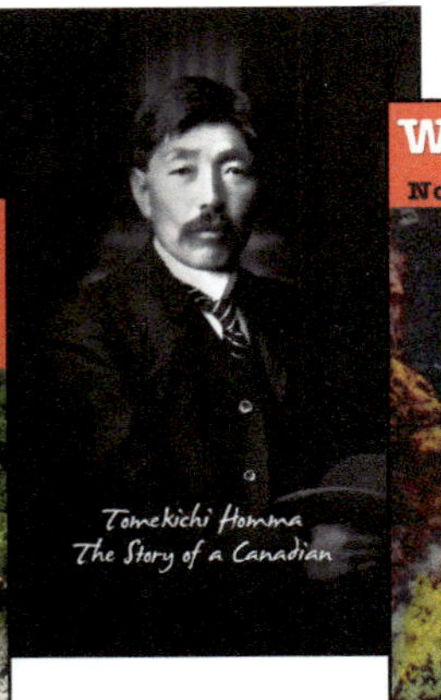

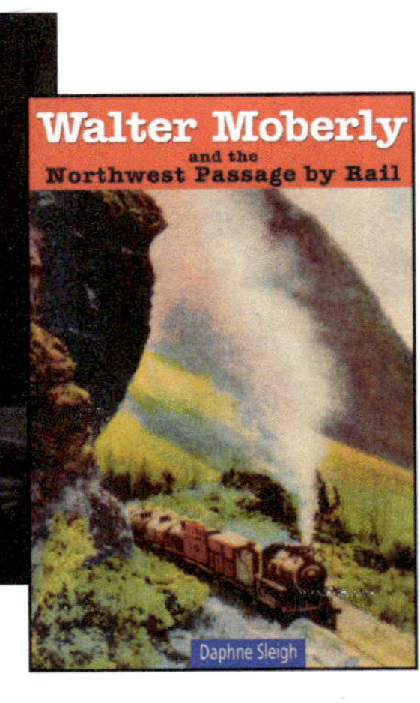

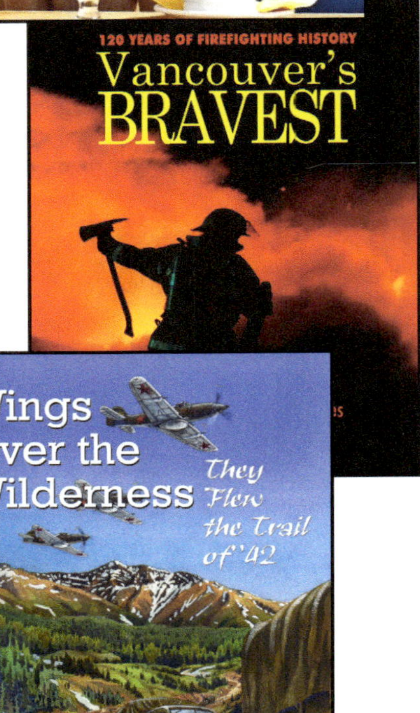

Amber River: a guide to unique pubs of Vancouver Island
Glen Cowley
ISBN 978-0-88839-075-2
5.5 x 8.5 • sc • 226 pages

Afloat in Time
Jim Sirois
ISBN 0-88839-455-1
5.5 x 8.5 • sc • 288 pages

Captain McNeill and His Wife the Nishga Chief
Robin Percival Smith
ISBN 0-88839-472-1
5.5 x 8.5 • sc • 256 pages

A Doctor's Notes
T.F. Godwin
ISBN 978-0-88839-654-9
5.5 x 8.5 • sc • 368 pages

Fraser Canyon
Lorraine Harris
ISBN 978-0-88839-182-7
5.5 x 8.5 • sc • 64 pages

Frontier Forts & Posts of the Hudson's Bay Company
Kenneth E. Perry
ISBN 0-88839-598-1
8.5 x 11 • sc • 96 pages

Gold Creeks and Ghost Towns (BC)
N. L. Barlee
ISBN 0-88839-988-X
8.5 x 11 • sc • 192 pages

Loggers of the BC Coast
Hans Knapp
ISBN 0-88839-588-4
5.5 x 8.5 • sc • 200 pages

Out of the Rain
Paul Jones
ISBN 0-88839-541-8
5.5 x 8.5 • sc • 272 pages

Outposts & Bushplanes
Bruce Lamb
ISBN 0-88839-556-6
5.5 x 8.5 • sc • 208 pages

Ruffles on my Longjohns
Isabel Edwards
ISBN 0-88839-102-1
5.5 x 8.5 • sc • 297 pages

Songs of the Pacific Northwest
Philip J. Thomas
ISBN 978-0-88839-610-5
8.5 x 11 • sc • 208 pages

Tomekichi Homma
K.T. Homma, C.G. Isaksson
ISBN 978-0-88839-660-0
5.5 x 8.5 • sc • 72 pages

Vancouver's Bravest
Alex Matches
ISBN 978-0-88839-615-0
8.5 x 11 • sc • 352 pages

Walter Moberly and the Northwest Passage by Rail
Daphne Sleigh
ISBN 0-88839-510-8
5.5 x 8.5 • sc • 268 pages

Wings Over the Wilderness
Blake W. Smith
ISBN 978-0-88839-595-7
8.5 x 11 • sc • 296 pages

Wild Canadian West
E. C. (Ted) Meyers
ISBN 0-88839-469-1
5.5 x 8.5 • sc • 208 pages